Southern Living

Cooking Across the South

Southern Living.

Cooking Across the South

A Collection and Recollection of
Favorite Regional Recipes

Lillian Bertram Marshall

Oxmoor House, Inc.
Birmingham

Copyright © 1980 by Oxmoor House, Inc.
Book Division of The Progressive Farmer Company
Publisher of *Southern Living*®, *Progressive Farmer*®,
and *Decorating & Craft Ideas*® magazines.
P.O. Box 2463, Birmingham, Alabama 35201

Eugene Butler   Chairman of the Board
Emory Cunningham   President and Publisher
Vernon Owens, Jr.   Executive Vice President

Conceived, edited and published by Oxmoor House,
Inc., under the direction of:

Don Logan   Vice President and General Manager
Gary McCalla   Editor, *Southern Living*
John Logue   Editor-in-Chief
Jean Wickstrom Liles   Foods Editor, *Southern Living*
Ann H. Harvey   Managing Editor
Jerry Higdon   Production Manager

Cooking Across the South

Designer: Faith Nance
Photographers: Jerome Drown: pages i, 149,
   150 (below), 169, 170, 204, 205, 206, 239; Taylor
   Lewis: cover, pages ii and iii, 29, 240; John
   O'Hagan: pages 150 (above), 203; Bert O'Neal:
   pages 100, 151; Bob Carter: page 99 (above); Mike
   Clemmer: page iv (below); Kent Kirkley: page 152;
   Bill Shrout: page 66
Artist: Barbara Shores

Assistant Editors: Susan Payne, Assistant Foods
   Editor, *Southern Living*; Annette Thompson
Production Assistant: Joan Denman
Editorial Assistants: Nita Robinson, Cecilia Robinson

Southern Living® and *Progressive Farmer*® are
federally registered trademarks belonging to The
Progressive Farmer Company. *Decorating & Craft
Ideas*® is a federally registered trademark belonging
to Southern Living, Inc.

Library of Congress Catalog Number: 80-80752
ISBN: 0-8487-0505-X

Manufactured in the United States of America
Second Printing 1980

Page i: *Covered dish dinners are an integral part of
Southern hospitality. Here's a sampling: Chicken Pie
With Sweet Potato Crust (page 105), Never-Fail Pan
Rolls (page 185), Milky Way Cake (page 200), Deep-Dish
Apple Pie (page 233), and Spiced Peaches (page 246).*

Pages ii and iii: *Horse-drawn vegetable carts are part of
the daily scene in Charleston, South Carolina.*

Page iv: *From Texas to Kentucky, outdoor barbecues are
a favorite Southern pastime. See pages 74 through 79 for
outdoor barbecue recipes that serve hundreds.*

Contents

To my children and to yours: a continuum

Collections and Recollections

Search for him everywhere, in the mountains or on the strand; in piny woods or verdant farmland; in back country or in towns—there is no such person as the typical Southerner. We are in fact rich and poor, fat and lean. We are black and white, or whatever the hue bequeathed to us by those who went before. We live in distress on Tobacco Road and in splendor at Tara. Lazy and industrious we are, ornery and sweet—and proud of it; we do have that in common.

Consider for a moment a few seemingly irrelevant facts about this Southland of ours: Texas boasts at least twenty-seven distinct ethnic cultures. Memphis has a larger Orthodox Jewish population than any city in the United States in proportion to its size. Tampa's annual Gasparilla Festival depends for its success upon the public-spirited cooperation of citizens from thirty-one different backgrounds. The most notable hallmark of the South and Southerners, it would then appear, is diversity.

Think next of the numberless peoples who have come to the Southern states by land and sea over the centuries and sunk generations of roots into the earth. Add them all to the fundamental American Indian culture, and what emerges is a United Nations of the South. And the culinary smorgasbord produced by our collective cook-fires is almost beyond imagining.

Who, then, is a Southerner? Where does he live, and what does he eat?

We tend to think of a Southerner as one whose ancestors came to the region ages ago and caused him to be born to its customs. He has stayed because he would not dream of living anywhere else. But a Southerner is also a person who moved to the South for any reason from anywhere at all, and stayed because he fell in step—or in love—with it and did not want to leave.

1

For purposes of this book, a Southerner lives in any one of some fifteen states, an area wrapped roughly around the lower right-hand third of the country. It is bounded on the south and east by water, on the west by New Mexico, and on the north by what most of us affectionately refer to as "the Nawth."

As to his diet, a Southerner has at his disposal one of the richest natural larders on earth. Contrary to myth, he does not live by fried chicken alone. Depending upon which home or restaurant is under scrutiny, the specialty of the house could well be potato latkes or sauerbraten or frijoles refritos or lasagna.

For the most part, a Southerner cooks with the same spices used in other parts of the country. But he may use them more lavishly, having a predilection for rich cakes and the native molasses sweets that call for huge quantities of ginger, mace, cinnamon, and nutmeg.

It may amuse him, on occasion, to sneak up on his guest with a dish that is superheated with cayenne, hot pepper sauce, or chilies. Add, in some localities, filé powder. He may season all his vegetables with salt-cured pork. But do not label him; he could use schmaltz instead, or peanut oil. In any case, his day is seldom complete without at least one dessert; although, if he is dieting strenuously, he may pass up the whipped cream.

City bred or farm fed, a Southerner will look back on the food of his childhood as being better than anything he has tasted since; in this I am no exception. My brothers and I were reared just slightly north of grits, black-eyed peas, and Tennessee. Our foodways were based on chicken for Sundays; on cured ham, bacon, and sausage for everyday eating; on fresh green beans and corn—and all the good things a garden, lovingly tended, could yield in return.

Ours was a pork-heavy, waste-not economy, with some fine by-products. At hog-killing time, the iron cauldron out by the smokehouse cooked the fat pork trimmings into a year's supply of snow-white lard (pastry has never again tasted so good) and cracklings for cornbread. That same kettle, at other times, boiled accumulated household grease mixed with lye into soap. My mother, like her peers, prided herself on the pallor of her soap, which she cut into bars and shaved into the laundry water. White clothes thus washed were then boiled in the iron cooker to whiten them further.

Later, with the advent of the incredible new Maytag wringer-type washer, that lye soap was still shaved into the wash where it cleansed with very little sudsing. Just for the luxury of it, my mother would purchase a box of "soap chips" two or three times a year. She would shake a spoonful or so onto the squirming wet wash and watch it bubble up like meringue. Everything but hosiery got starched with boiled water and flour, then ironed into sharp creases. The pillow cases, with the faintest air of lye soap still clinging, left scars on our cheeks that did not fade away until nearly noon.

Customs such as these certainly were not peculiar to Kentucky. The feasting we made at hog-killing time was probably similar to rural Louisiana's present-day boucherie. State lines are, after all, for political, not culinary, purposes. Foods and customs cross borders as though they did not exist.

Kentuckians are not alone in their fondness for air-dried apples, for example. The hilly states in the Southeast still prefer them to the dried apples prepared with sulphur. Sliced and dried, the apples turn a rich, rusty brown and keep forever, hung up in bags in a dry attic. They need only to be soaked, cooked, sugared, and spiced to fill the ginger-flavored layers we call "stack cake" which invariably turns up at an old-fashioned dinner-on-the-ground or family reunion.

The same rural high country areas still favor "shuck beans": green beans dried in their hulls. Sometimes known as "fodder beans" or "leather britches," they are another half-forgotten but delicious instance of the old air-drying method of food preservation. My mother broke up the beans, as for cooking, before putting them to dry on screens. Her sister threaded the whole pods on yard-long strings and hung them to dry on her back porch. The two sisters argued the merits of their respective methods all their lives.

There are many other sub-regions of the South, and they must enter into any discussion of Southern foodways. River delta natives, for example, share an ingrained fondness for catfish and hush puppies, just as folks living anywhere along the ocean's edge dote on shrimp and crabmeat. The Florida Panhandle votes with Alabama and Georgia when menus are made, while the remainder of the state goes tropical and cosmopolitan with its big cities and rich mix of international influences.

One should not, in short, simply go South and expect to eat "Southern Food" at every crossroad. Regionalism lives, in spite of jet travel, television, and the home freezer. In many instances old recipes and methods have had to be relegated to occasional use, but in the minds of older cooks there is a treasury of regional lore just waiting to be called forth. This book's chapter, "Southernisms," is such a calling forth of a wealth we can ill afford to forget.

It is possible, even easy, to ignore regional food completely when traveling. Almost every large Southern city points with pride to at least one superb continental-style restaurant. I love them all, but for my dining dollar, an exquisite French meal is of the same level of interest whether eaten in Miami or in Chicago. I will go out of my way to keep from seeing the same menu in Biloxi that I saw in Nashville.

How does one find the real food of a given region? It would be possible, I suppose, to stand on a street corner wearing a sign that pleads, "Take me with you and feed me a home-cooked meal," but such an action may be misconstrued.

Next to the street corner gambit, to which I have not yet succumbed, the best recourse is to cultivate the habit of talking with strangers. I recommend this procedure, in spite of a respectable upbringing. I have been known to enter a professional building, approach a smart-looking receptionist with my friendliest smile, and inquire for the best eating place in the neighborhood. Given a moment to rally from her surprise, she decides what I need and sends me off to a happy experience.

Proprietors of cookware shops are wellsprings of good restaurant information. Once, in Key West, I found an outstanding meal by presenting myself at The Cook's Bazaar. A staff member not only directed but accompanied me to La Conca Cupboard. Unprepossessing to look at, this little restaurant within a drugstore serves, without fanfare, the excellent Cuban food that is "home cooking" to so many Key Westers.

Further to the subject of food-finding in an unfamiliar place, we Southerners are known for our "pride of place." There is hardly a city or hamlet that does not boast a gem of a museum or a restored historic shrine: the Tullie Smith House in Atlanta; the Sophienburg Museum in New Braunfels, Texas; Ashton Villa in Galveston; Locust Grove and Farmington in Louisville; the Arkansas Territorial Capitol Restoration in Little Rock. There are literally hundreds of these. The point is that such spots, aside from the intrinsic interest they hold for the history-minded traveler, are staffed by docents drawn from members of a local historic preservation society. These folks know their town and they know their food. Engage the tour guide in conversation; explain that you are student of Southern food, stressing your interest in the food of that particular region. It was a charming docent at Ashton Villa in Galveston who made a restaurant sound so inviting that I took a cab straight to an early dinner.

Cab drivers are a separate study. In the South, you cannot have a better friend than a sympathetic taxi driver. Throw yourself on his/her mercy; take him/her into your confidence—you will be cared for as though you were visiting royalty. Once you have decided where to dine, by your methods or mine, call your cab. Then make a deal with the driver to come back for you after dinner. In San Antonio, Fred not only returned for me on schedule, he calmly came in and joined me for coffee because I had forgotten to watch the time while enjoying an unusually long, drawn out and delicious Mexican dinner.

In Galveston, Bobby took charge of my affairs, giving me his personally escorted tour of the city while driving me to appointments. Otherwise, I would not have seen the restoration work on The Strand, the fantastic cotton shipping facilities, the tea warehouses, and the yellow mountains of sulphur waiting on the docks to be exported all over the world. We had lunch at his favorite hometown bistro, stopping to visit a candy-making operation called La King's Confectionary.

John, in Key West, remembered Hemingway, and could "still just see Harry Truman walking down Duval Street." Slim, down in Lafayette, Louisiana, came back to get me an hour early from the boudin festival at Broussard. He knew, and I did not, that I would miss my flight out if I stayed as late as I had planned. And, for good measure, he gave me his special recipe for chicken.

Slim was one of the helpful people I met during my discovery of Louisiana's bewitching Evangeline country. The way I came to be in that neighborhood at all is probably the best illustration of my theory on "how to ask your way through the South like a cousin from out of town." It happened this way.

In New Orleans, a companion and I had been sent to a restaurant "really off the beaten path, where the natives like to eat," just the sort of place a visitor to that singular city hungers for. Sure enough, all the natives were there, and the waiting space was standing room only, located fortuitously alongside the bar.

During the interminable wait, perfect strangers became old friends, some of us nearing the point of promising to exchange letters. Two young men inching toward the tables with us happened to be students at the University of Southwest Louisiana. On learning that we were food professionals, they told us about a "boudin" festival to be held the following weekend at the little town of Broussard, Louisiana, just outside Lafayette.

Without knowing exactly what "boudin" meant, I promised to attend, and did so. Members of the Broussard Chamber of Commerce had taken possession of the local fairgrounds that day, and the television and radio people had come from as far away as Baton Rouge to cover the demonstration of boudin making. How could I not have known that boudin was sausage!

Standing on tiptoe, I could see Dudley Hebert (pronounced ay-bear), in a red coverall, pushing the sausage mixture through a narrow funnel into the prepared casings. If I had not known better, I would have sworn that funnel was a natural cow's horn! Once the media people finished their interviews and left, he switched to a sausage-stuffing attachment on the grinder, and the operation picked up speed.

Mrs. Hebert stood by, giving the long stuffed casings a deft twist every six inches, and soon a coil of chubby sausages lay on the table, ready for cooking. After a brief boiling, the boudin were served up, wrapped in paper napkins. With no bread or bun to absorb the peppery heat, I shed tears of boudin happiness along with the rest of the crowd. By a stroke of luck, plenty of cold beer had been provided to put out such brush fires.

Finally I was able to ask my question. "Yes," Hebert told me, "that's my granddaddy's cow horn, the one he always used for boudin. Not very fast, but it still works."

Before freezer storage became commonplace the cooked boudin was put down in crocks and covered with melted lard. Sealed off from the air, it would keep as long as necessary. On that principle, in other parts of the South fried sausage balls were put in jars and covered with the frying drippings. The only thing that tasted better was pork tenderloin, put by in the same way.

"We fun loving. Never too broke to have fun," a man said, with the characteristic Cajun French accent. The motto in Cajun country is *Laisser le bon temps rouler*—"Let the good times roll." A guest does well to bear that in mind; the only way he could feel unwelcome at a Cajun gathering would be to bring along his troubles for an airing. They play as hard as they work. When the fiddles and accordians strike up "Jolie Blonde," and the fais do-do begins, everyone dances.

Old and young alike take the floor (dancing fais do-do is outdoors on the ground). It is plain to see that the old people have been dancing all their lives, and if they have a care in the world, it does not show in their faces. A couple with their golden anniversary behind them may approach the floor with rheumatic twinges, but when the band's front man begins to shout the lyrics, all in French, they become as weightless as moon walkers.

No age barriers are in evidence as tots try out the dance steps, either alone or guided by a grandparent or teenaged sibling. As I watched, a young father swept up his toddler daughter and danced her to the center of the floor. The child clung fearfully to his neck with both arms—for two whole minutes. Soon she had relaxed and extended an arm, laughing, pretending to dance, although her feet were off the ground. By the time the next number had been announced, she was on the ground, holding her father's hands, unself-consciously dancing, toes stamping lightly forward into the giving earth, hips swaying saucily in time to the music.

Before Slim came for me, I had been invited to attend a boucherie the very next weekend in a nearby town. I had to postpone that pleasure; but it is good to know that it will be held next February right on schedule, because that is the way tradition works.

With the same assurance, one can plan to look in on St. Petersburg's Folk Fair in February of any year, or the Texas Folklife Festival in San Antonio any August, or the Kentucky Derby the first Saturday of any May, or to participate in the glorious celebration of Christmas in Williamsburg. Conviviality is one common denominator of the traditional festivals in the South; food is another. Our festivals remind us of our basic regionalism by serving the same delicious, predictable victuals every time around.

Good chili can be, and is, made in Virginia; passable mint juleps are stirred in Texas. But it may be that we owe it to ourselves someday to see our Southland at a leisurely pace, let our ears collect the many ways the American language can sound, and sample every possible dish on its home ground. Not that we cannot cook chicken-fried steak Oklahoma style, or bake a Mississippi pecan pie without having traveled there. The whole reason for having recipes and cookbooks is to make sure that we can.

Perhaps the senses only seem to respond better to chili when you are somewhere in Texas, and the sun goes down and the wind rises to roil your hair. By the same token, she-crab soup awakens the softer emotions when taken in salt air, with a spectacular view of Chesapeake Bay. Filé gumbo is not too difficult to make, but to eat it in New Orleans' French Quarter is a decidedly sensual experience. Just try shrimp-oyster stew in Southwest Louisiana, with a Cajun band playing and a new friend explaining the recipe over the din, and you will come away reeling from the total experience.

Once you have traveled to a food's place of nativity, the recipe can, with remembering, come alive in your own kitchen. I suppose it would even work for a New Yorker cooking turnip greens and pot likker, if he could look back on the same meal taken in the sociable atmosphere of a Tennessee family's dinner table.

The South is devoted to the past without being bound by it. We exchange ideas because we are communicators of the first water, and we happily adopt one another's foods. Each time I visit Savannah I come home and make benne seed wafers for weeks. Back from Memphis, I scour the market for fresh turnip greens and the salt pork it takes to flavor them right.

There still are excellent regional dishes, fine shades of difference in the ways we put the same raw materials together, and inborn leanings toward certain foods that have not yet become part of the typical American menu. It is these attitudes and differences to which this book is dedicated. In our diversity there is unity in this respect: while reaching for the new with one hand, we Southerners are holding tight to our traditions with the other.

Soups and Stews

Because soups range in consistency from liquid broths to semisolids such as gumbos, chili, stews, and burgoo, I have always categorized them mentally as "the wet foods." In any case, soups may be right behind barbecue in man's climb up the gastronomic ladder. Note how archaeologists examining prehistoric caves deciphered this recipe pictographed on the walls: "Make a bag from animal skin and put some water into it. Add well-broken bones from the day's kill. Heat stones in the fire and drop them into the water. Wait for the broth to get hot; then drink it, and gnaw the bones. . . . " Well, not in so many words, but the idea was there. Apparently no mention was made of seasoning; perhaps the family followed an animal path to the nearest salt lick or sipped a little seawater after dinner.

Eventually, of course, the day came when man contrived a pot that would withstand both fire and water. He must have realized in a flash that food would go further when diluted with water, no small consideration to a fellow with a large family to support. Imagine his jubilation as the meaty bones actually began to stew in the water, giving off the unmistakable aroma of soup. Did he decide to throw in some wild herbs, or did such embroideries await the inventiveness of succeeding generations?

Soups are probably closer to the heart of any country or region than any other item of its food. Always made of the most plentiful ingredients, soup is dependent upon local weather, availability of foods, and seasonal kitchen gardens. And in the American South there is no exception. A look into a Southerner's everyday soup pot tells whether his garden grows in a hot or cool climate, whether he lives near or far from the sea, and possibly even something of his ethnic background.

A study of Southern foodways quite logically begins with soups, for in them is found the most infinite variety. And by way of looking at the South's soups in some sort of order, one could well go straight to Texas and commence with chili. Texas occupies a larger chunk of the South than any other state, so if a Texan's story ever seems larger than life, it is only because the rest of us do not understand the principle of sheer bigness. Among the legends of Texas, none is more colorful than the story of chili. Chili was part of the life-support system in the vastness of Texas untouched by the sea; it could be made any time a beef or venison was slaughtered.

It must be remembered that during the nearly three hundred years of Spanish rule Texans consisted of Mexican, Irish, English, French, Italian, and African immigrants. It was not until the early 1800s that Southerners, most of North European extraction, poured in from Georgia, Tennessee, Alabama, and the Carolinas. Latecomers to Texas, then, found Mexican chilies there ahead of them, plenty of beef on the hoof, and dried beans (to be eaten alone or with chili) in every trail kit.

While the Indians maintain that they have been making chili for as long as there have been winters and that Texas stole chili from them, historians are fairly certain that "the world's greatest restorative" was first cooked in Texas border towns in the early 1800s. The dish remained somewhat localized until 1893 when "San Antonio Chilly" created a sensation at the Chicago World's Fair.

Frank X. Tolbert, in his witty treatise on chili called *A Bowl of Red*, recounts that when the West was young, chili was a staple on jailhouse menus. Villains, it was said, planned to stage their most daring escapades in or near towns whose jail cooks had the best reputations for making chili. The theory was that in case a particular crime did not pay, at least the food would be good during the lull while plans were laid for the next felony.

Will Rogers' reverent term for this native American dish was "a bowl of blessedness." He did not live to see the cheerful madness called "The Annual World Championship Chili Cook-Off," first held in Terlingua, Texas, in 1967. The ingredients at this gathering seem to have gotten out of hand, but spirits soar as contestants gather from everywhere plus England to vie for the championship pot of chili. Nothing is sacred as cooks throw in armadillo meat, tequila, peppers from Sri Lanka—even a handful of "mother earth, to sift out the impurities," as a Shawnee from Oklahoma remarked during the cook-off a few years ago.

There are many ways to make chili, and each method has its wild-eyed adherents. Meat cubed or coarsely ground, with or without beans, and so on. And on. The original San Antonio Chilly laid on the peppers and left out the beans. What chili recipes do have in common is their satisfying, delicious, rib-sticking quality. That is what sustained the weary cowpoke when the weather turned sour and threatened to freeze him to his horse. And no matter what the recipe, or how it laid waste to his taste buds, nothing could have been further from his mind than to express dissatisfaction with the chuck wagon cook's kettle of chili.

The first woman ever to win The Annual World Championship Chili Cook-Off was Allegani Jani, who named this recipe for the outfit she wore for the 1974 contest.

Hot Pants Chili

4 pounds beef stew meat, ground once
3 onions, chopped
2 tablespoons vegetable oil
Salt and pepper to taste
2 heaping teaspoons cumin seeds
6 garlic cloves
1 or 2 teaspoons water
1 (28-ounce) can tomatoes
1 teaspoon sugar
½ can beer
3 tablespoons chili powder

2 (2½-ounce) packs chili seasoning
1 tablespoon mole paste*
1 teaspoon hot sauce
1 teaspoon salt
1 quart water
4 jalapeño peppers, chopped (may be omitted)
½ cup masa flour* (All-purpose flour can be substituted for masa flour, although results will be less authentic.)

Brown the meat with the onions in the oil. Add salt and pepper. With a *molcajete* (a Mexican mortar-and-pestle-type grinder made of volcanic rock) or mortar and pestle, mash and grind together cumin seeds, garlic cloves, and 1 or 2 teaspoons water. Add to the meat mixture.

Place the tomatoes, sugar, beer, and chili powder in a blender. Add the chili seasoning or the alternate ingredients and blend until the tomatoes are broken up completely. Add to the meat mixture.

Add the mole paste, hot sauce, salt, 1 quart water, and jalapeño peppers. Simmer for 2½ hours, stirring well from time to time.

Combine the masa flour with enough water to make a runny paste. Add to chili while stirring quickly in order to prevent lumping. Cook 30 minutes more for the chili to thicken. Yield: 8 to 10 servings.

Note: To make your own chili seasoning, mix together the following ingredients. Store in airtight container.

1 teaspoon red pepper flakes
2 tablespoons ground coriander
2 tablespoons ground cumin
¼ cup paprika
2 teaspoons salt
4 teaspoons ground oregano

2 tablespoons dried onion flakes
1 teaspoon dried garlic flakes
¼ cup cornstarch
½ teaspoon ground black pepper

*Mole paste and masa flour are available at Mexican and Spanish groceries and specialty food stores.

For some insight into the foodways of the part of Texas that looks seaward, a sampling of the famed Gulf Coast gumbos at Galveston Island is a good beginning. Reached by a causeway across Galveston Bay, the island stretches for thirty miles along the southeast Texas coastline. It was here that the early German settlers landed in the mid-nineteenth century before moving inland to make their homes. In its early history the island was plagued by pirates, as was the entire Gulf Coast and the Eastern Seaboard. But it was the devastating hurricane of 1900 that almost wrote Galveston's epitaph. Heroically, the city rose to its feet, walled out the sea, and resumed its place as one of the most important seaports in the United States. Galveston is also, I found, a good place to be at dinner time.

Gumbo in Galveston usually means okra, but here is not the place to bring up the old debate as to whether okra pods or filé powder better serves to bring gumbo to the proper flavor and viscosity; that is a purely subjective matter. Nor will I enter the list to argue the origin of the word "gumbo." It is enough for us that the gods have smiled on the proud Southern gumbo in its every guise, including the exquisite Gumbo d'Herbes, which uses neither okra nor filé, depending for body only on the roux. Take this old recipe from southern Louisiana. Since all Southerners are born knowing the roux, the fat and flour measurements are left to the cook's judgment, as is everything else:

Gumbo D'Herbes

Roux   Greens (mustard, turnip,
Salt pork   spinach)
Water   Cooked rice

Combine roux and salt pork. Add water and boil 20 minutes. Grind all the greens (spinach, mustard greens, or whatever is available). Add to roux mixture and cook about 1 hour, or until thickened. Season to taste. Serve with rice.

The experienced cook merely eyes the supply of greens, cuts up a chunk of salt pork sufficient to season it, tries it out in the iron kettle, then makes the roux in quantity to thicken it to his satisfaction. Rice is cooked separately, and the gumbo spooned over it when serving.

After a mild beginning in Galveston, gumbo heats up in Port Arthur, Texas. A few years ago, the Cajun por Demain (Cajuns for Tomorrow) of Port Arthur, in cooperation with their local Chamber of Commerce, pulled off a heroic feat: For their part in the annual Texas Folk Life Festival, they transported by tractor-trailer and helicopter a 450-gallon cast-iron pot to San Antonio. The pot, said to be over 200 years old, was originally used for boiling cane syrup. But for this occasion, it was the vessel that cooked the world's largest gumbo. And here, courtesy of Cajun leader W.T. Oliver, is just what I had always wanted—the recipe for 450 gallons of gumbo.

Chicken-Sausage Gumbo

200 pounds smoked sausage	Beau coups (many) gallons
3,000 pieces chicken	roux
¼ acre green onions	Plus all the secret spices that
⅛ acre parsley	only Cajuns know
½ acre rice (1,100 pounds)	

Now that you have recognized that number for the typical Cajun leg-pull it really is, refer to page 20 for a Chicken-Sausage Gumbo that will work for you.

Pressing east to New Orleans where Creole (French-Spanish) and Cajun cuisines face off in a contest that is as delicious as it is perpetual, it is interesting to look for both similarities and differences.

Mrs. Marie Louise Comeaux Manuel, former Director of the School of Home Economics at the University of Southwestern Louisiana, and distinctly Cajun in her outlook, expressed the following comparisons during a symposium a few years back:

"The Acadian Cuisine, unlike the Creole Cuisine, uses the herbs, seasonings, and spices to bring out the full taste of the main ingredient, thus . . . the original flavor of the main ingredient predominates. Another difference is that the Acadian dishes are not as greasy; there is not excess fat."

On one point, the roux, there is no disagreement. Comeaux had this to say about it: "The roux: sprinkle flour slowly into shortening in an iron pot, brown it slowly, and stir continuously. Then the secret is to add cold water or stock gradually, then the spices and herbs. My mother always said, 'Add cold water to the roux; if hot water is added, your roux will be pale,' meaning hot water blanches the roux."

Getting to the heart of Cajun country is a matter of moving out of Texas via Interstate 10 into southwest Louisiana. The spirit of Evangeline haunts the bayous and inspires a people that are at once deeply religious and fun-loving.

Arriving in Lafayette, Louisiana, I located Chez Pastor, a restaurant frequented as much by the locals as by the tourists.

The seafood gumbo filé at Chez Pastor is hot and dark, sumptuous with shrimp and unctuous with oysters. Pat and Maugie Pastor gave me what I believe to be absolutely definitive directions for making their *spécialité de maison*. First the roux is made, using 1 cup vegetable oil and 1 cup all-purpose flour. Like this, says Pat Pastor:

Seafood Gumbo Filé Chez Pastor

"Heat 1 cup oil in a black iron pot until hot. Slowly stir in 1 cup flour with a spatula until all flour is added. Now stir constantly over medium heat until roux is a dark brown color; this should take about 15 minutes. The roux is a very important ingredient in our cuisine and is used in all our gumbo, stew, crawfish bisque, and étouffée. I usually make my roux by the gallon on a quiet evening

at home, so I always have it. It keeps wonderfully in a jar on the kitchen cabinet. Once the roux is made, it is just a matter of throwing everything into a big pot and letting it cook."

2 gallons chicken stock	1 tablespoon salt
1 cup chopped onion	1 teaspoon pepper
½ cup chopped celery	1 teaspoon cayenne pepper
½ cup chopped green pepper	5 dozen raw oysters
2 cloves garlic, chopped	Chopped green onion
¾ cup roux	Chopped parsley
¼ cup Worcestershire sauce	Hot cooked rice
2 pounds shrimp, peeled and deveined	

Put first 7 ingredients in a soup pot and cook over low heat for 2 hours. (You must cook it this long to complete cooking of the roux.) Keep covered so as not to lose liquid. This becomes the basic 'gumbo stock' and can be used for either seafood or chicken.

Add 2 pounds peeled and deveined shrimp which have been seasoned with 1 tablespoon salt and 1 teaspoon each of black and cayenne pepper. Cook 20 minutes. Just before serving, add 5 dozen raw oysters. You never add oysters ahead; they will overcook. To serve, sprinkle with chopped green onion and parsley. Guests add their filé as desired when served—of course with steaming white rice. Yield: 16 servings, with Chez Pastor's generous ladle.

Creole or Cajun in emphasis, "New Orleans à table" remains, in the estimation of many devotees, the nonpareil gastronomic experience in the country, if not the world. One can go for broke at the Royal Orleans, the Pontchartrain, or the Roosevelt-cum-Fairmont, any one of which will spoil one forever for the real world. I found quite another ambience at New Orleans' Bon Ton restaurant where the food adheres faithfully to the Acadian background of founder Al Pierce.

Pierce opened his restaurant in 1953, and it became one of the city's favorite watering places. It remains so, under the guidance of Pierce's nephew and his wife Debbie. Debbie discussed the house recipe for one of their specialties, crawfish bisque:

Crawfish Bisque À La Bon Ton

"The preparation is in two steps. First, the making of a bisque gravy, and second, the stuffing for the crawfish heads that go into the gravy to produce the completed soup.

"It is a lengthy process, so most Southern cooks prefer to make it in large quantities when they decide to take on the task. The end, however, does justify the means in this case."

Bisque Gravy:

½ cup all-purpose flour
½ cup vegetable oil
3 large onions, diced
1 clove garlic, finely chopped
2 stalks celery, chopped
½ green pepper, chopped
2 quarts water, divided
Dash of sugar
Salt and pepper to taste
½ cup crawfish fat
2 pounds crawfish tails, peeled
3 green onions, chopped
½ cup fresh parsley, chopped
4 hard-cooked eggs, chopped

Make a roux by adding flour to heated oil in a heavy-bottomed pan. Stir constantly over low heat until mixture is golden brown. Add onion, garlic, celery, and green pepper, and cook until tender while stirring to avoid burning. Add 1½ quarts water, sugar, salt, and pepper; allow mixture to simmer, stirring constantly.

While this mixture is cooking over low heat, combine remaining water with crawfish fat in a saucepan. Cook over medium heat, stirring constantly, until it comes to a boil. Add to roux mixture and let it simmer 1 hour. Add crawfish tails, green onion, and parsley. Simmer another 30 minutes; add Stuffed Heads. Serve in a soup plate over buttered, parsleyed rice; sprinkle each serving with half of a hard-cooked egg. Yield: 8 servings.

Crawfish Bisque Stuffed Heads:

1 cup vegetable oil
2 medium onions, chopped
2 green onions, chopped
2 cloves garlic, finely chopped
2 cups crawfish tails, cut into small pieces
Salt and pepper to taste
¼ cup parsley, chopped
3 eggs, well beaten and divided
2 cups breadcrumbs
30 crawfish heads, eyes and antennae removed
1 cup milk

Heat oil and simmer onion and garlic until tender in heavy-bottomed pan. Add crawfish tails, salt, and pepper. Cook over low heat, stirring, until liquid is absorbed. Add parsley, 2 beaten eggs, and breadcrumbs; mix well. Stuff mixture into cleaned crawfish heads. Dip heads into batter made with remaining beaten egg and milk. Deep fry for 3 to 5 minutes.

Northern Mississippi and Alabama may seem far removed from coastal influence, but their feet rest in the Gulf of Mexico, and I find the sea soups are as outstanding in Biloxi and Mobile as any on the coast. Gumbos are much in evidence as one follows the Gulf to Florida, but chowders, thick with fresh seafood, come into their own along the shore of the entire peninsula. Conch chowder is just one reason for visiting Key West.

Key West, Florida, is not on the way to or from anywhere else. One must drive 160

miles from the edge of Florida on U.S. 1 or go down to Miami and hop a plane owned by Air Sunshine. The plane, in turn, hops to Key West—usually. It is an informal little airline referred to by the natives as "Air Sometime." The island itself is 30 miles north of the Tropic of Cancer and, as someone suggested, appears to be a jungle undergoing rehabilitation.

Key West was a busy place as far back as the seventeenth century, but it was a spasmodic population composed of pirates and smugglers. No Conch Tour Train, no Margaret Truman Laundromat. No one seemed to think of the 2- by 4-mile coral island as real estate until 1822, when a rich New Orleans trader named J.W. Simpson plunked down $2,000 to buy it from a Spanish army officer.

In the 1830s, some folk from the Bahamas and Bermuda settled on the island. They were mainly descendants of British sympathizers who had left the United States during the American Revolution. Soon they were joined by other settlers from the Southern states. At times I fancied a faint British accent coming from a Key Wester whose family goes all the way back. The English legacy also accounts for the continuing popularity of duff, a steamed pudding customarily served with beans.

There is no recorded date for the important discovery that the muscle of the conch (say "konk") is edible. Since then, however, much research has gone into finding out how. Happily, modern day chowderists and fritter-makers find the going easy; thrice-ground conch meat is available now in fish markets and grocery stores.

Finding a bowl of good conch chowder in Key West can be as simple as strolling into a shop and asking the proprietor where he himself has lunch. I found conch chowder in Key West as it was meant to be, thick with conch meat long-cooked to chewability, thickened with potatoes, and pink with tomato—tomato for liquid, not milk, because there were no cows on the island when conch recipes were first devised. With Cuban bread, buttered and grilled, chowder makes a hearty meal.

Conch Chowder

2 cups fresh or frozen conch ground three times
4 cups peeled diced potatoes
2 quarts water
¼ pound salt-cured pork, diced

2 medium onions, chopped
1 green pepper, chopped
1 cup fresh or canned tomatoes, drained
1 to 1½ teaspoons salt
¼ teaspoon pepper

Place ground conch in 4-quart saucepan; add potatoes and water. Bring to a boil; reduce heat, and simmer 30 minutes. Fry pork in heavy skillet; add onion and green pepper. Sauté 5 minutes; add to kettle along with tomatoes. Season to taste; cover and simmer about 45 minutes, or until conch is tender and potatoes have dissolved and thickened the chowder. Yield: 8 servings.

Heading North, one might savor the distinctive soups of the Low Country of coastal Georgia and the Carolinas. One might then visit the Outer Banks off the coast of North Carolina. Foodways there have remained relatively unchanged from earlier days because of the islands' very real geographic isolation. In recent years, more people have discovered the delicate beauty of Ocracoke Island, but the residents have not allowed themselves or their island to be altered in any way for the tourist trade. An Ocracoker's friendly Southern accent is still tinged with Old English inflections, making it one of the most interesting of our many "languages." Upon leaving this island where tradition is not just observed but lived, a traveler may bear north as far as Baltimore to find she-crab soup so elegant it borders on decadence, before turning west to sample such landlocked traditions as Brunswick stew, Kentucky burgoo, and Arkansas egg soup.

When the American settler moved inland, his intrepid wife packed up her black iron kettle and shared his wilderness venture. His skill with the rifle kept the kettle simmering with squirrel and rabbit meat. But it was not until they had planted and harvested their first garden that she was able to throw together that imperishable Southern favorite, Brunswick stew.

Whether it is named for Brunswick, Georgia, or Brunswick, Virginia, does not matter. When game is in short supply in my kitchen, I use a fat hen instead and cut down the salt pork to one-half pound, and it is still Brunswick stew. In Georgia, this stew often accompanies a barbecue, just as burgoo goes with barbecue in Kentucky.

Brunswick Stew

3 squirrels or 2 rabbits
5 quarts boiling water
1 pound salt pork, cut into strips
1 large onion, minced
4 cups tomatoes, chopped
2 cups lima beans, canned or frozen
2 cups whole kernel corn, canned or frozen
8 to 12 potatoes, peeled and cubed
1 tablespoon salt
1 teaspoon black pepper
Dash of cayenne pepper
1 tablespoon plus 1 teaspoon sugar
½ cup butter or margarine
¼ cup all-purpose flour

Cut up squirrels or rabbits as for fricassee. Drop into boiling water in a large kettle. Add salt pork and onion. Cover and simmer 2 hours, removing foam at beginning of cooking. Add vegetables and seasonings and bring to a boil; cover and simmer 1 hour longer, stirring occasionally to prevent burning.

Make a paste of butter and flour; shape into small balls and drop into stew. Boil for 10 minutes, stirring to make a smooth stew. Add more seasoning, if necessary. Yield: 12 servings.

And just what is "real" Kentucky burgoo? It is just about anything the cook says it is. I have seen recipes calling for a thickening of rice or even oatmeal, which does seem to be stretching the definition a bit far. It would be difficult to choose among several "true" stories about its origin, but burgoo dates back to the time when hunting game was the major source of meat supply.

Burgoo recipes are fairly loose; some cooks use cabbage while others say cabbage has no place in it. Otherwise, there is general agreement that entire vegetable gardens must be sacrificed when a big burgoo is brewed.

Having worked with burgoo for a long time, I have developed a method for cooking it in the oven, obviating the need for the incessant stirring that serves not only to keep it from sticking to the pot but also tends to reduce the ingredients to a homogeneous mass. To be fair about it, burgoo is a bunch of trouble to make, so it makes sense to cook a large quantity at one time. It will keep several days in the refrigerator and is actually better made a day or two ahead and reheated. It freezes well, too. Burgoo will stand alone as a main dish, served with corn sticks, coleslaw, and a fruit cobbler for dessert.

Kentucky Burgoo

3 to 4 pounds beef chuck
2 to 3 pounds lamb or
    mutton
1 stewing hen
1 lemon
4 pounds potatoes
2 pounds onions
1 pound carrots
4 (1-pound) cans tomatoes (or
    use fresh)
⅓ cup Worcestershire sauce

1 (8-ounce) can tomato puree
⅔ cup vinegar
⅔ cup catsup
2 tablespoons salt
1 teaspoon cayenne pepper
6 ears cut or 1 (1-pound) can
    whole kernel corn
1 (1-pound) can lima beans
2 cups fresh or 2 (10-ounce)
    packages frozen sliced okra

You will need an 18- to 20-quart covered container, such as an enamel water-bath canner or roaster. Put the meats together in it, with enough cold water to cover. Simmer, covered, until meat is almost off the bones. Remove meat, cool, remove bones and fat, and put meat along with the lemon through the coarse blade of food chopper. Degrease the broth by skimming well or, preferably, refrigerating overnight, and lifting off fat in the morning. (Refrigerate the meat separately if you use this method.) Combine the meat with the vegetables, which have been peeled and chopped rather small; then mix in tomatoes, Worcestershire sauce, puree, vinegar, catsup, salt, and pepper. This mixing should be done in the large cooking vessel. Bring the broth to boiling in a separate container and pour enough broth over the vegetable-meat mixture to come within an inch of covering the mixture. Cover the cooking vessel.

Cook the burgoo in either of two ways: Barely simmer in a covered kettle on top of the stove for 7 to 8 hours, stirring occasionally; or bake, covered, at 210° for 18 to 20 hours. The latter method requires no stirring.

There are three ingredients left to be added: For the stove-top method, add corn, limas, and okra for the last hour of cooking. For the oven method, stir them in gently for the last 3 hours of cooking. In any case, taste after adding them and add salt, if needed. Yield: (loosely) 22 pounds.

Note: Use more or less okra, depending on amount of thickening needed. This is a loose-knit recipe; burgoo is that kind of thing. You can juggle the vegetables to your heart's content.

One of the most unusual wet foods I have encountered is cooked down in Lunenburg County, Virginia. They call it "Sheep Stew," but it is not the same as lamb stew, with which we are affectionately familiar. This is a hearty dish with onion being the only vegetable. If the school band needs new uniforms, or the church recreation room wants a piano, the fund raisers announce a sheep stew. Hungry donors turn out in droves, many bringing containers for carryouts to stock their freezers.

Sheep Stew

50 to 60 pounds fat lamb	7 tablespoons black pepper
3 pounds white fat pork	10 tablespoons salt
3 pounds smoked pork side meat	4 to 5 pounds butter or margarine
50 to 60 pounds onions	3½ to 4 loaves of bread, broken into pieces
3 tablespoons red pepper	

Dress lamb and place in refrigerator until well chilled. Saw the sides from the backbone and cut the meat into smaller portions. Place meat in a kettle with cold water (a 30- to 35-gallon washpot is good if you cook it outdoors). Start the fire. Add the finely cubed fat meat and side meat. Then add onion. When meat is tender, remove all bones, and add seasoning; taste and adjust seasoning. Add butter and bread.

To stir, use a pronged stick 5 feet long, or a long-handled fork. Stir enough to keep stew from sticking. When water is needed, add hot, not cold, water. Cook until thick enough to eat with a fork. This requires 6 hours or more. Serve hot. Yield: about 75 servings.

The savory Brunswick and other stews may be sampled as well at water's edge as inland and are among our most firmly entrenched traditions. The range of Southern soups is unlimited, and whether one is serving four or four thousand, the South has a soup for every occasion, every mood. One has only to choose, for any one of these recipes can be the making of a dinner—or a day.

"Trouble always sets heavy on an empty stomach."
Alice Hegan Rice

Soups and Stews

Fire Engine Chili

½ pound beef suet, chopped
2 pounds ground round steak
3 cloves garlic, minced
¼ cup chili powder
2 tablespoons paprika
1 tablespoon salt
½ teaspoon pepper
½ teaspoon cumin seeds
4 chili peppers, crushed
4 cups water
3 (15-ounce) cans kidney beans,
    drained

Lightly brown suet in a Dutch oven; do not drain. Add ground steak, garlic, and seasonings; cook until beef is light brown. Cover and simmer 2 hours, stirring occasionally.

Add water to meat mixture; cover and simmer 1 hour and 45 minutes, stirring occasionally. Stir in beans; simmer 15 minutes. Yield: 6 to 8 servings.

Hearty Baked Chili And Beans

5 cups water
2 teaspoons salt
1 pound dried pinto beans, washed
2 pounds ground beef
3 teaspoons salt
1 (28-ounce) can whole tomatoes,
    undrained
2 medium onions, chopped
1 clove garlic, minced
¼ cup chili powder
¼ teaspoon ground cumin
¼ teaspoon pepper

Bring water and salt to a boil in a Dutch oven; add beans, return to a boil, and boil 2

minutes. Remove from heat; cover and let soak 1 hour.

Brown beef in a skillet; add to beans. Stir in remaining ingredients; cover, and bake at 350° for 3½ hours or until beans are tender. Remove cover, and bake 30 minutes longer. Yield: about 8 servings.

Savory Chili

¼ cup olive oil
2 cloves garlic, minced
1 large onion, chopped
3 green onions, chopped
4 stalks celery with leaves, chopped
1 tablespoon chopped fresh parsley
2 pounds ground chuck
1 (6-ounce) can tomato paste
1 (15-ounce) can tomato sauce
5 to 6 cups water
1 (1½-ounce) can chili powder
1¼ teaspoons salt
Dash of pepper
1 cup cooked red beans (optional)
Condiments

Heat olive oil in a 5-quart Dutch oven. Add garlic, onion, celery, and parsley; sauté just until tender, about 5 minutes. Add ground beef, and brown, stirring occasionally.

Drain off pan drippings, reserving 3 tablespoons. Add reserved pan drippings to meat mixture. Stir in tomato paste, tomato sauce, water, chili powder, salt, and pepper. Bring to a boil; reduce heat, and simmer 1 hour. Add red beans during last 15 minutes, if desired.

Serve chili with the following condiments: shredded lettuce, shredded Cheddar cheese, diced onion, and tortilla chips. Yield: 8 to 10 servings.

Gregg Chili

1 pound dried pinto beans
2 teaspoons salt
¼ pound salt pork, sliced
¼ cup plus 2 tablespoons vegetable
 oil
6 pounds ground beef or game
9 onions, chopped
4 (14½- or 16-ounce) cans tomatoes,
 undrained
2 tablespoons salt
6 cloves garlic, minced
½ cup chili powder
4 teaspoons dried cilantro
2 teaspoons sugar
2 teaspoons hot pepper sauce
6 jalapeño peppers, seeded and
 chopped
2 teaspoons ground cinnamon

Wash beans thoroughly; cover with water, and soak overnight. The next day add 2 teaspoons salt and salt pork. Simmer over low heat until tender, about 2 hours.

Heat oil in a 12-quart pot; add meat and onions. Brown meat slowly. Add remaining ingredients except beans; simmer 1 hour. Stir in beans; simmer 30 minutes, stirring occasionally. Yield: 9 to 10 quarts.

Texas Championship Chili

2 large onions, chopped
3 cloves garlic, minced
1 jalapeño pepper, finely chopped
1 tablespoon peanut oil
3 pounds boneless chuck roast,
 finely diced
1 teaspoon cumin seeds
1½ tablespoons whole oregano leaves
1 (1½-ounce) can chili powder
1 (28-ounce) can whole tomatoes,
 undrained
3½ cups water
1½ teaspoons instant corn masa
 (optional)
Shredded Cheddar cheese (optional)

Sauté onion, garlic, and jalapeño pepper in oil until tender; set aside. Combine meat, cumin, and oregano in a Dutch oven; cook until meat is browned. Add onion mixture, chili powder, tomatoes, and water; bring to a boil. Reduce heat and simmer 2 to 3 hours, stirring frequently.

For thicker chili, combine corn masa with small amount of cold water to make a paste; add to chili, stirring constantly. Top with shredded cheese, if desired. Yield: 5 to 7 servings.

Super Hot And Spicy Chili

¼ pound dried pinto beans
2 (10-ounce) cans tomatoes with
 chiles
¼ cup margarine
1¼ pounds ground beef
½ pound ground pork
1¾ cups chopped green pepper
1 tablespoon vegetable oil
2½ cups chopped onion
¼ cup chopped fresh parsley
1 clove garlic, crushed
3 to 4 tablespoons chili powder
1 tablespoon salt
1 teaspoon pepper
1 teaspoon cumin seeds
1 teaspoon monosodium glutamate

Wash beans; cover with 2 inches water in a large Dutch oven, and soak overnight. Cook beans in same water, covered, until tender. Add tomatoes; simmer 5 minutes.

Melt margarine in 10-inch skillet. Add meat; cook until browned. Set aside.

Sauté green pepper in oil 5 minutes; add onion and cook until tender. Stir in meat mixture, parsley, garlic, and chili powder; cook 10 minutes over low heat. Add mixture to beans; stir in remaining ingredients. Cover and simmer 1 hour; uncover and simmer 30 minutes. Yield: 8 to 10 servings.

Chicken-Sausage Gumbo

1 (2-pound) broiler-fryer chicken
¼ cup vegetable oil, divided
3 tablespoons all-purpose flour
2 quarts water
1 pound smoked sausage, cut into
    ½-inch slices
½ cup chopped fresh parsley
1 green pepper, chopped
1 cup chopped celery
1 small clove garlic or 1 teaspoon
    garlic salt
2 tablespoons Worcestershire sauce
4 drops hot sauce
1 bunch green onions with tops,
    chopped
Hot cooked rice

Cut chicken into small pieces and brown in about 2 tablespoons oil. Remove chicken. Add flour and the remaining oil; stir continuously over low heat to a rich, dark brown. Gradually stir in water, blending well. Add next 7 ingredients. Simmer over low heat until tender, approximately 1 hour. Add green onion, and remove from heat. Serve over hot rice. Yield: 8 to 10 servings.

Crab Gumbo

12 large crabs
1 cup butter or margarine
3 medium onions, chopped
2 tablespoons all-purpose flour
1 cup chopped smoked ham
3 quarts cold water
Salt and pepper to taste
2 tablespoons filé powder
Hot cooked rice

Wash crabs, getting rid of all sand; remove feelers and gills. Cut crabs into quarters.

Heat butter in heavy soup kettle. Add onion and sauté carefully until it begins to brown; add flour. Cook over low heat, stirring constantly, until browned. Add crabs,

ham, and water. Season to taste. Cover; simmer 1 to 1½ hours. Just before serving, sprinkle in filé powder. Do not allow to boil after addition of filé. Serve over hot cooked rice. Yield: 10 to 12 servings.

Southern Gumbo

1 cup vegetable oil
1 cup all-purpose flour
8 stalks celery, chopped
3 large onions, chopped
1 green pepper, chopped
2 cloves garlic, minced
About ½ cup chopped fresh parsley
    (optional)
1 pound sliced okra
2 tablespoons shortening
2 quarts chicken stock
2 quarts water
½ cup Worcestershire sauce
Hot sauce to taste
½ cup catsup
1 large tomato, chopped
2 tablespoons salt
4 slices bacon, or large slice ham,
    chopped
1 or 2 bay leaves
¼ teaspoon dried thyme leaves
¼ teaspoon dried rosemary leaves
Red pepper flakes to taste (optional)
2 cups cooked chopped chicken
1 or 2 pounds cooked crabmeat
4 pounds boiled shrimp
1 pint oysters (optional)
1 teaspoon molasses or brown sugar
Lemon juice (optional)
Cooked rice

Heat oil in heavy iron pot over medium heat (or use oven method for cooking roux). Add flour very slowly, stirring constantly with a wooden spoon until roux is medium brown. This will take from 30 to 40 minutes.

Add celery, onion, green pepper, garlic, and parsley, if desired; cook an additional 45 minutes to 1 hour, stirring constantly. (You may cut cooking time at this stage, but the gumbo will not be as good.)

Fry okra in 2 tablespoons shortening until brown. Add to gumbo and stir well over low heat for a few minutes. (At this stage the mixture may be cooled, packaged, and frozen or refrigerated for later use.)

Add chicken stock, water, Worcestershire sauce, hot sauce, catsup, chopped tomato, salt, bacon or ham, bay leaves, thyme, rosemary, and red pepper flakes, if desired. Simmer for 2½ to 3 hours.

About 30 minutes before serving time, add cooked chicken, crabmeat, and shrimp; simmer for 30 minutes. Add oysters, if desired, during last 10 minutes of simmering period. Add molasses or brown sugar. Check seasonings and add more, if needed. A bit of lemon juice may be added at the very last, if desired. Put a generous amount of hot, cooked rice in soup bowls; spoon gumbo over the rice and serve immediately. Yield: 12 large servings.

Shrimp Gumbo

    2 cups sliced fresh okra or 1
        (10-ounce) package frozen
        sliced okra
    ⅓ cup vegetable oil
    ⅔ cup chopped green onion with
        tops
    3 cloves garlic, finely minced
    1½ teaspoons salt
    ½ teaspoon pepper
    1 pound peeled deveined shrimp
    2 cups hot water
    1 cup canned tomatoes
    2 whole bay leaves
    6 drops hot sauce
    1½ cups cooked rice

Sauté okra in oil about 10 minutes, stirring constantly. Add onion, garlic, salt, pepper, and shrimp; cook about 5 minutes. Add water, tomatoes, and bay leaves. Cover and simmer 20 minutes. Remove bay leaves. Add hot sauce. Place ¼ cup rice in each of 6 soup bowls; fill with gumbo. Yield: 6 servings.

Okra Seafood Gumbo

Earl Peyroux grew up in a New Orleans Creole family. A teacher of cooking and host for a television cook show in Pensacola, Peyroux makes this seafood gumbo with okra.

    3 pounds okra
    ¼ cup vegetable oil
    ⅓ cup vegetable oil
    ⅓ cup all-purpose flour
    4 medium onions, chopped
    4 teaspoons tomato paste
    4 cups water
    2 pounds shrimp, peeled and
        deveined
    1 pint oysters
    1 pound crabmeat
    1 cup diced ham
    ¾ cup chopped parsley
    2 cloves garlic, finely chopped
    3 bay leaves
    1 cup finely chopped celery
    Salt and pepper to taste
    Hot sauce to taste
    Hot cooked rice

Thinly slice okra and sauté in ¼ cup oil until thick; set aside. Combine ⅓ cup oil and flour in a heavy pot. Cook over medium heat, stirring constantly, until a rich brown roux is formed. Add onion, tomato paste, and water; blend well. Add okra, shrimp, oysters, crabmeat, and ham. Season with parsley, garlic, bay leaves, celery, salt, and pepper. Simmer, uncovered, about 1 hour. Add hot sauce and serve in soup bowls over rice. Yield: about 12 servings.

Catfish Chowder

The coastal areas are more famous for chowders than the inland South, of course, but anyone who has tasted catfish chowder will swear it holds up to any other. All along the South's river deltas the catfish is as much a mainstay in the soup kettle as it is in the frying pan.

Large, firm catfish bones
5 cups water
2 teaspoons salt
2 onions, minced
3 or 4 potatoes, peeled and diced
1 (16-ounce) can tomatoes, undrained
¼ teaspoon pepper
2 pounds catfish fillets, cubed
1 tablespoon lemon juice
2 tablespoons chopped parsley

Combine fish bones, water, and salt in a Dutch oven; bring to a boil. Reduce heat; simmer 10 minutes. Remove and discard bones. Add onion, potatoes, tomatoes, and pepper to liquid. Bring to a boil; reduce heat and simmer until potatoes are tender. Add fish; simmer until fish flakes. Add lemon juice and parsley. Serve hot with crisp hush puppies. Yield: 5 to 6 servings.

Ocracoke Clam Chowder

Dinner on Ocracoke, in a restaurant overlooking Silver Lake Harbor, might well start with a strong-flavored clam chowder. In common with Key West, Ocracoke offers its chowders cooked with a water base. Milk was not easy to come by in early days; canned milk was hoarded for the children's use.

1 (1-inch-thick) slice salt pork
2½ pounds potatoes, peeled and diced
1½ pints fresh minced clams
1 onion, chopped
3 quarts water
2¼ teaspoons salt

Fry salt pork over medium heat in a large Dutch oven until done. Remove pork, reserving drippings in pan.

Dice pork; combine with potatoes, clams, onion, water, and salt in Dutch oven. Bring to a boil, and reduce heat; cover and simmer 2 hours and 15 minutes or until potatoes are tender. Yield: 8 to 12 servings.

Creamy Fish Chowder

1 cup diced potatoes
1 cup boiling water
3 slices bacon, chopped
1 medium onion, chopped
¾ pound fish fillets, cubed
1 cup milk
½ teaspoon salt
⅛ teaspoon pepper
2 tablespoons chopped fresh parsley

Place potatoes in boiling water in a Dutch oven; cover and cook 10 to 15 minutes. Fry bacon until transparent; add onion, and cook until onion is soft and bacon is lightly browned. Add bacon, onion, bacon drippings, and fish fillets to potatoes. Simmer 10 minutes or until potatoes and fish are done. Stir in milk and seasonings; simmer 5 minutes. Sprinkle with parsley. Yield: 2 to 3 servings.

Corn Chowder

¼ pound salt pork, diced
1 large onion, chopped
2 cups whole kernel corn
2 cups peeled diced potatoes
10 saltine crackers
½ cup milk
Salt and pepper to taste
Ground nutmeg
Boiling water

Fry salt pork in heavy kettle until lightly browned; add onion, and sauté until tender. Add corn and potatoes. Soak crackers in milk;

add to vegetable mixture. Add seasonings to taste, and cover with boiling water. Cover and simmer 45 minutes, stirring occasionally. Yield: 6 servings.

Shrimp And Corn Chowder

1 tablespoon butter or margarine
¼ cup chopped green onion
1 clove garlic, minced
⅛ teaspoon pepper
2 (10¾-ounce) cans cream of potato soup, undiluted
2 cups milk
1 (3-ounce) package cream cheese, softened
1 (8¾-ounce) can whole kernel corn, undrained
1½ pounds fresh shrimp, peeled and deveined

Melt butter in a large Dutch oven; add onion, garlic, and pepper. Sauté until tender. Stir in soup, milk, cream cheese, and corn; bring to a boil, stirring occasionally.

Add shrimp; then cover, reduce heat, and cook 5 to 7 minutes. Serve hot. Yield: about 8 servings.

Hearty Cheddar Chowder

3 cups water
3 chicken bouillon cubes
4 medium potatoes, peeled and diced
1 medium onion, sliced
1 cup thinly sliced carrots
½ cup diced green pepper
⅓ cup butter or margarine
⅓ cup all-purpose flour
3½ cups milk
4 cups (1 pound) shredded sharp Cheddar cheese
1 (2-ounce) jar diced pimiento, drained
¼ teaspoon hot sauce (optional)

Combine water and bouillon cubes in a Dutch oven; bring to a boil. Add vegetables; cover and simmer 12 minutes or until vegetables are tender.

Melt butter in a heavy saucepan; blend in flour, and cook 1 minute. Gradually add milk; cook over medium heat until thickened, stirring constantly. Add cheese, stirring until melted.

Stir cheese sauce, pimiento, and hot sauce, if desired, into vegetable mixture. Cook over low heat until thoroughly heated (do not boil). Yield: 8 to 10 servings.

Ham 'N Cheese Chowder

½ cup water
Dash of salt
2 cups peeled cubed potatoes
3 tablespoons butter or margarine
1 cup chopped onion
3 tablespoons all-purpose flour
Dash of pepper
3 cups milk
1½ cups diced cooked ham
1½ cups (6 ounces) shredded Cheddar cheese
Croutons (optional)

Place ½ cup water and salt in a small saucepan; bring to a boil. Add potatoes, and reduce heat; cook 15 minutes or until potatoes are tender. Drain potatoes, reserving liquid. Set potatoes aside. Add enough water to potato liquid to make 1 cup; set aside.

Melt butter in a 3-quart Dutch oven; add onion, and sauté until tender. Blend in flour and pepper. Stir in milk and potato liquid; cook over medium heat until mixture is bubbly and slightly thickened. Add cooked potatoes and ham; heat gently. Remove from heat, and stir in cheese. Top with croutons, if desired. Yield: 6 to 8 servings.

Inlander's Clam Soup

2 tablespoons bacon drippings
1 bunch green onions, sliced
1 clove garlic, minced
1 cup chopped canned or fresh
    tomatoes
4 cups water
1 small green pepper, chopped
1 stalk celery, chopped
1 carrot, chopped
2 tablespoons chopped fresh parsley
¾ teaspoon dried thyme leaves
1 bay leaf
¼ teaspoon ground cloves
1 teaspoon salt
2 tablespoons tomato paste
2 tablespoons catsup
Pepper
2 (7½-ounce) cans minced clams,
    undrained

Heat bacon drippings in heavy soup kettle. Sauté onion and garlic until tender. Add remaining ingredients except clams; cover. Simmer 30 minutes, or until vegetables are tender. Add clams; simmer 10 minutes. Yield: 8 servings.

Fresh Vegetable And Chicken Stew

1 (4- to 5-pound) baking hen
2 to 3 tablespoons shortening
2 cups water
1 tablespoon salt
¾ teaspoon pepper
12 small white onions
1 cup sliced carrots
1 cup fresh green peas, lima beans,
    or snap beans
1 cup peeled diced potatoes
⅓ cup all-purpose flour
½ cup water

Cut hen into serving-size pieces and brown on all sides in hot shortening. Place in Dutch oven or saucepan with 2 cups water, salt, and pepper. Cover and cook over medium heat 1 hour, or until chicken is tender. Add vegetables about 30 minutes before cooking time is up. Combine flour and ½ cup water, and stir into stew. Cook over medium heat until thickened. Yield: 6 servings.

Mountain People's Brunswick Stew

1 (1½- to 2-pound) broiler-fryer
    chicken, cut into serving-size
    pieces
1 tablespoon salt, divided
Paprika to taste
¼ cup butter or margarine
2 medium onions, sliced
1 medium-size green pepper, diced
3 cups water
2 cups canned tomatoes, undrained
2 tablespoons chopped parsley
½ teaspoon hot sauce
1 teaspoon Worcestershire sauce
2 cups whole kernel corn
1 (10-ounce) package frozen lima
    beans, thawed
3 tablespoons all-purpose flour

Sprinkle chicken with 1 teaspoon salt and paprika. Heat butter in a Dutch oven; add chicken, and brown on all sides.

Add onion and green pepper to chicken; cook until onion is transparent. Add water, tomatoes, parsley, remaining salt, hot sauce, and Worcestershire sauce; bring to a boil. Cover; reduce heat, and simmer 30 minutes.

Add corn and lima beans; cook 20 minutes longer. Blend flour with a little cold water, and gradually stir into stew. Cook 10 minutes, stirring constantly. Yield: 4 to 6 servings.

A Small Burgoo

1 pound pork shank
1 pound beef shank
1 pound breast of lamb
1 pound veal shank
½ (4-pound) baking hen
4 quarts water
½ bunch parsley, chopped
1 cup chopped cabbage
1 green pepper, chopped
2 carrots, diced
2 onions, diced
2 potatoes, peeled and diced
2 cups chopped tomatoes
1 cup cut corn
1 red pepper, seeded and chopped
½ cup lima beans
2 teaspoons Worcestershire sauce
Cayenne pepper and salt to taste

Boil meat in water until tender. Remove meat from broth, reserving broth. Cool. Remove meat from bones, dice, and add to broth. Add remaining ingredients to meat stock and cook until thick. Yield: 12 servings.

Chuckwagon Stew

1 teaspoon sugar
¼ cup all-purpose flour
2 pounds lean beef for stewing
2 tablespoons melted shortening
2 teaspoons salt
¼ teaspoon pepper
1 teaspoon chili powder
¼ teaspoon dried thyme leaves
1 bay leaf
2 tomatoes, peeled and quartered
1½ cups beef broth
6 small potatoes, peeled and
    quartered
6 small carrots, cut into 2-inch pieces
6 small whole onions, peeled
4 stalks celery, cut into 2-inch pieces
1 cup frozen green peas

Combine sugar and flour. Cut beef into 1-inch cubes. Coat beef with flour mixture, and brown in hot shortening.

Add seasonings, tomatoes, and broth to meat; cover and simmer over low heat about 1½ to 2 hours or until meat is almost tender. Stir in vegetables except peas; cover and cook about 30 minutes. Add peas; cover and cook about 15 more minutes. Yield: 6 to 8 servings.

Brown Oyster Stew With Benne (Sesame) Seeds

Oyster stew, it seems to me, might more properly be called a soup. But tradition puts plump oysters into a creamy liquid so rich I have to drop my argument. Down around Charleston, I found an oyster stew that reinforced my faith in regional cooking; it contains parched benne (sesame) seeds. Parch the seeds by browning them either on top of the stove or in the oven; then make the stew.

4 slices bacon
1 large onion, sliced
2 tablespoons all-purpose flour
1½ cups oyster liquor or water
2 tablespoons parched benne
    (sesame) seeds
2 cups oysters

Fry bacon and onion until brown; drain and discard bacon and onion, reserving drippings in pan. Stir flour into reserved drippings and stir vigorously until flour is brown. Remove from heat and gradually stir in oyster liquor; cook over medium heat, stirring constantly, until the mixture is slightly thickened and smooth. Pound benne seed, using pestle and mortar, and add to sauce. Add the oysters and cook until the edges curl. Serve immediately over rice or hominy. Yield: 6 servings.

Oyster Stew

2 green onions, chopped
2 tablespoons melted butter or
    margarine
1 pint oysters, undrained
1 quart half-and-half or milk
Salt to taste
Red pepper to taste
Crackers

Sauté onions in butter; add oysters and their liquid and cook over low heat 3 to 4 minutes or until edges of oysters curl. Add milk, salt, and pepper; heat thoroughly. Serve with crackers. Yield: 8 servings.

Traditional Maryland Oyster Stew

1 pint oysters, undrained
1 quart milk
¼ cup butter or margarine
Salt and pepper to taste
Seafood seasoning (optional)

Cook oysters in liquor in a 4-quart pan over low heat just until edges of oysters begin to curl. Add milk, butter, salt, and pepper; cook over low heat until thoroughly heated, but do not boil. Sprinkle seafood seasoning on each serving, if desired. Yield: about 6 servings.

Papa's Favorite Quail And Oyster Stew

6 to 8 cleaned whole quail
1 teaspoon salt
3 quarts water
2 pints fresh oysters, undrained
¼ cup butter
Freshly ground pepper to taste
1 quart milk

Cook quail in salted water over medium heat in a 5- or 6-quart pot until meat is tender and done. Add oysters, butter, and pepper. Cook until oysters curl on edges, approximately 3 minutes. Add milk, and heat thoroughly. Do not allow to boil. Yield: 6 to 8 servings.

Shrimp And Ham Jambalaya

Jambalaya is not, strictly speaking, a soup. It is a stew, not too wet, made of ham, seafood, or chicken, or a combination of them, and rice. It is at home anywhere in the deep South. Earl Peyroux, who teaches cooking in Pensacola, makes it this way.

2 cups water
2 teaspoons salt
1 cup uncooked regular rice
2 pounds shrimp, peeled and
    deveined
1½ cups finely chopped onion
2 cloves garlic, minced
6 tablespoons butter or margarine
1 (16-ounce) can tomatoes, undrained
3 tablespoons tomato paste
½ cup finely chopped celery
¼ cup finely chopped green pepper
1 tablespoon finely chopped fresh
    parsley
3 whole cloves
½ teaspoon dried thyme leaves
1 teaspoon salt
½ teaspoon cayenne pepper
¼ teaspoon pepper
1 pound cooked ham, diced

Bring 2 cups water and 2 teaspoons salt to a boil in saucepan. Add rice; stir, cover, and reduce to low heat. Cook 18 to 20 minutes, or until water is absorbed; set aside.

Boil shrimp in salted water for 5 minutes or until pink; drain and set aside.

Sauté onion and garlic in butter in large skillet for 5 minutes. Add tomatoes and tomato paste, stirring to chop tomatoes; cook 5 minutes. Add next 8 ingredients; cook until thick enough to mound when dropped from a spoon. Add ham and cook 5 minutes. Add shrimp and cook 5 minutes. Add rice and stir over low heat until mixture is dry. Serve immediately. Yield: 8 to 10 servings.

Shrimp Jambalaya

¾ pound cooked peeled deveined shrimp or 3 (4½-ounce) cans shrimp, drained
8 slices bacon, chopped
3 tablespoons chopped onion
3 tablespoons chopped green pepper
1 clove garlic, finely minced
1 tablespoon all-purpose flour
½ teaspoon salt
½ teaspoon Worcestershire sauce
Dash of cayenne pepper
Dash of paprika
½ cup sliced pitted ripe olives
1 (16-ounce) can tomatoes, undrained
2 cups cooked rice

Cut large shrimp in half; set aside. Fry bacon until crisp. Add onion, green pepper, and garlic; cook until tender. Blend in flour and seasonings; add olives and tomatoes and cook until thick, stirring constantly. Stir in rice and shrimp; heat. Yield: 6 servings.

Shrimp Stew

¾ cup diced salt pork
1 tablespoon all-purpose flour
3 pounds shrimp, peeled and deveined
¼ cup diced onion
1 cup peeled diced potatoes
1 teaspoon salt
½ teaspoon pepper
2 to 3 cups water

Fry salt pork until brown. Add flour and brown slightly, stirring constantly. Add remaining ingredients, blending well. Cover and simmer over low heat until potatoes are tender, 20 to 30 minutes. Yield: 6 servings.

Katherine's Terrapin Stew

3 large terrapins
Salt to taste
1 onion, chopped
6 hard-cooked egg yolks
1 cup butter or margarine
3 tablespoons all-purpose flour
Juice and rind of 1 lemon
1 tablespoon Worcestershire sauce
1 teaspoon ground nutmeg
Red pepper to taste
2 cups half-and-half
6 hard-cooked egg whites, chopped

Cut off and discard heads of terrapins; dip body in boiling water for a short time, and carefully pull off and discard outer skin from the feet and all that will come off the back. With a sharp knife cut open the terrapins and remove the eggs; set eggs aside in small amount of cold water. Discard entrails and gall bags; reserve livers for use in other recipes. Leave all the legs on the backs and simmer in about 3 pints water, with salt and onion about 45 minutes (do not boil). When tender, remove meat from back and discard bones. Cut up meat across the grain to prevent stringing; chill stock until ready to prepare stew.

To prepare stew, combine egg yolks, butter, and flour; blend well, and set aside.

Bring reserved stock to a boil; add egg yolk mixture, lemon juice and rind, Worcestershire sauce, nutmeg, red pepper, salt, and reserved terrapin meat and eggs. Stir in half-and-half and egg whites. Heat thoroughly. Remove lemon rind before serving. Yield: 8 servings.

Firehouse Bean Soup

  1 pound Great Northern beans
  ¾ pound smoked bacon or ham,
      chopped
  2 quarts water
  1 pod red pepper
  1½ teaspoons salt
  ¼ teaspoon pepper

Wash beans thoroughly; place in soup kettle with water barely to cover. Bring to a boil over high heat; boil until water is almost evaporated. Add water and repeat cooking process 3 times, or until beans are fairly tender and puffy.

Add remaining ingredients. Bring to a boil; reduce heat and simmer until beans are tender. Remove 1 cup beans; mash, and return to soup to thicken. Yield: 8 servings.

Lentil Soup

  Bones from baked ham or roast lamb
  2½ quarts cold water
  2 tablespoons salt
  1 small clove garlic
  8 to 10 peppercorns
  1 medium onion, sliced
  1 cup celery leaves
  1 bay leaf
  4 sprigs parsley
  1½ cups quick-cooking lentils
  2 cups diced carrots
  ⅛ teaspoon pepper

Place bones in large kettle; cover with water. Add salt. Tie garlic, peppercorns, onion, celery leaves, bay leaf, and parsley in cheesecloth; add to kettle. Cover pot; simmer 3 to 4 hours.

Remove bones and cheesecloth bag. Skim fat from broth. Remove any meat from bones and return to broth. Add lentils; cover and cook over medium heat 30 minutes. Add diced carrots and pepper. Continue cooking for 30 minutes, or until lentils and carrots are tender. Yield: 6 servings.

Spanish Bean Soup

During the festivities attending Gasparilla Week in Tampa-St. Petersburg, tourists and natives alike line the streets to taste the free bean soup ladled out by white-aproned chefs. Garbanzo (Spanish bean) soup, richly yellow, is thick with potatoes and seasoned with chorizo sausage. It may not be the best choice for a first course, depending on one's will power, for this well-remembered heritage of the Spanish is filling enough to constitute a meal in itself.

  ½ pound garbanzo beans
  1 tablespoon salt
  1 beef bone
  1 ham bone
  2 quarts water
  ¼ pound white bacon
  Dash of paprika
  1 onion, chopped
  ¼ cup lard
  1 pound potatoes, peeled and
      quartered
  Dash of saffron
  Salt to taste
  1 chorizo (Spanish sausage),
      thinly sliced

Soak garbanzo beans overnight with 1 tablespoon salt in sufficient water to cover. Drain the salted water from the beans, and add beef bone, ham bone, and 2 quarts water to the beans. Cook 45 minutes over low heat. Fry bacon, paprika, and onion in lard. Add to beans along with potatoes, saffron, and salt. Cook over low heat until potatoes are done; remove from heat and add chorizo. Yield: 4 to 6 servings.

Southern Gumbo (page 20) is made with shrimp, crab, oysters, chicken, and ham, with a subtle seasoning of garlic, onion, and tomatoes.

Chili cook-offs are a popular event, especially in Texas, where cooks from everywhere gather to prepare their favorite chili recipe. Some of our favorites begin on page 18.

Traditional Borscht

2½ pounds beef brisket or beef
    stew meat
3 pounds beef bones, cracked
1 tablespoon salt
12 peppercorns
8 fresh beets (4 unpeeled, 4 peeled)
4 small carrots
6 to 8 stalks celery
1 large green pepper, finely chopped
1 small head cabbage, finely chopped
2 medium onions, finely chopped
1 clove garlic
1 (8-ounce) carton commercial sour
    cream

Place meat and bones in large kettle with
enough water to cover. Add salt and peppercorns. Chop unpeeled beets; add to meat
mixture. Bring to a boil; reduce heat and
simmer 2 hours. Drain mixture, reserving
liquid in kettle; skim fat. Shred meat and
return to soup. Discard beets and bones.

Cut 4 peeled beets, carrots, and celery in
julienne strips; add to soup along with remaining vegetables. Pierce garlic clove with
a wooden pick; add to soup. Cover; simmer
1½ hours, adding water as needed for desired consistency. Adjust seasoning, if necessary. Remove garlic before serving. Ladle
soup into serving bowls and garnish with sour
cream. Yield: 12 servings.

Cabbage Soup

1½ to 2 pounds meaty beef bones
1 bay leaf
6 peppercorns
1 (28-ounce) can tomatoes, undrained
1 medium head cabbage, coarsely
    chopped
¼ pound salt pork, cubed small
2 tablespoons all-purpose flour
1 teaspoon salt
¼ teaspoon pepper

Place bones in soup kettle; add bay leaf,
peppercorns, and enough water to cover.
Bring to a boil; reduce heat and simmer,
covered, about 1 hour.

Add tomatoes and cabbage to soup mixture; simmer about 1 hour. Remove bones;
remove meat from bones. Chop meat and
add to soup.

Fry salt pork until crisp. Add flour and stir
over medium heat until flour is light brown;
add to soup. Add a little soup to skillet,
stirring to loosen flour particles; stir into
soup. Stir in salt and pepper. Yield: about 12
servings.

Note: Smoked sausage or smoked ham
hocks may be substituted for the meaty beef
bones.

Country Ham Bone Soup

1 baked country ham bone
3 quarts water
1 cup sliced carrots
1 cup sliced celery
½ cup chopped onion
1 (10-ounce) package frozen whole
    kernel corn
1 (10-ounce) package frozen lima
    beans
1 (16-ounce) can black-eyed peas,
    undrained
1 (16-ounce) can tomatoes, undrained
2 cups cooked elbow macaroni
Salt and pepper to taste

Break ham bone into 2 or 3 pieces. Place in
large soup kettle. Add water; simmer 30
minutes. Remove bones; remove meat from
bones. Chop meat and return to broth. Add
carrot, celery, and onion; simmer 30 minutes. Add remaining vegetables; simmer 1 to
1½ hours. Add macaroni; season with salt
and pepper. Heat to serving temperature.
Yield: 15 to 20 servings.

Gazpacho

½ cup olive oil
¼ cup lemon juice
6 cups tomato juice
2 cups beef broth
½ cup finely minced onion
2 tomatoes, chopped
2 cups finely minced celery
¼ teaspoon hot sauce
2 teaspoons salt
½ teaspoon pepper
2 green peppers, finely chopped
2 cucumbers, diced small
Croutons

Beat together oil and lemon juice. Stir in tomato juice, broth, onion, tomatoes, celery, hot sauce, salt, and pepper. Taste for seasoning. The mixture should be well seasoned; more salt or hot sauce may be used, if desired. Chill the soup at least 3 hours. Pour into soup bowls. Add green peppers, cucumbers, and croutons separately to each serving. Soup will keep several days in the refrigerator. Yield: 8 to 10 servings.

Hamburg-Vegetable Soup

1 pound ground beef
1 medium onion, chopped
2 quarts water
½ cup chopped celery with leaves
1 cup pearl barley
3 potatoes, peeled and diced
1 tablespoon salt
¼ teaspoon pepper
1 (16-ounce) can tomatoes, undrained

Brown beef in heavy soup kettle, stirring to crumble; drain off drippings. Add onion, water, celery, and barley. Bring to a boil; reduce heat and simmer 1 hour. Add potatoes, seasonings, and tomatoes. Add more water, if needed, for desired consistency. Simmer 30 minutes, or until barley is soft but not mushy. Yield: about 12 servings.

Mushroom Barley Soup

½ cup (1 ounce) dried sliced
    mushrooms
3 (10¾-ounce) cans beef bouillon,
    undiluted
4 cups water
¼ cup pearl barley
1 tablespoon minced onion or 1
    teaspoon dried onion flakes
1 stalk celery
1 bay leaf
½ teaspoon salt
¼ teaspoon pepper

Soak mushrooms in cold water to cover overnight, or soak in boiling water 30 minutes. Drain; set aside. Combine bouillon and 4 cups water in saucepan; add barley and bring to a boil. Reduce heat; add onion, celery, and bay leaf. Simmer about 45 minutes or until barley is almost tender. Add mushrooms and continue cooking 20 minutes; add seasonings. Remove celery and bay leaf. Serve hot. Yield: 6 to 8 servings.

Okra Soup

3 pounds meaty beef soup bones
2 quarts water
2 cups freshly cut or frozen corn
4 cups fresh or frozen okra, sliced
3 cups chopped tomatoes, fresh
    or canned
2 teaspoons salt
¼ teaspoon pepper
¼ cup butter or margarine
1 tablespoon all-purpose flour

Place beef bones and water in soup kettle; simmer 1½ to 2 hours, or until meat is falling from bones. Remove meat from bones. Skim fat from broth; add meat and vegetables. Add seasonings. Simmer 1 hour, adding more water if necessary. Combine butter and flour, blending well with a fork. Stir flour mixture into soup; simmer 15 minutes longer. Yield: 12 to 15 servings.

Fried Okra Soup

2 cups fresh or frozen lima beans
2 cups fresh or frozen cut corn
3 potatoes, peeled and diced
¼ teaspoon pepper
¼ teaspoon salt
6 tomatoes, chopped
2 onions, chopped
2 stalks celery, chopped
2 tablespoons sugar
¼ head cabbage, chopped
¼ pound salt pork, finely diced
1 quart fresh or frozen okra, sliced

Combine first 9 ingredients in soup kettle, adding water to cover. Cover; simmer about 45 minutes or until vegetables are almost tender. Add cabbage.

Fry salt pork in skillet until done; reserve drippings Add pork to soup. Brown okra in drippings; add to soup. Add water as necessary for desired consistency. Simmer, covered, 20 minutes longer. Yield: about 12 servings.

Winter Okra Soup

2 onions, finely chopped
2 tablespoons butter or margarine
1 pint oysters, undrained
3 tablespoons uncooked regular rice
1 (16-ounce) can tomatoes, undrained
1 pod red pepper, seeded
1 (14½-ounce) can cut okra

Sauté onion in butter until onion is lightly browned. Drain oysters, reserving liquid. Add water to liquid to measure 3½ quarts.

Combine liquid mixture, onion, rice, tomatoes, and red pepper in a Dutch oven. Bring mixture to a boil; reduce heat and simmer 3 hours, stirring frequently. Add okra and simmer 5 minutes; add oysters and simmer until edges of oysters begin to curl. Yield: 10 to 12 servings.

Potato Soup With Butter Dumplings

¼ cup butter or margarine
1 medium onion, chopped
4 cups water
3 pounds potatoes, peeled and diced
1 stalk celery, chopped
1 tablespoon salt
¼ teaspoon pepper
2 tablespoons chopped fresh parsley
Dumpling Batter
1 (8-ounce) carton commercial sour cream

Melt butter in large soup pot; add onion and sauté until tender. Add water; bring to a boil and add potatoes, celery, salt, pepper, and parsley. Reduce heat and simmer 15 minutes. Drop dumpling batter into soup by teaspoonfuls. Cover and simmer 10 minutes. Remove from heat and gradually stir in sour cream. Heat thoroughly, but do not boil. Yield: 10 servings.

Dumpling Batter:

2 tablespoons butter, softened
¼ cup plus 2 tablespoons all-purpose flour
2 eggs, beaten
¼ teaspoon salt
Dash of ground nutmeg

Cream butter with flour; beat in eggs. Stir in seasonings, mixing well. Yield: about ½ cup.

Split Pea Soup

1½ cups dried split peas
2 bay leaves
8 peppercorns
1 pound ham hocks
½ cup finely diced carrots
1 cup finely diced celery
1½ cups finely diced onion
2 quarts boiling water
¾ teaspoon sugar
1 to 2 teaspoons salt
¼ teaspoon pepper
Dash of garlic powder

Wash peas; drain and place in soup kettle. Tie bay leaves and peppercorns in cheese-cloth bag; add to peas. Add ham hocks, vegetables, water, and sugar. Cover; simmer over low heat until peas are soft, about 2 to 3 hours, stirring occasionally. Remove ham hocks and cheese-cloth bag; stir in seasonings. Yield: 8 to 10 servings.

Note: Flavor improves upon standing. Soup will thicken upon standing at room temperature, but may be thinned with half-and-half. Keep soup hot in double boiler to prevent thickening.

Scotch Broth, Alabama Style

3 pounds chuck roast or other beef
    with bones
3 quarts water
½ cup pearl barley
¼ medium head cabbage, chopped
4 carrots, chopped
2 parsnips, chopped
3 or 4 turnips, chopped
3 medium potatoes, peeled and
    cubed
1 medium onion, chopped
2 tablespoons chopped fresh parsley
Salt and pepper to taste
2 cups fresh or frozen green peas
    (optional)

Place beef, water, and barley in soup kettle; cover, and simmer 2 hours. Add cabbage, carrots, parsnips, turnips, and potatoes. More water may be added as necessary. Cover and simmer 1 hour. Add remaining ingredients; simmer an additional 45 minutes. Serve hot. Yield: 12 servings.

Note: For a more traditional Scotch broth, use lamb instead of beef; sauté vegetables before adding; omit peas.

Shrimp Bisque

¼ cup butter or margarine
1 medium onion, sliced
2 stalks celery, sliced
1 small carrot, sliced
1 tomato, chopped
3 cups water
1 bay leaf
1 teaspoon salt
¼ teaspoon pepper
1 slice lemon
2 pounds shrimp, peeled and
    deveined
½ cup dry sherry, divided
1 cup whipping cream

Melt butter in large saucepan; add vegetables and cook, stirring occasionally, until tender. Add water, bay leaf, seasonings, and lemon. Add shrimp and half the sherry. Simmer 30 minutes. Remove from heat and allow shrimp to cool in the cooking mixture. Discard bay leaf and lemon. Puree entire mixture, using either blender or food mill. Pour mixture into top of double boiler; add remaining sherry and cream. Bring to serving temperature over hot water. Serve hot. Yield: 8 servings.

Oyster Tomato Bisque

1 (12-ounce) can fresh oysters,
    undrained
3 tablespoons butter or margarine
3 tablespoons all-purpose flour
3 cups milk
1 teaspoon salt
¼ teaspoon pepper
1 teaspoon grated onion
1 (10¾-ounce) can tomato soup,
    undiluted
½ cup whipping cream, whipped
6 whole cloves

Heat oysters in a small saucepan just until edges curl. Drain, reserving liquor. Melt butter in heavy saucepan; stir in flour. Slowly stir in reserved oyster liquor and milk. Cook over low heat, stirring constantly, until slightly thickened. Add salt, pepper, and onion. Stir in tomato soup. Add oysters, and remove from heat. Top each serving with a dollop of whipped cream and 1 whole clove. Yield: 6 servings.

Beaufort Cream Of Crab Soup

1 onion, finely chopped
1 tablespoon melted butter
1 cup chicken stock
1 quart half-and-half
1 tablespoon finely chopped parsley
½ teaspoon celery salt
½ teaspoon ground mace
⅛ teaspoon pepper
½ teaspoon salt, or to taste
Dash of red pepper
1 pound crabmeat
2 tablespoons all-purpose flour
¼ cup dry sherry

Sauté onion in butter until transparent in a large skillet. Add chicken stock and slowly pour in half-and-half; stir well. Add seasonings and crabmeat. Stir well, and simmer 15 minutes. Make a thin paste with the flour and a little water, and stir into soup to thicken it

slightly. Just before serving, remove from heat and add sherry. Stir once and serve immediately. Yield: 8 servings.

She-Crab Soup

This soup is so named because of the eggs which the she-crab contains. It can be made with any crabmeat, however. Crab is abundant in South Carolina's coastal waters, and this soup is as famous in the Charleston area today as it was in colonial times when it was served to George Washington during his visit to the city in 1791. He was so impressed that he spread its fame all the way back to New England!

1 pound white crabmeat and roe
6 tablespoons butter
1 tablespoon all-purpose flour
1 pint milk
2 cups half-and-half
½ teaspoon Worcestershire sauce
1 teaspoon grated lemon rind
¼ teaspoon ground mace
1 teaspoon salt
¼ teaspoon freshly ground white
    pepper
3 crackers, finely crumbled
3 tablespoons dry sherry
½ cup whipping cream, whipped
Paprika

Check crabmeat for bits of shell or cartilage. Melt butter in top of a double boiler over rapidly boiling water and blend in flour. Add milk and half-and-half, stirring constantly. Add Worcestershire sauce, grated lemon rind, mace, and crabmeat and roe. Stir well and cook slowly for 20 minutes. Season with salt and white pepper and add cracker crumbs. Allow to stand over hot water on back of stove for 10 or 15 minutes. Serve in heated soup bowls, add ½ tablespoon sherry to each bowl, top with a dollop of whipped cream, and sprinkle with paprika. Yield: 6 to 8 servings.

Iced Avocado Soup

    4 large ripe avocados
    6 cups clarified chicken broth,
        divided
    ¼ cup lemon juice
    ¼ cup dry sherry
    Salt and pepper to taste
    1 (8-ounce) carton commercial sour
        cream
    Minced fresh parsley

Skin and seed avocados; reserve seeds. Puree avocados in blender with 1 cup broth. Pour into bowl; blend in remaining broth, lemon juice, sherry, and seasonings to taste. Stir in sour cream. Chill thoroughly until serving time. (If made a day ahead, put avocado seeds in soup; they will help soup retain color. Remove seeds before serving.) Garnish each serving with parsley. Yield: 12 appetizer servings.

Broccoli Bisque

    2 (10-ounce) packages frozen
        chopped broccoli
    3 cups chicken broth
    1 medium onion, quartered
    2 tablespoons butter or margarine
    1 teaspoon salt
    1 teaspoon curry powder
    Dash of pepper
    2 tablespoons lime juice
    ½ cup commercial sour cream
    1 tablespoon chopped fresh chives

Bring broccoli and broth to a boil in a large saucepan; add onion, butter, salt, curry powder, and pepper. Reduce heat; simmer 10 to 12 minutes. Place half the mixture in container of electric blender; blend at low speed until smooth. Repeat with remaining mixture. Stir in lime juice. Refrigerate at least 4 hours.

Serve in chilled soup bowls with a dollop of sour cream and a sprinkling of chives on top. Yield: 6 to 8 servings.

Iced Cherry Soup

    1 lemon
    1 (16-ounce) package frozen cherries
    4 cups water
    2 cardamom seeds or ⅛ teaspoon
        ground cardamom
    2 teaspoons cornstarch
    2 tablespoons cold water
    3 tablespoons powdered sugar
    8 paper-thin slices lemon

Pare lemon as thinly as possible. Squeeze juice; reserve. Place lemon peel in saucepan with cherries, water, and cardamom; simmer 15 minutes, or until cherries are very tender. Puree in blender, one-third at a time. Return to saucepan. Mix cornstarch with cold water; add to cherry mixture. Add sugar. Stir and cook 5 to 10 minutes, or until slightly thickened and clear. Stir in lemon juice; chill. Garnish each serving with a slice of lemon. Yield: 8 servings.

Iced Cucumber Bisque

    2 large cucumbers
    1 small clove garlic, minced
    1 teaspoon salt
    ½ teaspoon dried dillweed
    1 tablespoon chopped chives
    1 teaspoon lemon juice
    2 (8-ounce) cartons commercial sour
        cream
    2 cups half-and-half
    1 to 2 cups milk
    8 to 10 slices cucumber, unpared

Peel and seed cucumbers; puree in blender with seasonings and lemon juice. Pour into mixing bowl; stir in sour cream, half-and-half, and enough milk to make desired consistency. Chill thoroughly before serving. Garnish each serving with cucumber slice. Yield: 8 to 10 appetizer servings.

Grapefruit-Avocado Soup

2½ cups grapefruit juice, divided
2 ripe avocados, peeled and seeded
1 (8-ounce) carton plain yogurt
½ teaspoon salt
1 teaspoon ground coriander
6 thin slices lemon

Combine 1 cup grapefruit juice, avocados, yogurt, and seasonings in container of electric blender. Process until smooth. Pour into bowl; blend in remaining grapefruit juice. Chill several hours or overnight. Garnish each serving with lemon slice. Yield: 6 to 8 appetizer servings.

Note: Reserve seeds from avocados. Place in soup as it chills to prevent mixture from darkening.

Cream Of Celery Soup

2 cups diced celery
1 quart water
2 tablespoons butter or margarine
3 tablespoons all-purpose flour
3 cups milk
Salt and red pepper to taste

Combine celery and water in a large saucepan; bring to a boil. Reduce heat and simmer until celery is very tender and about 2 cups liquid remains in the saucepan. Drain celery, reserving liquid. Puree celery. Set aside.

Melt butter in a large Dutch oven; stir in flour. Gradually stir in milk, mixing well. Stir in salt, pepper, reserved liquid, and celery, mixing well. Simmer for about 10 minutes, stirring frequently. Yield: 6 to 8 servings.

Cream Of Corn Soup

3 tablespoons butter or margarine
¼ cup minced onion
3 tablespoons all-purpose flour
4 cups milk
2 cups cream-style corn

Melt butter in a large Dutch oven; add onion and sauté until onion is tender. Add flour, stirring until smooth. Gradually stir in milk; cook over medium heat, stirring constantly, until slightly thickened. Stir in corn; cook over low heat until thoroughly heated, about 5 minutes. Yield: 6 servings.

Egg Soup

Every cuisine I have studied has a version of egg soup: the Greek avgolémono, the Chinese egg drop soup, the Dutch rivel soup, to name a few. But when an Ozark family remembers its tradition, the result is a chicken broth left over from stewing a fat hen, thickened and enriched with squares of baked egg. With the chicken broth every modern cook hoards in the deep freeze, this soup can be simplicity itself.

2 to 3 quarts chicken broth
¼ cup all-purpose flour
½ cup whipping cream
¼ cup butter or margarine
½ teaspoon celery salt
½ teaspoon rubbed sage
6 eggs, beaten
2 cups milk
Salt and pepper to taste

Heat broth in large heavy kettle over medium heat. Blend flour with cream and add to broth; add butter, celery salt, and sage. Cover and simmer over low heat for about 1 hour.

Combine eggs, milk, and seasonings to taste, mixing well. Pour into buttered 13- × 9- × 2-inch baking pan. Set pan in a larger pan and add water to measure ½-inch in bottom pan. Bake at 350° about 35 minutes, or until set. Cut into squares, and place in soup tureen. Pour hot soup over squares. Ladle into bowls. Yield: 8 to 10 servings.

Green Pea Soup

    4 quarts fresh green peas, unshelled
    2 quarts water
    1 cup milk
    2 teaspoons all-purpose flour
    Salt and pepper to taste
    3 egg yolks
    ½ cup half-and-half

Shell peas; reserve pods. Combine shells and water in soup kettle. Bring to a boil and boil 45 minutes; strain. Discard pods. Return liquid to kettle; add peas. Cover and simmer over low heat 45 minutes. Combine milk and flour, stirring until smooth; add to soup. Season to taste. Simmer 15 to 20 minutes, stirring occasionally.

    At serving time, beat egg yolks with half-and-half. Gradually add small amount of hot mixture to yolk mixture; then add to remaining hot mixture. Stir well; serve hot. Yield: 8 servings.

Creamy Peanut Soup

    ½ cup butter or margarine
    1 small onion, diced
    2 stalks celery, diced
    3 tablespoons all-purpose flour
    2 quarts hot chicken broth
    1 (8-ounce) jar creamy peanut butter
    1 teaspoon salt
    ¼ teaspoon celery salt
    1 tablespoon lemon juice
    ½ cup skinless peanuts, ground

Melt butter in a Dutch oven; add onion and celery, and sauté for 5 minutes or until limp. Stir in flour; cook, stirring, until bubbly. Stir in chicken broth, and simmer 30 minutes.

    Remove from heat; strain soup, and discard vegetables. Add peanut butter, salt, celery salt, and lemon juice; stir well. Simmer 5 minutes; sprinkle each serving with ground peanuts. Yield: 12 to 15 servings.

Crème Vichyssoise

    4 leeks with tops or 1½ cups
        minced onion
    3 cups peeled sliced potatoes
    3 cups boiling water
    4 chicken bouillon cubes
    3 tablespoons butter or margarine
    1 cup half-and-half or whipping
        cream
    1 cup milk
    1 teaspoon salt
    ¼ teaspoon pepper
    2 tablespoons minced chives
    ¼ teaspoon paprika

Finely chop leeks and green tops. Cook leeks and potatoes, uncovered, in boiling water about 10 minutes or until tender. Do not drain.

    Press mixture through a fine sieve into a double boiler. Add next 6 ingredients. Mix well; reheat. Chill thoroughly. Serve very cold, and top with chives and paprika. Yield: 6 servings.

Tomato Bisque

    2 (10¾-ounce) cans chicken broth,
        undiluted
    1⅓ cups canned tomatoes
    1 cup chopped celery
    2 teaspoons chopped onion
    1 cup chopped carrots
    1 teaspoon salt, divided
    6 tablespoons butter or margarine,
        divided
    ¼ cup all-purpose flour
    2⅔ cups half-and-half, scalded
    2 large tomatoes, peeled and
        chopped
    2 tablespoons sugar
    ¼ teaspoon soda
    Paprika

Combine broth, canned tomatoes, celery, onion, carrots, and ½ teaspoon salt in a saucepan. Heat to boiling point; reduce heat and simmer 20 minutes. Strain; reserve broth and discard the vegetables.

Melt 3 tablespoons butter in a saucepan; gradually stir in flour. Cook, stirring constantly, over low heat 2 minutes. Gradually add half-and-half, stirring constantly. Cook, stirring constantly, until thickened. Remove from heat; stir in reserved broth. Set aside and keep warm.

Melt remaining 3 tablespoons butter in a skillet. Add fresh tomato; sauté 2 to 4 minutes. Stir in sugar, remaining ½ teaspoon salt, and soda. Add to broth mixture, stirring well. Garnish with paprika. Yield: about 8 servings.

Cream Of Turkey Soup

½ cup chopped onion
¼ cup butter or margarine
1 tablespoon all-purpose flour
3 cups turkey or chicken broth
1 cup thin egg noodles
1 cup chopped celery
⅛ teaspoon pepper
1½ teaspoons salt
½ teaspoon poultry seasoning
2 tablespoons parsley flakes
1½ cups cream-style corn
2 cups milk
2 tablespoons chopped pimiento
2 cups cooked cubed turkey

Sauté onion in butter until tender. Add flour, stirring until smooth. Add broth, noodles, celery, and seasonings, mixing well. Simmer 20 minutes or until noodles and celery are tender. Add remaining ingredients; heat and serve. Do not boil. Yield: 5 to 6 servings.

Matzo Ball Soup

3 eggs
3 tablespoons rendered chicken fat
¾ cup matzo meal
1 teaspoon salt
3 tablespoons water
2 quarts water
1 tablespoon salt
6 cups seasoned chicken stock

Combine eggs and chicken fat; add matzo meal and 1 teaspoon salt. Add 3 tablespoons water, mixing well. Cover and refrigerate 45 minutes.

Combine 2 quarts water and 1 tablespoon salt in a 4-quart saucepan; bring to a boil. Shape matzo mixture into 8 balls. Drop balls into boiling water; reduce heat and simmer for 1 hour. Remove matzo balls.

To serve, bring chicken stock to a boil. Place 1 matzo ball in each soup plate; ladle broth over matzo balls. Yield: 8 servings.

Beef Broth

2½ pounds cut-up beef shanks
2 quarts water
1 carrot, cut into eighths
1 onion, quartered
2 stalks celery
1 bay leaf
2 cloves garlic
¼ teaspoon dried thyme leaves
Salt and pepper to taste

Roast meat at 400° for 20 minutes or until browned. Transfer meat to a large kettle and add remaining ingredients. Bring to a boil and simmer, covered, for 2 hours. Strain broth; reserve meat and vegetables for other uses. Cool and skim off fat. Cover and store in refrigerator until ready to use. Yield: about 1½ quarts.

Note: Canned beef broth, beef broth made with bouillon cubes, or beef concentrate may be substituted for freshly made beef broth.

Chicken Broth

4 pounds chicken pieces
1 onion, quartered
2 stalks celery
½ teaspoon dried parsley flakes
1 bay leaf
¼ teaspoon dried thyme leaves
⅛ teaspoon marjoram
2 quarts water
Salt and pepper to taste

Combine chicken and remaining ingredients in a large kettle. Cover and bring to a boil; reduce heat and simmer 3 hours or until meat falls from bones. Strain broth; reserve chicken and vegetables for other uses. Cool and skim off fat. Cover and store in refrigerator until ready to use. Yield: about 1½ quarts.

Note: Canned chicken broth, chicken broth made with bouillon cubes, or chicken concentrate may be substituted for freshly made chicken broth. Also, turkey pieces may be substituted for chicken in the above recipe to make turkey broth.

Fish Stock

2 pounds fish bones or heads
5 cups water
⅓ cup sliced carrot
⅓ cup sliced onion
⅓ cup sliced celery
½ bay leaf
½ teaspoon dried parsley flakes
Salt and pepper to taste

Combine all ingredients in a kettle; cover and simmer 30 minutes. Strain broth; discard residue. Cool and skim off fat. Cover and store in refrigerator until ready to use. Yield: about 1 quart.

Ham Stock

2 pounds ham and ham bone
5 cups water
1 carrot, sliced
1 onion, quartered
1 stalk celery, coarsely diced
½ teaspoon dried parsley flakes
½ bay leaf

Combine all ingredients in a kettle; cover and simmer 30 to 40 minutes. Strain broth; discard residue. Cool and skim off fat. Cover and store in refrigerator until ready to use. Yield: about 1 quart.

Iced Bouillon

2 (10¾-ounce) cans beef bouillon, undiluted
2 cups water
⅓ cup dry sherry
6 paper-thin lemon slices

Combine bouillon, water, and sherry. Chill. Float a slice of lemon on each serving. Yield: 6 appetizer servings.

Consommé With Custard

1 egg
1 egg yolk
2 teaspoons half-and-half
¼ teaspoon salt
4 cups canned consommé or clear homemade stock

Beat egg and yolk together; add half-and-half and salt. Butter 2 small custard cups; pour in egg mixture. Place cups on rack in kettle with ½ inch hot water in bottom. Cover tightly and poach 30 minutes, or until set.

Turn custard out of cups and rinse custard quickly under hot water to remove fat; place in cold water. When cold, thinly slice custard and cut into diamonds or other shapes as desired. Bring consommé to boil; ladle into serving bowls. Add custard shapes to each serving. Yield: 6 servings.

Fish and Shellfish

Europeans newly arrived on the American East Coast found an amazing variety and quantity of fish and shellfish, especially in the Tidewater area of Virginia. It is said that oysters there were so crowded together that they formed shoals around which ships had to navigate. The scientific explanation for this phenomenon is that the saltier the water, the greater the tendency of oysters to clump together. Other shellfish could be scooped up by the bushel, and fish could be speared from river banks.

The Indians knew harvesting techniques and utilized nature's gifts to the fullest. One of the most interesting of their fishing tricks was to use horse chestnuts or a similar natural drug (often poisonous) to stupefy fish in trapped pools. Once the settlers adopted the Indians' method of catching and keeping fish, their chances of survival increased markedly.

Fishing was America's first industry. The Continental Army marched on pickled fish, as did the English forces opposing them. The order for "Ten thousand barrels of fish, well pickled and saved for use," issued by the Continental Congress of 1778, was a profitable one for the commercial fisheries that filled it. Pickled fish were, and still are, prepared by layering the fish in barrels with salt. Brine is formed when the moisture of the fish combines with the salt.

By the time plantations were established, the seacoast and the rivers teemed with mercantile and fishing boats. Those who did not fish for themselves could buy fresh fish from those who did. There were market boats from which the family cook could purchase ingredients for the day's meals, including Indian seasonings and game. From the Rappahannock to the Rio Grande, those early Southern cooks seasoned and tasted their way to preeminence in seafood preparation—to this day, nobody does it better.

The unique, watery world of the Chesapeake Bay has been, from our earliest history, a miraculous treasury of shellfish. From the marshlands of the southern part of the Bay around Maryland and Virginia comes fully a quarter of the nation's oyster harvest. And more than half our soft steamer clams come from the prolific Bay, as well as half the crabmeat we consume every year. After shrimp, salmon, and tuna, crab is the most valuable fishery in the nation.

The South Atlantic and Gulf shores account for respectable quantities of these shellfish, too. Add the peculiar stone crab, the beast that re-grows his claw when the law-abiding crabber takes one claw and throws him back into the water. Add the Florida "spiny" lobster and the rock shrimp. Mainly, though, add the shrimp. The Gulf of Mexico is to the shrimp what the Chesapeake Bay is to the clam and crab, accounting for about eighty-five percent of our total annual consumption.

Fish (or "finfish," to distinguish them from their shell-bearing relatives of the deep) are still one of the South's basic assets. Florida alone harvests commercially some forty-seven varieties of finfish.

Commercialism aside, the fisherman's paradise is as large as the Southland. Cast a net for mullet in a Florida bayou, spear a lazy flounder in South Carolina's waters, but be in North Carolina when the shadbushes bloom in spring. That is when the incredibly bony shad leave salt water and swim into the rivers to conduct their spawning ceremonies. Just to sample such bounties of Southern waters would take a lifetime of dedication.

In the coastal areas, one of the favorite outdoor get-togethers is a seafood boil. Commercially packaged crab boil takes care of balancing the spices. The recipe is necessarily rather loose; the method consists largely of counting the house and cooking about twice as much as the guests could be expected to eat. Outdoor air has an insidious effect on appetites. To have a fine seafood boil one has, in addition, only to furnish soft butter, cocktail sauce for the shrimp, salt and pepper, plenty of napkins, cold beer, and chilled watermelon.

Bluffton Boil

½ cup salt
12 large potatoes in skins, halved
24 small onions, peeled
3 whole buds (not cloves) garlic
3 (3-ounce) packages commercial crab boil

4 to 6 lemons, halved
1 cup vinegar
1 to 2 dozen crabs, backs removed
12 ears corn, broken in half
10 pounds shrimp in shell

Fill a large container with water two-thirds full. Add salt; bring to a boil. Add potatoes and onions, and continue boiling for 20 minutes. Add garlic, crab boil, lemon, vinegar, and crabs; cook an additional 10 minutes.

Reduce heat, and add corn; simmer 5 minutes. Remove from heat, and add shrimp; let stand in water 5 minutes. Drain carefully, placing vegetables and seafood on a newspaper-covered picnic table. Yield: 12 servings.

Note: Recipe is based on 1 serving of vegetables per person.

From the days of an unlimited and affordable supply of shrimp in New Orleans, we have this classic dish, as popular then as it is now.

Remoulade À La St. Tammany

1 cup mayonnaise
¼ cup vegetable oil
2 tablespoons dry mustard
1 tablespoon chopped
    green onion
1 tablespoon chopped
    celery
1 tablespoon chopped
    fresh parsley

1 tablespoon horseradish
1 tablespoon vinegar
1 teaspoon paprika
½ teaspoon salt
½ teaspoon Worcestershire
    sauce
Dash of hot sauce
Cooked shrimp or crabmeat
Shredded lettuce

Combine all ingredients except shrimp and lettuce in blender container; blend until smooth. Chill thoroughly, and serve with shrimp or crabmeat on a bed of lettuce. Yield: about 1½ cups.

The first time I heard about Maryland baked shad, I was incredulous. Cook a fish for five hours, indeed! If I had not known my informant was a restaurateur in the Chesapeake Bay area, I would have thought him mad—or joking. Along with other food writers and teachers, I have done my share of lecturing that the "cardinal sin in seafood preparation is overcooking." "Ten minutes in the oven per inch of thickness of the fish is maximum" is another of our refrains.

Of course, it turns out that long oven-steaming is the choice method for handling the delicious fish with the crazy bone structure that defies filleting. After its five-hour sojourn in the oven, the shad's smaller bones seem to dissolve, and even the backbone becomes edible. To see and eat it is to believe it.

Oven-Steamed Shad

1 shad, 3 to 4 pounds
    dressed weight
Lemon and pepper seasoning
    (or salt and pepper) to
    taste
3 to 4 cups water

1 cup dry white wine
    (optional)
2 stalks celery, broken into
    pieces
1 small onion, chopped
2 bay leaves

Wash and dry fish. Sprinkle inside and out with lemon and pepper seasoning. Put fish on rack in baking pan. Add water to level just under fish. (Part of the liquid may be the cup of wine.) Add celery, onion, and bay leaves.

Cover tightly and steam in 300° oven for 5 hours. Baste frequently during cooking. Yield: 6 servings.

Although Maryland does not have a patent on planked shad, I always think of them together. Indian in origin, the planking of fish was carried out by the early housewife who propped the plank up in front of her fireplace. Boy scouts, fishermen, and campers have continued planking fish out-of-doors more or less enthusiastically, depending to a large extent on whether or not it is raining.

As a reformed camper, I join the Boy Scouts of America in suggesting that if you plan to plank a fish by an open fire, "Be Prepared." Take along not only the hardwood plank but also some large-headed nails; safety pins just will not do for attaching the fish to the plank. The ingredients are few: a plank, a fish, and simple seasonings. But a warning here: some woods can cause toxic reactions, so check out the chosen plank before using; also, the plank should be hardwood, as softwood may impart an unpleasant flavor. Preheat the plank slowly by placing it in the oven at the time the heat is turned on. Or, at campsite, prop the plank up at a safe distance from the blaze to warm it. Then oil it well before attaching the fish to it.

For campfire cooking, the split, cleaned fish is seasoned and attached, skin side down, to the board with the nails. The board is then propped in a standing position before a burned-down fire, with the thick meat down and the tail (or thinner end) toward the top of the board. The top slants back, a bit further from the meat, so that the flesh cooks evenly.

My mature judgment tells me that planking fish makes more sense at home than abroad; it is more appetizing to me fresh from the oven than newly fallen from a plank.

The following instructions are for those decadent persons who wish to prepare planked fish in the sinful luxury of their own kitchens.

Planked Fish

1 (4-pound) whole fish, dressed and opened flat
2 tablespoons salt
Vegetable oil
¼ cup melted butter
Pepper to taste
Juice of ½ lemon

Place plank in cold oven; set oven control at 450°. Dissolve salt in enough cold water to cover fish; add fish and soak for 3 minutes. Remove warmed board from oven; oil it well. Drain fish and place it on the board, skin side down. Brush with melted butter and sprinkle with pepper. Drizzle lemon juice over the top. Place in the oven and bake for 10 to 15 minutes, basting once or twice if necessary to keep it moist.

If fish is not done after 15 minutes, reduce heat to 350° and bake until flesh flakes easily with fork. Do not overcook. Yield: 4 to 6 servings.

When it is time for the Florida mullet fisherman to cook his catch, nine times out of ten he will already have soaked his hickory chips or sawdust overnight, by way of being ready. Smoked mullet is a prized delicacy along the Southern coast; it is done like this.

Smoked Mullet

6 (1-pound) dressed mullet
1 cup salt
1 gallon water
¼ cup vegetable oil

Soak 1 pound of hickory chips or sawdust in 2 quarts of water overnight. Thaw fish if frozen; remove the head just below the collarbone. Cut along the backbone almost to the tail. The fish should lie flat in one piece. Clean and wash fish. Add salt to water and stir until dissolved. Pour brine over fish and refrigerate for 30 minutes. Drain, rinse, and dry.

Make a charcoal fire in a barbecue grill with a cover or hood. Let fire burn down to a low, even heat. Cover with ⅓ of the wet chips. (The wet chips provide smoke.)

Place the fish on a well-greased grill, skin side down, 4 to 6 inches from coals. Baste with oil at the beginning and frequently during cooking. Cover and smoke for 1½ hours, or until flesh flakes easily with fork. Add remaining chips as needed to keep the fire smoking. Yield: 6 servings.

One of the lamentations most often heard when a coastal dweller moves inland is "How I miss the seafood in Baltimore," or Natchez, or Savannah. The lack of seafood on the hoof is a source of great sadness for me, also, and I have never even lived near the ocean. We who live in or near the larger cities take such comfort as we can from the seafoods flown in fresh from the Eastern and Southern coasts. Along with the salt-water imports, trout, bream, crappie, bass, and catfish have always been mainstays for the landlocked states, a fact of no small importance to the men and women who blazed the trails westward. Wisely, they wanted to keep the fish in good supply; one of the first conservation laws was enacted in 1726, prohibiting the poisoning of fish in streams. The penalties ranged from a fine of a few pounds to a prescribed number of lashes in the public square.

The modern-day sport fisherman is alert to conservation laws; he observes catch limits and keeps his license up-to-date because he knows that a skillet full of fresh fish just an hour out of the water is a memorable thing. We have fried a lot of fish over the years, but one occasion stands out in the minds of my camping family. We had been on a long camping trip to Ocracoke Island in tandem with another family who were friends from Ohio. We were somewhere in West Virginia, within a day's drive of home; it was our last night together before taking separate ways. The fishing gear was unpacked and the fishermen took to the nearby stream.

The cooks surveyed the depleted camp stores and hoped for the best. The best is what we got. Our crappie and bass dinner was voted "Best of Trip" by everyone except one son who likes to catch fish but draws the line at eating them.

The fish were dredged in pancake mix that day and fried in margarine. We had no choice; we had used up the shortening at the beach, making pies in the folding camp oven. And we had run out of bacon drippings 250 miles earlier. Cracker crumbs and cornmeal for coating were likewise no longer in stock. The feast included perfect tomatoes and melons picked up at a roadside stand at Fancy Gap, where we had crossed the mountains that morning. We said we were "making do," but as it turned out, we were making memories.

Delicious as fresh fish can be right out of the hot skillet, if kind providence hands me a plump several-pounder, I surely will bake him or poach him, thereby saving myself a mess of calories to spend in other ways. Sometimes the choice depends on size; if a fish is small enough to fit in the skillet, frying may still be the most practical method. On the other hand, whatever the catch, seafood lends itself to a wide choice of preparation techniques.

For all lovers of fish and/or seafood, here are ways to bake, fry, broil, escallop, and otherwise make the most of what is available.

I certainly was a sincere and competent eater in those days. On the breakfast menu were baked oysters and broiled oysters with strange sauces. I learned to like them even for breakfast, along with pancakes, fried potatoes, and fruit. . . . When I went home . . . I told my mother about these strange dishes . . . on which she faithfully experimented. For she, though naturally Republican and conservative in all things, even things culinary, was a doting and devoted mother. . .
William Allen White

Fish and Shellfish

Basic Baked Whole Fish

1 (3- to 4-pound) bass or other
    dressed fish
¼ cup melted butter or margarine
Salt and pepper

Place fish in greased baking dish; brush with butter. Sprinkle seasonings inside and outside of fish. Bake at 350° for about 40 minutes, or until fish flakes easily with a fork, basting occasionally with remaining butter. Yield: 4 to 6 servings.

Basic Broiled Fish

1 lemon, thinly sliced
2 pounds fresh trout or bass fillets
    or steaks
Salt and pepper
¼ cup melted butter or margarine
Juice of 1 lemon

Cover broiler pan with foil; arrange lemon slices on foil. Sprinkle fish with salt and pepper, and arrange over lemon slices; brush fish with butter and lemon juice. Broil about 4 inches from heat for 8 to 14 minutes, or until fish flakes easily with a fork; baste once during broiling, but do not turn. Yield: 4 to 6 servings.

Corned Fish

The oily types of fish, such as shad, mullet, mackerel, and bluefish, are best for this method of preparation.

Clean and wash fish thoroughly; fillet. Sprinkle both sides of fillets generously with salt; cover and let stand 30 to 40 minutes. Wash all salt off.

Make a small hole in the tail end of each fillet; thread twine or string through hole. Hang in a dry place where air can circulate. Dry fillets until they no longer feel moist or sticky (about 2 to 3 days).

To pan fry, melt enough butter to coat skillet; sauté fillets 5 to 10 minutes on each side, depending on the size of pieces, or until browned. Sprinkle fillets with pepper, if desired.

To broil, place fillets on a broiler pan; dot with butter, and sprinkle with pepper. Broil until lightly browned; turn and broil until done.

Serve with pan drippings and lemon slices, if desired.

Creole Fish Fillets

2 pounds fish fillets
1 teaspoon salt
2 tablespoons butter or margarine
1 small onion, minced
1 clove garlic
1 (16-ounce) can tomatoes
1 bay leaf
¼ teaspoon cayenne pepper

Sprinkle fillets with salt; place in greased shallow baking dish.

Heat butter in skillet; sauté onion and garlic until tender. Remove and discard garlic; add tomatoes, bay leaf, and cayenne, mixing well. Pour tomato mixture over fish and bake at 350° for 30 minutes, or until fish flakes easily with a fork. Yield: 6 servings.

Basic Oven-Fried Fish

2 pounds fish fillets
1 tablespoon salt
1 cup milk
1 cup dry breadcrumbs or cracker
    crumbs
¼ cup melted butter or margarine

Cut fillets into serving-size portions. Dissolve salt in milk. Dip fish in milk; roll in breadcrumbs. Place in greased baking dish; drizzle with butter. Bake on top oven rack at 500° for about 10 minutes, or until fish flakes easily with a fork. Yield: 4 to 6 servings.

Basic Poached Fish

1 quart water
1½ tablespoons salt
1 pound fresh fish fillets or steaks

Combine water and salt in a Dutch oven; bring to a boil. Lower fish into water; reduce heat and simmer 10 minutes, or until fish flakes easily when tested with a fork. Do not allow water to boil. Remove fish carefully and serve hot with a sauce; or flake, after cooling, for use in other recipes. Yield: about 2 cups.

Grilled Fish With Sesame

6 pan-dressed trout or other pan fish,
    fresh or frozen
¼ cup melted butter or margarine
¼ cup sesame seeds
Juice of 1 lemon
1 teaspoon salt
½ teaspoon pepper

Thaw fish if frozen; place fish on greased grill. Combine remaining ingredients, mixing well; brush fish with one-half the butter mixture. Cook about 4 inches from heat for 5 to 8 minutes. Baste with remaining sauce; turn and cook 5 to 6 additional minutes, or until fish flakes easily with a fork. Yield: 6 servings.

Pan-Fried Fish

12 medium fish
2 cups cornmeal
1 teaspoon salt
1 teaspoon pepper
1 teaspoon paprika
⅛ teaspoon cayenne pepper
1 cup shortening

Wash fish in salted water; dry on paper towels. Combine cornmeal and seasonings in paper bag; shake fish in bag to coat well.

Heat shortening in iron skillet. Fry fish in hot shortening about 4 minutes or until browned; turn and fry other side about 3 minutes, or until fish flakes easily with a fork. Yield: 6 to 8 servings.

Fillets Marguéry

2 pounds fish fillets
1 teaspoon salt
¼ teaspoon pepper
1 cup fish stock or water
18 fresh oysters
18 fresh shrimp
Sauce Marguéry
Paprika

Cut fish into serving-size portions; sprinkle with salt and pepper. Place in greased baking dish. Pour stock over fish and bake at 350° for 15 minutes, or until fish flakes easily with a fork. Remove fish carefully to greased broiler pan, reserving liquid.

Place reserved poaching liquid in small saucepan; add oysters and shrimp; simmer 3 minutes. Place 3 poached oysters and 3 poached shrimp on top of each fish serving; reserve liquid for Sauce Marguéry. Spoon Sauce Marguéry over each serving; sprinkle with paprika. Broil for 1 or 2 minutes, or until lightly browned. Serve immediately. Yield: 6 servings.

Sauce Marguéry:

Reserved poaching liquid from fish
1 cup butter or margarine
8 egg yolks, beaten
¼ cup dry white wine
2 tablespoons lemon juice

Combine poaching liquid with enough water in small saucepan to make 1 cup. Boil until mixture is reduced to ½ cup. Add butter; heat until melted. Slowly stir a little of the hot mixture into the beaten yolks; beat yolks into remaining hot liquid. Beat mixture over low heat until thickened. Stir in wine and lemon juice. Yield: about 1½ to 2 cups.

Stuffed Fillets With Egg Sauce

2 pounds fish fillets
1¼ teaspoons salt, divided
½ teaspoon pepper, divided
4 cups soft breadcrumbs
½ cup plus 2 tablespoons melted
    butter or margarine, divided
¼ cup milk
¼ cup finely chopped onion
2 teaspoons dried dillweed
1 tablespoon chopped fresh parsley
1 teaspoon dried thyme leaves
2 eggs, beaten
Egg Sauce
1 or 2 hard-cooked eggs, sliced

Sprinkle fillets with 1 teaspoon salt and half the pepper. Place half the fillets in greased 2½-quart baking dish. Combine breadcrumbs, ½ cup butter, milk, onion, dillweed, parsley, thyme, eggs, and remaining salt and pepper in a large mixing bowl, mixing well. Spread mixture on top of fillets. Place remaining fillets on top of crumb mixture; brush with remaining butter. Bake at 350° for 30 to 35 minutes, or until fish flakes easily with a fork. Top with Egg Sauce; garnish with sliced hard-cooked eggs. Yield: 6 servings.

Egg Sauce:

¼ cup butter or margarine
¼ cup all-purpose flour
1 teaspoon dry mustard
1 teaspoon salt
⅛ teaspoon white pepper
2 cups half-and-half
¼ teaspoon hot sauce
3 hard-cooked eggs, coarsely grated
2 tablespoons chopped fresh parsley

Melt butter in small saucepan; stir in flour, mustard, salt, and pepper. Gradually stir in half-and-half. Cook over low heat, stirring constantly, until thickened, but do not boil. Stir in hot sauce, eggs, and parsley. Yield: about 2½ cups.

Fillets Véronique

2 pounds fresh fish fillets
2 tablespoons lemon juice
2 teaspoons salt
1 cup dry white wine
1 cup (¼ pound) seedless green
    grapes
¼ teaspoon fines herbes
3 tablespoons butter or margarine
2 tablespoons all-purpose flour
Seedless green grapes

Sprinkle fillets with lemon juice and salt; arrange in greased skillet in 1 or 2 layers. Combine wine, 1 cup grapes, and fines herbes; pour wine mixture over fish, and heat to simmering. Cover and poach for 5 minutes, or until fish flakes easily with a fork. Carefully transfer fish to an oven-proof platter, reserving liquid.

Melt butter in small saucepan; blend in flour. Stir in reserved liquid gradually; cook, stirring constantly, until smooth but not thick. Pour mixture over fish; garnish with additional grapes. Place under broiler for about 2 minutes, or until delicately browned. Yield: 4 to 6 servings.

Sweet And Sour Fish

1 (11-ounce) can mandarin oranges
1 tablespoon cornstarch
½ cup commercial sweet-and-sour
    sauce
2 pounds fish fillets
1 small onion, thinly sliced and
    separated into rings

Drain oranges, reserving juice. Combine juice and cornstarch in a small saucepan; cook over medium heat, stirring constantly, until mixture thickens. Remove from heat and stir in sweet-and-sour sauce; set aside.

Arrange fish in a foil-lined 13- × 9- × 2-inch baking pan. Arrange oranges and onion over fish; top with sauce. Bake at 350° for 20 to 30 minutes, or until fish flakes easily with a fork. Yield: 6 to 8 servings.

Striped Bass Stuffed With Crabmeat

1 (3- to 5-pound) dressed striped bass
1½ to 2 teaspoons salt
Pepper to taste
½ cup butter or margarine
2 tablespoons chopped onion
¼ cup chopped celery
2 cups soft breadcrumbs
1 cup flaked crabmeat
1 tablespoon chopped fresh parsley or
    1 teaspoon dried parsley flakes
Salt and pepper to taste
1 cup milk
1 large onion, sliced
¼ cup melted butter or margarine
Lemon wedges
Chopped fresh parsley

Wash and dry bass. Lay fish flat on a cutting board; slit lengthwise down center of fish to tail. Cut flesh along both sides of backbone to the tail, allowing knife to run along the rib bones to form a pocket for stuffing; sprinkle inside and out with salt and pepper.

Melt ½ cup butter in heavy saucepan. Sauté onion and celery in butter until lightly browned. Remove from heat; stir in breadcrumbs, crabmeat, parsley, salt, and pepper.

Stuff fish and secure with skewers or sew it closed. Place fish in shallow baking dish and put milk and sliced onion in dish. Pour ¼ cup melted butter over fish.

Bake, uncovered, at 350° for about 45 minutes, or until fish flakes easily with a fork. Remove to warm platter and garnish with lemon wedges dipped in chopped parsley. Yield: 4 to 6 servings.

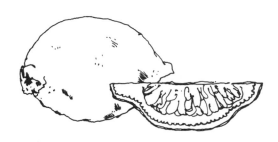

Orange Lake Amandine

½ cup slivered blanched almonds
¼ cup melted butter or margarine
12 large bass or trout fillets
Salt and pepper to taste
Dried thyme leaves to taste
Milk
All-purpose flour
½ cup vegetable oil
2 teaspoons chopped fresh parsley
Lemon wedges (optional)

Sauté almonds in butter until golden brown; set aside.

Sprinkle fillets with salt, pepper, and thyme; dip in milk, and dredge in flour. Fry fillets in hot oil over medium heat until golden brown on both sides. Drain on paper towels. Remove to serving dish; sprinkle with almonds and parsley, and garnish with lemon wedges, if desired. Yield: 6 to 8 servings.

Grilled Lake Bass
In Wine Sauce

6 large bass steaks or fillets, fresh or
    frozen
1 cup dry white wine
⅓ cup vegetable oil
1 (4-ounce) can mushroom stems and
    pieces, drained
¼ cup chopped green onion
2 tablespoons lemon juice
2 tablespoons chopped fresh parsley
2 teaspoons salt
¼ teaspoon cayenne pepper
¼ teaspoon dried thyme leaves

Thaw fish if frozen. Cut 6 pieces of heavy-
duty aluminum foil 18 inches square. Grease
foil lightly; place 1 fish on each square of foil.
Combine remaining ingredients; pour evenly
over each fish. Wrap fish with foil and seal
edges; place packets on grill 6 inches from
heat. Cook 20 to 25 minutes, or until fish
flakes easily with a fork. Yield: 6 servings.

Golden Fried Catfish

*A catfish restaurant in Columbus, Georgia,
many years ago displayed a huge sign in-
forming the customer that "The fish you are
eating slept in the river last night."*

6 small catfish, cleaned and dressed
1 teaspoon salt
¼ teaspoon pepper
2 cups self-rising cornmeal
Vegetable oil for deep frying

Sprinkle catfish with salt and pepper. Place
cornmeal in a paper bag; drop in catfish one
at a time, and shake until coated. Fry in deep
hot oil (375°) until golden brown; drain well.
Serve hot. Yield: 4 to 6 servings.

Fried Catfish

⅓ cup yellow cornmeal
2 tablespoons all-purpose flour
1 teaspoon salt
¼ teaspoon paprika
1 pound whole catfish, cleaned and
    dressed
¼ cup vegetable oil

Combine cornmeal, flour, salt, and paprika.
Dry fish thoroughly; coat both sides of fish
with cornmeal mixture.

Fry fish in hot oil over low heat about 4
minutes on each side, or until golden brown.
Drain on paper towels. Yield: 2 servings.

Note: Fish fillets may be substituted.

Shameful Bloody
Mary Croaker

2 pounds croaker fillets or other
    fish fillets, fresh or frozen
1 teaspoon salt
½ cup thinly sliced (¼-inch pieces)
    celery
½ cup thinly sliced green onion with
    tops
1 (2½-ounce) can sliced mushrooms,
    drained
2 tablespoons melted butter or
    margarine
1 (6-ounce) can Bloody Mary mix
1 tablespoon cornstarch
Chopped fresh parsley

Thaw fish if frozen; sprinkle with salt. Place
fish in a single layer in a greased 12- × 8- ×
2-inch baking dish.

Sauté celery, onion, and mushrooms in
butter in a 1-quart saucepan until tender.
Combine Bloody Mary mix and cornstarch;
add to vegetable mixture and stir over medium heat for 2 to 3 minutes or until sauce is
thickened. Pour sauce over fish; bake at 350°
for 20 to 25 minutes, or until fish flakes easily
when tested with a fork. Garnish with parsley. Yield: 6 servings.

Crab-Stuffed Flounder

¾ cup minced celery
½ cup minced onion
½ cup minced fresh parsley
¼ cup minced shallots
¼ cup minced green pepper
1 clove garlic, minced
½ cup melted butter or margarine
1 tablespoon all-purpose flour
½ cup milk
½ cup dry white wine
½ pound fresh lump crabmeat
1¼ cups seasoned dry breadcrumbs
¼ teaspoon salt
Dash of pepper
6 (10-ounce) flounder fillets
Mornay Sauce
Paprika
Hot cooked mashed potatoes
    (optional)
Minced fresh parsley (optional)

Sauté celery, onion, parsley, shallots, green pepper, and garlic in butter in a large skillet over medium heat; cook until vegetables are tender. Add flour and cook 1 minute, stirring constantly. Gradually add milk and wine; cook over medium heat, stirring constantly, until slightly thickened. Remove from heat, and stir in crabmeat, breadcrumbs, salt, and pepper.

Place 3 fillets in a greased 15- × 10- × 1-inch jellyroll pan; spoon about 1 cup crabmeat stuffing on each fillet. Cut remaining fillets in half lengthwise; place a fillet half on either side of stuffed fillets in baking pan, pressing gently into stuffing mixture. Top each portion with Mornay Sauce; sprinkle with paprika.

Bake at 425° for 15 to 20 minutes, or until fish flakes easily when tested with a fork.

Pipe or spoon hot cooked mashed potatoes around each portion, if desired. Garnish with additional paprika and parsley, if desired. Cut each portion in half to serve. Yield: 6 servings.

Mornay Sauce:

¼ cup butter
¼ cup all-purpose flour
2 cups milk
½ teaspoon salt
⅛ teaspoon white pepper
2 egg yolks
1 tablespoon whipping cream
¼ cup shredded Swiss cheese

Melt butter in a heavy 2-quart saucepan over low heat; add flour and cook 1 minute, stirring constantly. Gradually add milk; cook over medium heat, stirring constantly, until thickened and bubbly. Stir in salt and white pepper.

Beat egg yolks until thick and lemon colored; stir in cream. Stir some of hot mixture into yolks; add to remaining hot mixture, stirring constantly. Cook over medium heat, stirring constantly, until thickened (about 2 to 3 minutes). Add cheese; stir until melted. Remove from heat. Yield: about 2 cups.

Cheese-Topped Flounder

2 pounds skinless flounder fillets
    or other fish fillets
2 tablespoons grated onion
1½ teaspoons salt
⅛ teaspoon pepper
2 large tomatoes, thinly sliced
¼ cup melted butter or margarine
1 cup (4 ounces) shredded Swiss
    cheese

Cut fish into 6 portions. Place in single layer on large, greased, oven-proof platter. Sprinkle fish with onion and seasonings. Arrange tomato slices over fish; pour butter over tomatoes. Broil about 4 inches from heat for 10 minutes, or until fish flakes easily with a fork. Remove from heat; sprinkle with cheese. Broil 2 to 3 minutes longer or until cheese is melted. Yield: 6 servings.

King Or Spanish Mackerel

2 to 3 pounds mackerel steaks or
  fillets
6 tablespoons melted butter, divided
½ teaspoon salt
¼ teaspoon pepper
Juice of 2 limes
1 tablespoon Dijon mustard
¼ teaspoon ground fennel

Place fish in baking pan, skin side down.
Brush with about one-third of the melted
better; sprinkle with salt and pepper. Broil 5
inches from heat for 5 minutes. Mix remaining ingredients to make a mustard sauce.
Pour sauce over fish and return to broiler for
5 minutes, or until fish flakes easily with a
fork. Yield: 6 to 8 servings.

Herb-Seasoned
Spanish Mackerel

2 pounds Spanish mackerel fillets or
  other fish fillets, fresh or frozen
½ cup vegetable oil
2 tablespoons lemon juice
1 clove garlic, peeled and quartered
1 cup crushed herb-seasoned
  croutons
½ cup grated Parmesan cheese
¼ cup chopped fresh parsley
1 clove garlic, minced

Thaw fish if frozen; skin fillets. Cut fillets into
serving-size portions; place in a 13- × 9- ×
2-inch baking dish. Combine oil, lemon
juice, and quartered clove garlic, mixing
well. Pour mixture over fish; marinate for 30
minutes, turning once.
  Combine crushed croutons, cheese, parsley, and minced garlic. Remove fish from
marinade; reserve 2 tablespoons marinade.
Roll fish in crumb mixture. Place on a large,
well-greased, oven-proof platter; drizzle reserved marinade over fish. Bake at 500° for
10 to 15 minutes, or until fish flakes easily
when tested with a fork. Yield: 6 servings.

Tangy King Mackerel Steaks

2 pounds king mackerel steaks or
  other fish steaks, fresh or frozen
½ cup catsup
¼ cup vegetable oil
3 tablespoons lemon juice
2 tablespoons vinegar
2 tablespoons liquid smoke
1 teaspoon Worcestershire sauce
1 teaspoon salt
½ teaspoon grated onion
½ teaspoon dry mustard
¼ teaspoon paprika
1 clove garlic, minced
3 drops hot sauce

Thaw steaks if frozen; cut steaks into serving-
size portions. Place fish in a single layer in a
12- × 8- × 2-inch baking pan.
  Combine remaining ingredients, mixing
well. Pour mixture over fish; marinate for 30
minutes, turning once. Remove fish, reserving marinade for basting. Wash and grease
same pan; replace fish on pan. Broil about 5
inches from heat for 5 to 7 minutes. Turn
carefully; baste fish and continue broiling for
5 to 7 minutes, or until fish flakes easily when
tested with a fork. Yield: 6 servings.

Smoked Mullet Salad

½ pound smoked mullet
1 cup mayonnaise or salad dressing
1 teaspoon prepared mustard
½ teaspoon dried tarragon leaves
½ teaspoon salt
¼ teaspoon celery seeds
3 cups cooked sliced potatoes, chilled
2 cups sliced celery
⅔ cup sliced radishes
⅓ cup sliced green onion
Lettuce leaves

Remove skin and bones from fish; flake fish.

Combine mayonnaise, mustard, tarragon leaves, salt, and celery seeds in a large mixing bowl; mix well. Fold in sliced potatoes. Cover; chill several hours to blend flavors.

Add celery, radishes, onion, and flaked fish to potato mixture; mix carefully. Arrange in center of a lettuce-lined serving dish; garnish with additional sliced smoked mullet. Yield: 6 servings.

Lemon-Rice Stuffed Mullet

3 (1¼- to 1½-pound) dressed mullet, fresh or frozen
1½ teaspoons salt
Lemon-Rice Stuffing
2 tablespoons vegetable oil

Thaw fish if frozen; wash and dry fish. Lay each fish flat on a cutting board; slit lengthwise down center of fish to tail. Cut flesh along both sides of backbone to the tail, allowing knife to run along the rib bones to form a pocket for the stuffing. Sprinkle both sides of pocket with salt; stuff fish loosely with Lemon-Rice Stuffing. Close openings with small skewers or toothpicks.

Place fish on a greased 13- × 9- × 2-inch baking pan. Brush fish with oil. Bake at 350° for 30 to 35 minutes, or until fish flakes easily when tested with a fork. Baste occasionally with oil during cooking. Remove skewers. Yield: 6 servings.

Lemon-Rice Stuffing:

1 cup thinly sliced celery
½ cup finely chopped onion
3 tablespoons melted margarine or vegetable oil
1 (4-ounce) can sliced mushrooms, drained
2 cups cooked long grain and wild rice mix
2 tablespoons lemon juice
1 teaspoon grated lemon rind
½ teaspoon salt
½ teaspoon fines herbes

Sauté celery and onion in margarine until celery is tender. Add mushrooms and heat thoroughly. Add remaining ingredients; mix well. Yield: 2⅔ cups.

Key Lime Mullet

2 pounds mullet fillets or other fish fillets, fresh or frozen
1 teaspoon salt
Dash of pepper
¼ cup lime juice
3 tablespoons butter or margarine, melted
Paprika
Lime wedges

Thaw fish if frozen. Skin fillets; cut into serving-size portions. Place fish in a single layer in a 13- × 9- × 2-inch baking dish. Sprinkle with salt and pepper. Pour lime juice over fish and marinate for 30 minutes, turning once.

Remove fish, reserving marinade. Place fish on a greased broiler pan. Combine butter and reserved marinade; brush fish with butter mixture and sprinkle with paprika. Broil about 4 inches from source of heat for 8 to 10 minutes, or until fish flakes easily when tested with a fork. Serve with lime wedges. Yield: 6 servings.

Pompano En Papillote

1 (2-pound) pompano
1 bay leaf
½ lemon
1 stalk celery
Dash of dried tarragon, chervil, and
    basil leaves
⅛ teaspoon dry sherry
Ground nutmeg
Salt and pepper to taste
8 oysters
3 mushrooms, sliced
1 shallot, finely chopped
4 shrimp, peeled and finely chopped
1 cup fresh crabmeat
Dash of cognac
Dash of Pernod
3 egg yolks, well beaten

Fillet pompano. Place enough water to cover fish in a large pan; add bay leaf, lemon, celery, tarragon, chervil, basil, sherry, nutmeg, salt, and pepper; simmer. Wrap pompano with cheesecloth and gently drop into simmering water mixture. Bring just to the boiling point; remove pompano. Strain liquid and place in saucepan. Add oysters, mushrooms, shallot, shrimp, and crabmeat; boil approximately 1 minute; add cognac and Pernod. Stir in beaten egg yolks. Pour sauce over the fillets, which have been placed in a paper bag in a large baking pan. Seal bag and bake at 400° for 15 to 20 minutes. Remove from oven and serve immediately. Yield: 2 servings.

Buttermilk-Fried Redfish

2 pounds skinless redfish fillets or
    other fish fillets
1 cup buttermilk
1 cup commercial biscuit mix
2 teaspoons salt
Vegetable oil
Lemon wedges or malt vinegar

Cut fillets into serving-size portions; place in single layer in shallow dish. Pour buttermilk over fish; let stand 30 minutes, turning once. Combine biscuit mix and salt, mixing well. Drain and roll fish in biscuit mix. Heat oil ½ inch deep in skillet. Fry fish 4 to 5 minutes, or until browned; turn carefully and fry 4 to 5 minutes longer, or until fish flakes easily with a fork. Drain on paper towels. Serve with lemon wedges or malt vinegar. Yield: 4 to 6 servings.

Sea Squab Supreme

1 pound sea squab fillets or other
    fish fillets
¼ cup all-purpose flour
1 teaspoon salt
⅛ teaspoon pepper
¼ pound (5 to 6 strips) bacon
2 tablespoons chopped onion
1½ cups tomato juice
1 teaspoon prepared mustard
½ teaspoon persille
½ cup commercial sour cream
Hot cooked rice or toast points

Cut fillets into bite-size pieces. Combine flour, salt, and pepper, mixing well; coat each fillet with flour mixture. Fry bacon in a large skillet until crisp. Remove bacon from pan and drain, reserving drippings. Add onion and fish to drippings in skillet and sauté over medium heat until lightly browned. Reduce heat and stir in tomato juice, mustard, and persille. Simmer for 5 to 10 minutes until sauce thickens slightly. Remove from heat and stir in sour cream.

Serve at once over hot cooked rice or toast points. Crumble bacon and sprinkle on top of each serving. Yield: 6 servings.

Note: One-fourth teaspoon dried parsley flakes and ¼ teaspoon garlic powder may be substituted for persille.

Salmon Croquettes Supreme

1 (15½-ounce) can red or pink
    salmon
2 eggs, beaten
1 cup toasted breadcrumbs
½ cup shredded Cheddar cheese
Salt and pepper to taste
Onion salt to taste
All-purpose flour
Hot vegetable oil

Drain salmon; remove skin and bones. Flake salmon with a fork. Add remaining ingredients except flour and oil, blending well; shape mixture into croquettes. Coat with flour. Fry in hot oil in skillet until golden brown, turning only once. Yield: 6 servings.

Salmon Puffs

1 (7¾-ounce) can red salmon,
    drained
1 egg, beaten
½ teaspoon salt
Dash of pepper
⅔ cup all-purpose flour
⅓ cup cornmeal
½ teaspoon soda
1½ teaspoons baking powder
⅓ cup buttermilk
Vegetable oil for deep frying

Combine all ingredients except oil, mixing well. Drop batter by tablespoonfuls into deep oil heated to 370°; cook until golden brown, turning once. Yield: 6 to 8 servings.

Salmon Loaf

1 (15½-ounce) can salmon
3 tablespoons salmon liquid
1½ cups breadcrumbs
1 egg
2 teaspoons grated onion
⅓ cup evaporated milk
Salt and pepper
Butter Sauce

Combine all ingredients except Butter Sauce. Pack into a greased and floured 8½- × 4½- × 3-inch loafpan; bake at 350° for 35 minutes. Serve with Butter Sauce. Yield: about 4 to 6 servings.

Butter Sauce:

3 tablespoons butter or margarine
3 tablespoons all-purpose flour
Salt and pepper
1½ cups milk
2 egg yolks, beaten
1 teaspoon lemon juice

Melt butter in a small saucepan; stir in flour, salt, and pepper until smooth. Add milk slowly, and cook until thickened, stirring constantly. Beat some of the hot mixture into egg yolks; stir into remaining hot mixture. Cook 1 minute. Stir in lemon juice. Yield: about 2 cups.

Baked Snapper With Sour Cream Stuffing

3 or 4 pounds dressed red snapper
    or other fish
1½ teaspoons salt
Sour Cream Stuffing
2 tablespoons melted margarine or
    vegetable oil, divided

Wash and dry fish. Lay fish flat on a cutting board; slit lengthwise down center of fish to tail. Cut flesh along both sides of backbone to the tail, allowing knife to run along the rib bones to form a pocket for the stuffing. Sprinkle inside and out with salt. Stuff fish loosely with Sour Cream Stuffing. Close opening with small skewers or toothpicks. Place fish on a large greased oven-proof platter. Brush with small amount melted margarine; bake at 350° for 40 to 60 minutes, or until fish flakes easily with a fork. Baste occasionally during cooking with melted margarine. Remove skewers. Yield: 6 servings.

Sour Cream Stuffing:

¾ cup chopped celery
½ cup chopped onion
¼ cup melted margarine or
   vegetable oil
4 cups dry bread cubes
½ cup commercial sour cream
¼ cup diced peeled lemon
2 tablespoons grated lemon rind
1 teaspoon paprika
1 teaspoon salt

Sauté celery and onion in margarine until tender. Add remaining ingredients; mix thoroughly. Yield: 4 cups.

Stuffed Rainbow Trout

6 pan-dressed rainbow trout or other
   pan fish, fresh or frozen
2 teaspoons salt, divided
⅔ cup melted butter or margarine,
   divided
8 slices stale bread, coarsely
   crumbled
1 cup sliced fresh mushrooms
½ cup sliced green onion
2 tablespoons chopped fresh parsley
1 pimiento, chopped
Juice of ½ lemon
½ teaspoon dried marjoram leaves

Thaw fish if frozen. Rinse and dry fish thoroughly. Lay each fish flat on a cutting board, light side down; slit lengthwise down center of fish to tail. Cut fish along both sides of backbone to the tail, allowing the knife to run along the rib bones to form a pocket for the stuffing. Sprinkle both sides of pocket with 1½ teaspoons salt. Heat half the butter in skillet, and sauté breadcrumbs until lightly browned. Add mushrooms and onion; cook until vegetables are tender. Stir in remaining ingredients except butter, mixing well. Stuff fish with vegetable mixture; secure openings with skewers or sew with kitchen thread; arrange fish in baking pan. Brush with remaining butter. Bake at 350° for 25 to 30 minutes, or until fish flakes easily with a fork. Yield: 6 servings.

Trout Amandine

6 pan-size rainbow trout or 2 pounds
   trout fillets
¼ cup all-purpose flour
1 teaspoon seasoned salt
1 teaspoon paprika
¼ cup melted butter or margarine,
   divided
½ cup sliced almonds
2 tablespoons lemon juice
4 to 5 drops hot sauce
1 tablespoon chopped fresh parsley

Cut fillets into 6 portions. Combine flour, seasoned salt, and paprika. Dredge fish in flour mixture; place in single layer, skin side down, in greased baking pan. Drizzle half the butter over fish; broil about 4 inches from heat source for 10 to 15 minutes, or until fish flakes easily with a fork.

Sauté almonds in remaining butter until lightly browned, stirring constantly. Remove from heat; stir in lemon juice, hot sauce, and parsley. Pour over fish and serve at once. Yield: 6 servings.

Trout Dinner In One Pot

    2 pounds trout or other fish fillets,
        fresh or frozen
    ½ cup all-purpose flour
    3 teaspoons salt, divided
    1 teaspoon pepper, divided
    Vegetable oil
    1 medium onion, thinly sliced
    3 medium potatoes, parboiled and
        sliced
    1 (16-ounce) can tomatoes
    2 tablespoons catsup
    4 ounces mild Cheddar cheese, diced

Thaw fish if frozen; cut into serving-size pieces. Combine flour, 1 teaspoon salt, and ½ teaspoon pepper; dredge fish in flour mixture. Heat oil in skillet; brown fillets quickly on both sides. Drain excess oil. Arrange onion slices over fish; arrange potatoes over onion. Combine tomatoes, catsup, and remaining salt and pepper; pour over potatoes. Top with cheese; cover; simmer 20 minutes, or until onion is tender. Yield: 6 servings.

Herb-Flavored Smoked Trout

    6 pan-dressed trout or other pan fish,
        fresh or frozen
    1 cup commercial Italian dressing
    2 teaspoons salt
    2 cups herb-seasoned stuffing mix,
        finely crushed to make 1 cup
    ½ teaspoon dried oregano leaves
    3 tablespoons minced fresh parsley

Thaw fish if frozen; place in shallow baking dish. Pour dressing over fish; marinate 30 minutes. Drain; sprinkle with salt. Combine stuffing mix and seasoning and dredge fish; place on greased grill. Cook in smoke oven at 200° for about 1 hour, or until fish flakes easily with a fork. Yield: 6 servings.

Note: Marinating fish in salt solution is not necessary for this recipe; the Italian dressing marinade has the same effect.

Baked Tuna With Biscuits

    3 tablespoons melted butter or
        margarine
    6 tablespoons all-purpose flour
    3 cups milk
    1 teaspoon salt
    Pepper to taste
    2 (7-ounce) cans tuna, drained and
        flaked
    1 medium onion, chopped
    1 medium green pepper, chopped
    ½ cup shredded Cheddar cheese
    1 (11-ounce) can refrigerated
        buttermilk biscuits

Combine butter and flour; cook over low heat until bubbly. Gradually add milk; cook, stirring constantly, until smooth and thick. Season with salt and pepper.

Combine white sauce, tuna, onion, and green pepper. Spoon into a lightly greased 2-quart casserole dish, and top with cheese. Arrange biscuits on top, and bake at 375° for 40 minutes. Yield: 6 to 8 servings.

Tuna Chop Suey

    1 cup finely chopped onion
    1 cup finely chopped celery
    ¼ cup melted butter or margarine
    1 (10¾-ounce) can cream of chicken
        soup, undiluted
    1 (3-ounce) package cashew nuts,
        halved
    1 (9¼-ounce) can tuna, drained and
        flaked
    1 (3-ounce) can Chinese noodles

Sauté onion and celery in butter until transparent. Add chicken soup, nuts, and tuna; mix well. Spoon into a lightly greased 1½-quart casserole. Top with Chinese noodles. Bake at 350° for 20 to 30 minutes. Yield: 6 servings.

Crispy Frog Legs

6 pair frog legs
¾ cup lemon juice or vinegar
Crushed ice
1 cup milk
6 eggs, separated
2 tablespoons olive or vegetable oil
¼ teaspoon salt
Salt and pepper
1½ cups all-purpose flour
Vegetable oil for deep frying

Wash frog legs thoroughly. Place in a large Dutch oven; sprinkle with lemon juice, and cover with crushed ice. Refrigerate 1 to 3 hours. Combine milk, egg yolks, olive oil, and ¼ teaspoon salt; mix well. Beat egg whites until stiff; fold into batter.

Sprinkle frog legs with salt and pepper; dip each in batter, and dredge in flour. Fry until golden brown in deep oil heated to 375°. Drain on paper towels. Yield: 6 servings.

Fried Cooter (Soft-Shell Turtle)

2 pounds turtle, cut into 2- to 4-inch pieces
½ cup vinegar
1 teaspoon salt
½ cup all-purpose flour
¼ cup plus 1 tablespoon milk
2 eggs, separated
2 teaspoons olive or vegetable oil
⅛ teaspoon salt
Vegetable oil for deep frying

Combine turtle, vinegar, and 1 teaspoon salt. Cover with water; simmer 1 hour or until tender. Drain and set aside.

Combine flour, milk, egg yolks, oil, and ⅛ teaspoon salt; mix well. Beat egg whites until stiff; fold into batter.

Dip turtle pieces into batter; fry until golden brown in deep oil heated to 375°. Drain on paper towels. Yield: 4 to 6 servings.

Clam Fritters

1 egg, beaten
1 cup ground fresh or thawed frozen clams
1 small onion, chopped
1 cup all-purpose flour
1 to 1½ teaspoons salt
Pepper to taste
½ teaspoon sugar
1 tablespoon baking powder
Vegetable oil for deep frying

Combine egg, clams, onion, flour, salt, pepper, and sugar; beat well. Fold in baking powder.

Heat oil to 265°. Drop batter by heaping teaspoonfuls into hot oil, not crowding fritters. Fry until lightly browned; drain. Yield: 4 to 6 servings.

Deviled Crab Deluxe

1 pound fresh crabmeat
1½ cups cracker crumbs, divided
1 tablespoon lemon juice
1 teaspoon Worcestershire sauce
½ cup minced onion
Dash of hot sauce
Dash of cayenne pepper
1 teaspoon dry mustard
¼ cup dried parsley flakes
⅔ cup melted butter or margarine
¼ cup evaporated milk
Salt and pepper to taste
Butter or margarine

Remove all cartilage from crabmeat. Combine crabmeat, 1 cup cracker crumbs, and next 10 ingredients in a medium mixing bowl, mixing gently.

Spoon mixture into 6 individual shells or ramekins or a 1-quart casserole. Sprinkle with ½ cup cracker crumbs; dot with butter. Bake at 375° for 10 to 20 minutes, or until browned on top. Yield: 6 servings.

Eastern Shore Crab Cakes

1 pound fresh crabmeat
Salt and pepper to taste
1 egg, slightly beaten
1 hard-cooked egg, sliced
½ cup butter, melted
1 tablespoon lemon juice
1 tablespoon Worcestershire sauce
Soft breadcrumbs
Butter

Combine crabmeat, salt, pepper, eggs, butter, lemon juice, and Worcestershire sauce in a medium mixing bowl; mix well. Combine crabmeat mixture with just enough breadcrumbs to shape mixture into small cakes.

Heat small amount butter in a heavy skillet over medium heat. Fry cakes in butter until golden brown. Drain and serve. Yield: about 8 servings.

Low Country Seafood Boil

6 large potatoes, halved
4 large sweet onions, halved
1 tablespoon salt
1 dozen live blue crabs
1 (3-ounce) package crab boil
3 whole buds garlic
4 to 6 lemons, halved
1 cup vinegar
1 dozen ears fresh corn
5 pounds unpeeled shrimp
Melted butter
Cocktail sauce

Fill a 5- or 6-gallon pot about two-thirds full of water; bring water to a boil. Add potatoes, onion, and salt; cover and cook over high heat 20 minutes. Stir in crabs, crab boil, garlic, lemons, and vinegar; cook an additional 10 minutes. Reduce heat, and add corn; simmer 5 minutes. Remove from heat, and add shrimp; let stand in water 5 minutes.

Drain off water; arrange crab, shrimp, corn, and potatoes on serving platter. Serve with melted butter and cocktail sauce.

To remove meat from crab, pry off apron flap on underside of crab with thumb or knife. Lift off top shell, using thumb or knife. Then break off large claws, and set aside for eating later. Peel off the spongy substance on each side of crab body. Remove digestive organs and other parts in center body. This will expose hard, semitransparent membrane covering the edible crabmeat. Use a knife to remove the membrane or slice lengthwise through each half without removing membrane. Chunks of meat will be exposed. Crack the claws with a mallet, nutcracker, or knife handle, and remove meat. Yield: 8 to 12 servings.

Sautéed Crabmeat Plantation

¼ cup butter
5 to 6 slices bacon, minced
1 ounce salt pork, minced
¼ cup chopped green onion
¼ cup chopped green pepper
1 pound fresh crabmeat
½ teaspoon Worcestershire sauce
½ teaspoon salt, or to taste
¼ teaspoon white pepper
¼ cup dry white wine
1 cup hot chicken stock
2 eggs, beaten
¼ cup fine cracker crumbs
¼ cup grated Parmesan cheese,
    divided
Lemon wedges

Melt butter in heavy skillet; sauté bacon and salt pork in butter until meat is cooked. Add onion and green pepper; sauté until tender. Stir in crabmeat and cook 1 minute; stir in Worcestershire sauce, salt, pepper, wine, stock, and eggs at 1-minute intervals. Stir in cracker crumbs and half the cheese. Sprinkle remaining cheese on top; broil 3 to 5 minutes, or until top is evenly browned. Serve with lemon wedges. Yield: 4 to 6 servings.

Crawfish Étouffée

¾ cup butter or margarine
1 medium onion, chopped
½ green pepper, chopped
3 stalks celery, chopped
1 tablespoon all-purpose flour
1 to 1½ cups water
1½ pounds crawfish meat, unrinsed
1 teaspoon salt
¼ teaspoon pepper
¼ teaspoon hot pepper sauce
2 teaspoons Worcestershire sauce
¼ teaspoon dried thyme leaves
6 green onions, chopped
2 tablespoons chopped fresh parsley
    or 2 teaspoons dried parsley
    flakes
Hot cooked rice

Melt butter in heavy saucepan. Sauté onion, green pepper, and celery in butter until tender. Add flour and cook 1 minute, stirring constantly. Stir in enough water to obtain desired consistency of gravy; cook over low heat until thickened, stirring frequently. Simmer 15 minutes, stirring occasionally.

Add crawfish, salt, pepper, hot pepper sauce, Worcestershire sauce, thyme, onion, and parsley. Simmer 5 to 10 minutes. Serve over hot cooked rice. Yield: 4 to 6 servings.

Broiled Lobster

2 (1-pound) live lobsters
1 tablespoon melted butter or
    margarine
¼ teaspoon salt
Dash of white pepper
Dash of paprika
¼ cup melted butter or margarine
1 tablespoon lemon juice

Kill each lobster by placing it on its back and inserting a sharp knife between body shell and tail segment, cutting down to sever the spinal cord. Cut in half lengthwise. Remove the stomach (located just back of the head)

and the intestinal vein (runs from the stomach to the tip of the tail). Do not discard the green liver and coral roe; they are delicious. Crack claws.

Place lobster, open as flat as possible, on a broiler pan. Brush lobster meat with 1 tablespoon melted butter. Sprinkle with salt, pepper, and paprika. Broil about 4 inches from heat for 12 to 15 minutes, or until lightly browned. Combine ¼ cup melted butter and lemon juice, and serve with lobster. Yield: 2 servings.

Creamy Lobster

¼ cup butter or margarine
2 (7-ounce) cans lobster, drained
2 tablespoons chopped green onion
3 tablespoons all-purpose flour
½ to 1 teaspoon salt
Dash of cayenne pepper
⅛ teaspoon ground nutmeg
1½ cups milk or half-and-half
Buttered toast
Chopped fresh parsley

Melt butter in a Dutch oven. Add lobster and onion; sauté 5 minutes or until onion is tender. Combine flour, salt, cayenne, and nutmeg; stir into lobster. Gradually add milk and cook over medium heat, stirring constantly, until thickened and bubbly.

Spoon lobster over toast. Sprinkle with parsley. Yield: 4 to 6 servings.

Lobster Newburg

¾ pound cooked lobster meat
¼ cup butter or margarine
2 tablespoons all-purpose flour
1 teaspoon salt
¼ teaspoon paprika
Dash of cayenne pepper
1 pint half-and-half
2 egg yolks, beaten
2 tablespoons dry sherry
Baked patty shells

Cut lobster meat into ½-inch pieces. Melt butter; blend in flour and seasonings. Add half-and-half gradually and cook over medium heat until thickened and smooth, stirring constantly.

Stir a little of the hot sauce into egg yolks; add egg yolks to remaining sauce, stirring constantly. Add lobster meat; heat thoroughly. Remove from heat and slowly stir in sherry. Serve in patty shells. Yield: 4 to 6 servings.

Lobster Creole

3 slices bacon
3 tablespoons vegetable oil
2 onions, minced
1 cup sliced okra
1 (8-ounce) can tomato sauce
1 cup cooked regular rice
1½ cups cooked lobster meat
Salt and pepper to taste
Buttered breadcrumbs

Fry bacon until crisp; drain on absorbent paper, reserving drippings. Add vegetable oil to bacon drippings; sauté onion and okra until tender. Add tomato sauce, rice, and lobster. Season with salt and pepper.

Pour into a greased 1½-quart casserole. Sprinkle breadcrumbs over lobster mixture. Bake, uncovered, at 350° about 30 minutes. Yield: 6 servings.

Creamed Oysters And Eggs On Hot Biscuits

1 pint oysters, fresh or frozen, undrained
1 tablespoon butter or margarine
1 tablespoon all-purpose flour
½ teaspoon salt
1 (10¾-ounce) can cream of celery soup, undiluted
½ cup evaporated milk
2 hard-cooked eggs, sliced
1 (2-ounce) can mushroom stems and pieces, drained
2 tablespoons chopped pimiento
2 teaspoons chopped fresh parsley
4 large biscuits or patty shells

Thaw oysters if frozen; remove any remaining pieces of shell.

Melt butter in a 2-quart saucepan; add oysters and cook over low heat until edges curl, stirring constantly. Stir in flour and salt. Add soup and milk; cook, stirring constantly, until sauce is smooth and hot.

Add eggs, mushrooms, pimiento, and parsley; mix well and heat. Spoon over split hot biscuits or into patty shells. Yield: 4 servings.

Enjoy the true flavor of the Low Country with Low-Country Seafood Boil (page 60), Southern Turnip Greens and Ham Hock (page 139), Savannah Red Rice (page 148), Rosy Chutney (page 258), Buttermilk Corn Sticks (page 167), Old-Fashioned Coleslaw (page 133), and Old-South Carrot Cake (page 197).

Right: *Fried Catfish (page 51), Golden Hush Puppies (page 167), and Coleslaw (page 133) are integral to any summertime fish fry.*

Far Right: *In Florida Cracker country these local specialties abound: (clockwise) Crispy Frog Legs (page 59), Golden Fried Catfish (page 51), Orange Lake Amandine (page 50), Baked Cheese Grits (page 140), and Fried Cooter, better known as Soft-Shell Turtle (page 59).*

Below: *Crab-Stuffed Flounder (page 52) covered in Mornay Sauce is a Low Country specialty.*

Oysters Rockefeller

¼ cup chopped celery
¼ cup chopped green onion
    with tops
2 tablespoons chopped fresh parsley
¼ cup melted butter or margarine
1 (10-ounce) package frozen chopped
    spinach, thawed and drained
1 tablespoon anisette or other
    anise-flavored liqueur
¼ teaspoon salt
Rock salt
1 pint large fresh oysters
    (approximately 18), drained
¼ cup dry breadcrumbs
1 tablespoon melted butter or
    margarine

Sauté celery, onion, and parsley in ¼ cup melted butter in a small saucepan until tender. Drain spinach well.

Combine sautéed vegetables, spinach, anisette, and ¼ teaspoon salt in container of electric blender and process until finely chopped, not pureed. (Stop blender and scrape sides of container with a rubber spatula when necessary.)

Fill a shallow oven-proof serving dish with rock salt. Arrange 18 oyster shells or ramekins into salt bed. (The rock salt holds shells in place and keeps oysters hot.) Place 1 oyster in each shell; top each oyster with spinach mixture. Combine breadcrumbs and 1 tablespoon melted butter; sprinkle crumb mixture over oysters. Bake at 450° for 10 minutes. Use tongs to transfer oysters in shells to serving dishes. Serve immediately. Yield: about 6 appetizer servings.

The cry, "Shrimp boats are coming," promises good eating that night: (counterclockwise) Shrimp Gumbo (page 21), Boiled Shrimp (page 71), and the ever-popular Shrimp Jambalaya (page 27).

Bay Country Oyster And Fish Dish

¼ cup butter or margarine
1 cup finely chopped onion
1 pound fish fillets, cut into 4 pieces
1 (4-ounce) can sliced mushrooms
½ pint oysters
¼ cup dry sherry
½ teaspoon salt
⅛ teaspoon pepper

Melt butter in a large skillet; add onion and sauté until glazed. Spread onion evenly over pan and lay fish fillets over top.

Drain mushrooms, reserving liquid. Spread mushrooms over fish. Drain oysters, reserving liquor. Combine mushroom and oyster liquid; add enough water to mixture to make ½ cup. Combine sherry, salt, pepper, and mushroom and oyster liquids, mixing well; pour over fish. Cover and simmer 5 to 8 minutes, or until fish flakes easily when tested with a fork. Place oysters in pan juices around fish and simmer, uncovered, about 5 minutes or until edges of oysters curl, basting frequently. Yield: 4 servings.

Pan-Fried Oysters

2 eggs, beaten
2 tablespoons milk
1 teaspoon salt
Dash of pepper
1½ cups dry breadcrumbs
1½ cups all-purpose flour
1½ pints oysters, drained
Vegetable oil

Combine eggs, milk, and seasonings in a small bowl; mix well. Combine breadcrumbs and flour in another bowl; mix well. Dredge oysters in crumb mixture; dip in egg mixture, then roll again in crumb mixture. Sauté for about 5 minutes in hot oil, turning carefully once. Drain on absorbent paper. Yield: about 6 servings.

Old Line Oyster Pie

2 cups thinly sliced potatoes
Pastry for double-crust 9-inch pie
1 pint oysters
4 hard-cooked eggs, sliced
¼ cup butter or margarine
Celery salt to taste
Lemon and pepper seasoning
Oyster Sauce (recipe follows)

Cook potatoes in boiling water just until barely tender; drain well. Arrange potatoes into a pastry-lined 9-inch pieplate.

Drain oysters, reserving liquor for use in Oyster Sauce, and layer oysters over potatoes. Layer egg slices over oysters; dot with butter and sprinkle with seasonings. Roll out remaining pastry, and place over pie; seal edges. Cut slits in top to allow steam to escape.

Bake at 400° for 10 minutes; lower heat and bake at 375° for 30 minutes, or until crust is lightly browned. Let stand a few minutes before serving. (Drain off any excess liquid.) Serve with Oyster Sauce. Yield: 6 servings.

Oyster Sauce:

2 tablespoons butter or margarine
2 tablespoons all-purpose flour
1 cup milk
Reserved oyster liquor
Salt and pepper to taste

Melt butter in a medium saucepan and blend in flour. Gradually add milk. Add enough water to oyster liquor to measure ½ cup; add oyster liquor, stirring constantly. Cook over medium heat, stirring constantly, until mixture thickens. Add salt and pepper. Yield: about 1½ cups.

Oyster Kabobs

1 pint oysters, fresh or frozen
⅓ cup commercial French dressing
10 slices bacon, cut into thirds
1 pint cherry tomatoes
2 large green peppers, cut into
    1-inch squares
1 (16-ounce) can small whole
    potatoes, drained
¼ cup vegetable oil
1½ teaspoons salt
⅛ teaspoon pepper

Thaw oysters if frozen. Drain oysters and place in a shallow baking dish. Pour dressing over oysters and marinate 30 minutes.

Drain oysters, reserving marinade for basting. Wrap 1 piece bacon around each oyster. Alternate oysters, tomatoes, green pepper, and potatoes on 6 skewers. Place kabobs on a greased broiler pan.

Combine oil, salt, pepper, and reserved marinade; mix well. Brush kabobs with sauce. Broil about 4 inches from heat for 8 to 10 minutes. Turn kabobs carefully and brush with the remaining sauce. Broil 4 to 5 minutes longer or until the bacon is crisp. Yield: 6 servings.

Note: Three large, firm tomatoes may be substituted for cherry tomatoes. Cut each tomato into 6 wedges.

Scallops Amandine

2 pounds scallops, fresh or frozen
¼ teaspoon salt
Dash of pepper
½ cup all-purpose flour
½ cup slivered almonds
½ cup melted butter or margarine
2 tablespoons chopped fresh parsley

Thaw scallops if frozen; rinse and drain scallops. Sprinkle scallops with salt and pepper; roll in flour.

Sauté almonds in butter until lightly

browned. Drain almonds, reserving butter in pan. Add scallops and sauté for 4 minutes, turning scallops once. Sprinkle with parsley and almonds; serve immediately. Yield: 6 servings.

Superb Baked Scallops

2 pounds calico or bay scallops, fresh or frozen
2 cups round buttery cracker crumbs
¼ cup melted butter or margarine
¼ cup catsup
½ teaspoon salt
¼ teaspoon sugar
Dash of pepper
¼ cup sliced green onion with tops
1 tablespoon melted butter or margarine
Paprika

Thaw scallops if frozen; rinse and drain scallops. Cut large scallops in half crosswise.

Combine scallops, cracker crumbs, ¼ cup melted butter, catsup, salt, sugar, and pepper, mixing well. Spoon scallop mixture into 6 small greased casseroles or 1 greased shallow 1½-quart casserole. Combine green onion and 1 tablespoon butter; spoon on top of scallop mixture. Bake at 350° for 20 to 30 minutes, or until brown. Sprinkle with paprika. Yield: 6 servings.

Fried Scallop Puffs

3 pounds scallops
1 (16-ounce) package or 3 cups pancake and waffle mix
1 egg
1¾ cups water
1 teaspoon salt
Hot vegetable oil for deep frying
Tartar sauce

Rinse scallops in cold water; pat dry, and cut into bite-size pieces. Set aside.

Combine pancake mix, egg, water, and salt; stir until well mixed. Dip scallops into batter; add additional water if batter thickens. Fry scallops 2 to 5 minutes in deep oil heated to 375°. Drain on paper towels. Serve Scallop Puffs with your favorite tartar sauce. Yield: 50 appetizer servings.

Divine Shrimp Puff

1 (4½-ounce) can shrimp
5 slices stale bread
Mayonnaise
½ cup shredded mild Cheddar cheese, divided
1 tablespoon butter or margarine
2 eggs
1½ cups milk
¼ teaspoon salt
¼ teaspoon pepper
1 teaspoon Worcestershire sauce
Paprika

Drain shrimp, reserving liquid. Spread bread liberally with mayonnaise; cut bread into small squares. Layer half the bread, half the cheese, and half the shrimp in a greased 1½-quart soufflé dish. Repeat layers with remaining ingredients. Dot with butter.

Combine eggs, milk, reserved shrimp liquid, and seasonings, mixing well; pour over bread. Set aside for 8 to 10 minutes; sprinkle with paprika. Place dish in a shallow pan containing a small amount of water; bake at 350° for 45 to 50 minutes. Serve immediately. Yield: 4 servings.

Spicy Barbecued Shrimp

8 pounds shrimp, heads removed
1 cup butter or margarine
1 cup olive oil
1 cup chili sauce
3 tablespoons Worcestershire sauce
2 lemons, thinly sliced
3 tablespoons lemon juice
4 cloves garlic, minced
1 tablespoon chopped fresh parsley or
    1 teaspoon dried parsley flakes
2 teaspoons paprika
2 teaspoons dried oregano leaves
1 to 2 teaspoons crushed red pepper
1 teaspoon hot sauce
3 tablespoons liquid smoke

Spread shrimp in shallow baking pan. Combine remaining ingredients in saucepan; simmer 15 minutes. Pour sauce over shrimp. Marinate several hours in refrigerator, turning shrimp in marinade every half hour. Bake at 300° for 30 minutes, stirring gently at 10-minute intervals. Serve with French bread. Yield: 12 to 16 servings.

Shrimp Paste

1 pound cooked shelled shrimp
½ cup butter or margarine
½ teaspoon onion juice
½ teaspoon Worcestershire sauce
Dash of cayenne pepper
½ teaspoon seasoned salt

Grind shrimp very fine or reduce almost to a paste in food processor. Add butter, blending thoroughly. Add seasonings.

Line a deep 2-cup bowl with plastic wrap. Pack paste into bowl; chill several hours or overnight. Turn bowl over on serving plate; remove bowl, and peel off plastic wrap. Make an all-over design with tip of teaspoon, if desired. Surround with crisp crackers and provide a butter knife for serving. Yield: about 2 cups.

Shrimp Kedgeree

3 tablespoons butter or margarine
2 or 3 green onions, minced
2 cups cooked regular rice
1 cup cooked shrimp, minced
2 eggs, beaten
Salt and pepper to taste

Heat butter in skillet; sauté onion in butter until tender. Add rice; fry until heated through. Add shrimp and continue to cook over low heat until rice is slightly browned, stirring gently. Combine eggs and seasonings, mixing well. Pour egg mixture into rice and shrimp in a thin stream, stirring, and continue to cook just until egg is set. Serve for breakfast or supper. Yield: 4 servings.

Carolina Shrimp Casserole

3 quarts boiling water
1 tablespoon salt
2½ pounds shrimp, peeled and
    deveined
1 tablespoon lemon juice
3 tablespoons vegetable oil
2 tablespoons butter or margarine
¼ cup finely chopped green pepper
¼ cup finely chopped onion
¾ cup regular rice, cooked
1 teaspoon salt
⅛ teaspoon pepper
⅛ teaspoon mace
⅛ teaspoon cayenne pepper
1 (10¾-ounce) cream of tomato soup,
    undiluted
1 cup whipping cream
½ cup dry sherry
½ cup slivered almonds, divided

Combine boiling water and 1 tablespoon salt. Add shrimp and cook 5 minutes. Drain. Sprinkle shrimp with lemon juice and oil; refrigerate.

One to 1½ hours before serving, melt butter in a large skillet and sauté green pepper and onion in butter for 5 minutes. Add cooked rice, salt, pepper, mace, cayenne, soup, cream, sherry, and ¼ cup almonds. Add shrimp, reserving several for the top. Pour into a greased 2-quart casserole and bake at 350° for 35 minutes. Top with reserved shrimp and remaining ¼ cup almonds; bake 20 minutes longer, or until mixture is bubbly and shrimp lightly browned. Yield: 6 to 8 servings.

Shrimp Miami

  2 pounds peeled and deveined
     shrimp, fresh or frozen
  ¼ cup olive or vegetable oil
  1 teaspoon salt
  ¼ teaspoon white pepper
  ¼ cup extra-dry vermouth
  2 tablespoons lemon juice
  1 tablespoon chopped fresh parsley

Thaw shrimp if frozen. Heat oil in a large skillet; add shrimp, salt, and pepper. Cook over medium heat for 4 to 5 minutes, or until shrimp are pink, stirring frequently. Add vermouth and lemon juice. Cook 1 minute longer, stirring constantly.

Remove shrimp to a warm serving platter. Sprinkle with parsley. Yield: approximately 60 appetizer servings or 6 entrée servings.

Shrimp De Jonghe

  1 pound cooked peeled deveined
     shrimp, fresh or frozen, or 4
     (4½-ounce) cans shrimp,
     drained and rinsed
  ¾ cup toasted dry breadcrumbs
  ¼ cup chopped green onion
     with tops
  ¼ cup chopped fresh parsley
  ¾ teaspoon crushed tarragon leaves
  1 clove garlic, crushed
  ¼ teaspoon ground nutmeg
  ¼ teaspoon salt
  Dash of pepper
  ½ cup melted butter or margarine
  ¼ cup dry sherry

Thaw shrimp if frozen. Combine breadcrumbs, onion, parsley, and seasonings; stir in butter, sherry, and shrimp.

Place shrimp mixture in 6 greased individual baking shells or 6-ounce custard cups. Place shells in a 15- × 10- × 1-inch baking pan. Bake at 400° for 10 to 15 minutes or until brown. Yield: 6 servings.

Boiled Shrimp

  4 large bay leaves
 20 peppercorns
  1 teaspoon mustard seeds
  ½ teaspoon dried basil leaves
 12 whole cloves
  ⅛ teaspoon cumin seeds
  1 teaspoon crushed red pepper
  ⅛ teaspoon celery seeds
  ⅛ teaspoon fennel seeds
  ⅛ teaspoon caraway seeds
  ¼ teaspoon ground marjoram
  ¼ teaspoon dried thyme leaves
  4 to 5 quarts water
  1 teaspoon salt
  1 lemon, cut in half
  2 cloves garlic
  2 teaspoons dehydrated onion flakes
  5 pounds medium or large shrimp
  Lettuce leaves (optional)
  Lemon slices (optional)

Combine first 12 ingredients in a doubled cheesecloth bag; tie securely with string.

Bring water to a boil. Add salt, lemon halves, garlic, onion flakes, and herb bag; return to a boil, and cook 2 to 3 minutes. Stir in shrimp; return to a boil, and cook 3 to 5 minutes. Drain well; chill. Peel shrimp, and serve on lettuce leaves and garnish with lemon slices, if desired. Yield: 8 to 10 servings.

Low Country Paella

Use any combination of shrimp, chicken, pork, and clams.

1 pound boned chicken, pork,
    or other meat
Peanut oil
1 large green pepper, cut into
    1-inch strips
2 large tomatoes or 1 (8-ounce)
    can tomato sauce
1 clove garlic, minced
1 (8-ounce) can green peas
Clam juice
2 cups water
1 large onion, chopped
Dash of powdered saffron
Salt and pepper to taste
1 cup uncooked regular rice
1 pound shrimp, peeled and
    deveined
About 2 pounds clams, unshucked
    and well scrubbed

Brown chicken in oil in a Dutch oven; drain chicken, reserving oil in pan. Sauté green pepper in reserved oil until tender; drain pepper, reserving oil in pan.

Place tomatoes in container of electric blender and blend on medium speed until pureed. Sauté garlic in previously reserved oil until lightly browned; add tomatoes and cook over low heat for 5 minutes, stirring occasionally.

Drain peas, reserving liquid. Add enough clam juice to pea liquid to make 1 cup. Add water, clam juice mixture, and onion to tomato mixture; bring to a boil. Reduce heat and add chicken. Cook over low heat for 15 minutes, stirring occasionally.

Add saffron, salt, pepper, peas, and rice. Cook over high heat, without stirring, for 10 to 15 minutes. Add shrimp and clams and cook for 5 minutes. Remove pan from heat and let sit until rice absorbs remaining liquid. Garnish with green pepper strips. Yield: 8 to 10 servings.

Superb Seafood Casserole

¾ pound fresh or frozen shrimp,
    peeled and deveined
¾ pound scallops, fresh or frozen
½ pound blue crabmeat, fresh or
    frozen
6 tablespoons melted butter or
    margarine
¼ cup all-purpose flour
1 teaspoon salt
Dash of pepper
1½ cups milk
2 tablespoons dry sherry
1½ cups soft breadcrumbs
¼ cup shredded Cheddar cheese
2 tablespoons melted butter or
    margarine
Paprika

Thaw seafood if frozen, and remove any pieces of shell or cartilage. Cut large shrimp and scallops in half. Sauté shrimp and scallops in 6 tablespoons melted butter in a large saucepan over medium heat for 4 to 6 minutes or until tender.

Remove shrimp and scallops from pan, reserving butter in pan; stir flour, salt, and pepper into butter. Add milk gradually and cook, stirring constantly, until thickened. Stir in sherry; fold in crabmeat, shrimp, and scallops. Spoon into 6 individual baking shells or ramekins.

Combine breadcrumbs, cheese, and 2 tablespoons melted butter; sprinkle over seafood mixture. Bake at 350° for 10 to 15 minutes, or until heated thoroughly. Sprinkle with paprika. Yield: 6 servings.

Many wrecked homes, many divorces, many crimes have been traced directly to a bad digestion, the result of wrong methods of cooking.

Progressive Farmer magazine

Meats, Poultry, and Game

Swan, horse, dormouse, porcupine, hyena . . . man has been enriching his diet with meat since his very beginnings. This list may seem rather baroque as we look back on the evolution of our culinary prejudices, but it covers only a fraction of the meats civilized man has fattened for his table in the best of times. In periods of want, of course, anything becomes edible. Historians will recall that just over a hundred years ago, the entire Paris zoo was sacrificed to feed the citizens when the Prussians laid siege to the French city.

The raising of meat animals on a commercial basis is a relatively recent development, although people have been eating domesticated animals since about 3,000 B.C. In the seventeenth century, feed crops such as turnips and grain stabilized somewhat, enabling some cattle to be wintered over. Meat thus was available to some extent the year round. But it was not until the advent of refrigeration in the late eighteenth century that the foundation was laid for the dependable meat supply we take for granted today. Thus, good meat was still far out of reach of all but the wealthy in Europe when the would-be colonists took ship for America.

The Europeans who arrived on these shores in the seventeenth century must have been astounded to find so much game for the taking. It will be recalled that the upper class in England not only owned the land, they owned the game as well. Poachers were dealt with harshly. Because most of our forefathers could not be placed in the landowner category, it is likely that they were more used to being the hunted than the hunter.

What a heady experience it must have been for the colonists to take whatever game they needed without looking over their shoulders for the landowner's gamekeeper. Of course, they hunted large game such as venison and bear only in winter because of the spoilage problem. But small game was plentiful: rabbit, squirrel, raccoon, field birds. In winter, wild waterfowl covered Virginia's rivers.

In fact, the new Americans who moved westward out of the settled coastal areas achieved the distinction of eating more meat per capita than any other people in history. Authorities have estimated their consumption at nearly a pound a day of game alone.

The American mania for meat continues unabated. We not only produce more beef than any other country, we consume it; in all the world, only Argentina eats more beef per capita than we. Fine pork and veal are available to us, too, in terms undreamed of even fifty years ago. The South participates in the American rage for good meat. And we modestly believe that we deal with it as skillfully as anyone, foreign or domestic. We especially point with pride to two of our distinctive ways with meat: the preparation of pit barbecue and the curing of hams.

We can only surmise how stale and unprofitable eating must have been before the discovery of fire. But once our common ancestor lit the fire under the first barbecue, we entered the era of eating for pleasure as well as for sustenance. The extremes of temperature in the South notwithstanding, it is a rare household these days that does not boast some sort of facility for outdoor meat cookery. And entertaining at barbecues is as firmly entrenched in the South as it is in California.

Georgia takes a back seat to none when it comes to open air gambols. A "pig picking" feast usually occurs in the hottest weather, but that is no reason to turn down an invitation. It is customary to serve Brunswick stew along with the barbecued meat. You can also expect any or all of the following: sweet potatoes, corn on the cob, coleslaw, garden salad, pickles, onion, tomatoes, rye and white breads, lemonade, watermelon, boiled coffee, and gingersnaps.

For a typically lavish production of Georgia-style pit barbecue, you will need a pit, a pig, a basting solution, a buttery sauce, and these explicit instructions:

Georgia Pit Barbecue

The Pit:

Dig (or get someone else to dig) a pit 1½ feet deep, 4 feet wide, and about 1 foot longer than the pig to be barbecued. Fire it up with small green oak wood, and let it burn down to red coals. The pit is now ready for the pig.

The Pig:

Select a pig weighing from 35 to 50 pounds. Remove the head near the shoulders, and the feet just above the first joint. Open the pig down through the center of the backbone so it will lie perfectly flat. With a circular motion of the knife, cut out and discard the thin flanks on each side of the carcass.

Run sharpened iron or oak rods lengthwise through hams and shoulders, allowing extensions of both ends to catch the banks of the pit. This makes it easy to hold the carcass up and furnishes handholds for positioning the meat. The rods should be inserted near the skin and under the ribs in order that the neck, shoulders, and hams may go down lower into the pit, while the rods under the ribs prevent them from falling out when the meat becomes tender.

Laterally insert 3 or 4 small rods, iron or oak, so that they protrude at the sides. Again, this prevents the meat from dropping off when done. The rods should be fastened in place with wire. The pig is now ready for the pit; position it over the prepared coals, meat side toward the heat. Do not salt.

The Basting Solution:

Mix 1 quart strong salt water with 1 teaspoon cayenne pepper and keep it very warm at all times.

Georgia Barbecue Sauce:

2½ pounds butter
2 quarts apple vinegar
1 pint water
1 tablespoon dry mustard
½ cup minced onion
1 (5-ounce) bottle
   Worcestershire sauce
1 pint chili sauce

Juice of 2 lemons
½ lemon, seeds removed
   (used whole)
3 cloves garlic, finely
   chopped and tied in bag
¼ cup sugar
1 pint tomato catsup
4 teaspoons hot sauce

Mix ingredients; cook to meld flavors. Use a mop to baste meat when meat is three-fourths done. Keep sauce very warm at all times.

Meanwhile, back at the pit, when the meat is warm, turn it up and baste with the hot saline solution; continue to do so, as often as the meat becomes dry, until meat is nearly done. (The water prevents the meat from scorching.)

As the meat cooks, more heat may be applied. Keep the coals bunched under the shoulders and hams, allowing the thinner part of the pig less heat. When meat is nearly done, baste two or three times with plain warm water (always warm water, never cold). This drives the salt in and washes off exterior salt.

The meat side is kept to the fire, except when it is turned over just long enough to be basted. The skin is thus allowed to become hot from time to time and will be finished off when the meat is nearly done, as follows:

Turn skin side down and begin basting with the barbecue sauce. When done and very tender, remove some of the coals from the pit and allow the skin to brown and crisp, watching closely. The skin should be crisp, not "gummy." During this last cooking you will note that the meat side is up and is basted frequently with the barbecue sauce.

To sum up, it is important that the sauce, as well as the saline basting solution, be kept hot; remember the cooking is slow, up to 7 hours for a small carcass, longer for a larger animal. The meat should be hot before basting begins. The skin side is never applied to the heat except when meat is turned over for basting, then at the end of cooking, to crisp the skin. A clean dish mop is ideal for basting.

For serving, the meat is not so much carved as it is pulled apart, "picked" into pieces, then put into pans and kept warm. The crisp skin is put in a separate pan. If meat must be held for a while before serving, baste frequently with the barbecue sauce. No sauce on the skin, though; it must remain crisp.

Churches early recognized the potential of the barbecue as a fund-raising technique. In the heavily German-Catholic western half of Kentucky, many churches maintain permanent roofed-over pits for their annual barbecues that regularly draw thousands of hungry cash customers. Most of these large picnics serve burgoo along with the barbecued meats. At places like St. Mary Church at Whitesville, or St. Peter's Church at Stanley, Kentucky, the festival would be considered lightweight indeed if the mob consumed less than 600 gallons of burgoo and 5,000 pounds of meat.

You can draw more people to a political barbecue in Texas or Kentucky than you could to a public hanging. The late Vice President Alben W. Barkley of Kentucky probably delivered more orations with blistered lips than any other political figure in history, with the possible exception of the late President Lyndon B. Johnson. It is interesting to note, however, that they probably preferred different meats. In western Kentucky, mutton is king; in Texas, beef. Oddly enough, eastern Kentuckians consume practically no mutton or lamb.

Fancy Farm, Kentucky, is the traditional rallying place for office seekers to court the electorate. The church there is St. Jerome, with some 570 families as parishioners. The town itself numbers only about 350 inhabitants. The first public "picnic" at Fancy Farm took place in 1880. The combination of good food and high-powered politics now draws around 10,000 people annually.

The meat for the Fancy Farm barbecue is purchased by the church; the coleslaw is made by a group of volunteers in the school cafeteria; and the remainder of the food is brought in by the parishioners and the population at large with equal enthusiasm.

Bob Spalding has served more than once as general chairman for the Fancy Farm Picnic. His meat order for the event consists of 7,500 pounds of mutton and 5,500 pounds of pork shoulders. He told me that the optimum mutton for barbecue is a ewe weighing 150 pounds and dressing out to 85 pounds.

The concrete block pits at Fancy Farm are roofed over, as is customary in the area. They afford a total of 220 feet of cooking surface. Fires of oak and hickory wood, built outside the pits, are burned down to red coals, which are then shoveled into the bottom of the pits through holes at ground level.

After twenty-four hours of the gentlest cooking, the meat is ready, and the men who have tended the pits all night head for home and rest—red-eyed, grinning, and blinking from the smoke. The serving crew takes over, carrying the meltingly tender mutton halves and pork shoulders to a screened enclosure to be boned out for serving. Bottles of extra barbecue sauce are available for those who wish to live dangerously—when taken in quantity, it will cauterize the taste buds.

Joseph Carrico is an old-timer in the barbecue business at Fancy Farm. He has retired, and his son, Rudy, has made some slight changes in the family recipe for the barbecue sauce with which Joseph Carrico has delighted customers for over 50 years:

Joseph Carrico Barbecue Sauce

3 quarts vinegar	2 tablespoons paprika
1 quart water	2 tablespoons salt
2 tablespoons cayenne pepper	2 tablespoons sugar

"Now, when I say 'tablespoon,'" said Carrico, "I mean a big kitchen tablespoon, not one of those little measuring spoons. Mix together over low heat and this recipe will make you a gallon of sauce; and it will keep, so you'll have it on hand."

Other than sheer size, the Fancy Farm picnic differs from other western Kentucky barbecues in a couple of respects. Burgoo is not served, as it is at the others. And, once the midday feeding is over, politicians take to the speakers' platform, which has been constructed on a pair of flatbed trucks in front of St. Jerome Church. There is a 10-foot-high tree stump down in front of the speakers' stand. That monumental stump has been plastered over and whitewashed. It is kept standing, I am told, in memory of all the generations of Kentucky political speakers who have gone beyond. "It was a beautiful tree. The hot air killed it."

When you follow barbecue through west Tennessee, it is spelled "pork"; mutton does not cross the state line. A good source of barbecue lore in Memphis is Charles Vergos, a second generation Greek who has run his Rendezvous Restaurant here since 1948.

"Johnny Mills was the father of barbecue here in Memphis," according to Vergos. "He served barbecued shoulders in a little restaurant off Beall St. Leonard's; he branched off from there, and the rest came later. Ribs got lost until I started them up again, and now everybody's doing them."

Vergos claims to be the granddaddy of barbecued ribs in Memphis. To drive home the point, he cites his weekly meat (pork) order: 8,000 pounds, with ribs accounting for 6,000 pounds of the total. His barbecue formula is the same for ribs and other cuts of pork but is a secret known only to himself and his son, Nick. "We use hot vinegar and water first, then coat the meat with a dry mix we make ourselves." And that is as close as anybody is going to get to Vergos' recipe.

In Texas, again, I found similar thinking on the three imperatives of barbecuing: the dry mix, the mopping sauce, and the barbecue sauce. The mopping liquid, which usually does not even taste good, is used during cooking to flavor and moisten the meat. Barbecue sauce is served with the meat at the table.

While Texans like to emphasize beef, that is not to say good spareribs cannot be had in their state. They can indeed, as this three-part recipe illustrates.

Texas Barbecue

Dry Barbecue Mixture:

¼ cup celery seeds, bruised
¼ cup paprika (Spanish)
½ teaspoon sesame seeds
6 dried chili tipines (small, round hot peppers)

1 tablespoon chili powder
2 tablespoons salt

Combine all ingredients and mix thoroughly. Sprinkle over meat on the grill after it has begun to brown and its surface is moist enough to hold the mixture. Sprinkle a little at a time but repeatedly, at intervals, until surface of meat has a light but thorough coating. Excellent on spareribs. It may also be used on many oven-roasted meats. Try it on any pork roast. This is also fine sprinkled into the bone cavity of a boned shoulder of pork before roasting or braising. Yield: about ¾ cup.

Mopping Sauce For Barbecue:

1 cup strong black coffee
½ cup Worcestershire sauce
1 cup tomato catsup
¼ cup butter or margarine

1 tablespoon freshly ground black pepper
1 tablespoon sugar
1 tablespoon salt

Combine all ingredients and simmer 30 minutes. Stir frequently. Store in a tightly covered jar in a refrigerator until needed. Heat gently before using. This is wonderful, too, for oven pork roasts. Yield: 2½ to 3 cups.

Barbecue Sauce:

1 cup chopped onion
¼ cup butter
1 clove garlic, minced
1 cup chicken bouillon or stock
¼ cup vinegar
½ teaspoon dry mustard
4 teaspoons Worcestershire sauce

2 tablespoons chili sauce
1 tablespoon lemon juice
½ teaspoon hot sauce
1 bay leaf
¼ teaspoon ground cloves
2 tablespoons sugar
2 tablespoons all-purpose flour

Sauté the onion in butter in a heavy saucepan over moderate heat until golden; do not brown. Add garlic and cook 2 minutes. Add remaining ingredients except flour and simmer 20 minutes. Moisten flour with a little cold water and stir into sauce. Cook, stirring constantly, until sauce is thickened. If a hotter sauce is desired, add more hot sauce. Yield: about 1½ cups.

Note: Although I have said that this sauce is never used as a basting sauce, it may be used once or twice at the very end of the barbecue cooking time to give the meat additional flavor. If used before meat is done, it will burn.

Purists claim that when we put spicy red sauce on meat during the cooking we are not truly barbecuing. Convenience must be served, however, even in Texas; thus many barbecue recipes exist that can be easily prepared in the home kitchen.

Unlike barbecue, which we fondly believe to have its roots in the South, the story of sausage-making in the South is a compilation of methods, brought from all over the world, to use up the last morsels of precious meat. Give a side of pork, beef, or venison to a Mexican-American, a Texan of German background, an Appalachian or Ozark Mountain man, and an Italian-Floridian. The result will be four distinctly different sausages, each more delicious than the other.

In my childhood, hog-killing time was a period of generalized tension; all the meat had to be treated quickly even in cold weather. But when it was time to make the sausage, there came the annual crisis in my parents' marriage. My father liked it hot; my mother enjoyed a more delicate approach to the spicing. Here is my father's recipe.

Pork Sausage

1 pound salt
2 to 4 tablespoons rubbed sage
2 to 4 tablespoons black pepper

1½ tablespoons red pepper (3 tablespoons for hot sausage)
50 pounds pork, ¼ to ⅓ fat by weight

Combine seasonings and rub well into cut-up meat. Grind twice. Stuff into casings. Smoke 2 to 4 hours over green hickory and hang to store. If sausage is not smoked, it should be frozen after taking seasonings for 2 days.

My love for hot sausage is directly traceable to my upbringing. Nevertheless, as mentioned earlier, I was not prepared for the natural heat in the pork-rice sausage they call "boudin" down in Cajun country.

Natural casings had been soaked in warm water to soften them and tied at one end to make yard-long sacs for the ground mixture. Seasoned pork and rice had been cooked separately; it was my first time to see sausage made of precooked ingredients. Some raw green onion and parsley were ground in with the rice and pork along with plenty of "redpeppernotblack" (one word in Cajun circles).

Dudley Hebert, who demonstrated the making of *boudin blanc*, gave me the following sketch of his recipe:

"Cook 5 pounds of pork, including a little fat, with 2 pounds liver. Flavor the cooking water with onion, celery, and green pepper. Drain, grind, and mix with ground red pepper, salt, green onion with tops, and parsley. Mix with cooked rice and stuff in casings. No garlic, because I can't eat it," Hebert said.

"Tastes better without it," observed a bystander.

The sausages are boiled for 10 minutes after stuffing. They may be served as is or browned in a skillet or on the back of a barbecue grill.

The development of sausage in Texas is, to a large extent, the story of the German segment of the population. As did the Acadians of Louisiana, the early German settlers who came to Texas suffered murderous hardships. In 1844, the first wave in a planned German immigration arrived in Galveston. Led by Prince Carl of Solms-Braunfels, they went on to a "gathering place" at Indianola, and finally, after losing many of their number to disease in the unaccustomed climate, established a colony on the Comal River south of San Antonio. They named it New Braunfels, in honor of the Prince's Braunfels Castle on the Lahn River in Germany.

Three thousand more Germans came through Galveston in 1846 and went on to found other settlements. They brought with them their genius for making wurst. Modern Texan communities such as Fredericksburg, Elgin, New Braunfels, and others ship their famous sausage products, smoked, fresh, or barbecued, all over the country.

In Texas, as in other parts of the South where venison is hunted, a delicious sausage variation is made, using three parts of venison to one part pork. From the Hilmar Staats family ranch in Mission Valley, Texas, comes this set of instructions. The sausage is usually made in November or December, and venison is used instead of the beef called for in the recipe.

Sausage Making

Meat Proportions:

40 pounds meat (30 pounds beef, 10 pounds pork)
1 pound coarse salt

¼ cup coarsely ground pepper
2 tablespoons finely chopped garlic

Equipment:

1 or more sets of casings from a meat market
String for tying

1 sausage stuffer
1 smokehouse
1 smokepot

Two days before making sausage: Chop garlic; place it in ½ cup hot water. Allow to stand overnight.

One day before making sausage: Purchase casings at meat market. Turn and clean in warm water. Cut into 16-inch lengths and firmly tie off one end.

To prepare meat and seasonings, mix salt and pepper. Add juice of garlic. Blend well. Cut beef and pork into chunks. Sprinkle seasoning mixture over combined meats. Grind meat in coarse grind, and then grind in fine grind. Spread meat over large board or counter in smokehouse. Allow to sit overnight. Keep refrigerated if weather is warm.

Day of making sausage: In the morning, knead meat once to be sure seasoning is well distributed. Sausage meat can now be shaped into patties and placed in the freezer or stuffed into casings. If meat is to be stuffed into casings, a sausage stuffer will be needed. Using the stuffer, firmly press meat into casing, and tie off open end tightly with twine. Using a large needle, punch several holes in sausage to allow any air bubbles to escape and to allow excess moisture to drain out. Hang sausage on poles in smokehouse. Be sure to space them evenly. Allow to hang overnight before smoking.

Day after making sausage: In order to give sausage a good, smoked flavor, combine oak and mesquite wood that has been cut into chips. Place wood in a sturdy bucket and begin a fire within the pot. Place in smokehouse, making certain windows are closed. Be sure smokepot has a cover with some openings to prevent wood from flaming. As wood is smoking in the smokepot, the sausage will eventually develop extra flavor. If weather is not too warm, the sausage can be cured in about 8 days. Wrap links in freezer paper and store in freezer. Yield: about 40 pounds.

For those who are not storing up a year's supply of sausage, yet want to try their hand at creating what has become a specialty, here are some simple stuffing instructions.

For those recipes that require stuffing sausage into casings, natural casings (the cleaned intestines of pigs or sheep) are preferable to artificial ones, as they are edible. They are available, clean and ready to use, packed in salt. Meat packing companies will sell them, and many butcher shops will be happy to order them. They are inexpensive; for a dollar or two, the home sausage maker can have a season's supply, and with very little effort, can turn out professional-looking sausages.

To use the casings, take them out of the salt, estimating roughly 2 inches per 1 ounce of meat to be processed. The unused portion, closed and in a cool place, will keep indefinitely. Cut casings into manageable yard-long pieces and rinse away the salt by running tepid tap water through each length. Blot excess water; knot one end. Slip the open end over the sausage stuffing attachment, drawing the casing over the tube to within an inch of the knotted end.

Fill the casing, using the free hand to equalize the meat as it goes in. Or, if no sausage stuffing attachment is available, use a funnel or cake decorator without a tube attached. In any case, the casings should not be too tightly stuffed, lest they burst under the pressure. Fill to within about 2 inches of the end, leaving enough casing to tie off. Form individual sausages by twisting the finished casing at desired intervals. As an alternative, the sausage may be left in one long coil. Before freezing or serving, hang the stuffed sausage to dry for twenty-four hours outdoors in a breezy spot, or indoors with an electric fan blowing.

Recipes for utilizing homemade specialty sausages are to be found in most kitchen libraries. Once a cook becomes accustomed to keeping a supply of sausage in the freezer, his imagination will take over where the recipes leave off. Spicy country sausage is the main ingredient in one of the South's favorite dressings for poultry; kielbasa is delicious in a chicken-sausage gumbo; chorizo is needed in the elegant Spanish *boliche*. These and other sausage recipes begin on page 115.

It is the English settlers whom we can credit with planting the seeds of the present-day Virginia ham industry. It took several years for the colonists to stabilize their food supply, as starvation forced them to eat their breeding stock. Finally new brood stock was imported from England, and it became illegal to slaughter the animals until there were enough to assure a continuing meat supply.

Salt was as expensive as sugar in early days, so the Indian techniques of drying and smoking game were adapted for pork, allowing ham to be enjoyed by rich and poor alike. Most people kept their own pigs and many homes had outbuildings strictly for the smoking and storing processes.

By 1640, Virginia was exporting hams to England. Peanut-fed hams were a favorite delicacy in the royal household of Queen Victoria, who had a standing order for six hams per week. Prince Albert, as well remembered for his independence as for his dashing good looks, may have preferred Westphalian hams from his native Germany, but history seems to be silent on that point.

Not only Virginians, but connoisseurs all over the South, pride themselves on their ham curing methods. Here is a "very rare old receipt" from Virginia.

How To Cure A Fine Old Virginia Ham

Between Thanksgiving and Christmas, after heavy frosts, is hog-killing time in Virginia.

The next day, after the body heat is out of the meat, pack the hams down in salt. Use enough salt so that all the meat is heavily covered. Let the hams stay in the salt for a week or 10 days, at least.

Now take them out and wash them. Rub each ham all over with molasses, a dessert spoon of saltpeter and plenty of freshly ground black pepper.

Hang hams from rafters in the smokehouse, and smoke for 21 days, seeing that you use nothing but hickory wood—no other wood will do. Careful tending and slow, even smoking are the secrets of curing a good ham. These hams are not at their best until they have aged 2 years. They have no equal when properly cured and aged.

Tennessee and Kentucky have a friendly rivalry over their ham curing expertise, with an annual confrontation at the Kentucky State Fair. I offer no comparisons; both are delicious and I have cousins in both states who still cure hams the way my Tennessee-born grandfather used to do.

Kentucky-Tennessee Cured Ham

Get a wooden box large enough to hold one or two hams. Cover the bottom with salt ½ inch deep. Rub the meat well with salt and lay the ham, skin side down, in the box. Cover the meat with salt.

Let the ham lie in the box 10 days to 2 weeks. Then brush all salt from ham. Hang ham until moisture dries off; this will take about 2 weeks.

Wash with boiling water and allow to dry again. Then dust with black pepper, red pepper, and borax. Place in a large brown paper bag, then in a large white cloth bag, and hang up for future use.

Cured or fresh, pork is high on any Southerner's list of most loved meats and is right up there with chicken, the food probably most closely associated with Southern cooking. But as every culinary buff knows, the origins of this fowl are not in the South. Rather, every ancient civilization appears to have had chickens. The Incas on our side of the world kept them, and the Greeks probably brought them from Asia. Conquering Rome found that the Gauls already were raising chickens and geese.

Turkey is a different matter; it wears the stamp, "Made in America." When the Spanish arrived in the New World in the early 1500s, they found turkeys being raised and eaten in Mexico. There has been some controversy about whether Europeans really had turkey before that. But by now most authorities agree that the bird Europe knew as turkey was actually guinea fowl, so-called because it originated in Turkey.

Throughout history, the desirability of fowl has risen and fallen according to the supply. Plentiful, chicken or turkey became food for the poor, disdained by their betters, who feasted on peacocks and whole flocks of songbirds; scarce, poultry again entered the great halls. "A chicken in every pot" was a political slogan during our Depression days, but the idea was stolen from a French monarch of several centuries earlier, who used a similar line to curry favor with the masses.

Whether experiencing a depression or not, the American South seems to have a particular affinity for chicken, as witness the mystique surrounding "Southern Fried." To the surprise of some first-time visitors to our area, there is no standard recipe for it.

There are a few areas of agreement, however. Most cooks allow the chicken to "take salt" before cooking, sometimes by way of a good soak in salt water, although some soak it in milk. Southerners generally coat the pieces with seasoned flour, pancake mix and other dry mixtures being occasional variations. For an extra heavy crust, some cooks dip the floured chicken into cream, then into the flour again.

How much shortening to use, and what kind? Opinion is divided: old-timers prefer lard for the flavor, but solid vegetable shortening is more widely used nowadays. Oils are popular as well, but since foods tend to brown more slowly in oil, it is well to know that half a stick of butter or margarine added to it will promote browning.

Once the chicken is fried tenderly brown, and before the excess fat is poured away to make ready for gravy, some Kentuckians like to make "chicken biscuits." One simply makes a batch of baking powder biscuits and fries them in the very hot grease. If the grease does not cover them, turn them over once. These are made to be drowned in rich gravy, and they are a nice accompaniment for this early Georgia recipe for fried chicken.

Fried Chicken

Select a young chicken weighing from 1½ to 2 pounds. Dress and disjoint; chill. When ready, have a deep fry pan with grease at least two inches deep.

Sift enough flour in which to roll the chicken pieces (1½ to 2 cups). Add salt and pepper to the flour, roll each piece in flour, and place in the hot grease. Put the largest pieces in first and on the hottest part of the pan. When all are in, cover for 5 minutes. Remove top and turn when the underside is well browned. Replace top for another 5 minutes; remove and cook in open pan until the bottom side is browned. About 30 minutes is all that will be required for cooking chicken if it is not too large. Do not turn chicken more than once. The grease should be deep enough to cover pieces when it boils.

Cream Gravy:

Pour off the grease, leaving 2 to 3 tablespoons in the pan with the browned crumbs. Add 2 tablespoons butter and 4 tablespoons flour; blend and cook until a golden brown. Add 1 cup milk and 1 cup hot water. Stir until smooth and thick; add salt and pepper. Serve with hot biscuits or dry rice. Never pour gravy over chicken if you wish Georgia fried chicken.

Cooks in the South are as worldly as in any part of the country. Yet there is a quality of tenderness, a kind of respect, in our treatment of chicken, in particular, and all types of meats in general. Patience and delicacy of seasoning bring out the flavor in a way traditional in these parts but not often found elsewhere. Generations of families treasure recipes such as these on the following pages.

Eating is the first activity of living. Hunger is the deepest rooted of all the senses. The desire to eat created the mouth, and the nose, its guard. The eye was made by the same instinct, it is hungry for light; touch is closely related to the neutrative. The hands are food-gatherers. Hunger is the cause of activity.

Progressive Farmer magazine

Meats, Poultry, and Game

Denton, Texas, Barbecued Beef Brisket

⅓ cup molasses
⅓ cup prepared mustard
½ cup firmly packed brown sugar
3 tablespoons Worcestershire sauce
¼ teaspoon hot sauce
½ cup pineapple juice
¾ cup wine vinegar
1 teaspoon chili powder
1 tablespoon minced onion
1 (4- to 6-pound) beef brisket

Combine all ingredients except beef, mixing well. Place meat in heavy plastic bag and pour marinade over it. Squeeze air from bag, and fasten bag. Place bag in a 13- × 9- × 2-inch baking dish; marinate in refrigerator at least 4 to 6 hours, or overnight.

Drain meat and reserve marinade. Grill meat over medium heat until browned. Cover grill and cook 15 minutes. Turn meat and baste with reserved marinade. Grill 15 minutes longer.

Wrap meat in heavy foil, leaving room for marinade. Cut a hole in top of foil and pour marinade through hole over the meat. Continue grilling for 1½ to 2 hours, or until meat is very tender. To serve, slice thin diagonal slices. Yield: 12 to 15 servings.

Boliche

One of the jewels in the Spanish cuisine, as practiced in the vicinity of Tampa and St. Petersburg, is boliche, or stuffed eye of round of beef. There are variations, but most of the stuffings contain chorizo, that delicious Spanish sausage so hard for many of us to find. Since this is a fine beef dish everyone will want to make, there is, not coincidentally, a recipe for making chorizo elsewhere in this chapter (page 116). Some recipes call for a little ground beef in the stuffing instead of the cured ham, so feel free to substitute.

3 to 4 pounds eye of round plus small piece of suet
1 chorizo sausage, chopped
1 medium slice of cured ham, chopped
1 clove garlic, minced
1 medium Spanish onion, chopped
½ green pepper, chopped
Salt and pepper
Paprika
3 tablespoons bacon drippings
¾ cup hot water
1 bay leaf
4 whole cloves

Ask butcher to cut lengthwise pocket in center of beef, leaving opposite end closed. Mix sausage, ham, garlic, onion, and green pepper; stuff roast with sausage mixture, packing well but not too tightly. Secure open end with skewers or wire. Salt and pepper meat and sprinkle generously with paprika. Brown meat well in bacon drippings over medium heat, turning often to brown evenly. Stir in hot water, mixing well with pan drippings. Lay suet on top of meat; add bay leaf and cloves to liquid. Cover and bake at 325° about 3 hours or until the meat is fork tender, basting occasionally. Drain meat and serve with pan drippings. Yield: 10 to 12 servings.

Dallas Barbecued
Pot Roast Of Beef

1 (4-pound) pot roast or beef chuck
2 tablespoons vegetable oil
1½ cups onion slices
1 clove garlic, minced
2 teaspoons salt
½ teaspoon pepper
1 (8-ounce) can tomato sauce
¼ cup chili sauce
⅓ cup vinegar
2 tablespoons brown sugar
2 teaspoons Worcestershire sauce
½ cup water
2 teaspoons chili powder

Trim fat from meat. Heat oil in a Dutch oven and brown meat on all sides; add onion and garlic. Cook until onion is lightly browned. Stir in salt, pepper, and tomato sauce. Cover and cook over low heat 1½ hours, stirring occasionally. Stir in remaining ingredients and cook 1 hour longer, or until tender, stirring occasionally. Skim fat from gravy. Slice meat thinly to serve; delicious served over hard rolls. Yield: 10 to 12 servings.

Pot Roast With Brown Gravy

1 (5- to 6-pound) beef shoulder roast
Lard or shortening, melted
Salt and pepper
1 large onion, coarsely chopped
¼ cup all-purpose flour
2 cups water, divided
Hot cooked rice

Trim most of the fat from roast and melt it in Dutch oven. Add enough lard to melted fat to make about ¼ cup.

Rub salt and pepper into surface of meat; brown on all sides in hot fat. Add onion, and sauté until brown. Remove meat and onion; reserve drippings in pan.

Add flour to drippings and brown, stirring

constantly, over low heat, as in making a roux. When mixture is a rich brown, stir in 1 cup water; add meat and onion. Cover, and simmer over low heat 1 hour, stirring occasionally. Add remaining water; simmer over low heat until meat is tender, about 1 to 1½ hours, stirring occasionally. Serve with rice. Yield: 10 to 12 servings.

Note: Gravy can be doubled by using ½ cup each of fat and flour in place of only ¼ cup.

Roast Beef With
Yorkshire Pudding

For the grandest occasion, a standing rib roast is unequaled for elegance and simplicity, especially when it is served in the traditional English manner with Yorkshire pudding. And nobody does it better than a Marylander.

Standing beef rib roast
Salt and pepper
Yorkshire Pudding

Have a prime rib roast of beef at room temperature. Rub meat with salt and coarsely ground black pepper. With a sharp knife, criss-cross the fat side and sprinkle with salt and pepper. Place meat in a roasting pan, resting on bone ends, fat side up. Bake at 450° for 15 minutes; reduce heat to 300° and continue baking, allowing 20 minutes to each pound of meat (including the 15 minutes searing period) for medium rare beef. When done, remove to a heated platter and let stand for about 20 minutes before carving.

Yorkshire Pudding:

1 cup all-purpose flour
½ teaspoon salt
1 cup milk
2 eggs

Turn up oven to 450° when meat is removed. Leave about ¼ inch of beef drippings in the roasting pan and keep very hot. Sift flour and salt into a mixing bowl. Make a well in center of flour. Pour in milk and break 2 eggs into milk. Mix and beat vigorously for several minutes until batter is smooth and bubbly.

Pour into sizzling hot drippings in pan and bake for 15 minutes or until pudding has risen. Reduce heat to 350° and continue baking until crisp and golden (about 15 minutes longer). Cut in squares and place around roast to serve. Yield: 4 to 6 servings.

Grilled English-Cut Roast

    1 clove garlic, pressed
    1 cup soy sauce
    1½ tablespoons vinegar
    ¼ cup bourbon
    1 cup water
    1 tablespoon commercial meat
        tenderizer
    1 (6-pound) English-cut beef roast

Combine all ingredients except meat, mixing well. Place meat in a heavy plastic bag and pour marinade over it. Squeeze air from bag, and tie end securely. Place bag in a 13- × 9- × 2-inch baking dish. Marinate for 24 hours in refrigerator.

Drain meat; grill over medium heat for 35 to 45 minutes or to desired degree of doneness. Yield: 12 to 15 servings.

German Sour Roast

    1 (4-pound) beef rump roast
    1 tablespoon mixed pickling spices
    Vinegar
    2 tablespoons shortening
    1 cup beef stock
    1 tablespoon raisins
    1 tablespoon currants
    6 gingersnaps, finely crumbled

Place meat in stoneware crock with pickling spices; cover with vinegar and marinate in refrigerator for 3 or 4 days.

Heat shortening in Dutch oven. Drain meat well; brown meat on all sides in hot shortening. Stir in stock, raisins, and currants. Cover tightly and simmer over low heat for 3 hours, or until tender, stirring occasionally. Remove meat to warm platter. Add gingersnap crumbs to pan juices; stir over medium heat until thickened. Serve gravy with roast. Yield: 8 to 10 servings.

Beef Shortribs Supreme

    3 pounds beef shortribs
    2 teaspoons salt
    ½ cup water
    ½ cup chopped onion
    1 clove garlic, minced
    1 (6-ounce) can tomato paste
    1 cup catsup
    ¾ cup firmly packed brown sugar
    ½ cup vinegar
    2 tablespoons prepared mustard

Brown ribs on all sides in a large skillet (do not add oil or shortening). Cover and cook over low heat for 1 hour. Drain off pan drippings.

Combine remaining ingredients; pour over ribs. Cover tightly, and cook over low heat 1½ hours or until meat is tender. Yield: 4 to 6 servings.

Lemon-Topped Round Steak

¼ cup all-purpose flour
½ teaspoon salt
¼ teaspoon pepper
½ teaspoon paprika
1½ pounds (½-inch-thick) round
    steak
3 tablespoons shortening or
    vegetable oil
1 small lemon, thinly sliced
1 large green pepper, seeded and
    sliced into rings
1 large onion, sliced and separated
    into rings
¼ cup catsup

Mix flour with seasonings; rub into surface of meat. Heat shortening in heavy skillet; brown meat well in hot shortening.

Layer lemon, green pepper, and onion slices on top of meat. Pour catsup over vegetables; add boiling water to just cover bottom of casserole. Cover and bake at 325° for 1½ hours or until very tender; remove meat and vegetables to warm platter. To serve, cut meat into wedge-shaped pieces so that each serving has a share of topping. Yield: 4 to 6 servings.

Note: If gravy is desired, strain cooking liquid. For ½ cup gravy, combine 1½ teaspoons cornstarch and 1½ teaspoons water; mix well. Gradually stir mixture into ½ cup hot cooking liquid and cook, stirring constantly, until thickened.

Little Birds

2 pounds round steak, cut into
    6 pieces
Salt and pepper
6 hard-cooked eggs
6 dill pickle spears
¼ cup shortening
2 cups water, divided
¼ cup all-purpose flour

Pound steaks very thin with meat mallet. Sprinkle with salt and pepper. Place 1 egg and 1 spear of pickle on each steak; roll up each steak and secure with string or wooden picks.

Heat shortening in Dutch oven; brown meat rolls on all sides. Add 1 cup water; cover and simmer 1 hour or until tender. Remove meat to warm platter.

Combine remaining water with flour; stir into pan liquid. Cook until thickened, stirring constantly; pour over meat. Yield: 6 servings.

Chicken-Fried Steak

Back when the Western states were still territories, chicken-fried steak was the trail driver's hearty reward after a tough day's work. Whether it had its origins in Texas, Kansas, or elsewhere, "chicken-fry" somehow became the Great National Dish of Oklahoma. Ask an Oklahoman who makes the best chicken-fried, and he will say, "My mother." But many restaurants in the state are vying with Mom in down-home style round steak.

One of the best versions is to be found at Kay's Restaurant in Tulsa. Gerald Fenster bought Kay's in 1979 and still serves the steak with excellent cream gravy and hot rolls. Fenster's father, Louis, took the time to discuss the house recipe.

"The selection of choice inside round of beef and the proper preparation of the meat before cooking is probably even more important than the cooking itself. We think of the meat as being actually skinned or shaved of all fat, connecting tissue, and gristle. We use an inside round that weighs between 19 and 22 pounds. When it is trimmed the way we do it, the round opens up and separates into two pieces, at which point we complete the trimming."

Fenster's recipe for home use is strict; the beef must be choice, completely trimmed, and tenderized before cooking.

6 (6-ounce) ½-inch-thick steaks
1½ teaspoons salt
½ teaspoon pepper
1 cup all-purpose flour
1 cup milk
Shortening for frying
Cream Gravy

Score steaks ⅛ inch deep on both sides. Pound steaks to about ¼-inch thickness. Sprinkle lightly with salt and pepper. Dredge in flour; dip into milk and dredge again in flour.

Heat shortening in grill or skillet; fry steak approximately 2 to 3 minutes on each side. Reserve meat on warm dish while preparing gravy. Remove drippings from skillet to use in Cream Gravy. Yield: 6 servings.

Cream Gravy:

1 quart milk
½ cup butter or shortening
Steak drippings
½ cup all-purpose flour
2 teaspoons salt
1 teaspoon pepper

Heat milk to scalding in heavy 2-quart saucepan. Combine butter and drippings in skillet. Add flour and cook slowly over medium heat, stirring, for 5 minutes. Add the roux to the hot milk, stirring well. Cook, stirring, over low heat until desired consistency is reached. Season. Yield: about 1 quart.

Chateaubriand

1 (4- to 5-pound) beef tenderloin, trimmed of fat
1 clove garlic, cut in half
¼ cup Worcestershire sauce
Juice of 1 lime
1 to 2 teaspoons salt
½ teaspoon pepper

Rub meat all over with cut side of garlic; discard garlic. Combine Worcestershire sauce, lime juice, salt, and pepper; brush over meat. Let stand 1 hour.

Grill about 5 inches from heat for about 30 to 35 minutes for rare, or 40 to 45 minutes for medium. Yield: about 12 servings.

Ginger Beef

The South is dotted with Chinese restaurants. They range, as any other kind of eating places do, from excellent to poor. But the surprising thing is that our Chinese communities, while relatively small compared with those of New York or San Francisco, have a great impact on our dining-out habits. The Chinese have much to teach us about food: economy of meat, beauty in the cutting of vegetables, conservation of energy in foods quickly cooked. Ginger beef, for the cook as yet unfamiliar with this cuisine, is a fine place to start.

½ cup beef stock
2 tablespoons soy sauce
1 tablespoon dry sherry
1½ teaspoons sugar
3 tablespoons vegetable oil
1 large clove garlic, finely minced
2 tablespoons chopped fresh ginger
2 pounds lean beef sirloin, sliced diagonally into ⅛-inch strips
5 or 6 green onions with tops, sliced diagonally into ½-inch pieces
4 teaspoons cornstarch
4 teaspoons water
Hot cooked rice

Mix stock with soy sauce, sherry, and sugar; set aside.

Heat oil in a wok or large skillet. Sauté garlic and ginger in hot oil about 1 minute. Add meat and green onion, and stir-fry over high heat until meat is brown; add stock mixture and cover. Simmer about 3 minutes.

Mix cornstarch with water; stir into pan mixture. Stir constantly over high heat until liquid is slightly thickened. Serve immediately with rice. Yield: 6 to 8 servings.

Pocket Steak

3 pounds (2-inch-thick) sirloin steak
8 oysters, chopped
1 (4-ounce) can sliced mushrooms, drained
6 slices bacon, cooked and crumbled
2 tablespoons melted butter or margarine
Salt and pepper

With a sharp knife, make a slit in side of steak almost to the center; continue slitting around all sides of steak, leaving center uncut. Combine oysters, mushrooms, and bacon. Stuff steak with oyster mixture; sew opening securely with kitchen thread. Brush with butter; sprinkle with salt and pepper. Broil or grill over burned-down charcoal fire about 5 inches from heat for about 25 minutes or to desired degree of doneness, turning once. Remove thread; serve. Yield: about 10 servings.

Beef Ragout

¼ cup dried mushrooms
1 cup water
2 large onions, chopped
½ cup butter
4 pounds boneless beef, cut into 2-inch cubes
2 bay leaves
2 large onions, sliced
1 green pepper, chopped
2 large tomatoes, peeled and sliced
½ pound fresh mushrooms, sliced
2 cloves garlic, minced
1 to 2 teaspoons salt
½ teaspoon pepper
½ teaspoon paprika
1 tablespoon all-purpose flour (optional)
1 tablespoon water (optional)
½ teaspoon commercial brown bouquet sauce (optional)
Hot cooked noodles

Soak dried mushrooms overnight in water. In large, heavy kettle, sauté onion in butter until brown. Add meat, dried mushrooms, water in which mushrooms were soaked, and bay leaves. Cover and simmer for 1 hour, stirring occasionally. Add remaining vegetables. Add next 4 ingredients and simmer 1 hour, or until meat is tender, stirring occasionally. If desired, the ½ cup cooking liquid may be thickened with 1 tablespoon flour combined with 1 tablespoon water and bouquet sauce. Serve with hot cooked noodles. Yield: 12 to 15 servings.

City Chicken

½ pound beef steak, cut into 1-inch cubes
½ pound veal steak, cut into 1-inch cubes
½ pound lean pork, cut into 1-inch cubes
1 teaspoon salt
½ teaspoon pepper
1½ cups fine dry breadcrumbs
1 egg
1 tablespoon water
¼ cup shortening
½ cup water

Alternate cubes of beef, veal, and pork on 5-inch wooden skewers. Combine salt, pepper, and breadcrumbs. Beat egg with water. Roll skewered meat in seasoned breadcrumbs; dip in egg, and roll in breadcrumbs again.

Heat shortening in heavy skillet; brown meat on all sides in hot shortening. Add water; cover tightly and simmer for 45 minutes, or until meat is tender. Yield: 4 to 6 servings.

Dutch Stew With Dumplings

¾ pound beef, cut into cubes
½ pound pork, cut into cubes
½ pound beef liver, cut into cubes
2 quarts boiling water
2 small onions, sliced
1 teaspoon salt
¼ teaspoon pepper
¼ cup all-purpose flour
¼ cup water
Dumplings (page 191)

Combine meat and 2 quarts water in a large Dutch oven; cover, and simmer 1½ hours. Add onion, salt, and pepper and simmer 30 minutes.

Combine flour with ¼ cup water; stir into stew. Drop dumpling batter by teaspoonfuls into stew; cover and simmer 15 minutes. Serve at once. Yield: 6 servings.

Creamy Liver

¼ to ½ cup all-purpose flour
1 teaspoon salt
¼ teaspoon pepper
1 pound sliced calf's liver
3 tablespoons melted butter or
    margarine
1 small onion, thinly sliced and
    separated into rings
2 cloves garlic, minced
½ to 1 cup sliced fresh mushrooms
1 (10¾-ounce) can cream of
    mushroom soup, undiluted
3 tablespoons chopped fresh parsley
1 teaspoon dried basil leaves
Milk (optional)
Hot cooked noodles

Combine flour, salt, and pepper, mixing well. Dredge liver in seasoned flour. Brown on both sides in butter in a skillet; remove from skillet, and set aside.

Add onion, garlic, and mushrooms to skillet; cook about 1 minute. Stir in soup, parsley, and basil, scraping up browned bits from pan. Add milk if a thinner sauce is desired.

Return liver to skillet; cover and simmer 2 to 3 minutes or until thoroughly heated. Serve over cooked noodles. Yield: 4 to 6 servings.

Corned Beef And Cabbage, Southern Style

1 medium head cabbage
8 slices bacon, divided
2 teaspoons red pepper flakes
1 teaspoon sugar
½ teaspoon salt
3½ cups water
1 (12-ounce) can corned beef, sliced

Wash cabbage, and cut into 4 wedges; do not separate leaves. Cook 4 slices bacon until crisp in a heavy Dutch oven; drain and crumble. Reserve 3 tablespoons bacon drippings.

Place cabbage in Dutch oven; add crumbled bacon, reserved bacon drippings, red pepper, sugar, salt, and water. Place remaining bacon over cabbage; cook 30 minutes. Add corned beef; cook 30 additional minutes. Yield: 4 to 6 servings.

Corned Beef Casserole

2 tablespoons butter or margarine
1 medium onion, chopped
2 cups cooked egg noodles
1 (12-ounce) can corned beef, diced
1 (10¾-ounce) can cream of
    mushroom soup, undiluted
1 cup milk
1 to 2 cups (4 to 8 ounces) shredded
    Cheddar cheese

Melt butter; sauté onion in butter until transparent. Combine onion with noodles, beef, soup, and milk, mixing well. Pour into a greased 2-quart casserole. Bake at 350° for 30 minutes. Sprinkle with cheese; return to oven for 5 minutes or until cheese is melted. Yield: 4 servings.

Hub's Riverboat Goulash

3 tablespoons beef drippings or
    margarine
2 medium onions, sliced
1 (12-ounce) can corned beef, cut
    into chunks
1 clove garlic, minced
½ cup water
2 (16-ounce) cans tomatoes,
    undrained
4 to 5 potatoes, peeled and diced
1 (16-ounce) can pork and beans
Salt and pepper
Cornbread (optional)

Heat drippings in heavy pot; sauté onion
until transparent. Add beef, garlic, water,
tomatoes, and potatoes. Cover and simmer
over low heat for about 1 hour, stirring occasionally. Add pork and beans, and season to
taste. Cover and simmer 30 additional minutes. Serve hot with cornbread, if desired.
Yield: about 6 servings.

Easy Oven Hamburgers

*We're hooked on hamburgers! When we
aren't buying them at the fast food empori-
ums, we are budgeting them into the week's
food bill. Ways to serve ever-popular ground
beef are among our most sought-after recipes. This one brings praise every time it
turns up at a church youth rally or teenage
party, not to mention the family dinner table.
Multiply it for a multitude; vary the seasonings according to taste—it's a winner.*

1 pound ground beef
1 tablespoon grated onion
1 teaspoon salt
Dash of pepper
3 tablespoons chili sauce or catsup
1 teaspoon prepared mustard
8 hamburger buns

Combine first 6 ingredients, mixing well.
Divide into 8 equal balls. Arrange bottoms of

hamburger buns on a foil-lined baking sheet.
Flatten balls to fit buns; shape meat with a
ridge at the edge, and a depression in the
center, to keep meat juice on top when it
cooks. Bake at 375° for 20 minutes. Put top
halves of buns on hamburgers and return to
oven for 2 minutes, or just until hot. Yield: 8
servings.

Note: These may be made up several hours
ahead and refrigerated until baking time.
Serve plain or with lettuce and dill pickle
slices.

Poor Boy's Filets

1 pound ground beef
1 teaspoon Worcestershire sauce
¼ teaspoon garlic powder
1 teaspoon margarine
1 teaspoon salt
¼ teaspoon pepper
3 or 4 slices bacon

Combine meat, Worcestershire sauce, garlic
powder, margarine, salt, and pepper, mixing
well. Shape into 3 or 4 patties. Wrap each
patty with a slice of bacon, fastening with
wooden picks.

Place patties on broiler rack and broil 1
minute; turn and broil 1 minute longer. Turn
broiler off and allow patties to stay in broiler
30 minutes. Meat will be very juicy. Serve
with sautéed mushrooms, if desired. Yield: 3
or 4 servings.

Birrocks

*The world's cooks have known for cen-
turies how to stretch meat by wrapping it in
bread dough, then baking, frying, or boiling
it. This recipe is from Okeene, in northwest
Oklahoma, where the German heritage is
strong and wheat farming is closely tied in
with the lives of the people. I have had a
similar dish in Memphis containing no meat,*

the dough being filled with sautéed vegetables and served with pot roast and gravy. A thought for another time!

> ¼ cup melted butter or shortening
> ¾ cup warm milk
> 3 tablespoons sugar
> 1 teaspoon salt
> 1 package dry yeast
> ¼ cup warm water (105° to 115°)
> About 4 cups all-purpose flour, divided
> 1 egg, beaten
> Filling (recipe follows)

Stir butter into milk; add sugar and salt and stir well. Dissolve yeast in warm water. Stir 2 cups flour into milk mixture; add yeast mixture and mix well. Stir in egg. Add enough remaining flour to make a soft, workable dough. Knead dough lightly until smooth. Place in greased bowl; turn to grease all sides. Cover and let rise in a warm place (85°), free from drafts, until doubled in bulk.

Punch dough down and roll into a 15-inch square. Cut dough with sharp knife into 5-inch squares. Spoon filling evenly on each square. Pull edges of dough together and seal. Place dough, sealed edges down, on greased baking sheet. Let stand in warm place about 15 minutes or until dough rises slightly. Bake at 375° for 20 minutes, or until browned. Yield: 9 servings.

Note: Two (13¾-ounce) packages hot roll mix may be substituted for the dough recipe above.

Filling:

> 2 pounds ground beef
> 6 medium onions, diced
> ½ head cabbage, shredded
> Salt and pepper to taste

Sauté ground beef, stirring to crumble; drain drippings. Add onion and cabbage to beef; sauté until vegetables are tender. Season. Cool to lukewarm.

Piroshki

Quite similar to the German birrock is the Russian piroshki brought from Texas. This meat pie is fried, however, and it does not contain cabbage.

> 2 cups milk
> ¼ cup sugar
> 1 tablespoon shortening
> 2 teaspoons salt
> 1 package dry yeast
> ¼ cup warm water (105° to 115°)
> 6 to 8 cups all-purpose flour
> Meat Filling (recipe follows)
> Vegetable oil for deep frying

Scald milk. Add sugar, shortening, and salt to milk; cool to lukewarm.

Dissolve yeast in warm water and add to milk mixture. Add 3 cups flour, mixing well. Add enough remaining flour to make a soft dough. Place dough in greased bowl, turning to grease top. Cover and let rise in a warm place (85°), free from drafts, until doubled in size. Knead dough 5 to 10 minutes; cover and let rise again until doubled. Knead dough 5 to 10 additional minutes.

Divide dough into 16 equal balls; roll each ball into ¼-inch-thick ovals. Spoon filling evenly into center of ovals and carefully seal edges. Let piroshki rise for 10 to 15 minutes. Fry in deep hot oil (365°) until golden brown. Yield: 16 servings.

Meat Filling:

> 2 medium onions, chopped
> 3 tablespoons butter or margarine
> 1 pound ground beef
> 1 tablespoon all-purpose flour
> Salt and pepper to taste

Sauté onions in butter until slightly brown. Add meat and flour and continue to sauté until meat is done. Add salt and pepper. Cool before spooning into dough. Yield: about 2 cups.

Ground Beef 93

Poached Meatballs In Lemon Sauce

1 pound ground beef
½ cup seasoned dry breadcrumbs
1 egg
½ teaspoon salt
1 teaspoon grated lemon rind
1 cup water
2 beef-flavored bouillon cubes
1 tablespoon lemon juice
1 teaspoon cornstarch
2 tablespoons water
1 egg yolk, beaten

Combine meat, breadcrumbs, egg, salt, and lemon rind, mixing well. Shape into 12 meatballs.

Bring 1 cup water to boil in a medium saucepan; add bouillon cubes, stirring to dissolve. Gently drop meatballs into bouillon; reduce heat and simmer 10 minutes.

Remove meatballs to a warm bowl. Add lemon juice to bouillon. Dissolve cornstarch in 2 tablespoons water; stir into hot mixture and cook until thickened, stirring constantly. Add a small amount of hot bouillon mixture to egg yolk; stir egg mixture into remaining hot mixture. Remove from heat and pour over meatballs. Yield: 4 servings.

Meat Loaf With Herbs

1 egg, beaten
½ to 1 cup milk, divided
1 pound top round steak, ground
1 medium onion, finely chopped
2 medium potatoes, pared and
    shredded
1 carrot, shredded (optional)
1 teaspoon salt
¼ teaspoon pepper
1 teaspoon dried marjoram leaves
⅛ teaspoon oregano or summer
    savory
Mushroom Sauce (recipe follows)

Combine egg with ½ cup milk; add meat and mix well. Add remaining ingredients except mushroom sauce to meat mixture, adding more milk as necessary for proper consistency. Shape meat into a 9- × 5- × 3-inch loafpan; bake at 350° for 45 to 50 minutes. Serve with mushroom sauce. Yield: 4 or 5 servings.

Mushroom Sauce:

1 (4-ounce) can mushrooms
1 tablespoon cornstarch
1¼ cups water
1 beef bouillon cube
½ teaspoon Worcestershire sauce

Combine mushrooms and liquid with cornstarch in a small bowl. Heat water in small saucepan and dissolve bouillon cube. Add mushroom mixture and Worcestershire sauce. Cook, stirring, until thickened. Yield: about 1½ cups sauce.

Herb-Roasted Lamb Shanks

1 clove garlic, minced
1 teaspoon olive oil
Dash of salt
Dash of pepper
2 lamb shanks
⅛ teaspoon dried marjoram leaves
⅛ teaspoon dried thyme leaves
⅛ teaspoon dried rosemary leaves
1 teaspoon all-purpose flour
3 tablespoons dry white wine
1 tablespoon plus 1 teaspoon water

Mix garlic, olive oil, salt, and pepper; rub mixture into meat. Sprinkle with marjoram, thyme, rosemary, and flour; place in small roasting pan. Mix wine and water; pour over meat. Roast at 325° for about 2 hours or until tender. Baste occasionally with drippings, adding additional water as necessary. Yield: 2 servings.

Roast Leg Of Lamb

People who like lamb tend to be mad about it; few there are who take a middle-of-the-road attitude. My mother hated it and seized every opportunity to say so. Not surprisingly, I grew up without ever having tasted it. As soon as I was introduced to lamb, however, I became a partisan. Helen Exum, Food Editor of The Chattanooga News-Free Press, *remembers her Mississippi mother-in-law's company dinners which featured roast leg of lamb.*

    1 (6- to 7-pound) leg of lamb
    2 cloves garlic, sliced
    ¼ cup butter or margarine, softened
    ¼ cup minced carrot
    ¼ cup minced fresh parsley
    1 small bay leaf, crushed
    2 tablespoons minced onion
    2 tablespoons all-purpose flour
    2 tablespoons prepared mustard
    2 teaspoons salt
    ½ teaspoon pepper
    1 teaspoon paprika
    ¼ teaspoon dried thyme leaves

Place lamb on rack in roasting pan. Make several small slits with knife tip at frequent intervals over surface of lamb, and insert a slice of garlic in each. Mix remaining ingredients and spread evenly over meat surface. Bake at 425° for 20 minutes; reduce heat to 325° and roast 35 minutes per pound, or until meat thermometer registers 180°. Yield: 8 to 10 servings.

Lamb Fries

    1 pound lamb fries
    ¾ cup all-purpose flour
    1 teaspoon salt
    ½ teaspoon pepper
    2 eggs, beaten
    1½ to 2 cups fine cracker crumbs
    Vegetable oil or shortening
    Cream Sauce (recipe follows)

Place lamb fries in the freezer until they are about half frozen; this facilitates handling. Remove skin; slice ⅓ inch thick. Combine flour, salt, and pepper. Coat lamb fries with the seasoned flour; dip into beaten egg. Dredge well with cracker crumbs.

Heat oil in heavy skillet. Fry lamb fries 2 to 3 minutes on each side or until nicely browned. They should not be overcooked, as they will toughen. To serve, place cream sauce in deep platter; arrange lamb fries on top. Serve at once. Yield: 4 to 5 servings.

Cream Sauce:

    ¼ cup butter or margarine
    2½ tablespoons all-purpose flour
    1 cup milk or half-and-half
    1 cup chicken stock
    ½ teaspoon salt
    ¼ teaspoon pepper

Melt butter in small, heavy saucepan. Stir in flour; add milk and stock. Cook, stirring constantly, over medium heat until thick and smooth. Season to taste. Yield: 2 cups.

Lamb Curry

    ½ cup butter or margarine, divided
    1 to 2 teaspoons curry powder
    2 tart apples, peeled and diced
    2 medium onions, diced
    2 cups cooked cubed lamb
    1 tablespoon all-purpose flour
    1 cup beef bouillon
    Hot cooked rice

Melt half the butter in skillet; add curry, apples, and onion. Sauté lightly; remove from pan. Melt remaining butter; add lamb and sauté until lightly browned. Remove lamb from pan, reserving butter in pan. Stir flour into pan; gradually add bouillon and stir until smooth and slightly thickened. Add onion, apple, and lamb back to bouillon mixture; heat. Serve on rice with condiments of chutney, chopped peanuts, or chopped green onion. Yield: 6 servings.

Barbecued Lamb Chops

8 (2-inch-thick) lamb chops
Salt and pepper to taste
3 cloves garlic, halved
Dash of rosemary
½ cup wine vinegar
¼ cup vegetable oil

Sprinkle lamb chops with salt and pepper; rub with garlic. Combine rosemary, vinegar, and oil, mixing well. Baste chops well with sauce.

Place chops 5 to 6 inches from medium coals. Grill 6 to 7 minutes for rare, 9 to 10 minutes for medium, 12 or more minutes for well done, or until desired degree of doneness. Baste frequently with sauce during cooking. Yield: 4 servings.

Lamb Shish Kabobs

1 (3½-pound) boned leg of lamb
1 large onion, finely chopped
½ cup vegetable oil
½ cup dry sherry
1 to 1½ tablespoons cumin seeds
1 tablespoon salt
1½ teaspoons dried rosemary leaves
1 teaspoon coarsely ground black
    pepper
1 teaspoon garlic salt
1 (1-pint) carton cherry tomatoes
3 green peppers, cut into 1-inch
    squares
2 (16-ounce) jars boiling onions,
    drained

Remove fell (tissuelike covering) from lamb; cut lamb into 1½-inch cubes, and set aside.

Combine chopped onion, oil, sherry, and seasonings. Add lamb; cover and marinate 24 hours in refrigerator.

Remove meat from marinade. Alternate meat and vegetables on skewers. Broil 5 minutes; turn and broil an additional 5 minutes or to desired degree on doneness. Yield: 10 servings.

Baked Kibbe

For lessons in lamb cookery, apply to the nearest Eastern Orthodox community. The Middle Eastern heritage includes more lamb lore than any other culture I have found. St. Michael's in Louisville has an annual feast that attracts thousands and the traditional kibbe remains everyone's favorite thing, year after year. There are several ways of preparing the mixture of ground lamb and cracked wheat, but this recipe is typically delicious.

1 cup cracked wheat
1½ pounds ground lamb
1 tablespoon salt
1 teaspoon pepper
Dash of ground allspice
Dash of ground cloves
2 teaspoons crushed dried mint
    leaves
½ cup butter or margarine, divided
¼ cup pine nuts
3 large onions, chopped

Rinse cracked wheat 2 or 3 times in cold water; pour off most of water. Cover and allow to stand at least 30 minutes or until water is absorbed. (Overnight standing is optimal if time allows, but not necessary.) Knead wheat until smooth and holds together. Drain any moisture from wheat and add to meat. Add seasonings to meat and knead mixture well.

Melt ¼ cup butter and sauté pine nuts in butter just until pale gold. Remove nuts and sauté onion in butter until transparent; add nuts to onion mixture and set aside.

Divide meat mixture in half. Press half of meat in a 9-inch square pan; pour nut mixture over meat. Shape remaining meat over nut mixture. Dip spatula in water and cut diamond-shaped pattern in mixture. Melt remaining ¼ cup butter and pour over top. Bake at 400° for 20 to 25 minutes or until lightly browned and meat is done. Yield: 6 servings.

Irish Lamb Stew

2 pounds boneless lamb, cut into
    1-inch cubes
2 carrots, diced
2 turnips, diced
1 onion, sliced
1 teaspoon salt
¼ teaspoon pepper
1 bay leaf
Dumpling or biscuit dough (optional)

Place lamb in kettle; cover with water. Cover and bring to a boil; reduce heat and simmer 1 to 1½ hours. Add vegetables and seasonings; cover and simmer 30 minutes. Drop dumpling or biscuit dough by teaspoonfuls on top of stew, if desired; cover and cook 15 minutes. Yield: 6 to 8 servings.

Note: For dumpling recipe, *see* Index. Select recipe using 1 cup all-purpose flour.

Ragout Of Lamb

2 tablespoons butter or shortening
2 tablespoons all-purpose flour
2 quarts water
3 bay leaves
5 whole cloves
2 onions, chopped
2 to 3 teaspoons salt
½ teaspoon pepper
2 teaspoons chili powder (optional)
2 to 2½ pounds boneless lamb, cut
    into 2-inch pieces
6 potatoes, peeled and quartered

Melt butter in a Dutch oven; stir in flour, and cook over low heat, stirring constantly, until medium brown. Stir in water; stir to blend. Add bay leaves, cloves, onion, salt, pepper, and chili powder, if desired. Add meat when liquid is boiling. Reduce heat; cover and simmer 1 hour. Add potatoes; cover and cook for 30 minutes or until meat and potatoes are tender. Yield: 8 to 10 servings.

Note: Veal may be used instead of lamb.

Veal Birds

4 pounds (½-inch-thick) boneless veal
¾ cup butter or margarine, softened
    and divided
3 tablespoons chopped fresh parsley
½ cup all-purpose flour
1½ to 2 teaspoons salt
½ teaspoon pepper
1½ cups consommé or chicken stock
1 cup whipping cream

Cut veal into 3- × 2-inch pieces; pound veal very thin using a meat mallet. Mix ½ cup butter with parsley; spread butter mixture evenly on each piece of veal. Roll veal and tie with a string. Combine flour with salt and pepper; coat meat with flour mixture. Heat remaining ¼ cup butter in skillet; brown meat in butter. Pour consommé over meat; cover and simmer for about 1 hour, or until tender. Add cream during last 30 minutes of cooking, mixing gently. Adjust seasonings. Remove veal to warm platter; remove strings and spoon the gravy over veal. Yield: 10 to 12 servings.

Breaded Veal Cutlets

4 thin veal steaks
¼ cup all-purpose flour
1 egg, beaten
1 tablespoon water
¾ cup fine cracker crumbs
½ teaspoon salt
¼ teaspoon pepper
¼ cup vegetable oil or butter
¾ cup milk

Coat meat with flour. Mix egg and water, and dip meat in egg mixture; coat well with cracker crumbs. Season with salt and pepper. Heat oil in oven-proof skillet; brown meat quickly on both sides in oil. Pour milk over meat; cover and bake at 325° for 45 minutes. Yield: 4 servings.

Veal Divine

6 veal cutlets
1 egg, beaten
⅔ cup fine dry breadcrumbs
¼ cup butter or vegetable oil
3 thin slices ham, cut in half
1 (10¾-ounce) can cream of
    mushroom soup, undiluted
¾ cup water
½ cup shredded sharp Cheddar
    cheese
Paprika

Pound steaks thin using a meat mallet; dip in egg, and dredge in breadcrumbs. Heat butter in skillet; brown veal on both sides in butter. Place ½ ham slice on each cutlet. Mix soup and water; pour soup mixture over meat. Cover tightly and simmer 45 minutes. Remove cover, and sprinkle with cheese; cover and cook about 10 minutes or until cheese melts. Sprinkle with paprika and serve. Yield: 6 servings.

Veal In Casserole

¼ cup all-purpose flour
1 teaspoon salt
¼ teaspoon pepper
1½ pounds boneless veal, cut into
    1-inch cubes
1 medium onion, chopped
¼ cup bacon drippings
1 teaspoon paprika
¾ cup tomato sauce
½ cup commercial sour cream
Noodles or dumplings (optional)

Combine flour, salt, and pepper, mixing well. Dredge meat in flour mixture. Fry meat and onion in bacon drippings in a heavy skillet. Add paprika and tomato sauce; simmer over low heat 1½ hours, or until meat is tender. Stir in sour cream, and heat thoroughly. Serve with noodles or dumplings, if desired. Yield: 4 to 5 servings.

Vitello Michelangelo

Don and Mike Grisanti are their family's third generation in the Casa Grisanti restaurant, and under their guidance, "Casa" became Louisville's only Four-Star eating place. Vincenzo Gabrielle, Food and Beverage Manager, does not bring me a menu, he brings me food. And more food, like Veal Michelangelo.

16 (1½-ounce) thin slices veal
All-purpose flour
Clarified butter
1 cup Madeira wine
2 cups chicken stock
6 tablespoons butter or margarine
16 thin slices prosciutto ham
16 thin slices Jarlsburg cheese

Pound veal as thin as possible using a meat mallet. Dredge veal in flour, and sauté in small amount clarified butter for 30 seconds per side. Remove veal from pan; add Madeira to pan drippings. Stir in chicken stock and butter; simmer until liquid is reduced and mixture is thickened.

Top veal slices with ham and cheese slices. Return to pan and heat until warm. Serve with gravy immediately. Yield: 4 servings.

Veal Scallopini Valdosta

8 thin slices veal
2 tablespoons butter or margarine
2 tablespoons vegetable oil
½ cup dry white wine
8 slices Swiss cheese
⅓ to ½ cup grated Parmesan cheese

Pound veal as thin as possible using a meat mallet. Heat butter and oil in skillet; fry meat briskly for 7 minutes in butter mixture, turning once. Add wine; place slice of Swiss cheese on each piece of meat and sprinkle with Parmesan cheese. Cover and cook 2 more minutes or until cheese melts. Serve hot. Yield: 8 servings.

Right: *A classic Southern breakfast begins with Country Ham and Grits with Red-Eye Gravy (page 111).*

Below: *When made into links by means of a sausage stuffer, Homemade Sausage (page 117) is a hearty supper dish.*

Veal Paprika

4 slices bacon, diced
1 (1½-pound) boneless veal steak
2 tablespoons chopped onion
1 teaspoon paprika
1 teaspoon salt
½ cup tomato sauce
1 (8-ounce) carton commercial sour
    cream
Hot cooked noodles

Fry bacon until crisp; drain bacon, reserving drippings in skillet. Crumble bacon and set aside. Cut veal into serving-size pieces; fry in reserved bacon drippings. Add onion; fry until light brown. Add seasonings. Stir in tomato sauce; cover and cook 30 to 40 minutes. Stir in sour cream; heat thoroughly, but do not boil. Serve over noodles; sprinkle with bacon. Yield: 6 servings.

Casserole Of Veal And Mushrooms Devonshire

1 (1½-pound) veal steak
Salt and pepper
All-purpose flour
1 clove garlic, crushed
2 tablespoons butter or margarine
1 tablespoon vegetable oil
1½ pounds fresh mushrooms
1 cup consommé, divided
1 cup whipping cream
2 egg yolks, beaten
2 tablespoons Madeira
Grated rind of 1 lemon
2 tablespoons butter or margarine

Pound veal thin with a meat mallet and cut into 3-inch squares. Sprinkle veal with salt and pepper and dredge in flour; fry veal and garlic in 2 tablespoons butter and oil until

A typical Southern Sunday dinner features Best-Ever Fried Chicken (page 107).

browned. Transfer veal to shallow casserole; pour off all but 1 tablespoon of fat. Remove stems from mushrooms; slice stems and sprinkle over veal. Add ¼ cup consommé to reserved fat in pan, stirring well. Add whipping cream and remainder of consommé; boil rapidly until mixture is reduced by half and begins to thicken. Gradually beat ¼ of hot mixture into yolks, and add yolk mixture to remaining hot mixture. Stir in wine and lemon juice. Spoon sauce over veal. Bake, uncovered, at 350° for 40 minutes. Sauté mushroom caps in 2 tablespoons butter and arrange on top of casserole just before serving. Yield: 4 servings.

Veal Croquettes

1 cup half-and-half or beef stock
1 tablespoon all-purpose flour
3 tablespoons butter or margarine,
    softened
2 cups chopped cooked veal
1 tablespoon salt
½ teaspoon pepper
1 tablespoon lemon juice
1 teaspoon onion juice
4 eggs
2 cups fine dry breadcrumbs,
    divided
Vegetable oil for deep frying

Bring half-and-half to a boil in a large saucepan. Mix flour with butter; stir flour mixture into half-and-half. Add meat, salt, pepper, lemon juice, and onion juice. Reduce heat and simmer 2 minutes or until slightly thickened, stirring constantly. Beat 2 eggs; stir eggs into meat mixture. Add ½ to 1 cup breadcrumbs to make meat mixture very stiff. Chill meat mixture until firm.

Shape meat mixture into 6 or 8 croquettes. Beat remaining eggs. Dredge croquettes into remaining breadcrumbs; dip into egg, and dredge again in breadcrumbs.

Heat oil to 365°; fry croquettes until golden brown. Yield: 6 or 8 croquettes.

Chicken And Dumplings

Anyone who has grown up in a family that prizes good cooking certainly will number chicken and dumplings among his chief pleasures. Part of the nostalgia concerns watching the selection and processing of that fat hen from the barnyard to the cookpot to the table. The modern cook is spared the responsibility of chasing down the squawking bird, and children must collect other sorts of things to remember. But everyone should have chicken and dumplings.

1 (4- to 5-pound) hen, cut up
1 tablespoon salt
1 bay leaf
Several celery leaves or 1 stalk
    celery, sliced
1 slice lemon
1 slice onion
6 peppercorns
Rolled Dumplings (page 192)

Combine hen, salt, and water to cover in a large pot; bring to a boil. Add remaining ingredients except dumplings. Boil 10 minutes; skim surface, reduce heat, and simmer until tender, about 2 hours, adding water as necessary.

Drop dumplings into pot on top of chicken pieces. Cover; simmer about 30 minutes or until cooked through. Yield: 6 to 8 servings.

Note: Serve Chicken and Dumplings on deep platter. Liquid remaining in pot may be thickened, if necessary, with cornstarch or flour mixed with cold water, and poured over chicken.

Cream De Volaille

1 (4- to 5-pound) hen
1 tablespoon salt
1 bay leaf
1 slice onion
1 slice lemon
6 peppercorns
1 carrot, sliced
Celery leaves
2 eggs
2 tablespoons half-and-half
1 tablespoon dried thyme leaves
2 teaspoons salt
½ teaspoon pepper
1 to 2 teaspoons finely chopped
    fresh parsley
1 tablespoon butter or margarine
1 tablespoon all-purpose flour
1 cup milk
1 envelope unflavored gelatin
2 tablespoons cold water
Commercial mushroom sauce

Place hen in kettle with water to cover; add salt, bay leaf, onion, lemon, peppercorns, carrot, and celery leaves; cover. Bring to a boil; reduce heat and simmer 2 to 3 hours or until very tender. Drain meat, discarding cooking liquid; remove meat from bones and grind meat. Add eggs, half-and-half, thyme, salt, pepper, and parsley to meat, mixing well.

Melt butter in small saucepan; stir in flour. Cook over low heat 1 minute, stirring constantly. Gradually stir in milk and cook, stirring constantly, until thickened. Soften gelatin in water; add to hot milk mixture, mixing well. Combine with chicken mixture, mixing well.

Pour mixture into a greased 6-cup ovenproof mold; cover with foil. Place mold in larger pan and pour water into outer pan to come halfway up sides of mold. Place over low heat and steam for 1¼ to 1½ hours. Or bake in oven at 325° for 1½ hours. Serve hot with mushroom sauce. Yield: 8 servings.

Chicken With Onion

¼ cup butter or margarine
1 medium onion, diced
4 stalks celery, chopped
1 (3-pound) broiler-fryer, cut up
½ cup water
2 teaspoons salt
1 teaspoon caraway seeds
Hot cooked rice

Heat butter in large skillet; sauté onion and celery in butter until transparent. Add chicken, water, salt, and caraway seeds. Cover and simmer until tender, about 45 minutes; add additional water as needed. Serve with rice. Yield: 4 to 6 servings.

Country Captain

Something of an oddity in Southern cuisine is that well-entrenched traditional dish we call "country captain." There are several stories to account for the presence of curry flavor in it. One is that a mysterious sea captain drifted into Savannah with the spice trade and gave his favorite recipe to a friend in exchange for hospitality. No matter; this recipe is still among our most lavish dinner productions.

¾ cup all-purpose flour
1 teaspoon salt
¼ teaspoon pepper
1 (2½-pound) broiler-fryer, cut up
4 to 5 tablespoons butter or
  margarine
½ cup chopped onion
½ cup chopped green pepper
1 clove garlic, minced or crushed
1½ teaspoons curry powder
½ teaspoon dried thyme leaves
1 (16-ounce) can tomatoes, undrained
3 tablespoons currants
Toasted sliced almonds
Chutney

Mix flour, salt, and pepper; coat chicken in flour mixture. Heat 4 tablespoons butter in large, heavy skillet; add chicken and brown well on all sides. Add additional butter during cooking, if necessary.

Remove chicken and set aside; reserve drippings in skillet. Add onion, green pepper, garlic, curry powder, and thyme to drippings and sauté until tender. Add tomatoes. Return chicken to skillet, meat side up. Cover; cook over low heat for 20 to 30 minutes, or until chicken is tender. Stir in currants and heat thoroughly. Serve with almonds and chutney. Yield: 4 to 6 servings.

Chicken Divan

½ cup butter or margarine
½ cup all-purpose flour
2 cups milk
2 egg yolks, beaten
½ teaspoon salt
2 tablespoons dry sherry
½ teaspoon Worcestershire sauce
1½ teaspoons grated Parmesan
  cheese
½ cup whipping cream, whipped
2 (10-ounce) packages frozen broccoli
  spears
1 pound cooked sliced chicken
Grated Parmesan cheese (optional)

Melt butter in heavy saucepan; stir in flour. Add milk gradually, and cook over low heat until thickened, stirring constantly. Remove from heat. Stir a small amount of hot mixture into beaten eggs, mixing well. Stir egg mixture into remaining hot mixture, mixing well. Stir in salt, sherry, Worcestershire sauce, and cheese. Fold in whipped cream.

Cook broccoli according to package directions; drain, and arrange in buttered 2-quart shallow casserole. Cover with sliced chicken. Pour sauce over chicken and sprinkle with additional cheese, if desired. Place under broiler 3 or 4 minutes, or until lightly browned. Yield: 6 to 8 servings.

Chicken Roquefort

1 (3-pound) broiler-fryer, cut up, or
    3 whole chicken breasts, split
1 teaspoon salt
⅛ teaspoon pepper
2 tablespoons butter or margarine
4 ounces Roquefort cheese, crumbled
1 clove garlic, minced
1 (8-ounce) carton commercial sour
    cream

Season chicken with salt and pepper. Heat butter in large skillet; brown chicken lightly in butter. Place chicken in a 13- × 9- × 2-inch baking dish; reserve drippings in skillet. Add cheese, garlic, and sour cream to drippings, mixing well. Cook over low heat until thoroughly heated; pour over chicken. Bake, uncovered, at 350° for 1 hour. Yield: 4 to 6 servings.

Charcoal Broiled Chicken

2 (2- to 3-pound) broiler-fryers,
    halved
½ cup soy sauce
¼ cup water
½ cup vegetable oil
2 tablespoons instant minced onion
2 tablespoons sesame seeds
1 tablespoon sugar
1 teaspoon ground ginger
¾ teaspoon salt
½ teaspoon instant minced garlic
⅛ teaspoon red pepper

Place chicken in a plastic bag. Combine remaining ingredients; mix well. Pour marinade into bag; close bag tightly, and place in shallow pan in refrigerator at least 12 hours, turning occasionally.

    Remove chicken from marinade. Arrange, bone side down, on grill over slow coals. Grill 1 hour or until meat is tender and skin is crisp, turning and basting with marinade every 15 minutes. Yield: 4 servings.

Brandied Chicken

1 (3-pound) broiler-fryer, cut up
Salt and pepper
2 tablespoons vegetable oil
2 tablespoons butter or margarine
½ pound fresh mushrooms, sliced
6 shallots or green onions, chopped
1 teaspoon poultry seasoning
1 tablespoon tomato sauce
2 to 3 tablespoons brandy

Sprinkle chicken with salt and pepper. Heat oil and butter in a large skillet; fry chicken slowly until done and lightly browned. Transfer chicken to warm platter, reserving fat in skillet; sauté mushrooms and shallots in reserved fat until tender. Add poultry seasoning, tomato sauce, and brandy; mix well. Cook for 2 to 3 minutes; pour over chicken. Yield: 6 servings.

Chicken And Oyster Casserole

¼ cup all-purpose flour
1¼ teaspoons salt, divided
½ teaspoon pepper, divided
1 (4-pound) broiler-fryer, cut up
2 tablespoons shortening
½ cup boiling water
½ cup whipping cream
18 fresh oysters
2 tablespoons slivered almonds,
    toasted

Combine flour and half of salt and pepper, mixing well; dredge chicken in flour mixture. Heat shortening in skillet; brown chicken in hot shortening. Place chicken in 1½-quart casserole; add water and bake at 350° for 1 hour or until tender. Add whipping cream, remaining salt and pepper, and oysters. Cover and bake 10 minutes longer, or until edges of oysters curl. Sprinkle with almonds. Yield: 6 to 8 servings.

Smothered Chicken

½ cup all-purpose flour
1 teaspoon salt
¼ teaspoon pepper
½ teaspoon dried thyme leaves
    (optional)
1 (3-pound) broiler-fryer, cut up
¼ cup shortening
2 cups milk

Combine flour and seasonings, mixing well; dredge chicken in flour mixture. Heat shortening in Dutch oven; brown chicken in hot shortening. Pour off excess fat, if desired. Add milk; cover and bake at 325° for 45 to 60 minutes. Yield: 4 to 6 servings.

Note: For a delicious variation, substitute 1 (8-ounce) carton commercial sour cream mixed with 1 cup water for milk.

Chicken Pie With Sweet Potato Crust

3 cups diced cooked chicken
1 cup sliced cooked carrots
6 small white onions, quartered and
    cooked
1 tablespoon chopped fresh parsley
3 tablespoons all-purpose flour
1 cup milk
1 cup chicken broth
Salt and pepper to taste
Sweet Potato Crust

Layer chicken, carrots, onion, and parsley in greased 2½-quart casserole.

Combine flour and a small amount of milk in a saucepan, blending until smooth; gradually stir in remaining milk and chicken broth. Place over low heat; cook until thickened, stirring constantly. Add salt and pepper.

Pour sauce over chicken and vegetables in casserole dish. Cover mixture with Sweet Potato Crust, and bake at 350° about 45 minutes. Yield: 6 to 8 servings.

Sweet Potato Crust:

2 cups all-purpose flour
1 teaspoon baking powder
½ teaspoon salt
⅓ cup shortening
1 cup cold mashed sweet potatoes
1 egg, well beaten

Combine flour, baking powder, and salt; cut in shortening until mixture resembles coarse crumbs. Add sweet potatoes and egg, blending well. Roll dough out on lightly floured surface to ¼-inch thickness. Yield: crust for one pie.

Chicken-Wild Rice Casserole

1 cup uncooked wild rice
½ cup butter or margarine
½ cup chopped onion
¼ cup chopped celery
¼ cup all-purpose flour
1 (6-ounce) can sliced mushrooms,
    undrained
1½ cups chicken broth
1½ cups half-and-half
3 cups diced cooked chicken
¼ cup diced pimiento
2 teaspoons dried parsley flakes
1½ teaspoons salt
¼ teaspoon pepper
⅓ to ½ cup slivered almonds

Cook wild rice according to package directions; set aside.

Melt butter in heavy saucepan; sauté onion and celery in butter until tender. Stir in flour; cook over low heat for 1 minute, stirring constantly. Add mushrooms, broth, and half-and-half. Cook over medium heat, stirring constantly, until thickened.

Stir in rice, chicken, pimiento, parsley, and seasoning. Pour mixture into a greased 2-quart casserole; top with almonds, and bake at 350° for 25 to 30 minutes or until bubbly and brown. Yield: about 6 servings.

Chicken Soufflé

2 tablespoons butter or margarine
1 tablespoon all-purpose flour
2 cups milk
½ cup fine dry breadcrumbs
2 cups minced or ground cooked
    chicken
1 tablespoon chopped fresh parsley
1 to 2 teaspoons salt
¼ teaspoon cayenne pepper
Dash of black pepper
3 eggs, separated

Melt butter in heavy saucepan; stir in flour. Cook over low heat for 1 minute, stirring constantly. Add milk and stir constantly over medium heat until mixture comes to a boil. Add breadcrumbs and cook 1 minute. Remove from heat; add chicken and seasonings.

Beat yolks; stir into chicken mixture. Beat whites until soft peaks form; gently fold into chicken mixture. Grease only the bottom of an 8-cup soufflé dish; pour mixture into dish. Bake at 400° for 20 minutes or until puffed and browned. Yield: about 6 servings.

Creamed Chicken, Kentucky Style

¼ cup butter or margarine
¼ cup all-purpose flour
½ teaspoon salt
¼ teaspoon paprika
2 cups chicken broth
2 cups cubed cooked chicken
Diamond Points

Melt butter in heavy saucepan; stir in flour, salt, and paprika, mixing well. Cook over low heat for 1 minute, stirring constantly. Gradually stir in chicken broth and cook until thickened, stirring constantly. Add chicken, mixing well. Serve over Diamond Points. Yield: 4 servings.

Note: 1 cup half-and-half may be substituted for 1 cup broth.

Diamond Points:

1½ cups all-purpose flour
½ cup cornstarch
½ teaspoon salt
2 teaspoons baking powder
¾ to 1 cup half-and-half

Blend dry ingredients; stir in enough half-and-half to make a soft dough. Knead on floured surface until smooth; roll dough to ½-inch thickness. Cut dough with sharp knife into small diamonds about 2 inches long. Place on greased baking sheet and bake at 400° for about 15 minutes or until lightly browned. Yield: 4 servings.

Note: One-fourth cup butter or margarine plus ½ to ¾ cup milk may be substituted for half-and-half. Cut butter into dry ingredients, and stir in milk.

Buttermilk Fried Chicken

1¼ cups all-purpose flour
2½ teaspoons salt
½ teaspoon paprika
¼ teaspoon pepper
1 cup buttermilk
1 teaspoon baking powder
2 (2½- to 3-pound) broiler-fryers,
    cut up
Vegetable oil

Combine flour, salt, paprika, and pepper, mixing well. Combine buttermilk and baking powder, mixing well. Dip chicken in milk mixture; dredge in flour mixture. Arrange on flat pan and refrigerate for 2 hours.

Pour oil ½ inch deep in large heavy skillet; heat oil to 350°. Add chicken pieces and fry, uncovered, for about 40 minutes or until chicken is done and golden brown. Yield: 8 servings.

Best-Ever Fried Chicken

1½ to 2 cups all-purpose flour
1½ teaspoons salt
2 teaspoons dried thyme leaves
2 teaspoons paprika
1 egg, beaten
⅓ cup milk
2 tablespoons lemon juice
2 (2- to 3-pound) broiler-fryers,
    cut up
Vegetable oil
Cherry tomatoes
Parsley

Combine flour, salt, thyme, and paprika. Combine egg, milk, and lemon juice. Dredge chicken in flour mixture. Dip into egg mixture; then dredge in flour mixture again. Refrigerate at least 30 minutes.

Heat ½ inch of oil to 375° in an electric skillet. Place chicken in skillet; fry until golden brown on both sides. Reduce heat to 250°; cover, and continue to cook for 25 minutes. Drain on paper towels. Arrange chicken on platter and garnish with cherry tomatoes and parsley. Yield: 8 to 10 servings.

Tiny Fried Chicken Drums

2 to 2½ pounds chicken wings
1 (13-ounce) can evaporated milk
2 eggs, beaten
2 cups all-purpose flour
1 tablespoon salt
½ teaspoon pepper
1 teaspoon paprika
Vegetable oil for deep frying

Remove tips from wings; cut wings into 2 pieces. Combine milk and eggs, mixing well. Combine flour and seasonings, mixing well. Dip chicken pieces into milk mixture; dredge in flour mixture.

Heat oil to 365°. Fry chicken, a few pieces at a time, until golden brown. Drain on paper towels; serve from heated chafing dish. Yield: about 36 appetizer servings.

Chicken Salad With Apple

4 to 5 cups diced cooked chicken
6 hard-cooked eggs, thinly sliced
1 large or 2 small tart apples,
    unpeeled and chopped
¼ cup chopped sweet pickle
1 cup diced celery
1 teaspoon salt
½ teaspoon pepper
Cooked Dressing (recipe follows)
Mayonnaise
Lettuce cups

Combine first 7 ingredients; toss lightly. Gently fold in cooked dressing and enough mayonnaise to make desired consistency. Chill; serve on lettuce cups. Yield: about 8 servings.

Cooked Dressing:

2 eggs, well beaten
½ cup vinegar
⅓ cup plus 2 tablespoons water
½ cup sugar
¼ cup butter or margarine

Combine all ingredients in a medium saucepan, mixing well; cook over low heat, stirring constantly, until thick. Yield: about 1½ cups.

Chicken In Aspic

2 envelopes unflavored gelatin
¼ cup cold water
3 cups hot chicken broth
Salt and pepper
6 hard-cooked eggs, sliced
3 cups diced cooked chicken
Shredded lettuce

Soften gelatin in cold water. Dissolve gelatin mixture in hot broth. Season to taste; cool. Dampen a 1½-quart mold; arrange alternate layers of eggs and chicken along sides and bottom of mold. Pour cooled broth into mold. Refrigerate until firm. Unmold onto serving dish; garnish with lettuce. Yield: 12 appetizer servings or 8 entrée servings.

Chicken Mayonnaise

1 (5- to 6-pound) hen
1 tablespoon salt
1 bay leaf
1 slice onion
1 slice lemon
6 peppercorns
1 carrot, sliced
Celery leaves
2 envelopes unflavored gelatin
½ cup cold water
Juice of 1 lemon
2 cups chopped celery
3 hard-cooked eggs, diced
Salt and pepper to taste
2 cups mayonnaise
Lettuce cups or watercress

Place chicken in kettle; add water to cover, salt, bay leaf, onion, lemon, peppercorns, carrot, and celery leaves. Bring to a boil; reduce heat and simmer about 3 hours, or until thoroughly tender. Drain chicken, reserving 2 cups broth. Soften gelatin in cold water; stir into hot broth; cool.

Remove meat from bones and chop finely; add to gelatin mixture. Add lemon juice, celery, eggs, salt, and pepper. Allow mixture to cool; fold in mayonnaise. Pack into two 9- × 5- × 3-inch loafpans, and chill for several hours or overnight. Unmold; slice and serve on lettuce cups or watercress. Yield: 15 to 20 servings.

Chicken Mousse

3 egg yolks, beaten
1 cup highly seasoned chicken broth, divided
1 envelope unflavored gelatin
1¼ teaspoons salt
Dash of paprika
1 cup minced cooked chicken
1 cup whipping cream, whipped

Combine egg yolks and ¾ cup broth in top of double boiler, mixing well. Cook, stirring constantly, over hot water until mixture coats the spoon. Soften gelatin in remaining broth; stir into egg mixture. Add salt and paprika. Cool until syrupy; fold in chicken and whipped cream. Pour into an oiled 6-cup mold and refrigerate until firm, several hours or overnight. Yield: 6 to 8 servings.

Chicken Salad Piquant

2 cups diced cooked chicken
1½ cups celery, finely chopped
1 teaspoon salt
6 lettuce leaves
Cream Dressing (recipe follows)
1 tablespoon capers (optional)
6 small sweet pickles, sliced
Celery fans

Combine chicken, celery, and salt, mixing well. Mound chicken mixture on lettuce leaves; cover with cream dressing, and garnish with capers, pickles, and celery fans. Yield: 6 servings.

Cream Dressing:

1 teaspoon dry mustard
1 teaspoon salt
2 teaspoons all-purpose flour
2 teaspoons powdered sugar
Dash of cayenne pepper
1 teaspoon melted butter or margarine
1 egg yolk, beaten
¼ cup hot vinegar
½ cup whipping cream, whipped

Combine dry ingredients in top of double boiler. Stir in butter and egg yolk. Slowly stir in vinegar; cook over boiling water, stirring constantly, until thickened. Cool; fold whipped cream into dressing. Yield: about 1½ cups.

Cornish Hens With Basting Sauce

There is something appealing about sitting down to a party dinner and being presented with a Cornish hen, an entire bird to oneself! Not only is it quite the prettiest thing imaginable but also it is unequaled for delicacy of flavor. So mild, in fact, that it takes better than any other fowl to saucing of many kinds. This Cajun-style basting sauce, for example, will flavor a row of birds on a rotisserie.

¾ cup finely chopped onion
1 clove garlic, minced
¼ cup vegetable oil or olive oil
1 (12-ounce) can pear nectar
½ cup white wine vinegar
¼ cup honey
2 tablespoons Worcestershire sauce
1 teaspoon prepared horseradish
1 teaspoon dry mustard
1 teaspoon salt
½ teaspoon dried thyme leaves
¼ teaspoon dried rosemary leaves
¼ teaspoon pepper
4 to 6 (1- to 1½-pound) Cornish hens

Sauté onion and garlic in hot oil in a saucepan until tender. Add remaining ingredients except hens; simmer, uncovered, for 5 minutes.

Place Cornish hens on rotisserie over hot coals. Cook 50 to 60 minutes, or until tender, basting with sauce. Serve remaining sauce on table. Yield: about 3½ cups.

Roast Turkey

Start preparing stuffing a day or so ahead of time, but refrigerate dry ingredients and broth separately until time to use the dressing. Do not stuff turkey until time to roast it. For each generous serving of roasted whole turkey, allow ¾ to 1 pound of ready-to-cook weight for birds weighing less than 12 pounds, and ½ to ¾ pound for birds weighing 12 pounds and over.

Clean bird thoroughly. Salt inside of bird. Fill neck cavity loosely with dressing, if desired. Fold neck skin to back, fastening to backbone with a poultry pin. Fold wing tip over neck skin. Spoon dressing into body cavity, shaking bird to settle dressing; do not pack dressing. Place skewers across opening and lace shut with cord. Tie drumsticks securely to tail. Brush skin with vegetable oil.

Cover turkey with a tent of aluminum foil or a piece of thin cloth moistened with oil. Baste turkey several times during roasting. When roasting is about half-done, cut the string or skin to release legs. Turkey is done when leg joints move easily and flesh on the legs is soft and pliable when pressed with fingers. When a meat thermometer is used, it should register 185° placed in center of inside thigh muscle or in center of the thickest meaty part.

Use chart to determine how long to roast chilled turkeys of various weights.

	ROASTING CHART	
Weight in Pounds	Total Cooking Hours at 325° for Unstuffed Turkey	Total Cooking Hours at 325° for Stuffed Turkey
4 to 8	2 to 3	2½ to 3½
8 to 12	3 to 4	3½ to 4½
12 to 16	4 to 5	4½ to 5½
16 to 20	5 to 6	5½ to 6½
20 to 24	6 to 7	6½ to 7½

Turkey-Almond Casserole

½ cup slivered almonds
2 tablespoons butter or margarine
2 cups chopped cooked turkey
1 (10¾-ounce) can cream of
    mushroom soup, undiluted
2 cups cooked regular rice
1 cup milk
½ teaspoon salt
¼ cup dry white wine
1 cup buttered breadcrumbs

Sauté almonds lightly in butter until lightly browned. Combine all ingredients except breadcrumbs and place in buttered 1½-quart casserole; top with breadcrumbs. Bake at 350° for 45 minutes. Yield: 6 to 8 servings.

Note: Chicken or tuna may be substituted for turkey.

Turkey Hash, Pendennis Club Style

2 small onions, chopped
¼ cup butter or margarine
3 tablespoons all-purpose flour
4 cups chicken stock
4 cups diced cooked turkey
2 cups diced cooked potatoes
Salt and pepper

Sauté onions in butter in a Dutch oven until transparent. Stir in flour; cook over low heat 1 minute, stirring constantly. Add stock gradually, stirring constantly. Cook, stirring constantly, until slightly thickened; add turkey and potatoes. Season to taste. Simmer 20 minutes, stirring occasionally. Serve with hot corn muffins and butter. Yield: 12 to 14 servings.

Note: Turkey hash, along with country ham, belongs on Louisville's traditional Kentucky Derby menu.

Turkey Loaf

2 cups turkey or chicken stock
2 cups fine dry breadcrumbs
2 eggs, well beaten
1 teaspoon salt
1 small onion, finely chopped
1 cup chopped celery
1 cup milk
4 cups diced cooked turkey
Commercial mushroom sauce
    (optional)

Bring stock to a boil; pour over breadcrumbs. Cover and let stand 5 minutes. Add remaining ingredients except mushroom sauce; mix well. Pour into a greased 9- × 5- × 3-inch loafpan. Bake at 325° for 45 to 60 minutes. Loaf will shrink from sides of pan. Unmold and slice to serve. Serve with mushroom sauce, if desired. Yield: 8 servings.

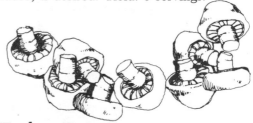

Turkey Tetrazzini

1 (5-ounce) package egg noodles
3 cups cubed cooked turkey
1 cup diced celery
1 tablespoon seasoned salt
1 teaspoon pepper
1 (10¾-ounce) can consommé,
    undiluted
2 (10¾-ounce) cans cream of
    mushroom soup, undiluted
2 (5-ounce) packages French-fried
    onion rings
½ cup sliced almonds

Cook noodles according to package directions. Combine all ingredients, mixing gently; pour into a greased 3-quart casserole, and bake at 325° for 45 minutes. Yield: 8 servings.

Golden Grilled Ham

1 (1-inch-thick) slice cooked ham
    (about 1½ pounds)
1 cup ginger ale
1 cup orange juice
½ cup firmly packed brown sugar
3 tablespoons vegetable oil
1 tablespoon wine vinegar
2 teaspoons dry mustard
¾ teaspoon ground ginger
½ teaspoon ground cloves

Score fat edge of ham. Combine remaining ingredients, mixing well. Pour over ham in a shallow baking dish. Refrigerate overnight or let stand at room temperature 1 hour, spooning marinade over ham several times.

Place ham on grill over slow coals; cook about 15 minutes on each side, brushing frequently with marinade. Heat remaining marinade; serve with ham. Yield: 4 servings.

Country Ham

1 (10- to 15-pound) country ham
4 quarts ginger ale

Put ham in a clean can or very large pot filled with hot water (just below the boiling point). Let boil 10 or 15 minutes. This step gives the ham a good cleaning and removes excess salt from the outside. Remove ham, and discard water.

Place ham in can, and fill half full with hot water. Add ginger ale, and put top loosely on can. Bring to a full rolling boil; boil 30 minutes. (The ginger ale helps to bring out the flavor of the ham.)

Place about 4 thicknesses of newspaper on the floor, and wet ham (still in can) on papers. Press can lid on tightly; pull papers around sides and top of can, and tie with string. Cover with quilts or blankets. Let sit for 10 to 14 hours according to size of ham. (A 12- to 13-pound ham requires about 10 hours.) Remove skin, and trim fat from ham. Glaze, if desired. Yield: 24 to 30 servings.

Country Ham And Grits With Red-Eye Gravy

Grits
Country Ham
Strong black coffee

Prepare grits according to package directions. Slice country ham about ¼ to ⅓ inch thick. Cut gashes in fat to keep ham from curling. Place slices in a heavy skillet and cook slowly, turning several times; cook until fat is transparent.

Remove ham from pan, and keep warm. Add a small amount of water to the skillet. For each pound of ham, add ¼ cup strong black coffee to pan drippings; bring to a boil, stirring well. Serve gravy over grits and ham.

East Tennessee Ham

1 (10- to 12-pound) country ham
2 cups blackstrap molasses
Unsweetened tea
1 tablespoon dry mustard
½ cup chili sauce
Whole cloves (optional)

Soak ham overnight in water to cover. Drain ham and scrub well; place in large roasting pan which will fit over 2 burners of stove. Pour molasses over ham; add enough tea to half-way cover ham. Cover roasting pan; simmer over medium-low heat for 3 hours, turning ham over once during cooking.

Remove ham from heat and peel off skin. Let ham cool completely in cooking liquid.

Place ham on rack in baking pan. Score ham in a diamond pattern, making cuts ¼ inch deep in ham fat. Mix mustard with chili sauce and spread over ham. Place cloves in scored design, if desired. Bake at 400° for 30 minutes; reduce heat to 325° and continue baking about 1 hour or until shank bone is loose. Yield: 20 to 24 servings.

Southern Maryland Stuffed Ham

Maryland's greens-stuffed country ham is legendary. Good Southern cooking is not always quick and easy, as its practitioners are aware, and this ham does take a bit of doing. When it is sliced thin and laid out on the platter, however, the compliments more than compensate for the time spent.

1 (12-pound) country ham
3 pounds kale
3 pounds watercress
2 pounds green cabbage
1 bunch celery, finely chopped
1 hot red pepper, finely chopped
¼ cup plus 2 tablespoons salt
2 tablespoons black papper
2 tablespoons ground red pepper
2 tablespoons mustard seeds
2 tablespoons celery seeds
2 teaspoons hot sauce

Choose a plump, thick ham, with a thin layer of fat. Parboil ham 20 minutes in water to cover. Drain ham and scrub well; remove all skin. Cool ham until comfortable to handle. Starting at butt end of ham, cut 3 lengthwise slits, 2 inches long, all the way through. Cut a second row of 2 lengthwise slits. Cut a third row of 3 lengthwise slits, cutting so that one slit for stuffing does not split into another.

Cut greens into 1- to 1½-inch pieces. Blanch greens, celery, and pepper in boiling water until limp; drain well. Add seasonings to vegetables and mix well. Stuff vegetable mixture into every slit, first from the top, and then from the under side. Spread remaining vegetable mixture over top of ham.

Place ham, skin side up, on a large square of clean cheese cloth; fold ends over tightly, and tie securely. Return ham to boiler; cover with water and simmer 15 minutes per pound. Let cool 2 hours in "pot likker." Chill in refrigerator overnight. Remove cloth and slice ham. Yield: about 48 servings.

Ham With Purple Plums

1 (29-ounce) can purple plums
1 (3-pound) fully cooked boneless ham
1 cup firmly packed brown sugar, divided
1 teaspoon ground cloves
½ cup plum preserves
¼ cup prepared mustard
Fresh parsley sprigs (optional)

Drain plums, reserving liquid; set both aside. Pierce ham all over with ice pick. Place ham on large sheet of heavy aluminum foil, cupping foil to form a bowl shape. Pour half the plum juice over ham; mix half the brown sugar and cloves, and sprinkle over ham. Seal foil over ham and bake at 350° for 40 minutes. Open foil and drain off juices.

Combine remaining plum juice and remaining sugar in a saucepan; bring to a boil and boil until syrupy; pour mixture over ham and bake, uncovered, for 30 minutes, basting frequently. Combine preserves and mustard, mixing well; spread mixture over ham. Bake 10 minutes. Remove to warm platter and garnish with plums and parsley, if desired. Yield: 12 servings.

Ham Loaf

½ pound fresh lean pork
1 pound smoked ham
1 tablespoon brown sugar
2 eggs
1 small onion, minced
¾ cup breadcrumbs
½ cup tomato sauce
Mustard Sauce (recipe follows)

Put pork and ham through meat grinder; add remaining ingredients except mustard sauce; mix thoroughly. Pack mixture into a 9- × 5- × 3-inch loafpan; set pan in a shallow pan of water. Bake at 350° for 1 hour. Serve hot with mustard sauce. Yield: 6 servings.

Mustard Sauce:

1 teaspoon dry mustard
1½ teaspoons prepared mustard
1 tablespoon sugar
½ teaspoon salt
Dash of cayenne pepper
3 egg yolks, beaten
½ cup vinegar
1 tablespoon butter or margarine
½ cup heavy cream, whipped

Combine dry ingredients in a medium sauce-pan; stir in egg yolks and vinegar. Cook over low heat, stirring constantly, until thick. Add butter; cook until butter melts. Allow to cool; fold in whipped cream. Yield: about 1¾ cups.

Ham Patties

5 slices white bread
½ cup milk
6 eggs, beaten
1 cup diced cooked ham
1 tablespoon chopped fresh parsley
1 teaspoon chopped chives
Shortening

Soak bread in milk; squeeze milk from bread, discarding milk. Crumble bread. Combine with eggs, ham, parsley, and chives; mix well.

Heat shortening ⅓ inch deep in skillet. Drop ham mixture by tablespoonfuls into hot shortening; fry until golden brown on both sides. Yield: 4 servings.

Jezebel Sauce For Ham

1 (16-ounce) jar pineapple or
    damson plum preserves
1 (5-ounce) jar prepared mustard
1 (16-ounce) jar apple jelly
1 (5-ounce) jar prepared horseradish

Mix all ingredients; store in refrigerator. Yield: about 5 cups.

Pork Chops With Potato Sauce

2 eggs
1 teaspoon paprika
1 small clove garlic, minced
½ teaspoon salt
⅛ teaspoon pepper
1 teaspoon dry mustard
6 pork chops
1 cup fine cornbread crumbs or
    cracker crumbs
Shortening
Potato Sauce

Beat eggs; add seasonings and blend well. Dip chops in egg mixture; coat well with crumbs.

Heat shortening ¼ inch deep in large skillet. Fry chops slowly over low heat until done and evenly browned on both sides. Remove chops from skillet; reserve oil in which chops were fried for Potato Sauce. Serve chops topped with Potato Sauce or pass sauce separately. Or place chops in baking dish, cover with sauce, and place in oven until ready to serve. Yield: 6 servings.

Potato Sauce:

Melted shortening
Reserved pan drippings
½ cup chopped onion
¼ cup shredded carrot
2 tablespoons chopped pimiento
3 tablespoons all-purpose flour
1⅔ cups water
½ to 1 teaspoon salt
¼ teaspoon pepper
1 small clove garlic, minced
2 cups diced cooked potatoes

Add melted shortening, if necessary, to reserved pan drippings to make 3 tablespoons. Heat drippings. Sauté onion, carrot, and pimiento in drippings until wilted. Stir in flour. Add water, stirring, and cook until thickened, stirring constantly. Add remaining ingredients; mix well. Serve hot, as directed above. Yield: about 4 cups.

Apple-Stuffed Pork Chops

1½ cups toasted ½-inch bread cubes
½ cup chopped apple
½ cup shredded sharp Cheddar
  cheese
2 tablespoons seedless golden raisins
¼ teaspoon salt
⅛ teaspoon ground cinnamon
2 tablespoons orange juice
2 tablespoons melted butter or
  margarine
6 (1½-inch-thick) pork chops, cut
  with pockets
Salt and pepper to taste

Combine bread cubes, apple, cheese, and raisins; sprinkle with salt and cinnamon. Add orange juice and butter; stir until bread cubes are coated.

Season pocket of pork chops with salt and pepper; stuff with bread cube mixture. Sprinkle chops with salt and pepper, and place in a shallow baking dish. Bake at 350° for 1 hour and 15 minutes. Cover and bake an additional 15 minutes. Yield: 6 servings.

Pork Tenderloin Braised In Wine

1 (4-pound) pork tenderloin
Marinade (recipe follows)
2 tablespoons rendered pork fat
⅓ cup currant jelly
Grated rind of 1 lemon

Cover tenderloin with marinade and refrigerate for 2 to 3 days, turning occasionally. Remove meat from marinade, and blot with paper towels; reserve marinade. Brown meat quickly in hot fat. Place meat in a large casserole. Bring marinade to a boil, and pour over meat. Cover casserole and bake at 325° for 2 to 2½ hours or until meat is tender.

Remove meat to warm platter. Strain liquid; reduce liquid to about 1 cup by boiling rapidly. Add jelly and lemon rind; simmer until jelly melts. Pour small amount of sauce over meat; serve remainder of sauce on the side. Yield: 8 servings.

Marinade:

3 cups dry red wine
2 large onions, coarsely chopped
1 carrot, coarsely chopped
1 large clove garlic, crushed
1½ tablespoons tarragon vinegar
½ teaspoon peppercorns
3 whole cloves
1½ teaspoons salt

Combine all ingredients in a saucepan; simmer 30 minutes. Cool. Yield: about 3½ cups.

German Pot Pie

2½ pounds pork shoulder cut into
  1½-inch cubes
5 stalks celery, cut into 1-inch pieces
3 medium onions, quartered
3 medium potatoes, quartered
1 teaspoon salt
¼ teaspoon pepper
Pastry (recipe follows)

Place meat, celery, and onion in 4-quart kettle; cover with water. Bring to boil; cover, reduce heat, and simmer about 45 minutes, or until meat is almost tender. Add potatoes and seasoning. Simmer 15 minutes; add water as necessary to keep liquid level barely covering vegetables. Drop pastry squares on top of simmering food; cover and simmer 45 minutes to 1 hour. Keep liquid level with pastry at all times. Yield: 6 to 8 servings.

Pastry:

2 tablespoons butter or margarine
1½ cups all-purpose flour
2 eggs, beaten
¼ teaspoon salt

Cut butter into flour with pastry blender; add eggs and salt, mixing until smooth. Roll dough ¼ inch thick on floured surface; cut into 3-inch squares.

German Gritz

2½ pounds lean pork shoulder, cut into cubes
½ pound unsliced bacon, cubed
2½ quarts water
2 tablespoons salt
1 tablespoon coarsely ground pepper
1 tablespoon ground cloves
5 cups steel-cut oats

Combine meat, water, and seasonings in kettle; bring to a boil, reduce heat, and simmer over low heat for about 4 hours. Drain meat, reserving water. Grind meat in meat grinder. Add oats to reserved meat liquid; cook until tender, about 20 minutes, stirring frequently. Combine oatmeal and meat, mixing well; pour into two 9- × 5- × 3-inch loafpans, and refrigerate up to 3 or 4 days, or wrap well and freeze. To serve, slice and fry. Serve with eggs for breakfast or brunch. Yield: about 6 pounds.

Note: Steel-cut oats can be found at food specialty shops or health food stores.

Cornmeal Scrapple

2 cups ground pork
2 cups ground beef
3 cups beef broth
2 teaspoons salt
¼ teaspoon pepper
1½ teaspoons rubbed sage
Dash of cayenne pepper
1 cup cornmeal
Hot vegetable oil

Combine pork, beef, and broth in a medium saucepan; bring to a boil, stirring to crumble. Add seasonings. Gradually sprinkle in cornmeal, stirring constantly; cook 30 minutes over low heat, stirring frequently.

Spoon into a greased 10-inch tube pan; chill until firm. Cut into ½-inch slices, and fry in ½-inch hot oil until brown, turning once. Yield: about 10 to 12 servings.

Bratwurst

Of the estimated 2,000 immigrants who entered the Oklahoma and Indian Territory annually between 1890 and 1914, Germans were the largest single ethnic group. In the northwestern third of Oklahoma, wheat farmlands expertly worked by the German descendants account for much of the state's productivity today. Wurst, especially bratwurst, is standard fare at Oktoberfests everywhere, including Oklahoma.

1 (3½-pound) pork shoulder or butt, about 30 percent fat
2 teaspoons salt
2 eggs
¼ teaspoon ground marjoram
¼ teaspoon dried coriander seeds
¼ teaspoon ground nutmeg
1 tablespoon chopped fresh parsley or 1 teaspoon dried parsley flakes
1 teaspoon white pepper
Few drops of soy sauce
Dash of grated lemon rind
¾ cup milk
Natural pork casings, soaked in warm water and rinsed

Cut meat into 2-inch chunks; mix with salt, and place in freezer 5 minutes. Grind meat twice in a meat grinder using fine blade. Add eggs, marjoram, coriander, nutmeg, parsley, pepper, soy sauce, and lemon rind to meat; mix thoroughly. Add milk, ¼ cup at a time, mixing well with hands after each addition. Fill casings loosely with sausage mixture (sausage expands upon cooking). If air pockets appear, prick with a needle. Tie sausage off in 4- to 5-inch lengths. Refrigerate sausage if it is to be cooked within a few days, or wrap sausage and freeze. Yield: about 3½ pounds.

Chorizo

Because so many Mexican recipes call for chorizo, and because so many cooks are hard put to find a supply, it is good to know that it can be made quite easily at home. Here is a recipe from Juanita Acevedo Olds, who with her husband James, opened Louisville's first authentic Mexican restaurant.

 2 pounds lean meat (pork and/or beef)
 2 teaspoons salt
 ¼ cup chili powder
 2 cloves garlic, crushed
 2 teaspoons dried oregano leaves
 ¼ cup vinegar
 Natural pork casings, soaked in warm water and rinsed

Grind meat coarsely in meat grinder or food processor. Add remaining ingredients and mix thoroughly. Stuff casings loosely with sausage mixture (sausage expands upon cooking). If air pockets appear, prick with a needle. Tie sausage off in 4- to 5-inch lengths. Refrigerate sausage if to be cooked within a few days, or wrap sausage and freeze. Yield: about 2 pounds.

Note: This recipe is for a mild chorizo, but to make it for Latin tastes, more chili powder and some crushed red pepper may be added. Some Mexican cooks like to add ¼ cup of brandy or tequila.

Black Beans And Rice

 1 cup black beans
 2 tablespoons olive oil
 ½ cup chopped onion
 1 cup uncooked regular rice
 4 cups boiling water
 6 to 8 ounces chorizo sausage, sliced

Soak beans in water to cover overnight. Drain beans and place in a heavy saucepan; cover with water, and bring to a boil. Reduce heat; cover and simmer 2 hours or until tender. Add water as needed during cooking. Drain beans, reserving ½ cup liquid.

Heat oil in heavy saucepan; add onion and sauté until tender; stir in rice. Add boiling water; cover and cook over low heat for 20 minutes, or until rice is tender.

Combine beans, reserved bean liquid, and rice in a Dutch oven; add sausage and cook over low heat 10 to 15 minutes or until sausage is done, adding a little boiling water, if necessary. Yield: 4 to 6 servings.

Italian Sausage

Homemade sausage, after one has made it a few times, becomes child's play. One of the most delicious is Italian sausage, indispensable in so many recipes. A member of Louisville's Italian community gave me his recipe.

 1 tablespoon crushed fennel seeds
 1 tablespoon ground red pepper
 2 teaspoons black pepper
 1 tablespoon paprika
 1 tablespoon salt
 1 (6-pound) pork shoulder or butt, 30 to 40 percent fat
 Natural pork casings, soaked in warm water and rinsed

Combine fennel, red and black pepper, paprika, and salt; mix well. Cut meat into 1-inch cubes and dredge in seasoning mixture. Grind meat in a meat grinder using a fine blade; mix well with hands. Fill casings loosely with ground meat. Tie sausage off in 3-inch lengths. Refrigerate sausage if to be used within 3 days, or wrap well and freeze. Yield: about 6 pounds.

Italian Sausage In Red Wine

 2 pounds Italian sausage
 2 cups water
 ½ cup dry red wine

Combine sausage and water in skillet; bring to a boil. Prick sausage with sharp fork to release fat. Reduce heat and simmer 20 minutes. Pour off any water remaining; brown meat in skillet, turning to brown evenly. Add wine; cover, and simmer 5 minutes. Serve hot with green salad and Italian bread. Yield: 4 to 6 servings.

Italian Sausage With Rice

½ cup butter or margarine, divided
2 onions, coarsely chopped and
    divided
1 cup uncooked regular rice
4 cups boiling chicken broth
1 teaspoon salt
¼ teaspoon pepper
½ pound Italian sausage, cut into
    2-inch lengths
4 to 6 chicken livers, halved
3 tablespoons tomato puree
3 tablespoons water
¼ cup grated Parmesan or Romano
    cheese (optional)

Melt ¼ cup butter in a large saucepan; add half the onion and sauté for 1 to 2 minutes. Stir in rice and broth; season with salt and pepper. Reduce heat, and cook until rice is tender, about 20 minutes.

Heat remaining ¼ cup butter in frying pan, and add remaining onion; sauté 1 or 2 minutes. Add sausage and liver; fry 5 minutes over medium heat. Mix tomato puree with water; pour over meat. Cover and simmer over low heat 20 minutes. Place meat in center of warm platter and surround with rice. Sprinkle with cheese, if desired. Yield: 4 to 5 servings.

Broiled Or Grilled Italian Sausage

Place sausage on rack in broiler pan. Broil 6 inches from heat source for 20 minutes or until done, turning frequently to prevent scorching. Prick sausage during cooking with a sharp fork to release fat.

Italian Sausage Casserole

1 pound Italian sausage, sliced
6 eggs
2 cups milk
1 teaspoon salt
1 teaspoon dry mustard
6 slices white bread, cubed
4 cups (1 pound) shredded mild
    Cheddar cheese
1 (4-ounce) can sliced mushrooms,
    undrained

Brown sausage in skillet over medium heat; drain sausage.

Beat eggs in a large mixing bowl; add milk, salt, and mustard, mixing well. Add bread, cheese, mushrooms, and sausage; mix lightly. Pour into a greased 3-quart casserole. Bake, uncovered, at 350° for 1½ hours. Yield: 6 to 8 servings.

Note: This casserole may be assembled 12 to 24 hours ahead of baking and refrigerated.

Homemade Sausage

25 pounds fresh pork (about 22
    pounds lean meat and 3
    pounds fat)
½ cup salt
½ cup firmly packed brown sugar
3 tablespoon ground sage
2 tablespoons pepper
2 tablespoons red pepper

Trim off any excess fat from pork. Cut pork into 2-inch cubes and spread out on waxed paper. Combine salt, brown sugar, sage, and pepper. Sprinkle over meat. Grind meat with seasonings in meat grinder two times, mixing ground mixture well with hands. Sausage can be canned, frozen, or stuffed into casings or bags. Yield: 25 pounds.

Kielbasa

Panna Maria, the oldest Polish town in North America, was established in central Texas in 1854–55. Other groups followed, and by 1900 there were 16,000 Poles in Texas. Of the many gifts we share from the Polish Southerners, none is more flavorful than kielbasa.

2 teaspoons salt
2 teaspoons dried marjoram leaves
1 teaspoon ground sage
1 teaspoon black pepper
½ teaspoon ground thyme
½ teaspoon ground nutmeg
1½ pounds pork butt, 25 percent fat, cut into cubes
¾ pound beef, 40 to 50 percent fat, cut into cubes
1 medium onion, finely chopped
1 clove garlic, minced
1 teaspoon prepared mustard
¾ cup water
Natural pork casings, soaked in warm water and rinsed

Combine all spices, mixing well; dredge meat cubes in spice mixture. Grind meat, onion, garlic, and mustard in meat grinder; mix well with hands. Add water gradually, mixing thoroughly. Fill casings loosely with sausage mixture; tie sausage off in 5-inch lengths. Refrigerate sausage if to be cooked within 3 days, or wrap well and freeze. Yield: about 2½ pounds.

Stuffed Spareribs

Salt and pepper
2 (3-pound) slabs spareribs
Stuffing (recipe follows)
Gravy (recipe follows)

Rub salt and pepper into meat. Spread stuffing on bony side of one slab of spareribs; cover with remaining slab. Tie spareribs securely with string. Place in roasting pan; cover and bake at 325° for 1½ to 2 hours, or until very tender. Uncover spareribs last 30 minutes to brown. Reserve 3 tablespoons drippings for gravy. Yield: 6 servings.

Stuffing:

3 cups 1-inch bread cubes
1 cup finely chopped unpeeled apple
1 cup chopped prunes or other dried fruit
1 medium onion, finely chopped
1 teaspoon salt
¼ teaspoon pepper
¼ to ½ cup chopped pecans (optional)
1 teaspoon ground sage

Combine all ingredients, mixing well. Yield: enough stuffing for 6 pounds spareribs.

Gravy:

3 tablespoons reserved pan drippings
3 tablespoons all-purpose flour
2 cups water or milk
Salt and pepper

Heat drippings in a saucepan; stir in flour. Gradually stir in milk and cook over medium heat, stirring constantly until thickened. Season to taste. Yield: about 2 cups.

Southern Barbecued Spareribs

2 cloves garlic, crushed
2 tablespoons melted butter or margarine
2 tablespoons prepared mustard
¼ cup firmly packed brown sugar
1 cup catsup
¾ cup chili sauce
1 tablespoon celery seeds
2 tablespoons Worcestershire sauce
1 to 2 dashes of hot sauce
½ teaspoon salt
1½ cups water
4 pounds pork spareribs or loin back ribs
Salt

Sauté garlic in butter 4 to 5 minutes. Add next 9 ingredients; bring to a boil.

Sprinkle spareribs with salt; place bone side down on grill over slow coals. Grill about 20 minutes; turn meaty side down and cook until browned. Turn meaty side up again, and grill ribs about 20 minutes longer. Brush meaty side with basting sauce. Continue to grill without turning 20 to 30 minutes, basting occasionally. Brush sauce on both sides of the ribs, and let cook 2 to 3 minutes on each side. Yield: about 4 to 6 servings.

Roast Wild Duck

Southerners have not lost their fondness for game and hunting. Arkansas and the Carolinas are known for the quality of their wild duck, fat from feeding on the rice crops. Fine duck and geese are hunted in all the states along the Mississippi Flyway, while numerous rivers and lakes attract large numbers of birds.

Many cooks soak wild duck and goose in water to which salt and soda have been added. The soda is said to dispel the "wild taste." Duck may be roasted for a short time at a high temperature and served very rare. This "bloody duck" method has many devotees who will patiently put up with their friends' ridicule. Others cook duck from 2 to 4 hours. The only tough duck I ever met had been cooked 1 hour, so the answer may be either to cook it a very short time or very long time. Here is a 3- to 4-hour recipe.

  2 wild ducks
Salt and pepper to taste
1 onion, chopped
1 apple, chopped
1 stalk celery, chopped
1 clove garlic, chopped
1 (10¾-ounce) can consommé, undiluted
1 cup dry red wine
2 tablespoons Worcestershire sauce

Rub ducks with salt and pepper inside and out. Stuff cavities of ducks with onion, apple, celery, and garlic. Place breast side down in roasting pan. Pour consommé and red wine over ducks. Sprinkle Worcestershire sauce over ducks. Roast at 325° for 3 to 4 hours, basting often. Turn breast side up and continue roasting for 30 minutes or until brown, basting often. Add water to maintain level of sauce, if needed. Yield: 4 to 6 servings.

Wild Goose With Sauerkraut

The goose, tame or wild, comes with more fat attached than is necessary or desirable. Before roasting goose, I like to pierce the skin over the breast and legs with a sharp knife tip. That done, and with a sliced apple and onion tucked into the cavity, it goes on a rack in a roasting pan, uncovered. One hour in a 375° oven gets rid of a great deal of excess fat, which is simply discarded along with the apple and onion, so that the cooking can proceed.

One of our special treats is wild goose stuffed with sauerkraut.

  1 goose, prepared as above and cooled
Salt to taste
3 (1-pound) cans sauerkraut
1 teaspoon caraway seeds

Sprinkle goose liberally with salt. Mix remaining ingredients and stuff into cavity of goose; truss. Place goose on rack in roaster, and add 1 cup water. Cover and bake at 275° for about 3 hours, or until tender; uncover during the last 30 minutes of baking. Yield: 5 to 6 servings.

Venison Parmesan

There is an Italian twist to this venison steak, with olive oil and two cheeses for flavoring.

> 1 (1-pound) venison steak, ¼ inch thick
> Salt and pepper
> 1 egg
> 2 teaspoons water
> ⅓ cup grated Parmesan cheese
> ⅓ cup fine dry breadcrumbs
> ¼ cup olive oil
> 1 onion, finely chopped
> 2 tablespoons butter or margarine
> 1 (6-ounce) can tomato paste
> 2 cups hot water
> 1 teaspoon salt
> ½ teaspoon dried marjoram leaves
> ½ pound sliced mozzarella or Swiss cheese

Cut steak into 6 or 8 pieces; sprinkle with salt and pepper. Beat egg with 2 teaspoons water. Combine Parmesan cheese and breadcrumbs, mixing well. Dip meat in egg; then roll in breadcrumb mixture. Heat oil in large skillet and fry 3 pieces at a time until golden brown on each side. Drain venison, reserving drippings in skillet. Lay venison in a 13- × 9- × 2-inch baking dish.

Sauté onion in butter and reserved drippings until soft. Add tomato paste, hot water, salt, and marjoram. Boil a few minutes, stirring well. Pour three-fourths of sauce over steaks. Top with thin slices of mozzarella cheese, then pour remaining sauce over cheese. Bake at 350° for about 30 minutes. Yield: 4 servings.

Venison Swiss Steak

The filet of venison called "backstrap" is as highly prized for its tenderness as is filet of beef. It may be sliced, wrapped in bacon, and grilled or pan-broiled in the same way.

Or it may be sliced, coated with seasoned flour, and deep fried. One tasty way to use the larger steaks is to "Swiss" them.

> All-purpose flour
> Salt and pepper
> 2 pounds venison steak, ½ to 1 inch thick
> 3 tablespoons shortening
> 1 small onion, chopped
> 1 small green pepper, chopped
> 1 (8-ounce) can tomato sauce

Pound flour, salt, and pepper into steak. Brown meat in hot shortening; add onion and green pepper. Pour tomato sauce over mixture and add enough water to cover. Cook slowly over low heat or bake at 325° until tender, about 1½ hours; add additional water if necessary. Yield: 6 to 8 servings.

Venison Stroganoff, Ozark Style

> 1½ pounds venison, cut into ½-inch cubes
> All-purpose flour
> 2 to 4 tablespoons shortening
> 1 (6-ounce) can sliced mushrooms
> 1 small onion, minced
> 1 clove garlic, minced
> 1 (10¾-ounce) can tomato soup, undiluted
> 6 drops hot sauce
> 1 tablespoon Worcestershire sauce
> ½ to 1 teaspoon salt
> 1½ cups commercial sour cream

Dredge meat in flour. Brown in hot shortening. Drain mushrooms; reserve liquid. Add mushrooms, onion, and garlic to meat. Combine soup with mushroom liquid and seasonings; pour over meat. Cover; simmer about 1 hour, or until tender. Just before serving, stir in sour cream; heat but do not boil. Serve over rice, noodles, or mashed potatoes. Yield: about 6 servings.

Doves

Pheasant, dove, and quail—even some wild turkey—still haunt the Southern woodlands, well protected by conservation laws. Those who hunt, and those fortunate enough to know the hunters, continue to enjoy the succulent wild birds. Braising is the most common method for cooking both dove and quail, as they are considerably tougher than their size would indicate. From Georgia comes an interesting variation in which dove is simmered down in a peppery sauce.

Salt
12 doves
Shortening
⅓ cup apple cider vinegar
⅔ cup water
1 teaspoon crushed red pepper
1 tablespoon Worcestershire sauce
½ teaspoon hot sauce
Juice of 2 lemons
2 tablespoons dry red wine (optional)
Garlic salt
Salt and pepper to taste

Wash, drain, and salt the doves. Melt shortening in large skillet to about ¼ inch deep. Add doves and cook until light brown, turning several times.

Add vinegar and water to skillet; cover, and simmer over low heat for 1 hour. Add red pepper, Worcestershire sauce, hot sauce, lemon juice, and wine, if desired. Sprinkle garlic salt over doves.

Cover and simmer for 45 to 60 minutes or until tender. Sprinkle salt and pepper over doves just before serving. Yield: about 6 servings.

Roast Pheasant

Pheasant may well be the most sought after of all game birds, since the flavor is slightly less "gamey" than others. Too, it is more available to nonhunters, as there are some farms that specialize in raising them. Pheasant under glass is not impossible to concoct at home: the glass bells required may be found at most restaurant supply houses. But it would be simpler to prepare it this way.

1 (2- to 3-pound) young pheasant
Salt and pepper
1 bay leaf
1 clove garlic, crushed
Few celery leaves
1 slice lemon
4 slices bacon
Melted butter or margarine
1 large onion, sliced
2 (4-ounce) cans mushrooms, undrained
1 cup chicken broth

Sprinkle pheasant inside and out with salt and pepper. Place bay leaf, garlic, celery leaves, and lemon in cavity of pheasant. Tie legs together with string. Turn wings under. Cover breast with bacon slices and cheesecloth soaked in melted butter. Place pheasant breast side up in baking pan. Arrange the onion slices and mushrooms around pheasant. Pour mushroom liquid and chicken broth over pheasant. Roast at 350° for about 30 minutes per pound, or until tender, basting frequently with liquid in pan. Remove cheesecloth and string. Yield: 3 to 4 servings.

Ranch-Style Creamed Quail

In Texas they know how to use cream to enhance the delicate flavor of quail. This recipe is very inexpensive to make if one owns a dairy herd, and delicious beyond belief

Salt and pepper
12 quail
2 cups butter
1 quart half-and-half
1 to 1½ cups toasted breadcrumbs

Salt and pepper quail. Melt butter in Dutch oven; add quail and simmer over low heat until tender. Add half-and-half; heat thoroughly. Remove quail to hot platter. Sprinkle browned breadcrumbs over quail, and pour cream gravy over quail. Yield: 12 servings.

Roasted Quail

Roasting of small birds may be carried out to good effect if one remembers to baste frequently to keep them moist. It is helpful to wrap the seasoned dove or quail in bacon and add a bit of butter to the roasting pan. Roasted tender, they are splendid served on crisp buttered toast, with the pan juices spooned over them. In North Carolina, they roast quail this way.

¼ cup water
3 tablespoons butter or margarine
½ cup dry sherry
¼ teaspoon dried marjoram leaves
Quail
Salt
Butter or margarine
All-purpose flour

Combine water, 3 tablespoons butter, sherry, and marjoram; mix well and set aside.

Sprinkle quail with salt; place about 2 tablespoons butter inside cavity of each bird. Rub birds with mixture of equal amounts of flour and butter. Bake at 275° for 1 hour, basting frequently with sauce.

Florida Stuffed Quail

8 quail, cleaned
2 to 3 teaspoons salt
Dressing (recipe follows)
Hearts and gizzards of quail
Shortening or vegetable oil
Salt and pepper
2 tablespoons all-purpose flour

Sprinkle birds inside and out with salt. Stuff lightly with dressing; tuck 1 heart and 1 gizzard into each bird. Close openings with skewers or sew with strong white thread.

Heat shortening ½ inch deep in heavy skillet. Brown quail on all sides in hot shortening, sprinkling with salt and pepper as they cook. When brown, add water to fill skillet two-thirds full. Cover, reduce heat, and cook until birds are tender, about 1 hour. Add a little more water as necessary. Serve gravy with quail. Yield: 4 servings.

Note: Make a paste of flour and a little water. Stir into pan juices and cook until thickened, about 5 minutes, stirring frequently. Thin with a little water if necessary. Season with salt and pepper.

Dressing:

4 cups breadcrumbs
1 medium onion, finely chopped
½ cup raisins
½ teaspoon salt
¼ teaspoon pepper
½ teaspoon ground sage
¼ teaspoon ground thyme
½ teaspoon paprika
½ cup vegetable oil

Combine all ingredients, mixing well. Yield: about 4 cups.

Vegetables and Side Dishes

When the first European colonists came ashore in the American Southeast, they found food in more abundance and variety than they had left behind, according to a fascinating piece of research into the history of colonial foods in Virginia by William R. Hess, Jr., of Virginia Polytechnical Institute and State University. A list of vegetables with which the English were already familiar, compared with the New World's cornucopia, is especially interesting.

The average European's diet was, at that time, very poor indeed. Root vegetables such as onions, leeks, beets, carrots, radishes, turnips, and parsnips were staples. They also knew about cabbage, lentils, and several berries and fruits that appeared in short growing seasons. When the English arrived on the East Coast, they found the Indians cultivating and eating an astonishing number of foods. Even discounting the seafood and game, the land was a vegetarian's paradise. But the newcomers apparently perceived the strange foods not as nourishment but as cultural shock.

Many of the settlers adopted the Indians' methods of preparing bread from corn, the principal grain of North America. But ground nuts (not peanuts, which came later from Brazil), squash, cranberries, gourds, watermelons, muskmelons, some kinds of beans or peas, tomatoes, artichokes, garden peppers, and sunflowers? How exotic! A whole new shopping list. In Florida and South Carolina, the Spanish found the Indians growing sweet potatoes; but it is doubtful that they were being used in Virginia when Jamestown was settled.

We must bear in mind that many of the settlers were not farmers at all; indeed, many of them wanted to get on with searching for gold, and some were eager to find a passage to the South Sea. By comparison, the Indians were superdomestic, with their cleared lands, systematic cultivation, methods of food preservation, and some cooking techniques different from those of the Europeans; for example, the Indians roasted their meat over an open fire, as opposed to the Englishmen's straight meat-boiling method.

It would appear that the settlers were slow in picking up on the Indians' expertise in matters of farming and food storage. In the process of becoming acclimatized, many starved, and some of that may have been unnecessary. True, clearing the land was a formidable and time-consuming undertaking. But an additional factor pointed up by Hess was that some of the Englishmen who comprised the first settlers were unaccustomed to doing manual labor and refused to do so, even to feed themselves.

Although to the immigrants this land was a forbidding wilderness, in the midst of which they felt helpless, the Indians knew the Atlantic Coast as a place of plenty. Just for the picking were raspberries, blackberries, whortleberries, gooseberries, huckleberries, strawberries, plums, cherries, crabapples, persimmons, and mulberries. The Indians dried them for winter food. The Gulf Coast natives had an even greater variety of fruits, owing to the semitropical growing conditions. Nuts could be stored, too, and were plentiful: hickory nuts, pecans, walnuts, butternuts, hazelnuts, chinkapins, and chestnuts.

Fibrous plants were utilized by the Indians for making baskets and textiles, but, again, the settlers failed to emulate them. Suffering marked the years while they familiarized themselves with the climate, the soil, the strange crops, and the habits of their new neighbors. They relied heavily on supplies from Europe, but each supply ship brought more people, thereby continually straining the economy.

The Indians' hostility was aroused as the newcomers, desperate for cropland, encroached on their clearings. Self-sufficiency was hampered, too, by the colonists' crude farming implements; it was several years before plows and other tools became available to ease and speed the labor.

As time passed, the colonists put their roots down more solidly and upgraded their hand-to-mouth existence. Food consumed depended on location: those who stayed in the coastal regions enjoyed the most variety, while frontiersmen had much less from which to choose. The average family, the equivalent of today's middle class, ate rather well compared with their European counterparts. Some form of cornbread accompanied the typical one-dish meal, which was cooked in a pot in the fireplace. Into the pot went such meat as was available plus whatever vegetables were in season. In summer, small game was used because of the danger of heat spoilage with large carcasses. Such a stew was, and is, a close relative of the French peasant's pot-au-feu, or "pot on the fire."

Plantation life evolved in Virginia Tidewater region, and there diet differed according to social class, the landowners eating high on the hog, while the poor made do with grits, peas, and salt pork. Entertaining became an art, as the wealthy planters vied with one another in the lavishness of their hospitality. Fine food mixed with good conversation marked the mid-afternoon dinner. Menus of the day list a profusion of meats and sweets, the assumption being that the vegetables bearing in the garden found their way to the table with no need to list them.

While well-to-do Virginia ladies built a graceful society patterned after the English country life, their Puritan women counterparts in New England busied themselves soberly with quilting and cornhusking bees. It would be impossible to treat the differing life styles between North and South during the country's formative period without saying straight out that Southerners who had acquired wealth replaced the serfs they had left behind with African laborers. Without these laborers to perform the menial domestic work, Southerners would have had as little time for frivolity as their Puritan brethren.

There is no doubt that the diet of the blacks of the period was poor. For the most part, they made do with salt meat, many times using only a little of it to flavor a vegetable main dish of greens or beans with pot likker and cornbread. But it seems to me that we err in defining the foodways of blacks with the limiting term "soul food," for we thereby exclude the poor white people who subsisted on the same diet.

One of the triumphs of Southern vegetable cookery is turnip greens; the dish recognizes no social or ethnic barriers. It was on the menu when President Jimmy Carter's son, Chip, visited Memphis and attended a dinner prepared by Mamie Gammon, a restaurateur and caterer. She, like most Southern cooks, seasons any kind of greens with salt-cured pork.

Turnip Greens

According to Mrs. Gammon, "Salt pork is not cured as long as it was years ago. But you can make up for that. Buy fat meat, cover it with salt to draw the moisture, and set it aside, covered and unrefrigerated. To use it, wash off the salt and boil the meat almost done. Then add your washed greens, cover the pot, and cook an hour or more. Add a red pepper pod, salt, and a little sugar. If necessary, add some bacon drippings toward the end."

Salt pork as seasoning is a common denominator in much of the South's vegetable cookery and is one of the main factors that sets it apart from that of other regions. Beans and peas, cooked Southern style, can taste remarkably meaty, and such a dish is almost always accompanied by cornbread. So it was hardly news to Southerners when nutritionists announced several years ago that beans or peas, eaten in combination with grain, put a near-perfect form of protein into the diet. It is these combinations that have sustained the South in good times and bad. Poor nutrition enters the picture only if and when the diet is lacking in fresh raw fruits and vegetables.

The upper South seems to prefer dried limas or pinto beans with cornbread. The deep South leans to black-eyed peas or red beans with rice. All over the South, though, New Year's Eve is the time to eat "hoppin' John." In its simplest form, hoppin' John is black-eyed peas soaked and cooked with salt pork, then combined with rice and simmered to make a moist, flaky consistency. Creole-style hoppin' John is made by adding tomatoes, green peppers, and onions to the peas. It is served over hot rice without mixing.

This variation, a black-eyed pea jambalaya from Louisiana, is an old one. "Ham or bacon may be added if . . . " Sometimes there was neither, in which case one hoped to season the dish with some bacon drippings.

Black-Eyed Pea Jambalaya

1 pound fresh black-eyed
   peas
1 onion, minced
½ clove garlic, minced
1 quart water

Salt to taste
2 cups regular rice, cooked
Chopped parsley
Green onion tops

Combine peas, onion, garlic, and water in a medium saucepan. Bring to a boil. Lower heat, and let simmer until beans are tender. Add salt. Add cooked rice, stirring until bean mixture coats rice. Add parsley and onion tops. Ham or bacon may be added if available. Yield: 8 servings.

Note: The jambalaya may just as well be made with dried peas, if they are soaked overnight. One pound dried peas, soaked, will make more, so double up on the remaining ingredients except the rice. Make that about 3 cups regular rice, cooked.

Southern cooks understand vegetables better than anybody, or so it seems to me. A dish of vegetables served up in the South is not merely an accompaniment but an entity. Cut fresh corn, for example, is not simply heated and buttered; it is lovingly fried or stewed with careful seasonings or perhaps made into a tender and creamy corn pudding. Okra, that dietary watershed between North and South, has been a staple since the seeds were brought to this country on slave ships from Africa. Many in the South still call it by its Bantu name of gumbo or gombo, which can be a source of confusion at times. The unique soup-stew called "gumbo" may or not contain okra, but Southerners can always fry or stew the okra that does not find its way into a gumbo.

Then the perennial green beans, Southern style, bear little resemblance to green beans outside the territory. We do not apologize for cooking them half a day, and if we are told the vitamin content is flowing out of them, we cheerfully promise to eat a salad to make up for it.

The vegetable section of this book is very special to me; I believe it represents and illustrates the Southern temperament better than any other category of recipes—with perhaps the exception of desserts.

Vegetables and Side Dishes

Asparagus Shortcake

2½ cups all-purpose flour
½ teaspoon salt
2½ teaspoons baking powder
½ cup shortening
½ to ⅔ cup milk
3 cups water
1 teaspoon salt
1½ pounds fresh asparagus, cut
    into 1-inch pieces
½ cup butter or margarine, divided
¼ cup all-purpose flour
½ teaspoon salt
2 tablespoons butter or margarine,
    softened
2 hard-cooked eggs, chopped

Combine 2½ cups flour, ½ teaspoon salt, and baking powder; mix well. Cut in shortening with pastry blender until mixture resembles coarse meal. Add enough milk to form a soft workable dough. Turn dough out on a floured surface; knead lightly and shape into a ball. Press dough evenly into a greased 9-inch cakepan. Bake at 425° about 20 minutes or until done.

Combine water and 1 teaspoon salt in a large saucepan; bring to a boil. Add asparagus; reduce heat, and simmer until asparagus is crisp-tender. Drain asparagus, reserving 2 cups cooking liquid.

Melt ¼ cup butter in a heavy saucepan over low heat; add ¼ cup flour, stirring until smooth. Cook 1 minute, stirring constantly. Gradually add reserved cooking liquid; cook over medium heat, stirring constantly, until thickened and bubbly. Stir in remaining ½ teaspoon salt and ¼ cup butter; stir in asparagus. Cook until thoroughly heated.

Remove shortcake from pan and slice in half horizontally; spread cut sides with 2 tablespoons softened butter. Place bottom layer on serving platter. Spoon half the asparagus mixture over bottom layer of shortcake; top with remaining layer of shortcake, cut side down. Spoon remaining asparagus mixture over shortcake, and sprinkle with eggs. Yield: 6 to 8 servings.

Asparagus Maltaise

½ cup butter or margarine
3 egg yolks
1 tablespoon orange juice
1 tablespoon lemon juice
⅛ teaspoon salt
⅛ teaspoon white pepper (optional)
Grated rind of ½ orange
Grated rind of ½ lemon
2 (10-ounce) packages frozen
    asparagus spears

Heat butter in small saucepan until bubbly; do not brown.

Combine next 5 ingredients in container of electric blender; blend until thick and lemon-colored. Add melted butter in a slow, steady stream, and continue to process until thick. Stir in grated rind. Place container of blender in a pan of warm, not hot, water while cooking asparagus. (Sauce cannot be reheated.)

Cook asparagus according to package directions; drain. Place spears in warm serving bowl; top with sauce mixture. Serve immediately. Yield: 5 to 6 servings.

Fried Green Apples

A favorite with fried country ham.

2 tablespoons shortening
2 tablespoons butter or margarine
6 cups sliced green apples
1 cup sugar
Dash of ground cinnamon

Heat shortening and butter in a large skillet; add apples, sugar, and cinnamon. Cook over low heat, stirring occasionally, for 20 minutes or until apples are browned and tender. Yield: 6 servings.

Alcachofras

(Artichokes)

4 artichokes
1 cup soft breadcrumbs
2 cloves garlic, minced
2 tablespoons shredded cheese
2 sprigs fresh parsley
2 tablespoons olive oil
½ cup water

Wash artichokes well, and trim stem even with base. Slice about ¾ inch off top of artichoke, and remove discolored leaves at base. Trim off thorny leaf tips.

Combine remaining ingredients except water; mix well. Sprinkle breadcrumb mixture behind leaves of artichokes. Pour water into a large skillet; add artichokes. Cover tightly, and bring to a boil; reduce heat and simmer 1 hour, or until leaves pull out easily. Remove artichokes from water, and arrange on a serving platter. Yield: 4 servings.

Baked Beans

1 pound dried navy beans
¼ pound salt pork, sliced
1 medium onion
4 whole cloves
1½ to 2 teaspoons salt
½ teaspoon pepper
¼ cup molasses
¼ cup catsup
½ cup firmly packed brown sugar

Wash beans well; place in a 2-quart bean pot or deep casserole. Cover with cold water, and soak overnight; do not drain. Push salt pork into center of beans. Stud onion with cloves; push onion into beans. Stir in salt, pepper, molasses, catsup, and brown sugar. Pour in boiling water to barely cover. Cover and bake at 300° for 3 to 5 hours, or until very tender; add boiling water once or twice during baking time, if necessary. Yield: 8 to 10 servings.

Pinto Beans

2 cups dried pinto beans
1 teaspoon salt
4 cloves garlic, minced
1 medium onion, sliced
¼ pound salt pork, sliced or diced
2 sprigs fresh coriander (cilantro)
    or ¼ teaspoon dried
    coriander leaves

Wash beans and place in a Dutch oven; cover with cold water and soak overnight. The next day add salt, garlic, onion, and pork. Simmer for approximately 4 hours, uncovered, until tender. Stir occasionally, and add more water during cooking as necessary. Add coriander during last 30 minutes of cooking. Yield: 6 servings.

Note: For special flavor, follow recipe above, but substitute 1 (12-ounce) can of beer for part of the water during cooking.

Red Beans And Rice

1 pound dried red beans
½ pound salt pork, sliced
1 onion, chopped
½ green pepper, chopped
1 small meaty hambone
Pepper to taste
Cayenne pepper to taste
1 bay leaf
1 tablespoon minced fresh parsley
1 clove garlic, minced
Dash of ground thyme
Dash of basil leaves
1 tablespoon butter or margarine,
    softened (optional)
1 tablespoon all-purpose flour
    (optional)
Salt (optional)
4 cups hot cooked regular rice

Wash beans; soak beans overnight in cold water to cover; drain.

Fry salt pork in a Dutch oven until done. Add onion and green pepper, and sauté until tender. Add beans and next 8 ingredients. Add enough cold water to measure 1 inch above beans. Cover and cook over low heat 2⅓ to 3 hours, stirring occasionally.

If beans need additional thickening, combine butter and flour, mixing well; stir butter mixture into beans during last 30 minutes of cooking. Add salt, if desired. Serve over rice. Yield: 6 to 8 servings.

Frijoles Refritos

1 pound dried pinto beans
½ teaspoon soda
1 small clove garlic
¼ pound salt-cured pork
1 medium onion, chopped
1 to 1½ teaspoons salt
1 teaspoon vinegar
¼ cup bacon drippings
1 cup (4 ounces) grated mild
    Cheddar or Monterey
    Jack cheese

Wash and pick over beans; place in a heavy 3- or 4-quart saucepan. Add soda; cover with cold water and let stand overnight. Do not drain. Add garlic and pork. Cover and cook over medium heat about 3 hours or until tender. Add boiling water from time to time during cooking. Water should be at least 1 inch deep when beans are done.

Remove from heat; add onion, salt, and vinegar. Heat drippings in heavy skillet; add beans and fry over medium heat, mashing with a potato masher and turning to prevent sticking. Fry for 12 to 15 minutes; stir in cheese and serve hot. Yield: 6 to 8 servings.

Shuck Beans

4 cups dried shuck beans
½ pound thick sliced bacon, cut into
    1-inch pieces
2 teaspoons salt

Wash beans several times; cover with cold water and soak overnight. Drain beans. Place bacon in a large kettle; add beans. Cover beans with water; bring to a boil. Reduce heat; cover and simmer about 4 hours or until tender. Add salt; continue to cook, uncovered, 2 hours or until most of liquid evaporates. Yield: 10 to 12 servings.

Old-Fashioned Green Beans And Corn

1 quart fresh green beans, cut
    into 1-inch pieces
2 ounces salt pork
½ to 1 teaspoon salt
¼ teaspoon pepper
4 ears fresh corn

Combine beans, salt pork, salt, and pepper in a large Dutch oven; add enough water to almost cover beans. Bring to a boil; cover, reduce heat, and simmer about 30 minutes or until beans are tender. Add corn; cover and simmer 10 minutes. Transfer beans and corn to separate serving bowls. Yield: 4 servings.

Southern-Cooked Green Beans

½ pound salt-cured bacon or
    hog jowl
1 quart water
3 quarts fresh green beans, cut
    into 1½-inch pieces
1 onion (optional)
1 red pepper (optional)
1 to 3 teaspoons salt

Combine bacon and water in a heavy 4-quart Dutch oven. Cover and simmer 30 minutes. Add green beans, onion, and red pepper, if desired; add enough cold water to cover. Cover and bring to a boil; reduce heat and simmer 3 to 4 hours, stirring occasionally. Add salt to taste during last hour of cooking. Lid may be removed during the last hour of cooking to allow liquid to cook down, if desired. Yield: 10 to 12 servings.

Saucy Green Bean Bake

4 cups fresh green beans, cut
    into 1-inch pieces
½ cup chopped onion
⅓ cup chopped green pepper
1 clove garlic, minced
2 tablespoons melted butter or
    margarine
1 (8-ounce) can tomato sauce
2 tablespoons chopped pimiento
1 tablespoon prepared mustard
¼ teaspoon salt
¾ cup (3 ounces) shredded process
    American cheese

Cook beans, uncovered, in boiling salted water 2 to 3 minutes; then cover and cook 20 to 30 more minutes or until tender. Drain and set aside.

Combine onion, green pepper, garlic, and butter in a medium skillet; cook over low heat until tender. Remove from heat; stir in tomato sauce, pimiento, mustard, and salt. Stir in beans, and spoon mixture into a greased 1-quart baking dish.

Cover and bake at 350° for 25 minutes. Remove cover, and sprinkle casserole with cheese. Bake 5 minutes or until cheese melts. Yield: 4 to 6 servings.

Cheese-Topped Green Beans

1 pound fresh green beans, cut
    into 1-inch pieces
¼ cup dry onion soup mix
1 cup water
3 tablespoons melted butter or
    margarine
⅓ cup toasted slivered almonds
3 tablespoons grated Parmesan
    cheese
½ teaspoon paprika

Combine green beans, onion soup mix, and water; cover and cook over low heat 20 to 30 minutes, or until beans are tender. Drain and spoon into a serving dish. Add butter, almonds, and cheese; toss lightly. Sprinkle with paprika. Yield: 4 to 6 servings.

Lima Bean Casserole

2 cups cooked lima beans
3 slices bacon
1 medium onion, chopped
2 cups canned tomatoes, chopped
½ teaspoon salt
¼ teaspoon pepper
2 slices bread, cubed
¼ cup grated Parmesan cheese

Place lima beans in a buttered 1½-quart casserole. Fry bacon until crisp. Drain and crumble bacon; reserve drippings in skillet. Sauté onion in reserved drippings until transparent; spoon onion and drippings over lima beans. Stir in tomatoes, salt, and pepper. Top with bread cubes; sprinkle with cheese. Bake at 350° for 20 to 25 minutes, or until heated thoroughly and lightly browned. Yield: 6 to 8 servings.

Fresh Lima Beans

4 cups fresh lima beans
1 tablespoon butter or margarine
2 tablespoons milk
2 tablespoons half-and-half

Wash beans. Cook beans with butter in boiling salted water until tender; drain beans. Add milk and half-and-half; heat thoroughly. Yield: 6 to 8 servings.

Beets In Sour Cream

2 (16-ounce) cans whole beets, diced and undrained
1 teaspoon salt
1 (8-ounce) carton commercial sour cream
1 bunch green onions, chopped

Bring beets and salt to a boil in a medium saucepan; reduce heat and simmer until thoroughly heated. Drain. Transfer beets to serving dish. Spread sour cream over top of beets, and sprinkle with onion. Yield: 6 to 8 servings.

Easter Beets And Eggs

1 (16-ounce) can sliced beets
6 hard-cooked eggs
¼ cup vinegar
2 (3- to 4-inch) cinnamon sticks
½ teaspoon whole cloves
¼ teaspoon salt
1 teaspoon sugar
Vinegar

Drain beets, reserving ¼ cup liquid in saucepan. Place beets and eggs in quart jar.

Combine reserved beet liquid, ¼ cup vinegar, cinnamon sticks, cloves, salt, and sugar in a small saucepan; bring to a boil. Pour liquid mixture over beets and eggs; fill jar to top with vinegar. Refrigerate, and use within 1 week. Yield: 6 servings.

Beets With Chutney

8 to 10 small beets, cooked and peeled, or 1 (16-ounce) can small whole beets, drained
2 tablespoons vinegar
2 tablespoons honey
¼ cup chutney

Combine all ingredients, mixing well. To serve cold, chill several hours or overnight. To serve hot, heat thoroughly in a small saucepan. Yield: 4 servings.

Broccoli With Pasta

½ pound bacon
3 cloves garlic
1 (10-ounce) package frozen chopped broccoli or 2 cups chopped fresh broccoli
2 cups shell macaroni
1½ cups (6 ounces) grated Romano cheese
¼ teaspoon pepper

Fry bacon until crisp; drain and crumble bacon, reserving ½ cup drippings. Sauté garlic until golden brown in reserved drippings; discard garlic and set drippings aside. Cook broccoli in boiling salted water just until tender; drain broccoli, reserving cooking liquid. Add enough water to cooking liquid to measure 2 cups; bring to a boil in a large saucepan. Add macaroni and cook until tender; drain. Combine macaroni, broccoli, bacon, reserved drippings, cheese, and pepper; mix well. Place mixture in an ungreased 2-quart casserole. Bake at 350° for 10 minutes, or until thoroughly heated. Yield: 4 servings.

Broccoli-Mushroom Casserole

> 2 (10-ounce) packages frozen
>   chopped broccoli or 4 cups
>   chopped fresh broccoli
> 1 pound fresh mushrooms, sliced
> 2 tablespoons melted butter or
>   margarine
> White Sauce (recipe follows)
> 1½ cups (6 ounces) shredded
>   Cheddar cheese
> Paprika

Cook broccoli in small amount boiling salted water just until tender; drain and set aside. Sauté mushrooms in butter until tender; drain mushrooms. Combine White Sauce, cheese, and mushrooms. Place broccoli in greased shallow 2-quart casserole; spoon White Sauce mixture over broccoli. Sprinkle with paprika; bake at 325° for 20 minutes. Yield: 6 to 8 servings.

White Sauce:

> ¼ cup butter or margarine
> ¼ cup all-purpose flour
> 2 cups milk
> ½ teaspoon salt
> ¼ teaspoon pepper

Melt butter in a heavy saucepan over low heat; add flour, stirring until smooth. Cook 1 minute, stirring constantly. Gradually add milk; cook over low heat, stirring constantly, until thickened and bubbly. Stir in salt and pepper. Yield: about 2 cups.

Sesame Broccoli

> 1 pound fresh broccoli spears or 1
>   (10-ounce) package frozen
>   broccoli spears
> 3 tablespoons butter or margarine
> 1 tablespoon sesame seeds
> ½ teaspoon salt

Cook broccoli in small amount of boiling salted water just until tender; drain. Place broccoli in a warm serving bowl. Melt butter in a small skillet; add sesame seeds and sauté 2 minutes. Pour sesame mixture over broccoli. Sprinkle with salt and serve. Yield: 4 servings.

Brussels Sprouts With Carrots

> ½ pound fresh brussels sprouts or
>   1 (10-ounce) package
>   brussels sprouts
> ½ cup chicken stock
> 1 cup water
> 1 pound carrots, cut into 2-inch
>   strips
> 2 tablespoons butter or margarine
> ¼ teaspoon ground ginger
> ½ teaspoon salt

Cook brussels sprouts in boiling chicken stock 8 minutes, or until barely tender; drain. Bring water to a boil; add carrots and cook until barely tender; drain. Melt butter in large skillet; add cooked vegetables and remaining ingredients. Cover, and cook over low heat 10 minutes or until heated through, shaking skillet occasionally to blend flavors. Yield: 6 servings.

Russian Cabbage Rolls

> 2 heads cabbage
> 1 cup uncooked regular rice
> ⅓ cup boiling water
> 1 pound lean ground beef
> 1 pound boneless pork loin, ground
> 1½ large onions, finely chopped
> 2 eggs
> 2 teaspoons salt
> Dash of pepper
> 1 (16-ounce) can sauerkraut
> Salt and pepper
> 2 (8-ounce) cans tomato sauce
> 1 (16-ounce) can whole tomatoes
> 1 onion, sliced
> 2 cloves garlic, chopped
> ⅛ teaspoon caraway seeds

Add cabbage to boiling salted water in a Dutch oven; reduce heat, cover, and cook over low heat until leaves are tender. Drain cabbage, reserving ¼ cup cooking liquid. Remove large leaves from cabbage; chop remaining cabbage and place in a Dutch oven.

Cook rice in ⅓ cup boiling water for 5 minutes or until approximately half cooked. Combine rice, meat, chopped onion, eggs, 2 teaspoons salt, and dash of pepper in a large mixing bowl; mix well.

Place a small amount of meat mixture on each cabbage leaf; roll up, turning edges in. Place cabbage rolls on top of chopped cabbage in Dutch oven. Spread sauerkraut over cabbage rolls, and sprinkle with salt and pepper; top with tomato sauce.

Layer tomatoes, sliced onion, and garlic over cabbage rolls; sprinkle with caraway seeds, salt, and pepper. Pour reserved cooking liquid over cabbage mixture.

Bring mixture to a boil; cover, reduce heat, and simmer for 1½ hours. Yield: 15 servings.

Coleslaw

    4 cups shredded cabbage
    1 cup finely grated carrot
    ¼ cup mayonnaise or salad dressing
    2 teaspoons lemon juice
    2 tablespoons sugar
    1 tablespoon evaporated milk
    Green pepper rings

Combine first 6 ingredients; mix well. Cover and chill thoroughly. Garnish with green pepper rings. Yield: 4 to 5 servings.

Note: Red cabbage may be substituted for 1 cup green cabbage.

Old-Fashioned Coleslaw

    10 cups shredded cabbage
    2 cups shredded carrots
    ½ cup sweet pickle salad cubes
    ½ cup mayonnaise or salad dressing
    ½ teaspoon salt
    ½ teaspoon sugar
    ½ teaspoon dry mustard
    ½ teaspoon pepper

Combine cabbage, carrots, and pickles; set aside. Combine remaining ingredients; mix well. Spoon over cabbage mixture and toss gently. Chill until serving time. Yield: 12 to 15 servings.

Tangy Coleslaw

    2 medium heads cabbage, shredded
        (about 4 quarts)
    3 large carrots, grated (about 3 cups)
    1 large green pepper, chopped
        (about 1½ cups)
    3 cups sugar
    1½ cups white vinegar
    1½ teaspoons salt
    1½ tablespoons celery seeds
    1½ teaspoons mustard seeds

Combine cabbage, carrot, and green pepper in a large bowl; set aside.

Combine sugar, vinegar, and salt in a medium saucepan; bring to a boil. Boil syrup 2 to 3 minutes; cool. Stir celery seeds and mustard seeds into syrup. Pour syrup over cabbage mixture; stir well. Cover and refrigerate 24 hours. Yield: about 5 quarts.

Note: Slaw may be stored several weeks in refrigerator.

Scalloped Cheese And Cabbage

1 medium head cabbage, shredded
2 cups (8 ounces) shredded
    Cheddar cheese
1 (10¾-ounce) can cream of celery
    soup, undiluted
Buttered breadcrumbs

Cook cabbage in boiling water for 7 minutes; drain well. Layer cabbage alternately with cheese in a greased 2-quart casserole. Pour soup over cabbage and cheese; top with buttered breadcrumbs. Bake at 425° for 15 minutes, or until bubbling and breadcrumbs are browned. Yield: 8 servings.

Sweet And Sour Cabbage

¼ pound salt pork, sliced
1 head cabbage, cut into small
    wedges
2 cups water
¼ cup firmly packed brown sugar
2 tablespoons vinegar
½ to 1 teaspoon salt
½ teaspoon pepper

Fry salt pork in Dutch oven until done. Add cabbage and water to pork; cover and cook over low heat about 25 minutes, or until tender. Add remaining ingredients, mixing well; simmer over low heat 10 minutes. Yield: 6 to 8 servings.

Gingered Carrots

1 pound small carrots, peeled and
    cut into julienne strips
1½ cups water
1 teaspoon salt
5 tablespoons sugar, divided
3 tablespoons melted butter or
    margarine
1 to 2 teaspoons grated fresh ginger

Combine carrots, water, salt, and 2 tablespoons sugar in a medium saucepan; bring to a boil. Cover; reduce heat, and simmer until carrots are crisp-tender, about 10 minutes. Drain; stir in butter, remaining sugar, and ginger. Pour into a buttered, shallow 1½-quart casserole; bake at 300° about 20 minutes or until carrots are glazed, stirring gently once or twice. Yield: 4 to 6 servings.

Carrot Ring

15 carrots, peeled and sliced (about
    2 pounds)
8 hard-cooked eggs
1 green pepper
1½ tablespoons finely grated onion
½ cup chopped fresh parsley
¼ cup melted butter or margarine
1½ to 2 teaspoons salt
½ teaspoon pepper
½ teaspoon paprika
Chopped fresh parsley
Cooked green peas or broccoli
    (optional)

Cook carrots in boiling salted water until tender; drain. Combine carrots, eggs, and green pepper in container of food processor; process until finely chopped using chopping blade. Stir in onion, ½ cup chopped parsley, butter, salt, pepper, and paprika. Pour mixture into a buttered 6-cup oven-proof ring mold. Bake at 350° for 25 to 30 minutes. Unmold onto warm platter; garnish with additional chopped parsley. Fill center of mold with green peas or broccoli, if desired. Yield: 8 to 10 servings.

Cauliflower Polonaise

1 head cauliflower
½ cup soft breadcrumbs
¼ cup melted butter or margarine
Juice of ½ lemon
1 teaspoon salt
¼ teaspoon pepper

Wash cauliflower, and remove large outer leaves. Cook, covered, in a small amount of boiling salted water about 20 minutes, or just until tender; drain. Remove to warm serving platter.

Sauté breadcrumbs lightly in butter in a small saucepan until browned. Stir in lemon juice, salt, and pepper. Sprinkle breadcrumb mixture over cauliflower just before serving. Yield: 4 servings.

Steamed Cauliflower With Green Pepper Sauce

1 large head cauliflower
1 small green pepper, chopped
¼ cup butter or margarine
2 tablespoons all-purpose flour
1½ cups milk
½ teaspoon salt
¼ teaspoon cayenne pepper
1 cup (4 ounces) shredded Cheddar cheese

Place cauliflower on rack in large Dutch oven. Fill pan with water to just below level of cauliflower. Bring water to a boil; cover and cook over medium heat about 20 minutes, or until tender. Remove from heat.

Melt butter in small saucepan; sauté green pepper in melted butter until tender. Add flour, stirring until smooth. Cook 1 minute, stirring constantly. Gradually add milk; cook over medium heat, stirring constantly, until thickened and bubbly. Add remaining ingredients, stirring until cheese melts. Transfer cauliflower to serving dish; pour sauce over cauliflower. Yield: about 6 to 8 servings.

Braised Celery With Carrot Sauce

3 hearts of celery (whole bunches minus outer stalks)
¼ cup butter or margarine
2 cups chicken broth
½ cup shredded carrot
1½ teaspoons salt
1½ teaspoons sugar
½ teaspoon white pepper

Cut tops from celery, leaving bunches about 6 inches long; trim any remaining leaves. Do not separate stalks. Cut stalks lengthwise into quarters. Melt butter in electric skillet or other large skillet. Add remaining ingredients; cover and cook over low heat until celery is crisp-tender. Remove celery to warm serving dish, reserving liquid in skillet; boil liquid until reduced by half. Pour liquid over celery; serve hot. Yield: 8 servings.

Tarragon Celery

A different cooked vegetable dish starring an old salad favorite.

3 cups sliced celery, diagonally sliced ⅜ inch thick
1 (10¾-ounce) can chicken broth, undiluted
¼ cup pale dry sherry
1 teaspoon dried tarragon leaves, crushed
Dash of freshly ground pepper
Butter or margarine

Combine first 5 ingredients in a medium saucepan; bring to a boil. Reduce heat and simmer about 8 to 10 minutes, or until crisp-tender. Drain and add butter; stir gently over low heat until butter melts. Yield: 4 to 6 servings.

Corn Fancy

2 cups cream-style corn
½ cup vegetable oil
½ teaspoon garlic salt
1 (2-ounce) jar chopped pimiento
4 eggs, well beaten
½ cup corn muffin mix
1½ cups (6 ounces) shredded mild
   Cheddar cheese

Combine first 6 ingredients, mixing well. Pour into a greased 1½-quart casserole. Bake at 300° for 30 minutes. Sprinkle with cheese; bake 15 minutes longer. Yield: 8 servings.

Corn Maquechou

3 to 4 tablespoons butter or
   margarine
2 cups fresh corn cut from cob
½ green pepper, chopped
1 large onion, chopped
1 large tomato, chopped
½ teaspoon sugar
½ to 1 cup milk
Hot sauce to taste (optional)
Salt and pepper to taste

Melt butter in heavy pan; add corn and cook over low heat for 10 minutes, stirring frequently. Add green pepper, onion, tomato, sugar, and ½ cup milk; stir well. Cook over low heat, stirring frequently for about 30 minutes or until done, adding more milk if necessary. Season. Yield: 4 to 6 servings.

Belmont Corn Pie

Pastry for double-crust 9-inch
   pie, divided
6 ears fresh corn
3 medium potatoes, diced
½ cup melted butter or margarine
1 teaspoon salt
¼ teaspoon pepper
6 hard-cooked eggs, sliced
About 2 cups milk

Roll half of pastry to ⅛-inch thickness; fit into a 9-inch piepan. Cut corn from cob; cook corn and potatoes in small amount of boiling water until barely tender; drain. Stir in butter, salt, and pepper.

Spoon half the corn mixture into piepan; top with half the sliced eggs. Repeat layers. Pour in enough milk to cover entire mixture.

Roll out remaining pastry to ⅛-inch thickness; carefully place over pie, leaving 1-inch rim beyond edge of pan. Seal and flute edges; cut slits in top for steam to escape.

Bake at 450° for 15 minutes. Reduce heat to 350°, and bake about 40 minutes. Serve immediately. Yield: 6 to 8 servings.

Corn Pudding Supreme

2 tablespoons melted butter or
   margarine
1½ cups milk
2 tablespoons all-purpose flour
1 teaspoon salt
1 tablespoon soy sauce
2 cups cream-style corn
1 egg, beaten
Buttered soft breadcrumbs

Combine butter, milk, flour, salt, soy sauce, corn, and egg in a medium mixing bowl; mix well. Pour into a greased 1½-quart casserole, and top with buttered breadcrumbs. Bake at 350° for 20 to 30 minutes or until firm. Yield: 6 servings.

Cucumbers And Onions

4 large cucumbers, sliced
¼ cup salt
2 medium onions, sliced
1 quart vinegar
1¼ cups sugar
1 cup water

Place cucumbers in a large bowl; sprinkle salt over cucumbers and add ice water to cover. Let stand 1 hour; drain, and add onion to drained cucumber.

Combine remaining ingredients in a large saucepan; bring to a boil, and boil 5 minutes. Pour hot mixture over vegetables. Refrigerate; use within 24 hours. Yield: 10 to 12 servings.

Oklahoma Cheese Dumplings

    2 (16-ounce) cartons small curd
        cottage cheese
    1 egg
    2 tablespoons finely chopped onion
    1 tablespoon half-and-half
    1 teaspoon salt
    ½ teaspoon pepper
    3 eggs, beaten
    1½ teaspoons salt
    ¼ cup plus 2 tablespoons milk
    3¾ to 4½ cups all-purpose flour
    2½ quarts water
    2 teaspoons salt
    Egg Topping (recipe follows)
    ¼ cup butter or margarine
    6 slices bread, cubed

Combine cheese, 1 egg, onion, half-and-half, 1 teaspoon salt, and pepper, mixing well; set aside.

Combine 3 eggs, 1½ teaspoons salt, and milk in a large mixing bowl. Stir in enough flour to make a stiff dough. Turn dough out on a lightly floured surface. Roll dough ⅛ inch thick; cut into 4½-inch squares. Place a heaping tablespoon of cheese mixture in center of each square; bring opposite corners together, and seal.

Combine water and 2 teaspoons salt in a large Dutch oven; bring to a boil. Drop dumplings into boiling water; boil gently for 5 minutes, or until dumplings are cooked. Drain; arrange dumplings in a large serving bowl. Spoon Egg Topping over dumplings.

Melt butter in a large skillet. Add bread cubes, and sauté until browned; sprinkle over Egg Topping. Yield: 8 servings.

Egg Topping:

    6 eggs
    1½ cups half-and-half
    1 teaspoon salt
    ¼ cup butter or margarine

Combine eggs, half-and-half, and salt; mix well. Melt butter in a large skillet; pour egg mixture into skillet. Cook over low heat, stirring gently, until done. Yield: about 8 servings.

Eggplant Casserole

    1 large eggplant
    ¼ cup vegetable oil or softened
        butter or margarine
    4 large tomatoes, peeled, sliced, and
        divided
    ¼ pound (about 32) soda crackers,
        crumbled and divided
    1⅓ cups (⅓ pound) shredded
        Cheddar cheese, divided

Peel eggplant and slice into ⅓-inch slices; arrange on greased baking sheet, and brush slices with oil. Bake at 350° for 15 minutes. Remove from oven; layer half the eggplant and tomato slices in a greased 2-quart baking dish. Sprinkle with half the cracker crumbs and half the cheese. Repeat layers using remaining ingredients. Bake at 350° about 30 minutes, or until lightly browned and bubbly. Yield: 8 servings.

Note: One (16-ounce) can of tomatoes, drained, may be substituted for fresh.

Eggplant Fritters

1 small eggplant, peeled and sliced
2 teaspoons vinegar
1 egg, beaten
½ teaspoon salt
½ teaspoon baking powder
¼ cup all-purpose flour

Cook eggplant in boiling water to cover about 10 minutes, or until tender. Gently stir in vinegar; drain immediately by pressing eggplant between paper towels. Mash eggplant and let cool. Beat in remaining ingredients. (Batter will be thin.)

Drop batter by tablespoonfuls onto a hot, lightly greased griddle or skillet. Cook until browned; turn to brown other side. Yield: 8 to 10 servings.

Shrimp-Stuffed Creole Eggplant

2 medium eggplant
1 large onion or 5 small green
    onions, chopped
½ cup minced celery tops
1 pound raw shrimp, peeled and
    deveined, or 2 (4½-ounce)
    cans shrimp, drained
2 cloves garlic, minced
2 tablespoons melted butter or
    margarine
5 to 7 slices stale bread
1 cup water
4 sprigs fresh parsley, chopped, or
    ¼ cup parsley flakes
1 teaspoon salt
⅛ teaspoon freshly ground black
    pepper
⅛ teaspoon red pepper
2 eggs, beaten
⅓ cup grated Parmesan cheese
Tomato Sauce (recipe follows)

Cook eggplant in boiling water about 15 minutes or until almost tender. Remove from

water and let cool. Cut each in half lengthwise. Carefully scoop out pulp, leaving shells intact; chop pulp.

Sauté onion, celery, shrimp, and garlic in butter until onion is clear and shrimp is tender.

Soak bread in water; squeeze out any excess water. Add bread, parsley, eggplant pulp, salt, and pepper to shrimp mixture; mix well. Cool slightly; then add beaten eggs, stirring well.

Arrange eggplant shells in a shallow baking dish; stuff each with shrimp mixture, and sprinkle with cheese. Bake at 400° for 20 to 25 minutes. Top with Tomato Sauce. To serve, cut into halves. Yield: 8 servings.

Tomato Sauce:

1 large onion, finely chopped
2 stalks celery, chopped
1 clove garlic, minced
3 tablespoons vegetable oil
1 bay leaf
1 teaspoon salt
½ teaspoon sugar
¾ teaspoon dried thyme leaves
¼ teaspoon red pepper
1 (16-ounce) can Italian-style
    tomatoes, undrained and
    chopped
4 to 6 sprigs fresh parsley, chopped,
    or ½ cup parsley flakes

Sauté onion, celery, and garlic in oil until tender. Stir in remaining ingredients. Simmer over low heat 50 minutes or until sauce is reduced by one-third. Discard bay leaf. Yield: 2½ cups.

Turnip Greens

1 large bunch turnip greens (about
    2 to 2½ pounds)
Salt
¼ pound salt pork, diced
½ cup boiling salted water
Vinegar or pepper sauce

Check leaves of greens carefully; remove pulpy stems and discolored spots on leaves. Wash thoroughly in several changes of warm water; add a little salt to the last rinse. Put greens in colander to drain.

Cook salt pork, covered, about 10 minutes in ½ cup boiling salted water. Add greens, a few at a time; cover and cook slowly until greens are tender. Do not overcook. Serve with vinegar. Yield: 8 to 10 servings.

Note: An alternate method is to wash greens carefully and put them into a large cooker with only the water that clings to leaves. Add salt and bacon drippings after the greens have cooked tender.

Collards

    2 pounds collards
    ½ pound salt pork, coarsely chopped
    1 gallon water
    4 medium potatoes, peeled
    Salt

Cut off and discard tough stems and discolored leaves from collards. Wash greens thoroughly.

Combine salt pork and water in a Dutch oven; bring to a boil, and cook 15 to 30 minutes. Add collards; cover and cook at low boil for 1½ hours. Add potatoes, and cook 30 minutes or until potatoes are tender. Season to taste with salt. Yield: 6 to 8 servings.

Southern Turnip Greens And Ham Hock

    About 1¾ pounds ham hock
    2 quarts water
    2 bunches (about 10 pounds) turnip
        greens with roots
    1 teaspoon salt
    1 tablespoon sugar

Wash ham hocks and place in an 8-quart Dutch oven; add water, and bring to a boil.

Reduce heat, and simmer 30 to 45 minutes or until tender.

Pick and wash turnip greens. Peel turnip roots; cut in half. Add greens, roots, salt, and sugar to Dutch oven; bring to a boil. Reduce heat; cover and simmer about 30 to 45 minutes or until greens and roots are tender. Yield: 8 to 12 servings.

Turnip Greens With Cornmeal Dumplings

    1 large ham hock
    3 to 4 pounds turnip greens
    1 cup stone-ground cornmeal
    1½ cups boiling water
    1 teaspoon sugar
    ¼ teaspoon salt
    1 egg
    All-purpose flour

Cook ham hock in boiling water to cover until tender. (If meat is very salty, pour off water and add fresh water halfway during cooking.) Wash greens thoroughly and drain. Add greens to ham hock and cook until tender, about 45 minutes.

Stir cornmeal gradually into 1½ cups boiling water. Add sugar and salt; let cool. Add egg to cornmeal mixture and mix well. Drop by rounded tablespoonfuls onto floured surface; roll into balls. Flatten balls slightly and dredge lightly with flour; drop into boiling greens mixture. Cover; reduce heat, and simmer about 15 minutes. Drain greens mixture; skin ham hock. Place ham hock in center of serving platter; arrange greens and dumplings around ham hock. Yield: 6 to 8 servings.

Baked Cheese Grits

6 cups water
2½ teaspoons salt
1½ cups uncooked regular grits
½ cup butter or margarine
4 cups (1 pound) shredded
    medium-sharp Cheddar cheese,
    divided
3 eggs, beaten

Combine water and salt; bring to a boil. Stir in grits; cook until done, following package directions. Remove from heat. Add butter and 3¾ cups cheese; stir until completely melted. Add a small amount of hot grits to eggs, stirring well; stir egg mixture into remaining grits. Pour grits into a lightly greased 2½-quart baking dish; sprinkle with remaining ¼ cup cheese. Bake at 350° for 1 hour and 15 minutes or until slightly firm. Yield: 6 to 8 servings.

Derby Day Grits Casserole

6 cups water
2½ teaspoons salt
1½ cups quick-cooking grits,
    uncooked
½ cup butter or margarine
Dash of cayenne pepper
2 (6-ounce) rolls garlic-flavored
    process cheese spread, cubed
3 eggs, separated
Paprika

Combine water and salt in a 4-quart Dutch oven; bring to a boil. Gradually stir in grits. Cook over low heat, stirring constantly, 1 to 2 minutes or until thickened. Remove from heat; stir in butter, cayenne, and cheese, stirring until cheese melts. Stir in egg yolks. Beat egg whites until stiff; fold egg whites into cheese mixture. Pour into greased 3-quart casserole, and sprinkle with paprika. Bake at 350° for 30 minutes. Yield: 10 to 12 servings.

Hominy Custard Casserole

4 cups canned hominy, drained
2½ cups milk
1 (6-ounce) roll garlic-flavored
    process cheese spread, cut
    into cubes
1 teaspoon salt
¼ teaspoon pepper
Hot sauce to taste
4 eggs, beaten

Place hominy in a greased 2-quart casserole. Combine milk and cheese in a heavy saucepan; cook over low heat, stirring constantly, until cheese melts. Add seasonings. Stir about one-fourth of hot mixture into eggs, beating constantly. Stir egg mixture into remaining hot mixture, mixing well. Pour sauce mixture over hominy; bake at 350° for 50 to 60 minutes. Stir mixture gently during baking to evenly distribute hominy. Yield: 8 servings.

Spanish Hominy

1 onion, finely chopped
1 green pepper, finely chopped
¼ cup bacon drippings
2 to 3 teaspoons chili powder
1 teaspoon ground cumin
1 (4-ounce) can tomato paste
1 (8-ounce) can tomato sauce
1 (4-ounce) can sliced mushrooms,
    undrained
1 to 2 teaspoons salt
½ teaspoon pepper
2 (29-ounce) cans hominy, drained
1 cup (4 ounces) shredded Cheddar
    or Monterey Jack cheese

Sauté onion and green pepper in drippings in a large skillet. Stir in remaining ingredients except cheese, mixing well. Pour into a buttered 3-quart casserole and top with cheese. Bake at 325° for 25 minutes. Yield: 8 to 10 servings.

Creamed Kale

    1 pound kale
    2 tablespoons butter or margarine
    2 tablespoons all-purpose flour
    1½ cups milk
    1 teaspoon salt
    1 teaspoon white pepper

Remove and discard roots, midribs, and wilted leaves of kale; wash thoroughly. Add kale to 1 inch of boiling salted water. Cover; reduce heat, and simmer 20 minutes. Drain well; chop finely, and set aside.

Melt butter in a heavy saucepan over low heat; add flour, stirring until smooth. Cook 1 minute, stirring constantly. Gradually add milk; cook over medium heat, stirring constantly, until thickened and bubbly. Stir in kale, salt, and pepper; cook 3 minutes. Yield: 4 servings.

Hot Sweet-Sour Lettuce

    4 slices bacon
    ½ pound lettuce, coarsely chopped
    Sweet And Sour Sauce (recipe
        follows)

Fry bacon until crisp; drain and crumble. Reserve drippings in pan for Sweet and Sour Sauce. Combine bacon and lettuce. Pour about one-half cup Sweet and Sour Sauce over lettuce and bacon, and toss lightly. Yield: 4 servings.

Sweet And Sour Sauce:

    Reserved bacon drippings
    1 cup sugar
    2 cups water
    ½ teaspoon salt
    1 egg, beaten
    1 tablespoon plus 1½ teaspoons
        cornstarch
    2 to 4 tablespoons vinegar

Combine reserved bacon drippings, sugar, water, and salt in skillet; bring to a boil.

Combine egg and cornstarch, mixing well. Stir into sugar mixture; cook, stirring constantly, until thickened. Remove from heat; add vinegar to taste. Yield: about 2¼ cups.

Note: Remaining dressing may be refrigerated and used within a week. Reheat to use. Dressing is also good on spinach.

Scalloped Mushrooms

    1½ pounds fresh mushrooms
    1 cup herb-flavored stuffing, divided
    ¾ cup half-and-half
    1 cup chicken stock
    3 tablespoons melted butter or
        margarine
    2 to 3 tablespoons dry sherry

Gently rinse mushrooms and pat dry. Remove stems from caps; chop stems. Combine mushroom stems and caps. Place half the mushrooms in a buttered shallow 2-quart casserole; sprinkle half the stuffing mix over mushrooms. Repeat layers; combine half-and-half, stock, butter, and sherry, mixing well; pour over mushroom mixture. Cover loosely with foil; bake at 350° about 40 minutes. Remove foil and bake an additional 10 minutes. Yield: about 8 servings.

Fried Okra

    ½ cup cornmeal
    ¼ cup all-purpose flour
    1 teaspoon salt
    ¼ teaspoon pepper
    4 cups young tender okra
    Bacon drippings

Combine dry ingredients in a paper bag; mix well. Rinse okra; while damp, shake okra in paper bag, coating well with dry ingredients. Heat drippings in skillet; fry okra in drippings, turning often until browned. Yield: about 6 servings.

Deep South Okra And Tomatoes

3 slices bacon
4 cups fresh or frozen okra, sliced
1 onion, finely chopped
1 teaspoon salt
½ teaspoon pepper
½ teaspoon ground cumin
¼ teaspoon garlic powder
2 (8-ounce) cans tomato sauce or
  1 (16-ounce) can tomatoes,
  undrained
Hot cooked rice (optional)
Toast points (optional)

Fry bacon until crisp; drain and crumble, reserving drippings in skillet.

Add okra and onion to drippings in skillet; sauté 5 minutes. Add salt, pepper, cumin, garlic powder, tomato sauce, and bacon. Cover and simmer 30 minutes, stirring occasionally. Serve over rice or toast, if desired. Yield: 6 servings.

Okra Pilâu

2 cups thinly sliced okra
3 slices bacon, diced
½ cup chopped green pepper
¼ cup chopped onion
1 cup uncooked regular rice
2 cups chicken broth
1 (16-ounce) can tomatoes, drained
  and chopped, or 3 medium
  tomatoes, peeled and quartered
1 teaspoon salt

Sauté okra and bacon in a large skillet until lightly browned. Add green pepper and onion, and continue cooking until vegetables are tender. Add rice, chicken broth, tomatoes, and salt; bring to a boil. Stir well; cover, reduce heat, and simmer 15 minutes, or until rice is tender. Fluff lightly with a fork and serve. Yield: 6 to 8 servings.

Honey-Glazed Onions

12 medium-size yellow onions,
  peeled
4 medium tomatoes, peeled and
  diced, or 1 (16-ounce) can
  tomato juice
Salt
½ cup honey
Butter or margarine

Cook onions until tender in boiling water to cover; drain.

Place tomatoes in a small saucepan; bring to a boil. Boil 5 minutes, stirring occasionally. Add enough water to tomatoes to measure 2 cups. Place onions upright in a buttered 2-quart casserole; sprinkle lightly with salt, and pour tomato juice over top. Drizzle honey over mixture, and dot each onion generously with butter. Cover and bake at 350° for one hour. Yield: 4 to 6 servings.

Onion Noodle Kugel

Most noodle kugels are sweet, but this dish is loaded with onions and is delicious with pot roast or roast beef.

1 (8-ounce) package wide egg noodles
¼ cup margarine
2 tablespoons vegetable oil
2 large onions, chopped
4 eggs, beaten
Salt and pepper to taste

Cook noodles according to package directions; drain.

Heat margarine and oil in skillet; add onion, and sauté until transparent. Add onion, eggs, salt, and pepper to noodles; mix well. Spoon noodle mixture into a greased shallow 2-quart casserole. Bake at 350° for 35 to 45 minutes or until top is golden and crisp. Cool 10 minutes, and carefully cut into squares. Yield: 6 to 8 servings.

Onions Au Gratin

    12 to 15 medium onions, peeled
    6 tablespoons butter or margarine,
        divided
    ¼ cup all-purpose flour
    2 cups milk
    ½ teaspoon salt
    1 cup (4 ounces) shredded process
        American cheese
    1 cup coarse soft breadcrumbs

Cook onions in boiling salted water to cover until tender; drain. Melt 4 tablespoons butter in a heavy saucepan over low heat; add flour, stirring until smooth. Cook 1 minute, stirring constantly. Gradually add milk; cook over medium heat, stirring constantly, until thickened and bubbly. Add salt and cheese, stirring until cheese melts.

    Combine onions and cheese sauce. Pour into a greased 2-quart casserole. Melt remaining 2 tablespoons butter in a small saucepan; add breadcrumbs, and stir until breadcrumbs are coated with butter. Sprinkle breadcrumbs over onions and bake at 425° for 20 minutes or until crumbs are browned. Yield: 4 to 6 servings.

Baked Parsnips

    8 to 10 parsnips, peeled
    ⅓ cup sugar
    Salt to taste
    Butter or margarine
    1 tablespoon hot water
    1 tablespoon whipping cream

Cook parsnips until tender in boiling water to cover; drain, and place in a buttered 1½-quart baking dish. Sprinkle sugar and salt over parsnips, and dot with butter. Pour water and whipping cream into dish. Bake at 350° for 25 minutes or until light brown. Yield: 4 to 6 servings.

Field Peas Hoppin' John

    1 cup dried field peas
    1 to 1½ quarts water
    ¼ pound slab bacon
    1 small pod red pepper
    1 cup uncooked regular rice
    Salt (optional)

Wash beans well; combine beans and 1 quart water in a Dutch oven, and soak overnight.

    Add bacon and pepper. Cover and cook over low heat for 1½ to 2 hours or until tender. Add rice; cover and cook over low heat, stirring frequently, until rice is cooked. Add additional water during cooking, if necessary. Add salt, if desired (jowl may make it salty enough). Yield: 8 servings.

Spicy Hoppin' John

    1 pound dried black-eyed peas
    8 cups water
    1 (16-ounce) can tomatoes
    1 (8-ounce) ham hock
    1 cup chopped onion
    1 cup chopped celery
    1 tablespoon salt
    2 teaspoons chili powder
    ¼ teaspoon dried basil leaves,
        crushed
    1 bay leaf
    1 cup uncooked regular rice

Combine peas and water in a Dutch oven; let soak overnight. (Or bring to a boil; cover, reduce heat, and simmer 2 minutes. Let stand 1 hour.) Do not drain. Drain tomatoes, reserving liquid; chop tomatoes. Add tomatoes and liquid to peas; add remaining ingredients except rice. Cover, and simmer until peas are tender, about 1 to 1½ hours. Remove ham hock; remove meat from bone. Dice meat; return to peas. Add rice; cover. Simmer for 20 minutes, or until rice is tender. Remove bay leaf. Yield: 14 servings.

Bollitos

1 pound dried black-eyed peas
1 teaspoon salt
2 or 3 cloves garlic
½ teaspoon cayenne pepper
Vegetable oil for deep frying

Cover black-eyed peas with cold water; soak overnight. Rub the peas together with the hands to loosen hulls; discard hulls and drain peas well.

Put salt on wooden board; peel and halve garlic cloves. Place garlic halves into salt, and with index finger pressing tip of metal spatula, work garlic and salt together into a paste.

Grind peas, using fine blade of grinder or a food processor. Add garlic-salt and cayenne. Blend well. Chill; drop by teaspoonfuls into oil heated to 360°. Fry until brown; serve hot as appetizer. Yield: about 1 dozen servings.

Note: For a side dish, drop mixture into oil by tablespoonfuls. Yield: 6 to 8 servings.

Toasted Peppers

6 large green peppers
½ cup vinegar
½ cup vegetable oil
Salt and pepper to taste
Dash of sugar

Wash peppers; place on a baking sheet, and broil about 3 inches from heat until brown and blistered on all sides. Cool peppers, and peel off skin; cut peppers into eighths, and remove seeds. Place peppers in serving dish. Combine remaining ingredients, mixing well; pour over peppers. Chill before serving. Yield: 6 to 8 servings.

Note: This dish will keep several weeks in the refrigerator. Use as relish or salad ingredient.

Scalloped Potatoes

6 large potatoes, peeled and thinly
    sliced
2 medium onions, chopped
2 cups (8 ounces) shredded mild
    Cheddar cheese
½ cup butter or margarine
1 to 1½ teaspoons salt
½ teaspoon pepper
¾ teaspoon celery seeds
1 tablespoon all-purpose flour
3 to 4 cups milk

Layer half the potatoes in a greased 3-quart casserole. Layer half the onion over potatoes, and sprinkle with half the cheese. Dot with half the butter; sprinkle with half the salt, pepper, and celery seeds. Combine flour and milk, mixing well. Pour half of milk mixture over vegetable mixture. Repeat procedure, using remaining ingredients. Cover loosely with foil; bake at 350° for 1 to 1½ hours, or until potatoes are very tender. Remove foil for the final 30 minutes of baking to brown top. Yield: 8 servings.

New Potatoes Steamed In Butter

2 pounds small new potatoes
½ cup butter or margarine
3 tablespoons water
1 teaspoon salt
½ teaspoon pepper
¼ cup chopped fresh parsley

Scrub potatoes; peel a strip around center of each potato, if desired. Melt butter in a heavy saucepan; add potatoes, water, and seasonings. Cover and cook over low heat about 25 minutes, or until tender, shaking pan to keep potatoes from sticking. Transfer to serving platter, and sprinkle with parsley. Yield: 6 to 8 servings.

Potato Latkes

4 large potatoes, peeled and grated
1 small onion, grated
¼ cup all-purpose flour
1 teaspoon salt
¼ teaspoon pepper
2 eggs, beaten
½ cup vegetable oil or schmaltz
Commercial sour cream or applesauce

Drain excess liquid from potatoes. Combine potatoes, onion, flour, salt, and pepper in a medium mixing bowl; mix well. Fold in beaten eggs. Heat oil in a heavy skillet; drop batter by tablespoonfuls into hot oil. Fry until brown on one side; turn and brown other side. Repeat procedure until all batter is used. Serve hot with sour cream or applesauce. Yield: 4 to 6 servings.

Sesame Hash Browned Potatoes

¼ cup butter or margarine
1 tablespoon minced green onion
¼ cup sesame seeds
4 large potatoes, baked, peeled, and diced
1 teaspoon salt
½ teaspoon pepper
¼ cup whipping cream

Heat butter in skillet; sauté onion in butter until tender. Add sesame seeds; cook until lightly browned. Add potatoes, salt, pepper, and cream. Cook, stirring occasionally, until potatoes are golden brown. Yield: 4 to 6 servings.

Potato Patties

4 large potatoes, peeled and grated
1 egg
½ teaspoon salt
1½ tablespoons all-purpose flour
1 tablespoon baking powder
2 teaspoons milk
Vegetable oil

Drain potatoes for 10 minutes in colander. Add remaining ingredients except oil; beat well. Shape mixture into small cakes and fry in hot oil in heavy skillet until brown, turning to brown both sides. Yield: 4 servings.

Russian-Style Fried Potatoes

6 large potatoes
4 tablespoons vegetable oil
2 large onions, sliced
4 cloves garlic, minced
Salt and pepper
4 to 5 green onions, chopped

Cook potatoes until tender in boiling salted water to cover. Drain potatoes, and let cool. Peel potatoes, and cut into ½-inch cubes. Heat oil in heavy skillet; add potatoes, onion, and garlic. Season to taste; fry until golden brown, turning to brown all sides. Sprinkle with green onion. Yield: 6 servings.

Dill Potatoes

1 (8-ounce) carton commercial sour cream or yogurt
1 teaspoon dillseeds
1 teaspoon chicken- or beef-flavored bouillon granules
2 tablespoons all-purpose flour
4 cups cubed boiled potatoes

Combine sour cream, dillseeds, bouillon granules, and flour in top of a double boiler; mix well. Cook over boiling water until bouillon granules dissolve and mixture is thickened. Spoon mixture over hot potatoes in a warmed serving bowl. Yield: 6 servings.

Home Fried Potatoes

6 medium potatoes, peeled and
thinly sliced
1 teaspoon salt
½ teaspoon pepper
½ to 1 teaspoon paprika
⅓ cup bacon drippings

Press potatoes between paper towels; sprinkle potatoes with seasonings. Heat drippings in a heavy skillet; add potatoes. Cover, and cook over low heat 5 minutes. Remove cover; fry over medium heat for about 20 minutes, turning to brown evenly. Drain on paper towels. Yield: 6 servings.

Hot Potato Salad, German Style

4 large potatoes
2 teaspoons minced onion
½ cup vinegar
¼ cup water
¼ cup sugar
2 teaspoons salt
¼ teaspoon pepper
½ teaspoon dry mustard
4 slices bacon, cooked and crumbled
¼ cup chopped fresh parsley

Cook potatoes until tender in boiling salted water; drain. Peel and slice potatoes. Combine onion, vinegar, water, sugar, salt, pepper, and mustard in a Dutch oven; bring to a boil. Add potatoes, bacon, and parsley, mixing carefully with a fork. Cook over low heat, shaking pan, until thoroughly heated. Yield: 4 servings.

Note: This salad is also good cold and may be varied by adding chopped celery and green pepper.

Old-Fashioned Soft Potato Salad

6 medium potatoes
1 large dill pickle, finely chopped
2 hard-cooked eggs, chopped
1 onion, chopped
½ cup vinegar
½ to 1 teaspoon celery seeds
1 teaspoon prepared mustard
1 teaspoon salt
½ cup sugar
Dash of cayenne pepper (optional)

Cook potatoes until tender in boiling salted water to cover. Drain and let cool. Peel and shred potatoes. Add remaining ingredients, mixing gently. Yield: 6 to 8 servings.

Candied Sweet Potatoes

4 medium or 3 large sweet potatoes
½ cup melted butter or margarine
1 cup sugar
¼ cup water

Peel potatoes, and cut into 2-inch slices. Combine butter, sugar, and water in an electric skillet; add sweet potatoes. Cover and simmer at 250° for 1 hour or until done, turning frequently. Yield: 4 servings.

Sweet Potato Logs

4 medium-size sweet potatoes,
cooked and mashed
1 teaspoon vanilla extract
1 cup sugar
1 egg, beaten
¼ cup milk
3 tablespoons all-purpose flour
1 teaspoon ground cinnamon
½ cup chopped pecans
½ cup raisins
All-purpose flour
1 cup grated coconut
½ cup melted butter or margarine

Combine first 8 ingredients, mixing well. Dredge raisins in flour; add raisins to sweet potato mixture, mixing well. Cool mixture; shape into 8 logs or croquettes, and roll in coconut. Place on greased baking sheet, and drizzle melted butter over logs. Bake at 375° about 20 minutes, or until browned and crisp. Yield: 8 servings.

Yummy Yams

4 pounds sweet potatoes, cooked and mashed
½ cup melted butter or margarine
¼ cup bourbon
⅓ cup orange juice
⅓ cup firmly packed brown sugar
¾ teaspoon salt
½ teaspoon apple pie spice
½ to ¾ cup pecan halves

Combine all ingredients except pecans in a large mixing bowl, mixing well. Pour into a greased 2½-quart casserole; arrange pecans around edge of dish. Bake at 350° for 45 minutes. Yield: 8 to 10 servings.

Pocketbooks

¾ cup raisins
1 cup hot water
1 large onion, diced
½ cup melted butter or margarine
1 (12-ounce) carton cottage cheese
½ teaspoon salt
¼ teaspoon pepper
2 tablespoons fine dry breadcrumbs
2 eggs, beaten
1 teaspoon salt
¼ cup milk
2½ to 3 cups all-purpose flour
2 quarts water
3 cups milk

Combine raisins and hot water; soak for 15 minutes, or until raisins are puffy. Drain.

Sauté onion in butter until tender. Combine cottage cheese, seasonings, bread-crumbs, raisins, and about ⅔ of the onion, mixing well; set aside. Combine eggs, 1 teaspoon salt, and ¼ cup milk in a large mixing bowl; stir in enough flour to make a stiff dough. Divide dough in half; turn half of dough out on a lightly floured surface, and roll into a ¼-inch-thick rectangle. Cut into 6 equal pieces; roll each piece into a 5-inch square. Spoon half of cottage cheese mixture evenly onto 6 squares. Bring opposite corners of dough together and seal. Repeat procedure with remaining dough and cottage cheese mixture.

Pour 2 quarts water in a large Dutch oven; bring to a boil. Carefully drop squares of dough into boiling water; cook, uncovered, for 20 minutes. Drain.

Combine 3 cups milk and remaining onion in a medium saucepan; heat thoroughly. Pour milk mixture over pocketbooks and serve immediately. Yield: 6 servings.

Risotto

5 tablespoons vegetable oil
1 medium onion, sliced
3 large cloves garlic, minced
1 cup uncooked regular rice
1½ cups hot chicken stock
1 (4-ounce) can mushrooms, undrained
1 cup dry sherry
Dash of whole saffron (optional)
½ to 1 teaspoon salt
¼ teaspoon pepper

Heat oil in a large skillet; sauté onion and garlic until transparent. Add rice; cook over low heat, stirring constantly, until browned. Combine stock and mushrooms; combine sherry and saffron, if desired. Alternately add stock and wine mixtures to rice mixture, 2 tablespoons at a time. Sprinkle with salt and pepper; do not stir. Cover skillet; cook over very low heat about 25 minutes, or until rice is tender and liquid is absorbed. Yield: 6 servings.

Savannah Red Rice

¾ cup diced onion
⅓ to ½ cup diced green pepper
2 tablespoons vegetable oil
1½ pounds cooked ham, finely
   chopped
2 (8-ounce) cans tomato sauce
2 cups water
2 tablespoons sugar
½ teaspoon salt
2 cups uncooked regular rice

Sauté onion and green pepper in oil in a
Dutch oven until tender. Stir in ham; cook
over medium heat about 3 minutes.

Add tomato sauce, water, sugar, and salt;
stir well. Bring mixture to a boil; add rice,
and reduce heat. Cover; simmer 15 minutes.

Cut a circle of brown paper large enough
to fit over top of Dutch oven, allowing 2-inch
overlap around edge of pot. Remove lid from
Dutch oven, and place paper over pot. Replace lid over paper; continue to simmer 15
to 20 minutes. Yield: 8 to 10 servings.

Rutabaga Au Gratin

6 tablespoons melted butter or
   margarine, divided
¼ cup all-purpose flour
2 cups milk
1 cup (4 ounces) shredded Cheddar
   cheese
1 teaspoon salt
⅛ teaspoon pepper
4 cups diced cooked rutabaga
½ cup soft breadcrumbs

Combine ¼ cup butter and flour in a heavy
saucepan over low heat. Cook 1 minute,
stirring constantly. Gradually stir in milk;
cook over medium heat, stirring constantly,
until smooth and thickened. Add cheese and
seasonings, stirring until cheese is melted.

Place rutabaga in a lightly greased 1½-
quart casserole; top with sauce. Combine

breadcrumbs with remaining 2 tablespoons
butter; sprinkle over casserole. Bake at 400°
for 15 minutes. Yield: 6 servings.

Creamy Rutabaga

1 small rutabaga, peeled and diced
1 tablespoon sugar
¼ cup evaporated milk
¼ cup firmly packed light
   brown sugar
2 tablespoons butter or margarine
Salt to taste
Ground nutmeg

Cook rutabaga in 1 inch of boiling salted
water 10 minutes. Stir in sugar, and cook
until very tender; drain well.

Combine all ingredients except nutmeg;
beat on high speed of electric mixer until
creamy. Sprinkle with nutmeg. Yield: 4 to 6
servings.

Baked Pumpkin

3 cups cooked mashed pumpkin
½ cup sugar
½ teaspoon salt
2 eggs, beaten
3 tablespoons all-purpose flour
¾ cup milk
1 teaspoon lemon extract
¼ cup melted butter or margarine

Combine all ingredients, mixing well. Spoon
into a greased 13- × 9- × 2-inch baking pan.
Bake at 350° about 30 minutes. Yield: about 6
servings.

---

*Shrimp, Parmesan cheese, and seasoned to-
mato sauce enhance the flavor of Shrimp-
Stuffed Creole Eggplant (page 138).*

Far Right: *Fried Peach Pie (page 235), fresh Turnip Greens (page 138), and Yellow Cornbread (page 166) provide true down-home eating.*

Right: *A typical Appalachian vegetable dinner provides hearty fare: (clockwise) Buttermilk Cornbread (page 165), Shuck Beans (page 129), Pickled Beets (page 260), and Tangy Coleslaw (page 133).*

Below: *When made into Corn Relish (page 259), the fresh, tender kernels of corn can be savored long after the garden season.*

Fresh Spinach

1 large bunch spinach (about 2 to
    2½ pounds)
Salt
¼ pound salt pork, diced
½ cup boiling salted water
Vinegar or pepper sauce

Check leaves of spinach carefully; remove pulpy stems and discolored spots on leaves. Wash thoroughly in several changes of warm water; add a little salt to the last rinse. Put spinach in colander to drain.

Cook salt pork, covered, about 10 minutes in ½ cup boiling salted water. Add spinach, a few at a time; cover and cook slowly until tender. Do not overcook. Serve with vinegar. Yield: 6 to 8 servings.

Note: An alternate method is to wash spinach carefully and put leaves into a large cooker with only the water that clings to leaves. Add salt and bacon drippings after the spinach has cooked tender.

Easy Spinach Supreme

2 (10-ounce) packages frozen
    chopped spinach
1 (8-ounce) package cream cheese,
    softened
¼ cup butter or margarine
Salt and pepper to taste
1 (8½-ounce) can artichoke hearts,
    drained
¼ cup melted butter or margarine
Croutons

Sweet potatoes are the basis of some of the South's favorite dishes: Candied Sweet Potatoes (page 146), Yummy Yams (page 147), and Sweet Potato Pie (page 237).

Cook spinach according to package directions; drain. Combine spinach, cream cheese, ¼ cup butter, salt, and pepper; mix well. Spoon mixture into a greased 1-quart casserole. Arrange artichoke hearts over top of spinach. Combine melted butter and croutons; toss lightly. Sprinkle croutons over casserole. Bake at 350° for 20 to 30 minutes. Yield: 4 to 6 servings.

Squash And Apple Bake

2 pounds butternut squash (about 2
    small)
2 cooking apples, cut into
    ½-inch slices
½ cup firmly packed brown sugar
¼ cup melted butter or margarine
1 tablespoon all-purpose flour
1 teaspoon salt
½ teaspoon ground mace

Cut each squash in half lengthwise; remove seeds. Peel squash, and cut into ½-inch slices. Arrange in a lightly greased 12- × 8- × 2-inch baking dish; top with apple slices.

Combine remaining ingredients, mixing well; spoon over apple slices. Cover tightly with foil. Bake at 350° for 1 hour and 15 minutes, or until squash is tender. Yield: 6 to 8 servings.

Squash Croquettes

2 cups finely chopped yellow squash
1 cup finely chopped onion
1 egg, beaten
1 teaspoon salt
1 teaspoon pepper
½ cup plus 1 tablespoon all-purpose
    flour
Hot vegetable oil

Combine first 5 ingredients; mix well. Stir in flour. Drop by tablespoonfuls into ½ inch of hot oil. Cook until browned, turning once; drain. Yield: 6 servings.

Winter Squash Soufflé

4 cups cooked mashed winter squash
½ cup butter or margarine
½ teaspoon salt
2 teaspoons vanilla extract
½ cup milk
3 eggs, beaten
1½ cups sugar
Topping (recipe follows)

Combine all ingredients, mixing well. Pour into 2-quart soufflé dish or deep casserole; spoon topping over mixture and bake at 350° for 35 to 45 minutes. Yield: 8 servings.

Topping:

2 (8-ounce) cans crushed pineapple, drained
½ cup all-purpose flour
2 eggs, beaten
½ cup sugar
½ cup melted butter or margarine

Combine all ingredients and blend well. Yield: about 1½ cups.

Note: Pumpkin or sweet potato may be substituted for squash.

Acorn Squash Casserole

1 acorn squash, peeled and sliced into ½-inch slices
1 cup (4 ounces) shredded Cheddar cheese
½ cup cottage cheese
4 eggs
¾ cup breadcrumbs
½ teaspoon salt
3 tablespoons butter or margarine

Combine squash, Cheddar cheese, cottage cheese, eggs, breadcrumbs, and salt. Spoon into a 13- × 9- × 2-inch baking dish. Dot with butter. Bake at 350° for 45 minutes. Yield: 6 servings.

Zucchini Casserole

½ cup chopped fresh mushrooms
¼ cup minced onion
Dash of instant minced garlic
½ cup melted butter or margarine
2 slices bacon, cooked and crumbled
2 medium zucchini, grated
1¼ cups cracker crumbs, divided
1 egg, beaten
½ teaspoon salt
¼ teaspoon pepper
½ cup (2 ounces) shredded Swiss cheese

Sauté mushrooms, onion, and garlic in butter just until tender. Combine bacon, mushroom mixture, zucchini, 1 cup cracker crumbs, egg, salt, and pepper; stir well. Pour zucchini mixture into a greased 1½-quart casserole.

Combine Swiss cheese and remaining ¼ cup cracker crumbs; sprinkle over zucchini mixture. Bake at 350° for 40 minutes. Yield: 6 servings.

Baked Stuffed Zucchini

4 medium-size zucchini
Chicken stock or salted water
1 teaspoon beef-flavored bouillon granules
½ cup fine dry breadcrumbs
1 teaspoon Worcestershire sauce
½ teaspoon sugar
Dash of ground thyme
Dash of hot sauce
Salt and freshly ground pepper
1 tablespoon minced onion
1 clove garlic, minced
2 tablespoons olive oil
¼ cup coarsely crushed cracker crumbs
1 tablespoon butter or margarine
4 strips bacon, cooked and crumbled

Wash zucchini thoroughly; cut off stem end. Cook zucchini in boiling chicken stock for 5 to 8 minutes or until tender. Drain and cool.

Cut zucchini in half lengthwise; remove pulp, leaving a firm shell. Drain pulp thoroughly in a colander. Combine pulp and bouillon granules; mash pulp. Add breadcrumbs, Worcestershire sauce, sugar, thyme, hot sauce, salt, and pepper, mixing well. Sauté onion and garlic in oil until slightly brown; add to zucchini mixture. Spoon mixture into zucchini shells. Top with cracker crumbs, and dot with butter; place on greased baking sheet, and bake at 350° for 15 minutes. Sprinkle with bacon before serving. Yield: 8 servings.

Zucchini Soufflé

¼ cup butter or margarine
¼ cup all-purpose flour
1⅓ cups milk
1 teaspoon salt
Dash of pepper
1 tablespoon minced onion
1¼ cups grated zucchini
5 eggs, separated
1 teaspoon cream of tartar
½ cup (2 ounces) shredded sharp
  Cheddar cheese

Melt butter in a heavy saucepan over low heat; blend in flour and cook 1 minute, stirring constantly. Gradually add milk; cook, stirring constantly, until smooth and thickened. Stir in salt, pepper, and onion; remove from heat, and let cool. Squeeze grated zucchini to remove as much liquid as possible; stir into sauce.

Beat egg yolks until thick and lemon colored; add to squash mixture; mix well. Beat egg whites and cream of tartar until stiff, but not dry; fold into squash mixture. Pour into a greased 2-quart casserole; sprinkle with cheese. Place dish in a baking pan filled with 1 inch of water. Bake at 350° for 1 hour and 15 minutes or until a knife inserted in center comes out clean. Yield: 6 to 8 servings.

Fried Tomatoes With Cheese Sauce

6 large tomatoes, barely ripe
Salt and pepper
¾ cup all-purpose flour
½ cup butter or margarine, divided
3 tablespoons all-purpose flour
2 cups milk or half-and-half
1 cup (4 ounces) shredded mild
  Cheddar cheese

Cut tomatoes into ¼-inch slices. Sprinkle with salt and pepper; dredge in ¾ cup flour. Melt ¼ cup butter in a heavy skillet; add tomatoes, and fry slowly until browned, turning once. Arrange tomatoes on warm deep serving platter.

Melt remaining butter in a heavy saucepan; add 3 tablespoons flour, stirring until smooth. Cook 1 minute, stirring constantly. Gradually add milk; cook over medium heat, stirring constantly, until thickened and bubbly. Add cheese, stirring until melted. Pour cheese sauce over tomatoes; serve immediately. Yield: 8 servings.

Fried Green Tomatoes

4 medium-size green tomatoes
Salt and pepper to taste
1 cup cornmeal
2 tablespoons bacon drippings

Cut tomatoes into ¼-inch slices. Season with salt and pepper; dredge in cornmeal. Heat bacon drippings in a heavy skillet; add tomatoes, and fry slowly until browned, turning once. Yield: about 4 to 6 servings.

Note: Squash may be fried the same way.

Turnip Au Gratin

　　2 cups peeled cubed turnips
　　1 tablespoon butter or margarine
　　1 tablespoon all-purpose flour
　　1 cup milk
　　¾ cup (3 ounces) shredded Cheddar
　　　　cheese
　　½ teaspoon salt
　　¼ teaspoon pepper
　　3 tablespoons melted butter or
　　　　margarine
　　½ cup soft breadcrumbs
　　Paprika

Cook turnips in boiling salted water to cover just until tender. Drain and spoon into a greased 1-quart casserole.

Combine 1 tablespoon butter and flour in a small saucepan; cook over low heat until bubbly. Gradually add milk; cook, stirring constantly, until smooth and thickened. Add cheese, salt, and pepper, stirring until cheese melts.

Spoon sauce over turnips. Combine melted butter with breadcrumbs, tossing well; sprinkle over casserole. Sprinkle with paprika. Bake, uncovered, at 350° for 15 minutes. Yield: 4 servings.

Parsleyed Turnips And Carrots

　　3 cups peeled diced turnips
　　3 cups peeled diced carrots
　　¼ cup melted butter or margarine
　　2 tablespoons minced fresh parsley
　　½ teaspoon salt
　　Dash of pepper

Cook turnips and carrots, covered, in small amount of boiling salted water for 20 minutes or until tender; drain. Add remaining ingredients; toss well. Yield: 6 to 8 servings.

Vegetable Pie With Peanut Butter Crust

　　3 tablespoons butter or margarine
　　¼ cup plus 1 tablespoon all-purpose
　　　　flour
　　3 cups milk
　　1 teaspoon salt
　　½ teaspoon celery salt
　　½ teaspoon paprika
　　16 small cooked onions
　　1 cup cooked green peas
　　1 cup cooked green beans
　　2 cooked sliced carrots
　　Peanut Butter Crust (recipe follows)
　　4 strips bacon, cooked and crumbled

Melt butter in a large heavy saucepan over low heat; add flour, stirring until smooth. Cook 1 minute, stirring constantly. Gradually add milk; cook over medium heat, stirring constantly, until thickened and bubbly. Stir in seasonings and vegetables. Pour mixture into a greased 13- × 9- × 2-inch baking dish; top with Peanut Butter Crust. Trim edges and flute pastry as desired. Make slits along top of pastry; sprinkle with crumbled bacon. Bake at 450° for 20 minutes. Yield: 6 to 8 servings.

Peanut Butter Crust:

　　1½ cups all-purpose flour
　　1 tablespoon baking powder
　　1 teaspoon salt
　　¼ cup creamy peanut butter
　　½ cup milk

Combine dry ingredients; add peanut butter and mix thoroughly with a fork. Add milk, stirring to form a soft dough. Turn dough out on a lightly floured surface. Roll dough to fit the top of baking dish. Yield: crust for 1 casserole.

Breads and Breadstuffs

When Pompeii was entombed beneath volcanic ashes in the first century A.D., commercial ovens filled with bread loaves were sealed up along with everything else in the city to be exhumed and studied centuries later. But at the time Pompeii perished, bread making was an art at least 3,000 years old.

Although Egyptian pyramids have yielded well-preserved loaves of bread put there to nourish the departed until he could get his bearings on the other side, even the Egyptians did not invent bread. Stone Age man left samples of a kind of bread which, according to archaeologists, was a sun-dried mixture of cereal seeds and water. It was not exactly what we would call bread nowadays, to be sure, but it was good enough to keep body and soul together until the Egyptians could work out the details.

Fermentation and leavening were Egyptian developments; they were the foundations of bread as we know it. Although fermentation is a form of leavening that uses the wild yeast from the air, we usually think of leavening as an agent deliberately added to dough to make it rise. The first leavened bread as we understand the term may have come about by accident. Some anonymous Egyptian may have thrown a handful of yeasty foam from his brewing vat into some dough. His friends must have thought him mad, at least until the bread was baked and served.

But in any case, the simple fermentation of a mixture of barley or wheat flour and water was an immense step forward. As a footnote to that historic discovery, the nineteenth century settlers and gold prospectors of the American West carried with them a direct link with the ancient past—sourdough starter.

Bread's importance in man's civilization can hardly be overestimated. Laborers were paid in bread; the city poor subsisted on bread doled out by their rulers. The truth is that the majority of people had nothing else to eat; without it, they simply starved. Even when stale and hard, bread was a treasure.

Such was the state of bread in England as late as the early sixteenth century. Only the wealthiest could afford the more refined breads. The city poor bought as much cheap bread as they could while their country cousins made bread from just about anything they were able to grind up. They used acorns, nuts, seeds, and such real cereal grain as they could grow. They had barley, rye, and a little wheat. Europe, of course, did not have corn.

Corn, to the early English settlers of the American East Coast, was almost manna from heaven. The soil was so rich that it was necessary only to poke holes in the ground with a sharp stick and drop in some seed corn, and it would grow. The New England colonies grew rye as well and mixed it with corn and molasses to make a common bread they called "Rye 'n Injun."

In the South, even after other grain crops became established, the people kept eating cornbread because they liked it, not because they had to. They invented a wide variety of breads made from corn, beginning with the elementary ones picked up from the Indians. The Indians who greeted the first settlers on the Eastern Seaboard used corn in many ways; it was their staple food. But unlike the tribes of the Southwest, they had no ovens. Their bread was a cornmeal mush or "platter" bread made of parched corn and baked in cakes by the sun's heat.

The story of Indian fry bread may be of interest at this point, as there may be others who labor, as I did, under the misapprehension that fry bread was made from corn. The Indians who gave corn cultivation and cookery to the colonists were not, at that time, making fry bread at all. And when they did, they made it from wheat flour.

The story of Indian fry bread is an unhappy one, as I received it from Mrs. Raymond Red Corn, of Pawhuska, Oklahoma. Claiming little or no Indian blood, Waltena Red Corn is Osage mostly by marriage. The Red Corns own the Ha-Pah-Shu-Tse Restaurant and are students of Indian history.

The origin of Indian fry bread runs like this. The Eastern tribes were moved off their lands in the early 1800s and relocated in the West. Their corn fields were left behind. The rations, or "commodities," issued by the government included flour, not cornmeal. "This was when they came up with a 'fry bread.' It had to be made of flour," said Mrs. Red Corn.

"It is made by different tribes in different ways. Ours is rolled and cut in squares; others pinch off a piece and flatten it by patting and pulling before dropping it in hot fat.

Indian Fry Bread

2 cups all-purpose flour
2 tablespoons baking powder

½ teaspoon salt
Vegetable oil for deep frying

Sift or stir dry ingredients in mixing bowl to blend thoroughly. Slowly add sufficient water to form a stiff dough. Cover bowl with towel; let stand 30 minutes. Pinch off balls of dough with floured hands, and work out into 5-inch circles. Drop into oil heated to 360°, and fry until golden brown. Yield: 7 or 8 fry breads.

"It was some time before the tribes were able to start farming on the new land allotted to them. When they did, they still used the 'platter' cornbread and do so today at special feasts and breakfasts. After ovens and stoves came into use, they made a delicious cornbread from grated fresh roasting ears."

Mrs. Red Corn's Fresh Corn Bread

1 dozen ears fresh corn
Salt and pepper to taste

¼ cup bacon drippings
Bacon drippings

Cut corn from cob, scraping all milk from the cob after cutting. Combine corn, salt, pepper, and ¼ cup bacon drippings. Grease a 10- × 12-inch baking pan with bacon drippings and pour in batter; bake at 475° for about 20 minutes, or until brown. The bread will be soft. Yield: 6 servings.

This bread is not served at the restaurant, as the labor cost would be prohibitive. She does serve fry bread, though, and grape dumplings and yellow corn soup. The Red Corns package and sell their own fry bread mix, based on flour. Very similar to biscuit mix, it is authentic.

Southern cooking without corn would be unthinkable, perhaps even impossible. If a desperate misfortune took away cornmeal, grits, and whole hominy, the calamity would be felt from breakfast through supper. Griddle cakes, hoecakes, pone, muffins and sticks, spoonbread—they are the staff of life. Some Southerners still mean cornbread when they say bread, just as they mean pork when they say meat. My mother, for example, would lay out a company dinner by first resolving to serve bread (corn sticks) and biscuits, meat (country ham) and chicken.

My best and shortest bread recipe is for my mother's hot water cornbread: "Salt and scald some meal and fry it." There is a captivating recipe for snow cakes in one of my very old cookbooks published in 1893. "Take one part Indian meal and two parts of dry snow or, if the snow be moist, use equal parts of meal and snow; mix well in a cold room. Fill the pans rounding full, and bake immediately in a very hot oven. This makes an excellent cake."

For cooks in the far South where snow is scarce and cold rooms a rarity, here is a more useful recipe.

Hot Water Hoecake

2 cups cornmeal
3 cups boiling water
2 tablespoons shortening
1 teaspoon salt

1 egg, beaten
About ½ cup milk
Butter

Stir cornmeal slowly into boiling water in a medium saucepan. Add shortening, salt, egg, and enough milk to make a stiff batter. Form into small ½-inch-thick cakes; fry on a hot greased griddle. Turn when brown on bottom side and brown on the other side. Serve hot with butter. Yield: about 20 small hoecakes.

From the simple hoecake to the elegant pone that looks like a handsome spongecake, corn is the South's number one breadstuff.

On the other hand, rice, while a staple grain that was introduced into the Low Country around Charleston and Savannah in 1694, made little impact on bread baking. However, two recipes I have found prompt the inclusion of rice in a discussion of Southern breads. Philpy is an interesting old rice bread from Charleston. And calas are fried cakes made from a rice batter. Women used to carry baskets of them, piping hot, through the New Orleans streets, crying "Belle calas tout chaud." They are delicious with café au lait at breakfast.

Philpy

½ cup milk
½ cup all-purpose flour
½ teaspoon salt
¾ cup soft cooked rice

2 teaspoons melted butter
1 egg, well beaten
Butter

Add milk slowly to flour and salt in a mixing bowl, beating to avoid lumping. Mash rice until fairly smooth. Combine with flour mixture; add melted butter and egg; bake in a greased 8-inch cakepan at 450° for 30 minutes. Slice while warm, split open, and butter generously. Yield: 4 to 6 servings.

Rice Fritters

½ cup uncooked regular rice
3 cups cold water
1 package dry yeast
3 tablespoons warm water
    (105° to 115°)
3 eggs, well beaten

⅓ cup sugar
1¼ cups all-purpose flour
½ teaspoon ground nutmeg
½ teaspoon salt
Vegetable oil
Powdered sugar

Add rice to cold water in saucepan; bring to a boil, and cook 25 minutes. Drain well. Place rice in a blender and puree; cool to lukewarm. Add yeast, which has been dissolved in 3 tablespoons warm water and blend. Cover and allow to stand overnight.

Next morning, add eggs, sugar, flour, nutmeg, and salt. Blend well and allow to stand 30 minutes before frying. Heat oil 1-inch deep in heavy pan to 375°. Drop batter by tablespoonfuls into hot oil, and fry 3 or 4 at a time until golden brown, turning once. Drain well; sprinkle with powdered sugar and serve immediately. Yield: about 2 dozen cakes.

But rice breads are a mere paragraph in the possible volumes that could be written on Southern breads. Next to cornbread, biscuits are the hallmark of Southern bread baking. Beaten biscuits, once known as Maryland biscuits, are not often seen nowadays. Small wonder—they require more time and brute strength than most of us can muster.

"Beat 300 times for family, 500 for company"; that used to be the rule of thumb before the invention of the beaten biscuit machine or "break." Residential streets in Southern towns once were filled with sounds like muffled drums in the early morning, as cooks applied their mallets to the dough.

One of the oldest cookbooks in my collection was written by Eliza Leslie of Philadelphia in 1857. After discouraging the reader with instructions to pound the biscuit dough for two to three hours, she had this to say:

"This is the most laborious of cakes, and also the most unwholesome. . . . We do not recommend it, but there is no accounting for tastes. Children should not eat these biscuits, nor grown persons either, if they can get any other sort of bread.

"When living in a town where there are bakers, there is no excuse for making Maryland biscuit. Believe nobody that says they are not unwholesome. Yet we have heard of families, in country places, where neither the mistress nor the cook knew any other preparation of wheat bread. Better to live on indian (*sic*) cakes." She said it herself; there is no accounting for tastes.

The weapons with which Southern cooks belabor beaten biscuits are formidable: baseball bat, heel of an axe, flatiron—they all work. There is a Kentucky woman who has taken many blue ribbons for her beaten biscuits at the State Fair. She does not own a biscuit break; she uses an old rolling pin with one handle missing, rhythmically beating blisters into the dough with the handleless end of the pin. It works, too. This recipe is a typical one.

Sally's Beaten Biscuit

4 cups all-purpose flour
Dash of salt
1 tablespoon sugar
1 teaspoon baking powder
4 to 5 tablespoons pure lard
About ¾ cup milk

Sift dry ingredients together in a large mixing bowl; cut in lard. Add just enough milk to make a stiff dough. Work dough through a roller (dough break) until it snaps and is shiny. Cut into biscuits about ½ inch thick; prick with a sharp 3-tine fork, making 3 rows of holes. Bake at 350° about 45 minutes or until light brown. Yield: about 2 to 3 dozen.

Note: May be frozen baked or unbaked.

But beaten biscuits have been seen only at parties and special occasions in recent years. For day-in, day-out plain good eating, Southern cooks bake up biscuits fluffy and light with baking powder or with soda and buttermilk. To say we dote on hot biscuits is to understate the case. They are so easy to make that they are daily fare in many homes.

Before baking powder was invented in 1850, bakers had to mix their own soda and cream of tartar and guess how much it would take to make their biscuits and other quick breads rise. The quality was certainly uneven.

Then came dependable commercial baking powder, removing the guesswork, and Southern cooks raised a floury cloud that has never subsided. Many bakers embraced self-rising flour and cornmeal when they became available, with excellent results. And for special occasions, we have the ultimate "riz" or "angel" biscuit wherein the standard baking powder or buttermilk recipe is bolstered with yeast.

Unique to the South, it appears to me, is our use of the ever-present dumpling. Not content to serve them just with chicken, we cook them on top of fresh butter beans, stewed tomatoes, black-eyed peas, dried beans of all kinds, soups, stews, and sauerkraut. Cornmeal dumplings, of course, go with greens and some pork dishes.

Dumplings are breadstuff, to be sure, but Southerners do not necessarily use them as a bread substitute; we blithely serve them up at the same meal with bread and/or biscuits. Calorie counters are on their own at such meals; the cook is not responsible if the guests eat some of everything.

Dressing is another of our specialties. Again, we have a breadstuff served in addition to, not instead of, bread at a meal. Loaded with sausage or oysters, dressing would be a respectable meal even without the poultry or meat it accompanies.

In pointing up the breads and breadstuffs that set the South apart from other sections of the country, I do not mean to imply that our yeast baking lags behind. Far from it; everyone knows that Southern cooks serve light rolls that melt in the mouth. And our rich ethnic mix gives us access to as many shapes and flavors as are to be found anywhere.

Some people like to remind one another that "to eat it today is to wear it tomorrow." That line always gives me a twinge when I bake something as tempting as Moravian Love Feast Buns or German Sugar Kuchen. Never mind—this is the kind of sweet adversity that builds the Southern character.

The North thinks it knows how to make corn bread, but
this is mere superstition.
Mark Twain

Breads and Breadstuffs

Baking Powder Biscuits

    2 cups all-purpose flour
    1 teaspoon salt
    2½ teaspoons baking powder
    3 tablespoons shortening
    ¾ to 1 cup milk

Stir dry ingredients together in a medium mixing bowl; cut in shortening until mixture resembles coarse meal. Gradually stir in enough milk to make a soft dough. Turn dough out on a floured surface; knead lightly 3 or 4 times. Roll dough to ½-inch thickness. Cut with a floured biscuit cutter. Place biscuits on a lightly greased baking sheet; bake at 425° about 15 minutes or until lightly browned. Yield: 1 to 1½ dozen.

Buttermilk Biscuits

    2 cups all-purpose flour
    1 teaspoon salt
    ½ teaspoon soda
    1 teaspoon baking powder
    3 tablespoons shortening or butter
    ¾ to 1 cup buttermilk

Combine flour, salt, soda, and baking powder; cut in shortening until mixture resembles coarse meal. Stir in enough buttermilk to make a soft dough. Turn dough out onto a floured surface; roll to ½-inch thickness, and cut with floured biscuit cutter. Bake at 400° for 12 to 15 minutes. Yield: 12 to 16 biscuits.

Little Party Biscuits

    2 cups self-rising flour
    1 teaspoon salt
    ¼ cup lard or shortening
    ¾ cup buttermilk

Combine flour and salt, mixing well. Cut in lard until mixture resembles coarse meal. Stir in buttermilk; knead lightly 3 or 4 times. Turn dough out onto a floured surface, and roll to ½-inch thickness. Cut with a floured 1-inch biscuit cutter. Place on a lightly greased baking sheet, and bake at 400° for 10 to 12 minutes. Yield: about 2½ dozen.

Sweet Potato Biscuits

    1½ cups all-purpose flour
    2 teaspoons baking powder
    ½ teaspoon salt
    ½ cup cold shortening
    1 cup milk
    1½ cups mashed cooked sweet
        potatoes

Combine flour, baking powder, and salt in a medium mixing bowl; cut in shortening until mixture resembles coarse meal. Combine milk and sweet potatoes, mixing well; add to flour mixture and stir quickly. Turn dough out on a lightly floured surface and knead lightly. Roll to ½-inch thickness; cut with a floured biscuit cutter. Place on greased baking sheets and bake at 425° for 12 to 15 minutes. Yield: about 2 dozen.

Note: For sweeter biscuits, add a little sugar and a few drops of vanilla extract to dough.

Corn Biscuit Strips

1 (8¾-ounce) can cream-style corn
2 cups biscuit mix
¼ cup melted butter or margarine

Combine corn and biscuit mix. Turn dough out onto a floured board and knead 15 times. Pat dough into rectangle; cut into 3- × 1-inch strips. Roll strips in melted butter; place on ungreased baking sheets. Bake at 450° for 12 to 15 minutes. Yield: 20 biscuit strips.

Raised Potato Biscuits

1 medium potato, peeled and sliced
1 package dry yeast
¼ cup warm water (105° to 115°)
1 egg, beaten
1½ cups milk
½ teaspoon soda
1 teaspoon baking powder
1½ teaspoons salt
⅓ cup sugar
About 6 cups all-purpose
    flour, divided
¾ cup melted butter or margarine,
    divided

Cook potato until tender in boiling water to cover. Do not drain; mash potato and water together. Dissolve yeast in ¼ cup warm water, and add to potato mixture. Stir in egg, milk, soda, baking powder, salt, sugar, and 2 cups flour; beat well. Cover and let rise in a warm place (85°), free from drafts, for 45 minutes or until bubbly. Stir in ½ cup melted butter and enough remaining flour to make a soft, workable dough. Turn dough out on a floured surface and knead until smooth and elastic. Roll dough to ½-inch thickness.

Cut into rounds with a floured biscuit cutter. Dip biscuits in remaining melted butter and place on ungreased cookie sheets. Cover and let rise in a warm place about 30 minutes; bake at 425° about 15 minutes or until browned. Yield: about 4 dozen.

Derby Breakfast Yeast Biscuits

1 package dry yeast
1 cup warm buttermilk (105° to 115°)
½ teaspoon soda
1 teaspoon salt
2 tablespoons sugar
2½ cups all-purpose flour
½ cup shortening
Melted butter or margarine

Dissolve yeast in warm buttermilk; set aside. Combine soda, salt, sugar, and flour in a medium mixing bowl; cut in shortening until mixture resembles coarse meal. Add yeast mixture to flour mixture; stir until blended. Turn out on a lightly floured surface and knead lightly. Roll dough to ½-inch thickness. Cut with a floured biscuit cutter; dip in melted butter and place on an ungreased baking sheet. Cover and let rise in a warm place (85°), free from drafts, for 1 hour. Uncover and bake at 400° for 12 minutes. Yield: about 2½ dozen.

Crackling Cornbread

2 tablespoons bacon drippings
2 cups cornmeal
½ cup all-purpose flour
1 teaspoon salt
2 teaspoons baking powder
½ teaspoon soda
1 cup buttermilk
1 egg, beaten
1 cup cracklings, chopped

Place drippings in a 9-inch skillet; set skillet in oven and heat oven to 425°.

Combine cornmeal, flour, salt, and baking powder in a medium mixing bowl; mix well. Add soda to buttermilk; stir into dry ingredients. Add egg; beat well. Stir in cracklings. Pour into hot greased skillet, and bake at 425° about 20 to 25 minutes or until browned. Yield: 8 servings.

Light Cornbread

1 cup milk
6 tablespoons sugar
2 teaspoons salt
½ cup butter or margarine
½ cup warm water (105° to 115°)
2 packages dry yeast
2 eggs, beaten
3½ cups all-purpose flour
1¾ cups yellow cornmeal

Combine milk, sugar, salt, and butter; heat until milk is scalded and butter is melted. Cool to lukewarm.

Combine warm water and yeast, stirring until yeast is dissolved. Add milk mixture, eggs, flour, and cornmeal; beat until well mixed (about 2 minutes). Batter will be stiff.

Spoon batter into 2 greased 8-inch round cakepans or 2 greased 9- × 5- × 3-inch loafpans. Cover; let rise in a warm place (85°) until doubled in bulk (about 1 hour). Bake at 375° for 30 to 35 minutes. Yield: 2 loaves.

Southern Lacy Edge Corn Cakes

1 cup cornmeal
1 cup boiling water
¼ cup all-purpose flour
1 teaspoon salt
1 teaspoon sugar
1 tablespoon baking powder
1 egg, well beaten
½ to ¾ cup milk
Butter or margarine

Scald cornmeal with enough boiling water to make a mushlike consistency in a medium bowl. Let cool about 10 minutes. Add flour, salt, sugar, baking powder, egg, and milk; beat well. Batter should be very thin.

Drop batter by tablespoonfuls onto a hot, lightly greased griddle. Cook until brown on one side; turn and brown other side. (Cakes will have a crusty, lacy edge.) Serve at once with butter. Yield: about 3 dozen.

Buttermilk Cornbread

1 tablespoon shortening
1¾ cups white self-rising cornmeal
⅓ cup self-rising flour
1½ cups buttermilk

Heat shortening in an 8-inch iron skillet at 500° until very hot. Combine remaining ingredients in a medium mixing bowl, mixing well. Pour batter into hot skillet, and bake at 500° for 20 to 25 minutes or until browned. Yield: 6 to 8 servings.

Southern Cornbread

2 eggs
2 cups buttermilk
2 cups cornmeal
1 teaspoon salt
1 teaspoon soda
2 teaspoons baking powder
2 tablespoons bacon drippings, melted

If skillet or muffin irons are to be used, grease and place in oven when it is turned on; they should be smoking hot. If tin pan or muffin rings are used, simply grease them.

Beat eggs in a medium mixing bowl; add buttermilk. Combine dry ingredients; stir into egg mixture. Stir in drippings.

Pour into a hot, well-greased 9- or 10-inch skillet or 18 muffin cups or one 9-inch square baking pan. Bake at 475° about 25 minutes if using skillet or baking pan, and about 15 to 20 minutes for muffins. Serve hot with butter. Yield: one 9- or 10-inch loaf or 1½ dozen muffins.

Note: To use cornbread in making dressing, cool and crumble.

Yellow Cornbread

1 cup all-purpose flour
¼ cup sugar
1 tablespoon plus 1 teaspoon baking
   powder
¾ teaspoon salt
1 cup yellow cornmeal
2 eggs
1 cup milk
¼ cup melted shortening

Combine flour, sugar, baking powder, and salt; stir in cornmeal. Beat eggs with a fork just enough to blend; stir milk and shortening into egg. Add dry ingredients and stir to blend thoroughly, beating just until smooth. Pour into a greased 8-inch square baking pan or a 10-inch iron skillet. Bake at 425° about 25 minutes or until done. Yield: 8 servings.

Note: For Buttermilk Cornbread, use 1 tablespoon baking powder and add ¼ teaspoon soda. Substitute buttermilk for milk.

Old-Fashioned Corn Lightbread

About 7 cups cornmeal, divided
4 cups boiling water
2 cups cold water
1 teaspoon soda
1 cup all-purpose flour
1 cup sugar

Add 2 cups cornmeal to boiling water in a 4-quart Dutch oven. Stir constantly for 2 minutes, or until meal swells; do not cook. Remove from heat; cool 30 minutes. Add cold water, stirring until smooth. Stir in 2 cups cornmeal. Cover and let stand in a warm place (85°), free from drafts, for 18 to 24 hours or until soured.

Stir batter well. Combine soda, flour, and 1 cup cornmeal; stir into batter. Add sugar and enough cornmeal to make a very stiff batter, about 2 cups.

Pour into a well-greased deep 9-inch skillet or Dutch oven with tight-fitting lid. Cover; bake at 350° for 2 hours. Allow to cool in pan, covered, for 1 hour or until crust is soft; complete cooling on wire rack. Store, covered, in a cool place. Yield: 12 to 16 servings.

Delicate Cornmeal Muffins

½ cup boiling water
½ cup cornmeal
2 tablespoons melted butter or
   margarine
½ cup all-purpose flour
½ teaspoon salt
2 tablespoons sugar
2 teaspoons baking powder
1 egg, lightly beaten
½ cup milk

Pour boiling water over cornmeal in a medium mixing bowl; add butter and mix thoroughly. Cover; let stand at least 1 hour. Stir in flour, salt, sugar, and baking powder. Stir in egg and milk; mix thoroughly. (Mixture will be quite thin.) Bake in a heated, buttered muffin pan at 400° about 25 minutes. Yield: 1 dozen small muffins.

Cornmeal Rolls

2 cups milk
½ cup shortening
½ cup cornmeal
½ cup sugar
1 teaspoon salt
2 eggs, beaten
1 package dry yeast
¼ cup warm water (105° to 115°)
4½ to 5 cups all-purpose flour

Scald milk. Add shortening, cornmeal, sugar, and salt to milk; stir until shortening melts. Stir in eggs. Dissolve yeast in warm water and add to milk mixture. Add enough flour to make a soft dough. Chill.

Shape dough into rolls; cover and let rise

in a warm place (85°), free from drafts, until doubled in size. Bake at 400° for 12 to 15 minutes. Yield: 2 to 3 dozen rolls.

Note: Dough may be stored in refrigerator for 3 to 4 days before shaping into rolls.

Corn Sticks

1¼ cups yellow cornmeal
⅔ cup all-purpose flour
¼ cup sugar (optional)
1 tablespoon baking powder
½ teaspoon salt
1 egg, beaten
1 cup milk
¼ cup vegetable oil

Combine dry ingredients. Add egg, milk, and oil; mix lightly. Pour batter into 2 well-greased corn-stick pans. Bake at 425° for 12 to 15 minutes or until golden brown. Yield: 14 corn sticks.

Buttermilk Corn Sticks

1⅓ cups cornmeal
⅓ cup all-purpose flour
1 teaspoon baking powder
½ teaspoon soda
½ teaspoon salt
1 tablespoon sugar
1 cup buttermilk
1 egg, beaten
2 tablespoons melted shortening

Combine first 6 ingredients; stir in buttermilk and egg just until dry ingredients are moistened. Stir in shortening.

Place a well-greased cast-iron corn-stick pan in a 400° oven for 3 minutes or until hot. Remove pan from oven; spoon batter into pan, filling two-thirds full. Bake at 400° for 12 to 15 minutes or until lightly browned. Yield: about 15 corn sticks.

Seafood Corn Sticks

Batter for Southern Cornbread (page 165)
1 cup flaked crabmeat or finely chopped shrimp
1 teaspoon Worcestershire sauce
Dash of cayenne pepper

Combine cornbread batter, crabmeat, Worcestershire sauce, and cayenne in a large mixing bowl; mix well. Pour into a greased cast-iron corn-stick pan or muffin tins and bake at 425° for 15 to 20 minutes. Yield: about 1½ to 2 dozen.

Golden Hush Puppies

2 cups self-rising cornmeal
1 small onion, finely chopped
¾ cup milk
1 egg, slightly beaten
Vegetable oil or shortening

Combine cornmeal and onion; add milk and egg, stirring well. Carefully drop batter by tablespoonfuls into deep hot oil (370°); cook only a few at a time, turning once. Fry until hush puppies are golden brown (3 to 5 minutes). Drain well. Yield: about 2 dozen.

Hush Puppies

1¾ cups white cornmeal
1½ teaspoons salt
1 teaspoon baking powder
½ teaspoon soda
1 egg, beaten
1 cup buttermilk
¼ cup finely chopped onion
Vegetable oil

Combine dry ingredients; add egg and buttermilk, mixing lightly. Stir in onion.

Drop batter by tablespoonfuls into deep hot oil (370°); turn once. Cook until hush puppies are golden brown (3 to 5 minutes). Drain well. Yield: 1½ dozen.

Cracker Hush Puppies

1¼ cups commercial hush puppy mix
1 (8-ounce) can whole tomatoes, drained and chopped
1 small onion, chopped
¼ cup chopped green pepper
1 egg, beaten
⅓ cup beer
¼ teaspoon salt
¼ teaspoon pepper
¼ teaspoon crushed red pepper
⅛ teaspoon garlic powder
Dash of baking powder
Vegetable oil

Combine all ingredients except vegetable oil; stir well. Drop batter by tablespoonfuls into deep hot oil (370°); turn once. Cook until hush puppies are golden brown (3 to 5 minutes). Drain. Yield: about 1½ dozen.

Boone Tavern Spoon Cakes

1½ cups white cornmeal
¼ teaspoon soda
½ teaspoon baking powder
½ teaspoon salt
1 cup buttermilk
¼ cup water
4 eggs, beaten
¼ cup melted butter

Sift dry ingredients. Add buttermilk and water; beat. Add eggs; beat. Add melted butter last and stir, mixing well. Drop by teaspoonfuls onto a hot greased griddle. A large skillet may be used, if desired. Serve hot. Yield: 6 to 8 servings.

Owendaw

2 cups hot cooked grits
3 tablespoons butter or margarine
4 eggs, well beaten
2 cups milk
½ teaspoon salt
About 1 cup cornmeal

Mix hot cooked grits with butter in a medium mixing bowl; add eggs. Stir in milk gradually; stir in salt and enough cornmeal to make batter the consistency of thick custard. Pour into a greased deep 2-quart casserole; bake at 350° for 45 minutes to 1 hour. Yield: 6 to 8 servings.

Note: This old plantation recipe complements any entrée.

Virginia Spoonbread

1½ cups cornmeal
3 tablespoons butter or margarine
About 1½ cups boiling water
1 egg, beaten
2 cups milk
1 tablespoon baking powder
1 teaspoon salt
1 tablespoon all-purpose flour
1 tablespoon sugar

Place cornmeal and butter in a medium mixing bowl; add boiling water, stirring until well moistened. Beat in egg and milk. Combine baking powder, salt, flour, and sugar; beat into batter. Pour into a greased 1½-quart baking dish, and bake at 450° about 30 minutes or until set and browned. Yield: 6 servings.

These homemade yeast breads are favorite accompaniments to any meal: (clockwise from top) New Orleans French Bread (page 177), Plaited White Bread (page 182), Black Bread (page 176), Sally Lunn (page 180), and Whole Wheat Sourdough Bread (page 181).

Rice Spoonbread

3 tablespoons white cornmeal
1 cup boiling water
¼ cup all-purpose flour
1 tablespoon sugar
½ teaspoon salt
1½ tablespoons butter or margarine
2 eggs, separated
1 cup cooked regular rice
1 cup milk
2 teaspoons baking powder

Combine cornmeal and 1 cup boiling water in top of a double boiler. Combine flour, sugar, and salt; add to cornmeal mixture. Cook over boiling water until thickened, stirring constantly. Remove from heat and stir in butter.

Beat egg yolks; add rice, milk, and baking powder to yolks. Stir yolk mixture into cornmeal mixture.

Beat egg whites until stiff but not dry; fold egg whites into cornmeal mixture. Pour mixture into a buttered 2-quart baking dish, and bake at 350° about 45 minutes or until set and browned. Yield: 6 to 8 servings.

Apple Fritters

1 cup all-purpose flour
1 teaspoon baking powder
1 teaspoon powdered sugar
¼ teaspoon salt
¼ cup milk
1 egg, beaten
2 apples, peeled and chopped
Vegetable oil
Powdered sugar

Combine dry ingredients in a medium mixing bowl. Combine milk and egg; stir into dry ingredients. Stir in apple. Drop batter by teaspoonfuls into deep hot oil (365°); fry fritters until browned, turning once. Drain on paper towels. Sprinkle with powdered sugar. Yield: 1 dozen.

Note: Other fruit may be substituted.

Berlin Jelly Doughnuts

4 cups all-purpose flour, divided
¼ cup sugar
1 teaspoon salt
1 package dry yeast
1 cup warm milk (105° to 115°), divided
1 egg, beaten
2 tablespoons vegetable oil
2 teaspoons rum
½ cup jelly or marmalade
1 egg white, slightly beaten
Vegetable oil or shortening
Powdered sugar

Combine flour, ¼ cup sugar, and salt. Soften yeast in ¼ cup of the milk in a medium mixing bowl; stir in ¾ of the flour mixture. Add egg, 2 tablespoons oil, rum, and remaining milk. Add enough remaining flour mixture to make a soft dough. Cover; let rise in warm place (85°), free from drafts, for 1 hour or until doubled in bulk. Punch down; roll out on a floured surface to ¼-inch thickness. Cut into 2½-inch rounds with a floured biscuit cutter. Place a teaspoonful of jelly in center of half the rounds; brush edges with egg white. Top with remaining dough rounds; pinch edges to seal. Let rise in a warm place (85°) on a floured surface for 20 minutes or until slightly raised.

Fry in deep hot oil (360°), a few at a time; cook about 2 minutes or until browned on one side. Turn and brown other side. Remove from oil with slotted spoon; drain on paper towels. Sprinkle with powdered sugar while still warm. Yield: about 1½ to 2 dozen.

Light Cornbread (page 165), Hush Puppies (page 167), and Corn Sticks (page 167) are just three variations of old-fashioned Southern cornbread.

Crullers

1½ cups sugar
2 eggs, beaten
1 cup buttermilk or sour milk
2 tablespoons melted butter or
    margarine
½ teaspoon ground nutmeg
½ teaspoon ground cinnamon
1 teaspoon salt
1 teaspoon soda
4½ to 5 cups all-purpose flour
Vegetable oil or shortening
Powdered sugar

Beat sugar with eggs in a medium mixing bowl; add buttermilk and butter. Combine nutmeg, cinnamon, salt, soda, and 4½ cups flour. Blend flour mixture into egg mixture; add additional flour if necessary to form a soft dough. Knead lightly 3 or 4 times. Turn dough out onto a floured surface; roll to ¼-inch thickness. Cut with floured doughnut cutter; drop into deep hot oil (365°) and fry about 2 minutes, turning once. Drain on paper towels; sprinkle with powdered sugar. Yield: 3 to 3½ dozen.

Knee Caps

¾ cup milk
3 tablespoons shortening
¼ cup sugar
1 teaspoon salt
1 egg, beaten
1 package dry yeast
¼ cup warm water (105° to 115°)
3½ to 4 cups all-purpose flour,
    divided
Vegetable oil or shortening
Syrup and butter (optional)
Powdered sugar (optional)

Scald milk in a small saucepan; add shortening, sugar, and salt. Stir to dissolve; cool. Pour into a medium mixing bowl; stir in egg. Dissolve yeast in water; stir into cooled milk

mixture. Beat in 1½ cups flour; add enough remaining flour gradually to make a soft, workable dough.

Turn dough out on a lightly floured surface and knead until smooth and elastic. Place in a greased bowl, turning to grease top. Cover and let rise in a warm place (85°), free from drafts, about 1 hour or until doubled in bulk. Punch dough down. Divide dough into 18 equal pieces. Roll each piece into a ball; pull each ball to make it thin in center. Drop into deep hot oil (365°), and fry until browned on both sides. Serve hot with syrup and butter, or dredge with powdered sugar. Yield: 1½ dozen.

Pancakes

1 cup soft breadcrumbs
¼ teaspoon soda
1 cup buttermilk
1 egg, well beaten
1 teaspoon baking powder
1 tablespoon sugar
Dash of salt
About 1 cup all-purpose flour

Place breadcrumbs in a medium mixing bowl. Dissolve soda in buttermilk and add to breadcrumbs. Add egg, beating well. Stir baking powder, sugar, and salt into breadcrumb mixture. Add enough flour to make proper consistency. Drop by tablespoonfuls onto a hot greased griddle or skillet. Cook until brown on one side; turn and brown other side. Yield: about 10 pancakes.

German Pancake

3 eggs
3 tablespoons all-purpose flour
4 tablespoons sugar, divided
¼ cup plus 2 tablespoons milk
Juice of ½ lemon
¼ teaspoon ground cinnamon
¼ cup melted butter or margarine
Powdered sugar
Jam, jelly, or applesauce

Beat eggs with flour, 1 tablespoon sugar, and milk in a medium mixing bowl. Pour batter all at once into a generously buttered 9-inch heavy skillet. Bake at 425° about 8 minutes. Reduce heat to 375°; bake 8 minutes longer or until pancake puffs up above sides of skillet and is a delicate brown. Place on a hot platter. Sprinkle with lemon juice, remaining 3 tablespoons sugar, cinnamon, and melted butter; roll up. Dust with powdered sugar and serve at once with jam, jelly, or applesauce. Yield: about 3 servings.

Orange-Apple Nut Bread

⅓ cup frozen orange juice
    concentrate, undiluted
1½ cups chopped apple
⅓ cup shortening
1 cup sugar
1 egg
2 cups all-purpose flour
1 teaspoon baking powder
½ teaspoon soda
¾ cup raisins
¾ cup chopped nuts

Combine orange juice and apple in a small bowl; set aside. Blend shortening and sugar in a medium bowl until creamy; add egg, beating well. Stir in apple mixture. Combine flour, baking powder, and soda; beat into creamed mixture. Stir in raisins and nuts. Pour into a greased 10-inch tube or Bundt pan. Bake at 350° for 45 minutes or until done and brown. Yield: 1 loaf.

Apple Nut Bread

1 cup vegetable oil
2 cups sugar
3 eggs, well beaten
2 cups diced peeled apples
1 cup chopped nuts
3 cups all-purpose flour
1 teaspoon soda
1 teaspoon salt
2 teaspoons vanilla extract

Combine oil and sugar in a medium mixing bowl; beat well. Add eggs, beating well. Stir in apples and nuts. Combine flour, soda, and salt; blend into batter. Stir in vanilla; pour into a greased and floured 9-inch tube pan or two 8½- × 4½- × 3-inch loafpans. Bake at 350° for 60 to 75 minutes for tube pan, and about 50 minutes for loaves, or until bread tests done. Cool on wire rack. Yield: one 9-inch cake or 2 loaves.

Apricot Nut Loaf

1 cup sugar
2 tablespoons shortening
1 egg, beaten
¾ cup milk
¾ cup orange juice
1 tablespoon plus 1 teaspoon
    grated orange rind
3 cups all-purpose flour
1 tablespoon plus ½ teaspoon
    baking powder
1 teaspoon salt
1 cup chopped dried apricots
¾ cup chopped nuts

Mix sugar, shortening, and egg in a medium mixing bowl. Combine milk and orange juice. Combine orange rind, flour, baking powder, and salt. Alternately add milk and flour mixtures to batter, mixing well. Stir in apricots and nuts. Pour into a greased 9- × 5- × 3-inch loafpan; let stand 20 minutes. Bake at 350° for 70 minutes. Yield: 1 loaf.

Banana Bread

½ cup butter or margarine
1 cup sugar
2 eggs
¼ teaspoon soda
¼ cup buttermilk
2 to 3 bananas
2 teaspoons baking powder
½ teaspoon salt
2 cups all-purpose flour
1 teaspoon vanilla extract

Cream butter and sugar until light and fluffy. Add eggs to butter mixture and mix well.

Combine soda and buttermilk; peel bananas and pour buttermilk mixture over them. Mash bananas in buttermilk mixture; stir banana mixture into creamed mixture. Combine baking powder, salt, and flour. Stir flour mixture and vanilla into creamed mixture. Pour into a greased 9- × 5- × 3-inch loafpan, and bake at 350° about 45 minutes or until done. Cool slightly; remove from pan and complete cooling on a wire rack. Yield: 1 loaf.

Banana-Peanut Butter Bread

2 cups all-purpose flour
2 teaspoons baking powder
½ teaspoon soda
½ teaspoon salt
1 cup sugar
½ cup butter or margarine, softened
2 eggs, well beaten
2 large bananas, mashed
½ cup crunchy peanut butter

Combine flour, baking powder, soda, and salt in a small mixing bowl; set aside. Cream sugar and butter in a large mixing bowl; add eggs, mixing well.

Mix mashed bananas with peanut butter; add banana mixture and flour mixture alternately to sugar mixture, mixing well. Pour into a greased and floured 9- × 5- × 3-inch loafpan. Bake at 350° for 50 to 60 minutes. Cool in pan on wire rack for 10 minutes. Remove from pan and complete cooling on wire rack. Yield: 1 loaf.

Old-Fashioned Brown Bread

2 cups whole wheat flour
½ cup all-purpose flour
2 teaspoons soda
1 teaspoon salt
2 cups buttermilk
½ cup molasses
1 cup raisins

Combine all ingredients in a large mixing bowl; mix well. Spoon mixture into 3 well-greased 1-pound coffee cans; let stand for 30 minutes. Bake, uncovered, at 350° for 45 to 50 minutes. Cool in cans 10 minutes. Remove from cans and cool on wire racks. Yield: 3 loaves.

Cranberry Bread

2 cups all-purpose flour
1 cup sugar
1½ teaspoons baking powder
½ teaspoon soda
1 teaspoon salt
Juice and grated rind of 1 orange
2 tablespoons vegetable oil
About 2 tablespoons boiling water
1 egg, well beaten
½ cup chopped nuts
1½ cups cranberries, coarsely
  chopped

Combine flour, sugar, baking powder, soda, and salt in a large mixing bowl. Pour orange juice into a measuring cup; add orange rind, oil, and enough boiling water to make ¾ cup. Combine orange juice mixture and egg.

Stir liquid mixture into dry ingredients just until dampened. Fold in nuts and cranberries. Pour into a greased and floured 9- × 5- × 3-inch loafpan. Push batter up into corners of pan, leaving center slightly hollowed. Let stand 20 minutes. Bake at 350° for 45 to 60 minutes. Remove from pan and cool on wire rack. Wrap tightly and store overnight for easier slicing. Yield: 1 loaf.

Date Nut Bread

2 cups boiling water
1 cup sugar
1 cup chopped dates
1 teaspoon salt
2 tablespoons shortening
2 teaspoons soda
1 egg, beaten
2 teaspoons baking powder
1 cup chopped nuts
3 cups all-purpose flour
2 teaspoons vanilla extract

Pour boiling water over sugar, dates, salt, shortening, and soda in a medium mixing bowl. Stir; let cool. Add remaining ingredients; mix well. Pour batter into 2 greased and floured 8½- × 4½- × 3-inch loafpans. Bake at 350° for 45 minutes. Yield: 2 loaves.

Grapenut Bread

1 cup nutlike cereal nuggets
2 cups sour milk or buttermilk
½ cup sugar
4 cups all-purpose flour
¼ teaspoon salt
2 teaspoons baking powder
1 teaspoon soda
2 eggs, beaten

Combine cereal, milk, and sugar in a medium mixing bowl; let stand for 1 hour or until cereal is softened. Combine dry ingredients; add to cereal mixture alternately with beaten eggs, blending well. Pour into a well-greased 9- × 5- × 3-inch loafpan. Bake at 350° for about 40 minutes or until bread tests done. Cool on wire rack before slicing or wrapping. Yield: 1 loaf.

Marmalade Bread

3 cups all-purpose flour
1 tablespoon baking powder
1 teaspoon salt
1 teaspoon soda
1½ cups orange marmalade, divided
1 egg, beaten
¼ cup vegetable oil
¾ cup orange juice
1 cup chopped nuts

Combine flour, baking powder, salt, and soda in a large mixing bowl. Stir in 1¼ cups marmalade, egg, vegetable oil, orange juice, and nuts. Pour into a greased 9- × 5- × 3-inch loafpan, and bake at 350° for 1 hour.

Remove loaf from pan; place on a greased baking sheet. Spread top of loaf with remaining ¼ cup marmalade; return to oven for 1 minute. Remove and cool. Yield: 1 loaf.

Whipped Cream Nut Loaf

1 cup golden raisins
1 cup whipping cream
1 egg
1 cup sugar
1 teaspoon grated lemon rind
1 cup walnuts or pecans, chopped
1¾ cups all-purpose flour
1½ teaspoons baking powder
¼ teaspoon salt

Combine raisins and water to cover in a small saucepan. Bring to a boil and boil 5 minutes. Drain and set aside.

Whip cream in a medium mixing bowl until soft peaks form; beat in egg and sugar until thoroughly blended. Add grated rind; fold in walnuts and raisins. Combine flour, baking powder, and salt; fold into cream mixture. Spoon batter into a greased 9- × 5- × 3-inch loafpan. Bake at 325° for 1 hour and 10 minutes or until done and brown.

Cool 15 minutes in pan on a wire rack. Remove from pan and cool completely before slicing. Yield: 1 loaf.

Olive Bread

        1½ cups all-purpose flour
        1½ cups whole wheat flour
        1½ teaspoons salt
        2 teaspoons baking powder
        ½ teaspoon soda
        ½ cup molasses
        1¾ cups milk
        1 cup coarsely chopped ripe olives

Combine flour, salt, and baking powder. Stir soda into molasses in a large mixing bowl. Add milk; gradually add dry ingredients, mixing thoroughly. Stir in olives. Pour into a greased 9- × 5- × 3-inch loafpan. Bake at 350° for 1 hour or until done and brown. Yield: 1 loaf.

Pumpkin Bread

        2 eggs
        ½ cup vegetable oil
        ⅓ cup water
        ¾ teaspoon salt
        ¾ teaspoon ground cinnamon
        ½ teaspoon vanilla extract
        1½ cups firmly packed light brown
            sugar
        1 cup cooked mashed pumpkin
        1½ cups all-purpose flour
        1 teaspoon soda
        ½ cup chopped walnuts or pecans
        ½ cup raisins

Combine eggs, oil, and water in a large mixing bowl. Add salt, cinnamon, vanilla, and sugar; beat well on low speed of electric mixer. Add pumpkin, mixing well. Mix flour with soda; stir into batter. Fold in walnuts and raisins. Pour into 2 greased 1-pound coffee cans or 2 greased 8½- × 4½- × 3-inch loafpans. Bake at 350° for 1 hour or until loaves test done. Cool in pans on wire racks. Yield: 2 loaves.

Walnut Pumpkin Bread

        5 cups all-purpose flour
        4½ cups sugar
        1 tablespoon soda
        2½ teaspoons salt
        1½ teaspoons ground cinnamon
        1½ teaspoons ground nutmeg
        1½ cups vegetable oil
        1 cup water
        6 eggs
        1 (29-ounce) can pumpkin
        1½ cups chopped walnuts
        Softened butter or cream cheese

Combine flour, sugar, soda, salt, cinnamon, and nutmeg in a large mixing bowl; mix well. Add oil, water, eggs, and pumpkin; beat at medium speed of an electric mixer until thoroughly blended. Stir in walnuts.

Pour batter into 6 greased 8½- × 4½- × 3-inch loafpans. Bake at 350° for 1 hour, or until loaves test done and tops are golden brown. Serve hot or cold with butter or cream cheese. Yield: 6 loaves.

Black Bread

        1 package dry yeast
        2 cups warm water (105° to 115°)
        2 tablespoons sugar
        2 teaspoons salt
        2 tablespoons shortening, melted
            and cooled
        4 to 5 cups all-purpose flour, divided
        3 tablespoons dark molasses
        3 cups rye flour
        1 tablespoon caraway seeds
        1 tablespoon dillseeds
        Melted butter or margarine

Dissolve yeast in warm water in a large bowl. Add sugar, salt, shortening, and 3 cups all-purpose flour; beat well. Add molasses, rye flour, caraway seeds, and dillseeds. Stir in enough additional all-purpose flour to form a stiff dough.

Turn dough out on a floured surface, and knead until smooth and elastic (about 8 to 10 minutes). Place in a well-greased bowl, turning to grease top. Cover and let rise in a warm place (85°), free from drafts, until doubled in bulk.

Divide dough in half, and shape each half into a smooth ball. Place each on a greased baking sheet, and lightly press to flatten bottom. Cover; let rise in a warm place, free from drafts, until doubled in bulk. Bake at 400° for 30 minutes or until loaves sound hollow when tapped. Brush hot loaves with melted butter. Remove from baking sheets; cool on wire racks. Yield: 2 loaves.

Cheese Bread

        7 cups all-purpose flour, divided
        2 tablespoons sugar
        1 tablespoon salt
        2 packages dry yeast
        2¼ cups milk
        3 tablespoons butter or margarine
        2 eggs, beaten
        4 cups (16 ounces) shredded
            extra-sharp Cheddar cheese

Combine 2½ cups flour, sugar, salt, and yeast in a large mixing bowl. Combine milk and butter in a small saucepan; bring to boil over medium heat. Cool to lukewarm; add to flour mixture and beat until blended. Add 1 cup flour; beat well. Stir in eggs, cheese, and remaining flour. Turn dough out onto a floured surface; knead until dough is smooth and elastic. Place in a greased bowl, turning to grease top. Cover; let rise in a warm place (85°), free from drafts, until doubled in bulk.

Punch dough down and divide into 2 loaves; place in greased 9- × 5- × 3-inch loafpans. Cover and let rise in a warm place, free from drafts, until doubled in bulk. Bake at 375° for 35 to 45 minutes. Remove loaves from pans at once and cool on wire racks. Yield: 2 loaves.

New Orleans French Bread

        2 tablespoons shortening
        1 tablespoon sugar
        1 tablespoon salt
        1 cup boiling water
        1 cup cold water
        1 package dry yeast
        5½ to 6 cups all-purpose flour,
            divided
        Egg White Glaze (recipe follows)

Combine shortening, sugar, salt, and boiling water in a large bowl; stir occasionally to melt shortening. Add cold water, and allow mixture to cool to 105° to 115°. Sprinkle yeast over liquid mixture; let stand 5 minutes, and stir to dissolve. Gradually beat in 4 cups flour; add enough remaining flour to form a stiff dough.

Turn dough out onto a floured surface, and knead until smooth and elastic (about 5 minutes). Place in a well-greased bowl, turning once to grease top. Cover and let rise in a warm place (85°), free from drafts, 1 to 1½ hours or until doubled in bulk. Punch down, and cover. Let rise 30 minutes or until doubled in bulk.

Turn dough onto a floured surface; knead slightly to press out gas bubbles; shape into a 14- to 16-inch cylinder on a greased baking sheet. Cover; let rise until doubled in bulk.

Cut ¼-inch-deep slashes in top of loaf with a sharp knife; then brush with Egg White Glaze. Bake at 375° for 40 to 50 minutes or until bread is golden brown. Remove from baking sheet and cool on wire rack. Yield: 1 loaf.

Egg White Glaze:

        1 egg white
        2 tablespoons cold water

Combine egg white and water, beating until frothy. Yield: glaze for 1 loaf.

Dill Bread

  ¾ cup commercial sour cream
  1 package dry yeast
  ¼ cup warm water (105° to 115°)
  2 tablespoons sugar
  1 teaspoon salt
  2 tablespoons shortening
  1 egg, beaten
  1 tablespoon dillseeds
  1 tablespoon dillweed
  2¼ cups all-purpose flour, divided

Heat sour cream in a small saucepan over low heat just until lukewarm. Dissolve yeast in warm water in a medium mixing bowl. Stir in lukewarm sour cream, sugar, salt, shortening, egg, dillseeds, dillweed, and 1½ cups flour; beat until smooth. Stir in remaining flour until smooth. Cover; let rise in a warm place (85°), free from drafts, about 30 minutes or until doubled in bulk.

Punch batter down and divide equally between two greased 9- × 5- × 3-inch loafpans. (Batter will be sticky.) Smooth batter into shape with floured fingers. Cover and let dough rise in a warm place, free from drafts, for 30 minutes. Bake at 350° about 1 hour or until golden brown. Cool on wire racks. Yield: 2 loaves.

Rich Homemade Bread

  3 packages dry yeast
  ½ cup warm water (105° to 115°)
  1 cup shortening
  ⅓ cup sugar
  2 teaspoons salt
  2 cups milk
  6 eggs, well beaten
  8 cups all-purpose flour
  Melted butter or margarine

Soften yeast in water. Combine shortening, sugar, salt, and milk in a large saucepan; scald. Cool. Stir in yeast; alternately add eggs and flour, beating well. Place dough in a

greased bowl; turn to grease all sides. Cover and let rise in a warm place (85°), free from drafts, until doubled in bulk. Punch dough down and divide evenly into 4 greased 9- × 5- × 3-inch loafpans. Cover and let rise in a warm place until doubled in bulk. Bake at 350° about 45 minutes or until done. Brush crust with melted butter. Cool slightly; remove from pans and finish cooling on wire racks. Yield: 4 loaves.

Irish Bread

  ¾ cup raisins
  2½ to 2¾ cups all-purpose flour, divided
  3 tablespoons sugar
  ½ teaspoon salt
  ½ teaspoon soda
  1 package dry yeast
  1 cup buttermilk
  2 tablespoons butter or margarine

Combine raisins and water to cover in a small saucepan. Cover and bring to a boil. Remove from heat and let set until raisins are plumped. Drain and set aside. Mix 1 cup flour with sugar, salt, soda, and yeast in a medium mixing bowl. Combine buttermilk and butter in a small saucepan and cook over low heat almost to boiling. (Mixture will look curdled.) Cool to lukewarm and gradually beat into flour mixture. Add ¼ cup flour and beat again. Stir in raisins and enough additional flour to make a soft workable dough. Form dough into a ball; place in a greased bowl, turning to grease both sides. Cover and let rise in a warm place (85°), free from drafts, for 1 hour or until doubled in bulk.

Turn dough out onto a floured surface and knead 20 times. Form dough into a ball; place on a greased baking sheet. Flatten ball to an 8-inch circle. Cover; let rise in a warm place, free from drafts, until almost doubled in bulk.

Sprinkle dough lightly with flour. Cut a shallow cross on top with a sharp knife. Bake at 350° for 30 minutes. Remove from baking sheet and cool on wire rack. Yield: one 10-inch loaf.

Note: In Ireland, the loaf is broken along the cross marks into 4 pieces. Each fourth or "farl" is then placed, broken side down, on a board and sliced.

Dutch Loaf (Potato Bread)

1 medium potato, peeled
1 package dry yeast
1 cup milk
5 cups all-purpose flour, divided
½ cup shortening and butter (mixed)
½ cup sugar
2 eggs
2 teaspoons salt
Melted butter or margarine

Boil potato in water to cover until tender; drain potato and reserve ½ cup cooking liquid. Mash potato. Stir yeast into reserved lukewarm cooking liquid and let stand a few minutes.

Scald milk; cool to lukewarm. Combine milk, yeast mixture, 1½ cups flour, and potato in a medium mixing bowl; beat for 3 minutes. Cover; let stand in a warm place (85°), free from drafts, for about 1½ hours or until doubled in bulk.

Cream shortening and butter in a medium mixing bowl; add sugar and beat until light. Add eggs and salt; beat well. Stir egg mixture into yeast mixture; add remaining flour to make a very soft dough, mixing well.

Place dough in a greased bowl, turning to grease top; cover, and let stand in a warm place until doubled in bulk. Punch dough down; turn dough out onto a lightly floured surface. Knead lightly 3 or 4 times. Place dough in a greased 2-quart casserole dish; brush top with melted butter.

Cover and let dough rise again in a warm place until doubled in bulk. Bake at 350° for 50 minutes or until done. Yield: 1 loaf.

Oatmeal Bread

2 cups boiling water
1 cup quick-cooking oats, uncooked
½ cup firmly packed brown sugar
2 tablespoons vegetable oil
½ cup whole wheat flour
1 tablespoon salt
1 package dry yeast
½ cup warm water (105° to 115°)
About 5 cups unbleached flour
Melted butter or margarine

Pour boiling water over oats, brown sugar, oil, whole wheat flour, and salt in a large mixing bowl. Stir well, and cool to lukewarm. Dissolve yeast in ½ cup warm water; add to batter. Stir in enough flour to form a soft dough; turn out on a floured surface and knead 5 minutes. Place in a greased bowl; turn to grease all sides. Cover, and let rise in a warm place (85°), free from drafts, for 1 hour or until doubled in bulk.

Punch dough down and let rise again in a warm place until doubled in bulk. Shape into three loaves and place in 3 greased 9- × 5- × 3-inch loafpans. Cover and let rise again until not quite doubled in size. Bake at 350° for 45 minutes or until done and brown. Remove from pans; brush tops with melted butter and cool. Yield: 3 loaves.

Raisin Bread

1 (15-ounce) box raisins
4½ to 5 cups all-purpose flour,
    divided
1 cup butter or margarine
2 cups sugar
4 eggs
1½ teaspoons ground nutmeg
1 package dry yeast
2 cups warm milk (105° to 115°)

Combine raisins with ½ cup flour; stir to coat raisins well. Combine butter and sugar in a large mixing bowl; beat until smooth and creamy. Add eggs, one at a time, beating well after each addition. Stir 4 cups flour with nutmeg and yeast. Add to batter alternately with milk, starting and ending with flour mixture. Add enough remaining flour to make a workable dough. Stir in raisins. Place in a greased bowl, turning to grease all sides. Cover and let rise in a warm place (85°), free from drafts, for about 1 hour or until doubled in bulk.

Punch dough down; turn out onto a floured surface. Divide dough in half; form into two loaves. Place in 2 greased 9- × 5- × 3-inch loafpans; cover and let rise in a warm place until almost doubled in bulk.

Bake at 325° for 1¼ to 1½ hours or until brown and done. Turn loaves out of pans immediately and cool on wire racks. Yield: 2 loaves.

Sally Lunn

1 package dry yeast
¼ cup warm water (105° to 115°)
¾ cup warm milk
½ cup butter or margarine, softened
⅓ cup sugar
3 eggs, well beaten
4 cups all-purpose flour
1 teaspoon salt

Combine yeast and water in a small bowl; let stand 5 minutes. Stir in milk. Cream butter

and sugar until light and fluffy in a large bowl; add eggs, blending well.

Combine flour and salt; add to creamed mixture alternately with milk mixture, beginning and ending with flour. Mix well after each addition. (Batter will be very stiff.) Cover and let rise in a warm place (85°), free from drafts, for about 2 hours or until doubled in bulk.

Spoon batter into a well-greased 10-inch tube pan or Bundt pan. Cover and let rise in a warm place, free from drafts, until doubled in bulk. Bake at 350° for 50 to 60 minutes. Remove from pan; cool on wire rack. Yield: one 10-inch loaf.

Raspberry Breakfast Bread

1 package dry yeast
1 cup warm water (105° to 115°)
⅓ cup sugar
1 teaspoon salt
2½ cups all-purpose flour, divided
1 egg
¼ cup shortening
1 teaspoon grated orange rind
¼ cup chopped nuts
¼ cup raisins
¼ cup raspberry preserves

Dissolve yeast in water in a medium mixing bowl. Stir in sugar, salt, and 1½ cups flour; beat about 2 minutes. Add egg, shortening, orange rind, nuts, raisins, and remaining flour, mixing well.

Pour batter into a greased and floured shallow 1½-quart baking dish. Cover and let rise in warm place (85°), free from drafts, for 1½ hours or until doubled in bulk. Gently make 3 long depressions in dough with the floured handle of a wooden spoon. Carefully spoon preserves into the depressions. Bake at 375° for 30 minutes. Cool in pan for 10 minutes. Yield: 1 loaf.

Whole Wheat Sourdough Bread

Many American pioneers leavened their breads by saving part of the dough from one baking to the next, which came to be known as sourdough. An adaptation of that same principle is used in bread making today— sourdough starter.

The starter used in this bread can be kept active by adding sugar and storing in the refrigerator. But: always let starters come to room temperature before using.

> 1½ cups boiling water
> ½ cup shortening
> 1 package dry yeast
> 1 teaspoon sugar
> 1 egg, well beaten
> ½ cup sugar
> ½ teaspoon salt
> 1 cup Sourdough Starter, at room
>   temperature (recipe follows)
> 3 cups all-purpose flour, divided
> 2 cups whole wheat flour

Combine boiling water and shortening in a large bowl; allow to cool to 105° to 115°. Add yeast and 1 teaspoon sugar; let stand 15 minutes. Add egg, ½ cup sugar, salt, Sourdough Starter, and 2½ cups all-purpose flour; beat at medium speed of electric mixer 3 minutes. Gradually stir in ½ cup all-purpose flour and whole wheat flour.

Turn dough out on a floured surface, and knead about 5 minutes or until smooth and elastic. Place dough in a greased bowl, turning to grease top. Cover and let rise in a warm place (85°), free from drafts, 1½ to 2 hours or until dough is doubled in bulk.

Divide dough in half, and place on a floured surface. Roll each half into an 18- × 8-inch rectangle. Roll up, beginning at narrow edge; as you roll the dough, press firmly to eliminate air pockets. Pinch seams and ends together to seal. Place seam side down in 2 well-greased 9- × 5- × 3-inch loafpans.

Cover and let rise until doubled in bulk. Place in a cold oven. Bake at 400° for 15 minutes; reduce heat to 350°, and continue baking 20 minutes or until loaves sound hollow when tapped. Remove from pans; cool on wire racks. Yield: 2 loaves.

Sourdough Starter:

> 1 package dry yeast
> 3 cups warm water (105° to 115°)
> 3½ cups all-purpose flour

Combine yeast and water; set aside 5 minutes. Gradually add flour, beating at medium speed of electric mixer until smooth. Cover and place in a warm spot (85°), free from drafts, until bubbles appear on surface (about 24 hours). If starter has not started to ferment after 24 hours, discard it and start over.

Stir starter well; cover and return to warm place. Let stand 2 days or until foamy.

Stir well, and pour into an airtight glass container. Store in refrigerator. Stir before using, and allow to come to room temperature. Yield: about 4 cups.

Note: Starter may be stored in refrigerator several weeks, but it should be used weekly. If not used regularly, add 1 teaspoon sugar, stirring well. This will keep yeast active.

White Bread

6 cups all-purpose flour, divided
3 tablespoons sugar
2 teaspoons salt
1 package dry yeast
1 cup milk
1 cup water
3 tablespoons butter or margarine

Mix 2 cups flour, sugar, salt, and yeast in a large mixing bowl.

Combine milk, water, and butter in a medium saucepan. Cook over medium heat until lukewarm; slowly beat milk mixture into flour mixture. Add 1 cup flour; beat for 2 minutes. Stir in remaining 3 cups flour. Turn dough out onto a floured board. Knead about 8 minutes or until smooth and elastic. Shape into a ball; place in a greased bowl, turning to grease top. Cover and let rise in a warm place (85°), free from drafts, for 1 hour or until doubled in bulk.

Punch dough down; knead a few times more. Divide dough in half; cover and let stand 15 minutes. Form into 2 loaves; place in 2 greased 9- × 5- × 3-inch loafpans. Cover and let rise in a warm place, free from drafts, for 45 minutes or until doubled in bulk. Bake at 400° for 30 minutes or until brown. Yield: 2 loaves.

Plaited White Bread

1 package dry yeast
2 cups warm water (105° to 115°)
⅓ cup sugar
2 teaspoons salt
1 egg, well beaten
6 to 7 cups all-purpose flour, divided
3 tablespoons vegetable oil

Combine yeast, warm water, sugar, salt, and egg in a large bowl; set aside 5 minutes. Gradually add 3 cups flour, beating well. Add vegetable oil and 3 to 4 cups flour to form a stiff dough.

Turn dough out on a floured surface, and knead until smooth and elastic (5 to 8 minutes). Place in a well-greased bowl, turning to grease top. Cover and let rise in a warm place (85°), free from drafts, 1½ to 2 hours or until doubled in bulk.

Punch dough down, and divide into thirds. Shape each third into a 14- to 16-inch rope. Place ropes on a greased baking sheet, and firmly pinch ends together at one end to seal. Braid ropes together, and pinch loose ends to seal. Cover; let rise in a warm place, free from drafts, until doubled in bulk. Bake at 350° for 20 to 25 minutes or until lightly browned. Yield: 1 loaf.

Honey Muffins

1 cup butter or margarine
1 cup sugar
1 egg
1 cup honey
2 cups all-purpose flour
1 teaspoon soda
½ teaspoon salt
1 cup commercial sour cream

Cream butter and sugar in a medium mixing bowl; beat in egg and honey. Combine dry ingredients; beat into batter. Stir in sour cream. Spoon into greased and floured muffin tins. Bake at 325° about 18 minutes, or until browned and done. Yield: about 1 dozen muffins.

Bran Muffins

¾ cup all-purpose flour
2½ teaspoons baking powder
¼ teaspoon salt
⅓ cup sugar
1 egg, beaten
¾ cup milk
3 tablespoons shortening, melted
1½ cups wheat bran flakes cereal

Combine flour, baking powder, salt, and sugar in a medium mixing bowl, mixing well.

Combine egg and milk; stir into flour mixture. Add shortening; mix only to dampen flour. (Dough will be lumpy.) Fold in bran flakes. Pour mixture into greased muffin tins, filling two-thirds full. Bake at 425° for 15 to 20 minutes. Yield: 8 muffins.

Note: Batter may be prepared the evening before, stored in the refrigerator, and baked the next morning.

Oatmeal Muffins

    1 cup quick-cooking oats, uncooked
    1 cup buttermilk
    1 cup all-purpose flour
    1 teaspoon baking powder
    ½ teaspoon salt
    ½ teaspoon soda
    1 egg, slightly beaten
    ⅓ cup firmly packed brown sugar
    ⅓ cup vegetable oil

Soak oats in buttermilk for 15 minutes in a medium mixing bowl. Combine flour, baking powder, salt, and soda; stir into oatmeal mixture. Stir in egg, brown sugar, and oil just until blended. Bake in greased muffin tins at 400° for 20 to 25 minutes. Yield: 12 large muffins.

Never-Fail Popovers

    1 cup all-purpose flour
    ¼ teaspoon salt
    2 eggs, slightly beaten
    1 cup milk
    1 teaspoon melted butter or
        margarine

Combine flour and salt in a medium mixing bowl. Combine eggs, milk, and butter, mixing well. Add liquid mixture to flour mixture and stir until blended.

Spoon into greased 6-ounce custard cups, filling about one-half full with batter. Place cups on a baking sheet and put in a cold oven. Heat oven to 425° and bake for one hour. Yield: 8 to 10 popovers.

Pineapple-Nut Muffins

    2 cups all-purpose flour
    1 teaspoon salt
    2 teaspoons baking powder
    ⅓ cup sugar
    ½ cup canned crushed pineapple,
        drained
    ½ cup chopped nuts
    1 egg, beaten
    ½ cup milk
    ¼ cup vegetable oil

Combine flour, salt, baking powder, and sugar in a medium mixing bowl; add pineapple and nuts. Stir in egg, milk, and oil, mixing just enough to dampen dry ingredients. Bake in greased muffin tins at 400° for 20 to 25 minutes. Yield: 12 to 14 muffins.

Squash Muffins

    1 egg
    1 cup milk
    ⅔ cup grated yellow squash
    ½ cup sugar
    2 cups all-purpose flour
    1 tablespoon baking powder
    ¼ teaspoon salt
    2 tablespoons vegetable oil

Beat egg in a medium mixing bowl; add milk and squash. Combine dry ingredients; stir into squash mixture. Stir in oil. Grease muffin tins and heat at 350° until hot. Spoon batter into tins, filling cups two-thirds full. Bake at 350° about 20 minutes or until done and brown. Yield: about 1 dozen.

Bran Rolls

½ cup shortening
½ cup boiling water
⅓ cup sugar
¾ teaspoon salt
½ cup wheat bran flakes cereal
1 package dry yeast
½ cup warm water (105° to 115°)
1 egg, beaten
3 cups all-purpose flour, divided

Combine shortening, boiling water, sugar, salt, and bran in a medium mixing bowl. Stir until shortening is melted; cool to lukewarm. Dissolve yeast in warm water. Add to bran mixture. Add egg and beat well. Add 1 cup flour and beat well. Add remaining flour and mix well. Cover and place in refrigerator overnight. Punch dough down; divide dough into 24 pieces and shape into rolls. Place on greased baking sheets. Cover and let rise in a warm place (85°), free from drafts, until doubled in size. Bake at 400° for 15 to 20 minutes. Yield: 2 dozen rolls.

Butterflake Rolls

2 cups buttermilk, warmed
½ teaspoon soda
½ cup sugar
1 tablespoon salt
¼ teaspoon powdered alum
½ cup butter or margarine, softened
3 eggs, beaten
2 packages dry yeast
1 cup warm water (105° to 115°)
10 to 11 cups all-purpose flour, divided

Combine buttermilk and soda in a very large mixing bowl. Stir in sugar, salt, alum, butter, and eggs. Dissolve yeast in water, and stir into buttermilk mixture. Add 2 cups flour and beat well.

Stir in enough remaining flour to make a soft workable dough. Turn dough out onto a floured surface and knead 3 or 4 times. Form

dough into a ball; place in a greased bowl, turning to grease top. Cover and let rise in a warm place (85°), free from drafts, about 1 hour or until doubled in bulk.

Punch dough down; divide dough in half. Shape half of dough into 36 balls; place in greased muffin pans. Bake at 400° for 15 to 20 minutes or until golden. Repeat procedure with remaining dough. Yield: 6 dozen rolls.

Cinnamon Rolls

1 cup milk
1 teaspoon salt
½ cup plus 2 tablespoons sugar, divided
2 tablespoons vegetable oil
1 package dry yeast
¼ cup warm water (105° to 115°)
3 to 4 cups all-purpose flour
Vegetable oil
2 tablespoons butter or margarine, softened
2 tablespoons ground cinnamon

Scald milk; stir in salt, 2 tablespoons sugar, and 2 tablespoons oil; cool to lukewarm. Dissolve yeast in water and add to milk mixture. Stir in enough flour to make a firm, but not stiff, dough. Turn dough out onto a floured board. Knead until dough is smooth and elastic. Put dough into a greased bowl; brush top with oil. Cover and let rise in a warm place (85°), free from drafts, until doubled in bulk.

Punch dough down; knead lightly. Roll dough into an 18- × 9-inch rectangle. Spread dough with butter; sprinkle with a mixture of ½ cup sugar and cinnamon. Starting at one long side, roll up tightly jellyroll fashion, and seal edge well. Cut into slices about 1 inch wide. Place rolls, cut side down, on a greased baking sheet. Cover and let rise in a warm place until doubled in bulk. Bake at 375° about 25 minutes. Serve hot. Yield: about 1½ dozen rolls.

Quick Herb Rolls

1 package dry yeast
¾ cup warm water (105° to 115°)
2½ cups biscuit mix
½ teaspoon celery seeds
1 teaspoon poultry seasoning

Dissolve yeast in warm water in a medium mixing bowl. Stir in biscuit mix and herbs and beat vigorously for 2 to 3 minutes. Turn dough out onto a surface dusted with biscuit mix and knead until smooth. Divide dough into 21 equal portions; shape each portion into a ball.

Arrange 13 balls around the inside edge of a greased 8-inch cakepan, with balls not quite touching each other. Arrange 8 balls in an inner circle, leaving a 2-inch hole in center of pan. Cover with a damp cloth. Let rise in a warm place (85°), free from drafts, about 1 hour or until doubled in size. Bake at 400° about 20 minutes or until golden brown. Serve hot. Yield: 21 rolls.

Love Feast Buns

3 packages dry yeast
7 cups warm water (105° to 115°), divided
4 eggs
4 cups sugar
1 cup softened butter and shortening (mixed)
2 tablespoons salt
1 cup warm mashed potatoes
8 pounds (about 32 cups) all-purpose flour
Half-and-half or melted butter

Dissolve yeast in 1 cup water; set aside. Beat eggs in a very large mixing bowl; add sugar, butter and shortening, salt, potatoes, yeast mixture, and remaining water. Stir in enough flour to make a soft dough.

Turn dough out onto a lightly floured board and knead until smooth. Place in large greased bowl, turning to grease top. Cover; let rise in a warm place (85°), free from drafts, for 1½ to 2 hours or until doubled in bulk.

Shape dough into buns about 4 inches in diameter. Place on greased baking sheets, 2 inches apart; cover and let rise in a warm place until light or almost doubled in bulk. Bake at 425° for 20 minutes or until golden brown. Brush with half-and-half or melted butter immediately after removing from oven. Yield: about 4 dozen buns.

Note: To halve recipe, use 2 packages yeast; to quarter it, use 1 package.

Never-Fail Pan Rolls

¾ cup sugar
¾ cup shortening
1 cup boiling water
2 packages dry yeast
1 cup warm water (105° to 115°)
2 eggs, slightly beaten
6 to 7 cups all-purpose flour, divided
1 teaspoon salt
1 teaspoon baking powder
½ teaspoon soda

Cream sugar and shortening until light and fluffy. Add boiling water, mixing thoroughly; set aside to cool.

Dissolve yeast in 1 cup warm water; set aside. Add eggs to cooled shortening mixture, mixing well; stir in yeast mixture. Combine 5 cups flour with salt, baking powder, and soda; add to yeast mixture, and mix well. Turn dough out on a well-floured surface; knead in enough remaining flour until dough is no longer sticky.

Roll dough into 1½-inch balls and place in 2 greased 9-inch round cakepans. Cover and let rise in warm place (85°), free from drafts, for about 1½ hours or until doubled in bulk. Bake at 400° for 20 minutes or until golden brown. Yield: about 3 dozen.

Note: Dough may be stored in refrigerator until ready to use; brush surface with vegetable oil, and place in a covered container.

Nut And Poppy Seed Rolls

2 packages dry yeast
½ cup warm milk (105° to 115°)
1 teaspoon salt
1 cup butter or margarine
3 tablespoons sugar
3 eggs, beaten
1 (8-ounce) carton commercial
    sour cream
About 6 cups all-purpose flour
Poppy Seed Filling (recipe follows)
Nut Filling (recipe follows)

Dissolve yeast in milk. Blend salt, butter, and sugar. Beat in eggs and sour cream. Add yeast mixture and gradually blend in enough flour to make a soft workable dough.

Knead dough on a lightly floured surface; shape into a smooth ball. Divide dough into 4 equal parts. Roll each part into a rectangle about ⅓ inch thick. Spread 2 rectangles with Poppy Seed Filling; spread remaining 2 with Nut Filling. Roll up jellyroll fashion, starting with long edge; seal edges. Place jellyrolls, seam side down, on greased baking sheets. Cover and let rise in a warm place (85°), free from drafts, about 45 to 60 minutes or until doubled in bulk. Bake at 350° for 35 to 40 minutes or until well browned. Slice; serve warm or cool. Yield: 24 to 36 servings.

Poppy Seed Filling:

1 cup milk
½ pound ground poppy seeds
¾ cup sugar

Scald milk; stir in poppy seeds and sugar. Cool. Yield: about 2 cups.

Nut Filling:

½ cup milk
½ pound ground walnuts or pecans
½ cup sugar
1 teaspoon vanilla extract

Scald milk; stir in remaining ingredients. Cool. Yield: about 1½ cups.

Refrigerator Rolls

¾ cup sugar
1 cup shortening
1 cup boiling water
2 packages dry yeast
1 cup warm water (105° to 115°)
2 eggs, beaten
2 teaspoons salt
7 to 7½ cups all-purpose flour

Cream sugar and shortening in a large mixing bowl; pour boiling water over creamed mixture, mixing well. Cool to lukewarm. Dissolve yeast in warm water; add to creamed mixture. Beat in eggs and salt. Stir in enough flour to make a soft workable dough. Turn dough out on a floured surface; knead lightly and shape into a ball. Place in a greased bowl, turning to grease top; cover and refrigerate up to 4 or 5 days. To prepare, punch dough down and shape into rolls as desired. Place on greased baking sheets; cover and let rise in a warm place (85°), free from drafts, about 45 minutes or until light. Bake at 375° about 18 to 20 minutes. Yield: about 5 dozen.

Spoon Rolls

1 package dry yeast
2 cups warm water (105° to 115°)
¼ cup sugar
¾ cup vegetable oil
1 egg
4 cups self-rising flour
¼ cup self-rising cornmeal

Dissolve yeast in water in a medium mixing bowl; add remaining ingredients. Mix well and store in refrigerator until ready to bake. Spoon into greased muffin tins. Bake at 425° for 20 minutes. Yield: 1½ to 2 dozen rolls.

Two-Hour Whole Wheat Rolls

2 packages dry yeast
1¼ cups warm milk (105° to 115°),
    divided
2 eggs, beaten
1 cup all-purpose flour
⅓ cup vegetable oil
⅓ cup sugar
1½ teaspoons salt
3 cups whole wheat flour
Butter or margarine

Dissolve yeast in ¼ cup milk; add eggs to yeast mixture. Stir in all-purpose flour. Combine oil, sugar, salt, and remaining 1 cup milk; add to yeast mixture along with whole wheat flour, mixing well. Shape into rolls and place on greased baking sheets. Cover and rise in a warm place (85°), free from drafts, about 1 hour or until doubled in size. Bake at 400° for 15 to 20 minutes or until brown. Brush with butter. Yield: about 2 dozen rolls.

Bagels

1 package dry yeast
1½ cups warm water (105° to 115°)
1 teaspoon salt
2 tablespoons sugar
About 4 cups all-purpose flour
1 egg white, slightly beaten

Dissolve yeast in water in a medium mixing bowl. Add salt and sugar; stir to dissolve. Gradually beat in enough flour to make a stiff workable dough. Turn dough out on a floured surface, and knead about 12 minutes or until smooth and elastic. Form into a ball and place in a greased bowl, turning to grease top. Cover and let rise in a warm place (85°), free from drafts, for 1½ to 2 hours or until doubled in bulk.

Punch down dough and divide into 12 equal parts. Roll each piece between the hands into a strip 10 to 12 inches long. Join ends of each strip to form circles, sealing ends firmly. Let rise in a warm place 15 to 20 minutes. Fill a large kettle half full with water and bring to boil. Drop bagels into boiling water. Remove bagels with a slotted spoon as they rise to the surface, holding spoon briefly over a towel to drain water; place bagels on ungreased baking sheets. Brush with egg white and bake at 375° for about 20 minutes or until golden and crisp. Yield: 1 dozen.

Polish Sweet Bread

1 cup raisins
8 egg yolks
2 eggs
2 cups powdered sugar
2 packages dry yeast
1 teaspoon baking powder
1 cup warm water (105° to 115°)
1 cup melted butter or margarine
½ cup milk
2 teaspoons salt
8 to 10 cups all-purpose flour
1 egg, beaten

Combine raisins and water to cover in a small saucepan. Bring to a boil and boil 5 minutes. Drain.

Beat yolks, eggs, and sugar in a large mixing bowl. Dissolve yeast and baking powder in water; add to egg mixture, beating well. Add butter, milk, and salt to egg mixture; stir in raisins. Add enough flour, 1 cup at a time, to make a soft dough. Turn dough out on a floured surface and knead briefly; form into a ball. Place in a greased bowl, turning to grease top. Cover and let rise in a warm place (85°), free from drafts, at least 1 hour or until doubled in bulk.

Punch dough down; divide into four equal parts and form each into a round loaf. Place in 4 greased 9-inch cakepans. Brush with beaten egg and let rise in a warm place about 30 minutes or until doubled in bulk. Bake at 350° for 35 to 40 minutes or until done and browned. Yield: 4 loaves.

Sweet Breads and Coffee Cakes 187

Sunday Morning Coffee Cake

¼ cup shortening
1 cup sugar
2 eggs, separated
1½ cups all-purpose flour
2 teaspoons baking powder
½ teaspoon salt
½ cup milk
1 cup powdered sugar
1 tablespoon ground cinnamon
3 tablespoons butter or margarine

Cream shortening and sugar in a medium mixing bowl. Add egg yolks; beat well. Mix flour, baking powder, and salt; add alternately with milk to creamed mixture. Beat egg whites until stiff but not dry; fold into creamed mixture. Pour into a greased and floured 13- × 9- × 2-inch baking pan.

Mix powdered sugar, cinnamon, and butter with a fork until crumbly; sprinkle over top of cake. Bake at 375° for 25 to 30 minutes. Yield: 1 coffee cake.

Texas Coffee Cake

¼ cup shortening
¼ cup sugar
1 egg, beaten
1½ cups all-purpose flour
1 tablespoon baking powder
¼ teaspoon salt
½ cup milk
1 teaspoon vanilla extract
Filling (recipe follows)

Cream shortening and sugar in a medium mixing bowl. Add egg, mixing well. Combine flour, baking powder, and salt; add to creamed mixture alternately with milk. Stir in vanilla. Spread half the batter in a greased and floured 8-inch square baking pan; cover with half the filling. Add remaining batter and top with remaining filling. Bake at 400° for 25 to 30 minutes. Yield: 6 servings.

Filling:

½ cup firmly packed brown sugar
2 tablespoons all-purpose flour
2 teaspoons ground cinnamon
2 tablespoons butter, softened
½ cup chopped nuts

Mix dry ingredients thoroughly; cut in butter until mixture is of crumbly consistency; stir in nuts. Yield: about 1 cup.

Fruit Kuchen

2 cups all-purpose flour
2 teaspoons baking powder
4 tablespoons sugar, divided
½ cup butter or margarine
1 egg
¾ cup milk
2 cups thinly sliced fruit or berries
1 teaspoon ground cinnamon

Combine flour, baking powder, and 3 tablespoons sugar in a medium mixing bowl; cut in butter until mixture resembles coarse meal. Blend in egg and milk. Press mixture lightly into a greased 9-inch square baking pan. Cover with fruit; sprinkle with cinnamon and remaining sugar. Bake at 350° for 45 minutes. Yield: 9 servings.

German Sugar Kuchen

1 package dry yeast
¼ cup warm water (105° to 115°)
1 cup milk
¾ to 1 cup butter or margarine, divided
2 egg yolks
1 egg
½ cup sugar, divided
1 teaspoon vanilla extract
3 cups all-purpose flour, divided
1 teaspoon salt

Dissolve yeast in warm water. Heat milk with ½ cup butter in a small saucepan until butter is melted; cool to lukewarm. Beat egg yolks and egg in a large mixing bowl until thick and lemon colored. Beat in ¼ cup sugar and vanilla. Add dissolved yeast and 1 cup flour, beating well. Add milk mixture, salt, and remaining flour; beat 5 minutes or until dough is smooth and elastic. Cover and let rise in a warm place (85°), free from drafts, for 1 hour or until doubled in bulk. Punch dough down and divide in half; arrange in 2 greased 9-inch round cakepans. Spread dough with half the remaining butter and sprinkle each with half the remaining sugar. Bake at 350° for 15 minutes. Remove from oven; spread with remaining butter and sprinkle with remaining sugar. Return to oven and bake about 5 minutes longer or until done and brown. Cool in pan on wire racks. To serve, cut in half, then cut into perpendicular slices across the first cut. Yield: two 9-inch cakes.

Snapdoodle

　½ cup shortening
　1 cup sugar
　3 cups all-purpose flour
　½ teaspoon salt
　1 tablespoon baking powder
　1½ cups milk
　1 tablespoon ground cinnamon
　1 cup firmly packed brown sugar

Combine shortening and sugar, creaming until smooth and fluffy. Combine flour, salt, and baking powder; add to sugar mixture alternately with milk, mixing well. Pour into a greased 13- × 9- × 2-inch baking pan or two greased 9-inch round cakepans. Combine cinnamon and brown sugar, mixing well; sprinkle over top of batter. Bake at 350° for 50 minutes or until done and brown. Cut into squares and serve hot or cold. Yield: 8 to 10 servings.

Moravian Sugar Cake

　½ cup sugar
　½ cup butter or margarine
　1 cup cooked mashed potatoes
　1 package dry yeast
　¼ cup warm water (105° to 115°)
　2 eggs, well beaten
　All-purpose flour
　Brown sugar
　Ground nutmeg
　Butter or margarine

Cream ½ cup sugar, ½ cup butter, and potatoes in a medium mixing bowl. Dissolve yeast in warm water; add to sugar mixture with eggs and enough flour to make a soft pliable dough.

Cover; let rise in a warm place (85°), free from drafts, for 12 hours or overnight.

After dough has risen, punch it down; press dough into 2 greased 9-inch square baking pans. Cover and let dough rise in a warm place (85°), free from drafts, until doubled in bulk. Firmly punch dents in the top of dough using fingertip; sprinkle generously with brown sugar and nutmeg, and dot with butter. Bake at 375° for 15 to 20 minutes. Let cool on wire racks. Cut into squares and serve warm or cold. Yield: two 9-inch cakes.

Cornbread Dressing

1 recipe Southern Cornbread
(page 165)
2 to 3 cups coarse dry breadcrumbs
¼ cup melted butter or margarine
2 to 3 cups boiling chicken broth
6 to 8 green onions with tops,
chopped
3 to 4 stalks celery, chopped
4 eggs, beaten
1 teaspoon salt
¼ teaspoon pepper

Crumble cornbread in a large bowl; add dry breadcrumbs. Pour melted butter over top. Pour 2 cups broth over breadcrumb mixture; let stand 15 minutes. Add onion, celery, and eggs, mixing well. If mixture is too dry, add more broth to obtain desired consistency. Stir in salt and pepper. Pour into greased 13- × 9- × 2-inch baking pan; bake at 325° about 1 hour. Yield: about 12 servings.

Note: Mixture may also be used to stuff a 12-pound turkey.

Louisiana-Style Dressing

1 recipe Southern Cornbread
(page 165)
2 pounds ground beef
1 pound ground pork
1 large green pepper, chopped
2 small white onions, chopped
1 bunch green onions, chopped
1 clove garlic, minced
1 to 2 tablespoons minced fresh
parsley
3 large tart apples, pared and
chopped
1 cup chopped pecans or walnuts
2 eggs, beaten
1 cup milk, divided
1½ to 2 teaspoons salt
½ teaspoon pepper

Crumble cornbread; reserve. Combine meats, green pepper, onion, garlic, parsley, apples, pecans, and eggs in a very large mixing bowl. Mix thoroughly. Add crumbled cornbread, mixing well. Add half the milk, mixing well. Season to taste. Pour into a greased 3-quart baking dish; pour remaining milk over top. Bake at 350° about 45 minutes. Yield: about 16 servings.

Note: Mixture may also be used to stuff a 16-pound turkey; roast according to any turkey recipe.

Oyster Dressing

¼ cup butter or margarine
½ medium onion, chopped
4 stalks celery, chopped
1 pint oysters, drained and chopped
4 small potatoes, cooked and mashed
10 cups coarse breadcrumbs
1 egg, beaten
Hot chicken broth
1½ to 2 teaspoons salt
½ teaspoon pepper

Melt butter in a skillet over medium heat; sauté onion and celery until transparent. Add oysters; sauté for 2 minutes. Stir in potatoes.

Place breadcrumbs in a large mixing bowl. Add onion mixture; mix well. Stir in egg and enough broth to obtain desired consistency. Season with salt and pepper. Pour into a greased 13- × 9- × 2-inch baking dish; bake at 325° about 45 minutes. Yield: about 12 servings.

Note: Mixture may also be used to stuff a 12-pound turkey; roast according to any turkey recipe.

Southern Pecan Dressing

1 turkey liver
12 slices bread, toasted and
    crumbled
¼ cup butter or margarine
3 tablespoons lard or shortening
1 teaspoon salt
1 teaspoon pepper
1 teaspoon crushed dried celery
    seeds
1 teaspoon dried thyme leaves
1 tablespoon chopped fresh parsley
½ teaspoon ground nutmeg
¼ teaspoon ground mace
1 large onion, chopped
1 tablespoon lard or shortening
6 hard-cooked eggs, chopped
2 cups salted pecans, chopped
1 (8-ounce) can mushrooms, drained
    and chopped
½ cup dry sherry

Cook liver in boiling water the day before making stuffing. Combine crumbled bread, butter, 3 tablespoons lard, salt, pepper, celery seeds, thyme, parsley, nutmeg, and mace, mixing well. Sauté onion in 1 tablespoon lard until transparent. Add onion, eggs, pecans, mushrooms, and sherry to crumb mixture; toss lightly. Add enough boiling water to make desired consistency for dressing, and stuff bird loosely; truss and roast bird. Yield: about 5 cups.

Baking Powder Dumplings

1 cup all-purpose flour
2 teaspoons baking powder
½ teaspoon salt
About ⅓ cup milk

Combine dry ingredients; stir in enough milk to make a stiff dough. Drop by teaspoonfuls on top of simmering sauerkraut or other food. Cover; simmer 20 minutes. Yield: 4 servings.

Note: Recipe may be doubled.

Buttermilk Dumplings

1 cup buttermilk
¼ teaspoon soda
1½ teaspoons baking powder
½ teaspoon salt
1 egg, well beaten
1¼ to 1½ cups all-purpose flour

Combine buttermilk with soda and baking powder in a small mixing bowl; stir until mixture foams. Add salt and egg; stir in enough flour to make a soft dough. Drop by teaspoonfuls on top of simmering food; cover and simmer 15 minutes or until done. Yield: 4 to 5 servings.

German Dumplings

3 eggs, beaten
1 teaspoon salt
½ cup water
3½ cups all-purpose flour
1 tablespoon baking powder

Beat eggs with salt and water in a medium mixing bowl. Add flour and baking powder to egg mixture, beating until smooth. Drop by tablespoonfuls into simmering salted water or stock. Cover; simmer about 15 minutes or until done. Yield: about 8 servings.

Quick Dumplings

1 (10-ounce) can refrigerator biscuits

For thin, firm dumplings, roll out each biscuit; let stand at room temperature 1 hour. Roll to ⅛-inch thickness; cut into bite-size pieces. Drop on top of simmering food; cover and simmer 20 minutes.

For fluffy dumplings, roll out each biscuit to ⅛-inch thickness; cut immediately without allowing them to stand. Drop on top of simmering food; cover and simmer 20 minutes. Yield: 4 servings.

Potato Dumplings

Salt
1 onion, chopped
2¾ cups boiled potatoes, riced or
    mashed
⅓ cup all-purpose flour
1 teaspoon salt
¼ cup farina
1 egg, beaten
2 teaspoons milk

Fill a 4-quart Dutch oven half-full with water. Add salt and onion, and simmer.

Combine potatoes, flour, salt, farina, egg, and milk in a medium mixing bowl; beat until smooth. Form dough into 1-inch balls. Drop into boiling water; simmer, uncovered, about 15 minutes or until dumplings float and are done. Serve with pot roast. Yield: 4 to 6 servings.

Note: May be cooked in stock or in soup or stew in place of onion-flavored water.

Rolled Dumplings

2 cups all-purpose flour
2 teaspoons baking powder
1 teaspoon salt
⅓ cup shortening
1 egg, beaten
½ cup milk

Combine dry ingredients; cut in shortening until mixture resembles coarse meal. Combine egg and milk; stir in enough of the egg mixture to dry ingredients to make a firm dough. Roll dough to ¼-inch thickness on floured surface. Cut into strips, squares, or diamonds with sharp knife. Drop onto simmering food; cover and simmer 10 minutes or until done. Yield: 6 to 8 servings.

Noodles

2 eggs, beaten
1 teaspoon salt
¼ cup milk
2½ to 3 cups all-purpose flour

Combine eggs, salt, and milk; stir in enough flour to make a stiff dough. Turn dough out on a floured surface; knead until smooth.

Roll dough to ⅛-inch thickness. Fold corners of dough to center and roll to ⅛-inch thickness. Repeat rolling and folding process 10 times, adding as little flour as possible. Roll dough as thin as possible. Roll dough tightly, jellyroll fashion. Cut roll crosswise to make noodles of desired width. Carefully unroll noodles and lay on a board to dry for 30 minutes. Drop noodles into boiling salted water and cook until done, about 10 minutes. Yield: about 8 servings.

Note: Noodles may be rolled, cut, and filled for use with stuffed dumpling recipes.

*"There's a heap o' women to be pitied, child, but of all
things deliver me from livin' with a man that has to
have hot bread three times a day. Milly Amos used to
say that when she died she wanted a hot biscuit carved
on her tombstone. . . ."*
Eliza Calvert Hall

Sweets and Desserts

Anytime a Southerner cannot "save room for dessert," his general state of health may be called into question. Americans consume more sugar per capita than any country in the world today with the exception of the United Kingdom.

But sugar has not always been in plentiful supply in America—or the world. Refined sugar is, in fact, a comparative newcomer to man's diet although the hunger for a taste of sweetness is as old as man himself.

Wild honey was prized in ancient Egypt where it was used in pastries. Honey came to symbolize a life of ease and luxury in Biblical times. While not everyone could hope to live out his days in a land flowing with "milk and honey," the good life could nonetheless figure in the dreams of the lowliest man.

Historians believe that sugarcane originated in India, but apparently the juice was used in liquid form until about the eighth century, when some refining may have taken place in Egypt. It is known that by 1,000 A.D. the Egyptians had discovered how to refine sugar commercially. Sugar came to Spain with the Moors and spread to the rest of Europe via the Crusaders.

Except for some early and not very definitive work by the Chinese centuries earlier, the refining of sugar from beets is a fairly recent industry. Napoleon is credited with encouraging its development by offering a prize to anyone who could find a way to make beet sugar commercially. The cash prize and the rank of baron was awarded to a man named Delessert.

Sugar came to America with Columbus on his second voyage, and the Spanish started sugar plantations in all their tropical territories. But it was not until the 1700s that sugar became a fairly common element in the average person's diet. The catch was that the sugarcane had to be taken to Europe for refining, then shipped back in sugar form. By the time all that had taken place, only the wealthiest could afford to buy it.

Most of the colonists, then, had to make do with wild honey from the forest, and they learned about maple syrup from the Indians. When the South's refineries were established in the eighteenth century, sugar and its by-product, molasses, came into general use. Every home had a molasses jug on the table, along with the vinegar cruet and the sugar bowl. Filling that jug from the master supply in cold weather was such a lesson in patience that the expression "slow as molasses in January" came to describe anything exhibiting little or no motion.

Molasses remained a mainstay in Southern households even after sugar became affordable, and it is still an important ingredient in our desserts. After all, it is sweet, and sweets are one of our most deeply rooted traditions. Ask a hundred Southerners to jot down their favorite recipes. The result will be approximately eighty dessert recipes and twenty miscellaneous recipes for salads, meats, and so on. Then examine the postmarks accompanying the dessert recipes, and you will find some weather-caused differences among the more traditional recipes. From the colder regions come dried apple cakes and pies, black walnut and hickory nut confections. From the warmer parts of the South come the peach, fig, and pecan creations. Other sweets, such as butter-laced cakes and the good-anytime bread puddings, come from every section.

Southern sweets as we know them came into flowering on the plantations south of the Potomac: the Virginia Tidewater, the Low Country of the Carolinas and Georgia, the moss-hung bayous of Louisiana. It was here that luxury evolved, and the landed gentry created and lived their own myths. Our history is larded with menus and descriptions of feasts written in letters home by visitors to plantations with romantic names such as Monticello, Mount Vernon, and Shadows-on-the-Teche.

Thomas Jefferson was a product of three generations of this plantation life. He was not only born to it, he enlarged upon it. While serving as the first American Minister to France, he deliberately studied French cooking; he wrote down recipes, imported ingredients, and had his own cooks taught the fine points of classic French cuisine. More than any other single influence, Jefferson gave the upper South a touch of European continentalism that was native, in this country, only to Louisiana.

Of all the accounts of lavish entertaining that have come down to us, Jefferson's parties read the most like fiction. Even to the guests at his board, they must have seemed a little unreal, as his French-trained cooks served up gâteaux, soufflés, ices, and sauces tinctured with wine. The Old Dominion had not seen the likes of such extravagance, and there were those who were critical of his expenditures on food and entertaining that kept him on the verge of bankruptcy most of his life.

While ice cream was not common in the late eighteenth century American households, it was not unknown: George Washington, who may have learned about it from the Marquis de Lafayette, had an ice cream freezer as early as 1784. But it was Jefferson who became enamored of ice cream while in France and brought back recipes for delicate ices as well as for rich frozen creams. As a footnote to our gastronomic history, he may well have been the first Southerner to say, "Make mine vanilla"; in 1791, he ordered fifty vanilla pods from Paris.

Ice cream may have been on the menu that day at Monticello when Jefferson delighted his guests with the first meringues glacé they had ever seen; another of his Paris finds, the recipe he had jotted down started with "12 *blanc d'oeufs.*" Did he also serve fruit tarts, a sherried trifle, perhaps, and blancmange? On the great tables, several desserts made their appearance at the same meal. Ambrosia, that hallowed combination of sliced or segmented oranges and sweet, shredded coconut, was as popular in Jefferson's day as it is now in our own.

While I know of no place, public or private, now serving meals such as were the rule on the plantations, there are two spots in Virginia which, averaged together, might come close: restored Colonial Williamsburg and The Greenbrier Hotel.

Williamsburg, that fascinating living history lesson, is splendid at any time of the year. But a week before Christmas, The Grand Illumination signals the beginning of one of the loveliest festivals in the South. It is a time to give in and let the costumed carolers roll back the time two hundred years. Fifes and drums proceed down Duke of Gloucester Street, and, magically, brightly lit candles appear in every window.

Choose to dine at Christiana Campbell's, the King's Arms, or Chowning's; the food is above reproach and probably faithful to the best public dining traditions prevailing when Jefferson, Washington, and Madison were in town learning politics. On the menu, I see cherry tarts, cream pie flavored with rum, and tea cakes; I will skimp on the rest of my meal and have one of each. Luxurious? To me, maybe. But modest compared with the list of sweets on the dessert tables of the great plantations.

The Greenbrier overwhelms me with its spectacular desserts; I could subsist on them for the rest of my days. How Jefferson would have loved the pastries here, so bewitching, so temptingly French. But he would not have stopped at wolfing them, as I must; he would have charmed the recipes right out of the chef's safe and carried them back to Monticello. And there his little army of cooks would have used them to crown a Jeffersonian feast, more elegant than Williamsburg, more homey than The Greenbrier.

Cream pie, napoleons, cherry tarts, pâté à choux—they all came together at Monticello. But influential as plantation society was in the evolution of Southern cooking, it did not have an immediate effect upon the life-style of the general population. In our desserts we have a picture of the coexistence of plantation cooking and that of the less privileged folk. To the cooks of modest means we owe the survival of delicious pies made from sweet potatoes, molasses, and pumpkin; puddings made from bread and rice; and cakes requiring little more than kitchen staples.

Our sweet-cooking is as richly varied as all the influences that went before us. We have only to choose a recipe, flavor it to taste with peach or pecan, chocolate or vanilla. And so long as it is sweet, a Southerner will be happy.

Sweets and Desserts

Old-Fashioned Stack Cake

> 1 cup firmly packed brown sugar
> 1 cup shortening
> 1 cup molasses
> 1 cup buttermilk
> 2 eggs, beaten
> 1 teaspoon soda
> 1 teaspoon ground ginger
> Dash of salt
> 5½ cups all-purpose flour
> About 6⅔ cups apple butter
> Dried apples (optional)

Combine sugar, shortening, and molasses; beat until smooth. Add buttermilk, eggs, soda, ginger, and salt; mix well. Add flour, about 1 cup at a time, beating after each addition just until blended. (Do not overbeat.)

Divide dough into 10 parts, and place each on a greased cookie sheet; pat into a 10-inch circle. Bake each layer at 350° for 5 to 7 minutes. Carefully remove to cooling rack.

Spread about ⅔ cup apple butter between each layer and on top of cake. Garnish with dried apples, if desired. Yield: one 10-inch layer cake.

German Apple Cake

> 1 cup sugar
> ½ cup shortening
> 2 eggs
> 2¼ cups all-purpose flour
> ½ cup firmly packed brown sugar
> 2 teaspoons soda
> ¼ teaspoon salt
> 1 cup sour milk or buttermilk
> 2 cups grated raw apple
> Topping (recipe follows)

Cream sugar and shortening in a medium mixing bowl; add eggs, mixing well. Combine flour, brown sugar, soda, and salt; add alternately with sour milk to sugar mixture. Fold in grated apple; pour batter into a greased 13- × 9- × 2-inch baking pan and sprinkle with topping. Bake at 375° for 40 to 45 minutes. Yield: 12 servings.

Topping:

> ¼ cup firmly packed brown sugar
> ¼ cup sugar
> ½ teaspoon ground cinnamon
> ½ cup chopped nuts

Combine all ingredients in a small mixing bowl; mix well. Yield: about 1 cup.

Tennessee Stack Cake

> 1 cup sugar
> 1 cup butter
> 1 cup molasses
> 2 eggs
> 6 cups all-purpose flour
> 1 teaspoon soda
> 1 teaspoon salt
> ½ teaspoon ground ginger (or to taste)
> 1 tablespoon baking powder
> ½ cup buttermilk
> Apple Filling (recipe follows)

Cream sugar and butter together in a medium mixing bowl. Beat in molasses; add eggs, one at a time, beating well after each addition. Combine flour, soda, salt, ginger, and baking powder; add to butter mixture alternately with buttermilk. Mix thoroughly.

Shape dough into 7 balls; roll each ball out to a 9-inch circle on a well-floured surface.

Place in a greased 9-inch skillet or greased 9-inch cakepans; bake each circle at 450° about 10 minutes. (Clean and grease skillet after each circle is baked.) Cool and spread Apple Filling between stacked layers. Yield: one 9-inch cake.

Apple Filling:

    1 pound dried apples
    ½ cup sugar
    1 cup firmly packed brown sugar
    2 teaspoons ground cinnamon
    ½ teaspoon ground cloves

Cover dried apples with water in a large saucepan, and cook over medium heat until tender; mash thoroughly. Add sugar and spices; mix well. Cool thoroughly before spreading between layers of cake. Yield: enough filling for one 9-inch stack cake.

Note: This cake should be left to stand at least 12 hours before cutting.

Blackberry Cake

    1½ cups sugar
    ½ cup shortening
    2 eggs
    1 cup drained blackberries,
        canned or fresh
    2 cups all-purpose flour
    ½ teaspoon baking powder
    1 teaspoon ground allspice
    1 teaspoon ground nutmeg
    1 teaspoon ground cinnamon
    ⅔ cup buttermilk
    1 teaspoon soda

Combine sugar, shortening, eggs, and blackberries in a medium mixing bowl; beat for 2 minutes. Combine dry ingredients; combine buttermilk and soda and add alternately with flour mixture to sugar mixture. Beat for 2 minutes. Pour batter into a greased and floured 13- × 9- × 2-inch baking pan; bake at 350° for 25 to 30 minutes or until tests done. Yield: 12 servings.

Old-South Carrot Cake

    2 cups all-purpose flour
    2 cups sugar
    1 teaspoon baking powder
    ¼ teaspoon soda
    ¼ teaspoon salt
    1 teaspoon ground cinnamon
    4 eggs
    1 cup vegetable oil
    2 cups grated carrots
    Deluxe Cream Cheese Frosting

Combine dry ingredients; stir gently, and set aside. Combine eggs and oil, beating well. Fold in dry ingredients and carrots.

Spoon batter into 3 greased and floured 9-inch cakepans; bake at 375° for 25 minutes or until cake tests done. (Cake layers will be thin.) Cool 10 minutes in pans; remove from pans, and cool completely. Spread Deluxe Cream Cheese Frosting between layers and on top and sides of cake. Yield: one 3-layer cake.

Deluxe Cream Cheese Frosting:

    ½ cup butter or margarine, softened
    1 (8-ounce) package cream cheese,
        softened
    1 (16-ounce) package powdered sugar
    2 teaspoons vanilla extract
    1 cup chopped pecans
    1 cup flaked coconut

Combine butter and cream cheese; cream until light and fluffy. Add sugar and vanilla, mixing well. Stir in pecans and coconut. Yield: enough frosting for one 3-layer cake.

Coconut Cake

½ cup butter
1⅓ cups sugar
2 cups all-purpose flour
2½ teaspoons baking powder
¾ teaspoon salt
⅔ cup milk
2 eggs, slightly beaten
1 teaspoon vanilla extract
¼ cup milk
Coconut Filling
Seven-Minute Frosting
1 medium coconut, grated, or 2
    (6-ounce) packages frozen
    flaked coconut

Cream butter and sugar in a large mixing bowl until light and fluffy. Combine flour, baking powder, and salt; beat into butter mixture. Add ⅔ cup milk; beat well. Add eggs, vanilla, and remaining ¼ cup milk, beating until smooth.

Pour batter into 2 greased and floured 9-inch cakepans. Bake at 350° for 20 to 25 minutes or until golden brown. Layers will shrink slightly from sides of pan and toothpick inserted in center will come out clean when done. Cool in pans 10 minutes; turn out and complete cooling on wire racks. Split each layer in half, making 4 thin layers. Spread Coconut Filling between layers and on top of cake; cover with Seven-Minute Frosting. Sprinkle with ½ cup coconut; reserve remaining coconut for Coconut Filling. Yield: one 9-inch layer cake.

Coconut Filling:

2 cups sugar
¼ cup cornstarch
2 cups milk or 1 cup milk and
    1 cup coconut milk
Reserved coconut
1 teaspoon vanilla extract
1 tablespoon butter or margarine

Combine sugar and cornstarch in a heavy saucepan. Stir in milk gradually; cook over medium heat, stirring constantly, until thick. Remove from heat and stir in coconut, vanilla, and butter. Cool. Yield: about 3½ cups.

Seven-Minute Frosting:

2 egg whites
1½ cups sugar
5 tablespoons cold water
1½ teaspoons light corn syrup
2 teaspoons vanilla extract

Combine first 4 ingredients in top of double boiler. Cook over boiling water, beating constantly with rotary beater, for 7 minutes. Remove from heat; add vanilla, and continue to beat until mixture cools and reaches spreading consistency. Yield: enough frosting for one 9-inch cake.

Quickie Cake

2 eggs
1 cup sugar
1 cup all-purpose flour
1 teaspoon baking powder
¼ teaspoon salt
4 tablespoons butter or margarine,
    divided
½ cup plus 2 tablespoons milk,
    divided
1 cup flaked coconut
⅓ cup firmly packed brown sugar

Beat eggs until light in a large mixing bowl. Beat in sugar. Combine flour, baking powder, and salt; add to egg mixture, mixing well.

Combine 1 tablespoon butter in a small saucepan with ½ cup milk; heat to boiling point. Remove from heat and beat into egg mixture. Pour into a greased 12- × 8- × 2-inch baking pan. Bake at 350° for 20 minutes or until a toothpick inserted in center comes out clean.

Remove cake from oven; sprinkle coconut over top. Heat 3 tablespoons butter, brown sugar, and 2 tablespoons milk in a small saucepan over low heat. Bring to a boil; pour over coconut topping. Bake at 350° for 5 to 10 minutes or until lightly browned. Yield: 9 to 12 servings.

Crazy Cake

1½ cups all-purpose flour
1 cup sugar
3 tablespoons cocoa
1 teaspoon soda
½ teaspoon salt
¼ cup plus 2 tablespoons
    vegetable oil
1 tablespoon vinegar
1 teaspoon vanilla extract
1 cup water

Stir first 5 ingredients together in a medium mixing bowl. Make 3 depressions in the mixture; pour oil in one, vinegar in another, and vanilla in the third depression. Pour the water over all; stir only enough to mix. Pour batter into an ungreased 9-inch square baking pan. Bake at 350° for 25 to 30 minutes or until tests done. Yield: 12 servings.

Buttermilk Chocolate Cake

½ cup butter
1½ cups sugar
2 eggs
2 (1-ounce) squares unsweetened
    chocolate, melted
2 cups sifted cake flour
1 teaspoon salt
1 cup buttermilk
1 teaspoon vanilla extract
1 teaspoon soda
1 tablespoon vinegar
Icing (recipe follows)

Cream butter in a large mixing bowl; add sugar and beat until creamy. Add eggs, one at a time, beating well after each addition; stir in chocolate. Combine flour and salt; add alternately with buttermilk to chocolate mixture. Stir in vanilla; dissolve soda in vinegar and slowly stir into chocolate mixture. Pour batter into 2 greased and floured 8- or 9-inch cakepans. Bake at 350° for 30 to 35 minutes. Cool in pans 10 minutes; remove from pans. Complete cooling on wire racks before frosting. Yield: one 8- or 9-inch cake.

Icing:

½ cup butter or margarine, softened
3 cups sifted powdered sugar
3 (1-ounce) squares unsweetened
    chocolate, melted
1 teaspoon vanilla extract
Half-and-half or milk (optional)

Cream butter in a small mixing bowl; add sugar and beat well. Stir in chocolate and vanilla. Thin with a drop or two of half-and-half, if necessary. Yield: enough icing for one 8- or 9-inch cake.

Chocolate Walnut Loaf

1 cup butter or margarine
2 cups sugar
5 eggs
2 (1-ounce) squares unsweetened
    chocolate, melted
1 teaspoon vanilla extract
2½ cups all-purpose flour
1 teaspoon soda
¼ teaspoon salt
1 cup buttermilk
1 cup chopped English or black
    walnuts

Beat butter and sugar in mixing bowl until creamy. Beat in eggs, chocolate, and vanilla. Combine dry ingredients; add alternately with buttermilk to chocolate mixture. Fold in walnuts. Pour into 2 greased and floured 9- × 5- × 3-inch loafpans. Bake at 325° about 1 hour or until loaves test done. Yield: 2 loaves.

Milky Way Cake

8 (1⅞-ounce) chocolate-covered
    malt-caramel candy bars
½ cup melted butter or margarine
2 cups sugar
½ cup butter or margarine, softened
4 eggs
1 teaspoon vanilla extract
1¼ cups buttermilk
½ teaspoon soda
3 cups all-purpose flour
1 cup chopped pecans
Milk Chocolate Frosting

Combine candy bars and ½ cup melted butter in a saucepan; place over low heat until candy bars are melted, stirring constantly. Cool. Cream sugar and ½ cup softened butter until light and fluffy. Add eggs, one at a time, beating well after each addition; stir in vanilla. Combine buttermilk and soda; add to creamed mixture alternately with flour, beating well after each addition. Stir in candy bar mixture and pecans.

Pour batter into a greased and floured 10-inch tube pan; bake at 325° for 1 hour and 20 minutes or until done. Cool in pan 1 hour; remove. Complete cooling on wire racks. Frost with Milk Chocolate Frosting. Yield: one 10-inch cake.

Milk Chocolate Frosting:

2½ cups sugar
1 cup evaporated milk, undiluted
½ cup melted butter or margarine
1 (6-ounce) package semisweet
    chocolate pieces
1 cup marshmallow cream
Milk

Combine first 3 ingredients; cook over medium heat until it reaches soft-ball stage. Remove from heat; add chocolate pieces and marshmallow cream, stirring until melted. If necessary, add milk to make spreading consistency. Yield: frosting for one 10-inch cake.

Black Cake

1 cup butter or margarine
2 cups sugar
4 eggs, beaten
2¼ cups all-purpose flour
1 tablespoon ground cloves
1 tablespoon ground cinnamon
1 tablespoon ground allspice
1 tablespoon ground nutmeg
1 cup raisins
1 teaspoon soda
½ cup molasses
½ cup hot coffee
1 cup sour milk or buttermilk
2 (1-ounce) squares unsweetened
    chocolate, melted
Cream Cheese Icing

Cream butter and sugar in a medium mixing bowl; add eggs and blend.

Combine flour, spices, raisins, and soda; combine molasses, coffee, and milk. Add flour mixture alternately with molasses mixture to butter mixture; stir in chocolate.

Pour into a greased and floured 13- × 9- × 2-inch baking pan or 3 greased and floured 9-inch cakepans. Bake at 350° for 25 to 35 minutes, or until wooden pick inserted comes out clean. Let layers cool in pans for 10 minutes; then remove from pans and cool completely on wire racks. Frost with Cream Cheese Icing. Yield: 12 servings or one 9-inch cake.

Cream Cheese Icing:

1 (8-ounce) package cream cheese,
    softened
½ cup butter or margarine, softened
1 (1-pound) package powdered sugar,
    sifted
1 teaspoon vanilla extract

Blend cream cheese and butter well in a small mixing bowl. Add sugar gradually, beating until mixture reaches spreading consistency. Stir in vanilla. Yield: enough for one 13- × 9- × 2-inch or one 9-inch layer cake.

Chocolate Pound Cake

 1 cup butter, softened
 ½ cup shortening
 3 cups sugar
 5 eggs
 ½ cup cocoa
 3 cups all-purpose flour
 ½ teaspoon baking powder
 ¼ teaspoon salt
 1 tablespoon vanilla extract
 1 cup milk

Cream butter, shortening, and sugar in a medium mixing bowl. Add eggs, one at a time, beating well after each addition. Beat at high speed of an electric mixer for 2 minutes or until fluffy.

Combine cocoa, flour, baking powder, and salt. Add vanilla to milk; add milk mixture alternately with flour mixture to butter mixture. Pour batter into a greased and floured 10-inch tube pan; bake at 325° for 1 hour and 25 minutes. Yield: one 10-inch cake.

Old-South Date Nut Cake

 3 eggs, separated
 1 cup sugar
 ⅛ teaspoon salt
 1 teaspoon vanilla extract
 ½ teaspoon almond extract
 ⅔ cup cracker crumbs
 ½ cup chopped dates
 1 cup chopped pecans
 1 teaspoon baking powder
 Whipped cream

Beat egg yolks well in a medium mixing bowl; add sugar, salt, and flavorings, mixing well. Combine cracker crumbs, dates, pecans, and baking powder; add to egg yolk mixture, mixing well. Beat egg whites until stiff; fold into egg yolk mixture. Pour into a greased and floured 13- × 9- × 2-inch baking pan and bake at 325° for 30 to 35 minutes. *Do not overbake.* Serve with whipped cream. Yield: 12 to 16 servings.

Fig Cake

 2 cups all-purpose flour
 1 cup sugar
 1 teaspoon salt
 1 teaspoon soda
 1 teaspoon ground cinnamon
 1 teaspoon ground cloves
 1 teaspoon ground nutmeg
 1 cup vegetable oil
 3 eggs, beaten
 ¾ cup buttermilk
 2 cups fig preserves, chopped
 1 cup chopped nuts
 1 tablespoon vanilla extract
 Sauce (recipe follows)

Combine dry ingredients in a medium mixing bowl. Add oil; mix well. Add eggs; beat well. Gradually add buttermilk, fig preserves, nuts, and vanilla, mixing well. Pour batter into a greased and floured 10-inch tube pan. Bake at 325° about one hour or until wooden pick inserted comes out clean. Pour sauce over cake while hot and still in pan. Yield: one 10-inch cake.

Sauce:

 ½ cup buttermilk
 1 cup sugar
 1 tablespoon light corn syrup
 ½ teaspoon soda
 ½ cup margarine
 1 teaspoon vanilla extract

Combine first 5 ingredients in a medium saucepan; bring to a boil over medium heat, stirring constantly. Boil 3 minutes, stirring constantly; remove from heat and stir in vanilla. Yield: about 1½ cups sauce.

Date Nut Cake

    1 cup all-purpose flour
    ½ teaspoon salt
    2¼ teaspoons baking powder
    1 cup sugar
    4 eggs, beaten
    1 teaspoon vanilla extract
    1 pound English walnut halves
    1 pound pitted whole dates

Combine flour, salt, baking powder, sugar, eggs, and vanilla in a large mixing bowl; mix well. Stir in nuts and dates. Pour batter into a greased and floured 10-inch tube pan and bake at 300° for 1 hour or until cake shrinks from sides of pan. Yield: one 10-inch cake.

Japanese Fruit Cake

    2 cups sugar
    1 cup butter, softened
    4 eggs
    3¼ cups all-purpose flour
    1 tablespoon baking powder
    ¾ cup milk
    1 teaspoon vanilla extract
    1 teaspoon ground cinnamon
    1 teaspoon ground allspice
    ½ teaspoon ground cloves
    1 cup chopped raisins
    Filling (recipe follows)
    White Icing (recipe follows)

Cream sugar and butter in a medium mixing bowl; add eggs, one at a time, beating well after each addition. Combine flour and baking powder; add alternately with milk to sugar mixture, mixing well. Stir in vanilla. Divide batter into 2 equal portions; stir spices and raisins into one portion. Pour plain batter into 2 greased and floured 9-inch cakepans; pour spiced batter into 2 greased and floured 9-inch cakepans. Bake at 350° for 25 to 30 minutes. Spread Filling between layers; frost top and sides with White Icing. Yield: one 9-inch cake.

Filling:

    Juice of 2 lemons
    Grated rind of 1 lemon
    1½ cups flaked coconut
    2 cups sugar
    1 cup boiling water
    Dash of salt
    2 tablespoons cornstarch
    ½ cup water

Combine first 6 ingredients in a medium saucepan and bring to a boil over medium heat. Dissolve cornstarch in ½ cup water; add to coconut mixture and cook over medium heat, stirring constantly, for 5 minutes or until mixture will drop in thick lumps from the spoon. Remove from heat and cool. Yield: about 3 cups filling.

White Icing:

    1 cup sugar
    Dash of salt
    ⅛ teaspoon cream of tartar
    ⅓ cup boiling water
    1 egg white
    ½ teaspoon vanilla extract

Combine sugar, salt, cream of tartar, and boiling water in the top of a double boiler; place over boiling water. Add egg white; beat by hand with a rotary beater about 7 minutes or until mixture is of spreading consistency. Stir in vanilla. Yield: enough icing to frost a 9-inch cake.

A bountiful apple crop is the basis for these outstanding dishes: (clockwise) Apple Butter (page 258), Old-Fashioned Stack Cake (page 196), Crabapple Jelly (page 261), and Fried Apple Pies (page 232).

Far Right: *Favorite Pecan Pie (page 237), Barbecued Pecans (page 253), and Buttermilk Pecan Pralines (page 246) take full advantage of the season's bounty of pecans.*

Left: *Pound cakes, such as this Million Dollar Pound Cake (page 214) and Butterscotch-Mocha Pound Cake (page 214), can be the dessert for any special occasion.*

Below: *Special cookies are as much a part of the holidays as hanging the Christmas stockings: (clockwise from top left) Coconut Island Cookies (page 219), Date-Nut Pinwheel Cookies (page 223), Black-Eyed Susans (page 222), Cherry Delights (page 220), Date-Nut Balls (page 219), Fruitcake Cookies (page 220), Frosted Apricot Jewels (page 218), Candy Cane Cookies (page 222), Lemon Cheese Logs (page 224), and Cream Cheese Crescents (page 222).*

Louisiana Fruit Cake

        5 cups all-purpose flour
        2 teaspoons baking powder
        1 teaspoon soda
        ½ teaspoon salt
        2 teaspoons ground cinnamon
        2 teaspoons ground nutmeg
        1 teaspoon ground cloves
        2 cups butter or margarine, softened
        1 cup sugar
        8 eggs, separated
        ¼ cup honey or syrup
        1 cup fruit juice (any flavor)
        1 cup strawberry preserves
        1 cup fig preserves
        2 cups muscadine or peach preserves
        1½ cups watermelon rind preserves
        1 cup fig conserve or blackberry jam
        1 cup grape jelly or orange preserves
        4 cups chopped nuts

Sift flour, baking powder, soda, salt, and spices together 3 times; set aside. Cream butter and sugar in a large mixing bowl; add egg yolks, beating well. Add honey; blend in fruit juice alternately with half of flour mixture. Mix remaining flour mixture with preserves, jams, and nuts; stir into batter. Beat egg whites until stiff; fold into batter.

Pour batter into 2 greased and floured 9- × 5- × 3-inch loafpans and 2 greased and floured 10-inch tube pans. Bake at 275° about 3 hours for loaves and 4½ to 5 hours for tube pans. Place a shallow pan of water in the bottom of the oven during baking time; remove during the last hour of baking. Yield: two 9-inch loaves and two 10-inch cakes.

Note: Other preserves may be substituted. Cakes keep well with little or no soaking.

Rich Peach Ice Cream (page 245) is just one way to enjoy the fresh fruit of the season.

Kentucky Jam Cake

Jam refers to blackberry, dewberry, etc. The cake is a "must" not only for Kentucky and Tennessee folk, but for families whose roots stem from these states.

        ¾ cup butter or margarine, softened
        1 cup sugar
        3 eggs
        3 cups all-purpose flour
        2 teaspoons baking powder
        1 teaspoon soda
        ¼ teaspoon salt
        1 teaspoon ground cinnamon
        1 teaspoon ground allspice
        ½ cup sour milk or buttermilk
        1 cup thick jam
        Fruit Frosting

Cream butter and sugar in a large mixing bowl; add eggs and beat again. Sift dry ingredients together three times; add to creamed mixture alternately with sour milk. Fold in jam. Pour into 2 greased 9-inch cakepans. Bake at 350° about 35 to 45 minutes or until golden brown. Cool in pans 10 minutes; remove from pans and complete cooling on wire racks. Spread warm Fruit Frosting between layers and on top and sides of cake. Yield: one 9-inch cake.

Fruit Frosting:

        1 cup pitted dates
        1 cup figs
        1 cup raisins
        1 orange, peeled
        1 lemon, peeled
        ⅓ cup sugar

Grind dates, figs, and raisins. Cut orange and lemon in quarters; remove seeds, and grind. Combine all ingredients in a medium saucepan. Cook over medium heat until mixture thickens, stirring constantly. Spread warm frosting on cake. Yield: enough frosting for a 2-layer cake.

Mayflower Grape Cake

½ cup shortening
¾ teaspoon salt
1½ teaspoons vanilla extract
1½ cups sugar
2¾ cups all-purpose flour
1 tablespoon baking powder
½ cup milk
½ cup water
4 egg whites, stiffly beaten
Grape Filling
Grape Frosting

Blend shortening, salt, and vanilla in a large mixing bowl. Add sugar and cream well.

Combine dry ingredients and add to creamed mixture alternately with milk and water, beating well after each addition. Fold in egg whites.

Bake in 2 greased and floured 9-inch cake-pans at 350° for 25 minutes. Cool in pans 10 minutes; remove from pans and complete cooling on wire racks. Spread Grape Filling between layers, reserving ½ cup filling to decorate top of cake. Frost top and sides of cake with Grape Frosting and decorate with reserved Grape Filling. Yield: one 9-inch cake.

Grape Filling:

½ cup grape juice
½ cup water
3 tablespoons cornstarch
¼ teaspoon salt
½ cup sugar
¼ cup lemon juice
1 tablespoon butter or margarine

Scald grape juice and water in top of double boiler. Combine cornstarch, salt, and sugar, mixing well; add to grape juice mixture. Cook over direct medium heat until thick, stirring constantly. Cook over boiling water 15 minutes, stirring occasionally. Add lemon juice and butter and blend well. Cool. Yield: about 1½ cups or enough frosting for one 9-inch layer cake.

Grape Frosting:

1 egg white
¾ cup sugar
3 tablespoons grape juice
½ teaspoon light corn syrup

Mix all ingredients in top of double boiler and cook over low heat, beating constantly, until mixture holds a peak. Remove from heat and beat until thick enough to spread. Yield: about 1 cup.

Misty Mountain Gingerbread

1 cup sorghum or molasses
1 cup lard or shortening
1 cup sugar
1 tablespoon ground cinnamon
1 tablespoon ground ginger
1 teaspoon ground allspice
1 teaspoon ground cloves
2¼ cups all-purpose flour
1 teaspoon salt
1 cup buttermilk
2 eggs, beaten
1 teaspoon soda
¼ cup hot water
Butterscotch Sauce or whipped cream

Bring first 7 ingredients to boil, heating until lard is melted. Combine flour and salt; beat in boiled mixture. Add buttermilk and eggs, beating well. Dissolve soda in water; stir into batter. Pour into a greased and floured 12- × 7½- × 1½-inch baking pan; bake at 350° for 50 to 60 minutes or until tests done. Cool on rack. Serve with Butterscotch Sauce or whipped cream. Yield: 8 servings.

Butterscotch Sauce:

½ cup firmly packed brown sugar
½ cup sugar
½ cup cold water
2 tablespoons light corn syrup
1½ tablespoons butter or margarine
½ teaspoon vanilla extract
¼ cup hot water

Combine first 4 ingredients in small saucepan; cook until mixture forms a firm ball when tested in cold water (about 245°). Remove from heat; beat in butter, vanilla, and hot water. Cool slightly before serving. Yield: about 1 cup sauce.

Lane Cake

   3 cups cake flour
   2 teaspoons baking powder
   1 cup butter, softened
   2 cups sugar
   1 cup milk
   1 teaspoon vanilla extract
   8 egg whites
   Coconut Filling

Sift flour and baking powder together in a small mixing bowl. Cream butter and sugar together in a medium mixing bowl until light and fluffy. Combine milk and vanilla; stir into butter mixture alternately with flour mixture. Beat well, scraping bowl frequently. Beat egg whites until stiff but not dry; fold into batter. Pour batter into 3 greased and floured 9-inch cakepans. Bake at 350° for 20 to 25 minutes or until sides of cake pull away from pan. Cool in pans for 5 minutes before removing to wire racks to completely cool. Spread Coconut Filling between layers and on top of cake. Yield: one 9-inch cake.

Coconut Filling:

   8 egg yolks
   1 cup sugar
   ½ cup butter or margarine, softened
   1 cup sweet white wine
   1 to 2 cups chopped pecans
   1 fresh coconut, grated, or 1
       (7-ounce) package frozen
       coconut, thawed, or 1 (4-ounce)
       can flaked coconut
   1 cup chopped white raisins

Combine egg yolks, sugar, and butter in the top of a double boiler; beat until thick and lemon colored. Cook over boiling water for 30 to 45 minutes, stirring constantly, until mixture has thickened. Remove from heat and stir in wine.

Combine pecans, coconut, and raisins in a large mixing bowl; pour yolk mixture over pecan mixture and mix thoroughly. Yield: enough icing to fill and frost one 9-inch cake.

Patriotic Cake

   1 teaspoon soda
   1 tablespoon water
   2 tablespoons half-and-half or milk
   1 pound (about 2 cups) risen White
       Bread dough (see Index)
   1 cup butter or margarine, softened
   2 cups firmly packed brown sugar
   3 eggs, beaten
   1 teaspoon ground cloves
   ½ pound currants
   ½ pound raisins

Dissolve soda in water and half-and-half; add to dough and knead in a large mixing bowl. Add butter and continue to knead dough until it is smooth and elastic. Add sugar, eggs, and cloves, beating thoroughly until smooth.

Pour boiling water over currants and raisins; drain and dry on a paper towel. Add to batter, mixing thoroughly. Pour into a greased and floured 10-inch tube pan and bake at 350° for 1 hour or until toothpick inserted in center of cake comes out clean. Cool in pan 10 minutes; remove to a wire rack and cool completely. Serve cake plain or frosted with a thin caramel frosting. Yield: one 10-inch cake.

Lady Baltimore Cake

3½ cups sifted cake flour
1 tablespoon plus 1 teaspoon
    baking powder
1 teaspoon salt
1 cup butter, softened
2 teaspoons vanilla extract
2 cups sugar, divided
1 cup milk
1 cup egg whites (7 or 8)
Lady Baltimore Frosting

Combine flour, baking powder, and salt; set aside. Cream butter until light and fluffy in a large mixing bowl. Add vanilla. Gradually add 1½ cups sugar and cream well until mixture resembles whipped cream.

Add flour mixture and milk alternately in small amounts to sugar mixture, beginning and ending with flour. Mix thoroughly after each addition. Beat egg whites until stiff, gradually adding ½ cup sugar. Beat until glossy. Fold egg whites into batter and mix thoroughly.

Spoon batter into 3 brown paper-lined, greased, and floured 9-inch cakepans. Tap filled pans against table to remove large air bubbles. Bake at 375° for 25 minutes or until done. Allow to cool in pans a few minutes; remove from pans and complete cooling on wire racks. Spread Lady Baltimore Frosting with fruit between layers, and frost top and sides of cake with remaining frosting. Yield: one 3-layer cake.

Lady Baltimore Frosting:

1½ cups sugar
½ teaspoon cream of tartar
½ cup water
3 egg whites
1 teaspoon vanilla extract
½ cup chopped nuts
½ cup chopped raisins
½ cup chopped dates
½ cup chopped candied cherries

Mix sugar, cream of tartar, and water in a medium saucepan. Bring to a boil over medium heat and stir until sugar is dissolved. Cook, without stirring, until mixture reaches soft ball stage (240°).

Beat egg whites until stiff in a medium mixing bowl, and gradually pour hot syrup over egg whites; continue beating until mixture will stand in soft peaks. Add vanilla, mixing well.

Remove about one-third of the frosting and add to it the fruit and nuts; use this mixture for the filling. Yield: enough frosting to fill and frost a 3-layer cake.

Marble Cake

½ cup butter, softened
1 cup sugar
2 eggs
2 cups all-purpose flour
1 teaspoon soda
1 teaspoon baking powder
1 teaspoon vanilla extract
1 cup commercial sour cream
¼ cup sugar
1 tablespoon ground cinnamon
¼ cup melted butter

Cream ½ cup butter and 1 cup sugar together in a medium mixing bowl; add eggs, one at a time, beating well after each addition. Combine flour, soda, and baking powder; stir into butter mixture, and add vanilla. Stir in sour cream.

Spoon ⅓ of batter into a greased 10-inch tube pan; combine ¼ cup sugar and cinnamon and sprinkle half of mixture on top of batter. Spoon half the remaining batter on top; sprinkle with remaining sugar-cinnamon. Add remaining batter. Pour melted butter over top; cut through the batter with a spoon to make a marbled effect. Bake at 375° for 40 to 50 minutes. Yield: one 10-inch cake.

Nameless Cake

1½ cups sugar
¾ cup shortening
3 eggs
1¾ cups all-purpose flour
½ teaspoon baking powder
½ teaspoon salt
½ teaspoon soda
¾ teaspoon ground nutmeg
1 teaspoon ground cinnamon
2 tablespoons cocoa
¾ cup buttermilk
1 teaspoon vanilla extract
1 teaspoon lemon extract
½ cup coarsely chopped nuts
Icing (recipe follows)

Cream sugar and shortening in a medium mixing bowl; add eggs and blend thoroughly. Combine flour, baking powder, salt, soda, nutmeg, cinnamon, and cocoa; add alternately with buttermilk to sugar mixture. Blend in flavorings and nuts. Pour batter into 2 greased and floured 8- or 9-inch cakepans; bake at 350° for 25 to 30 minutes. Cool in pans 10 minutes; remove from pans and complete cooling on wire racks. Spread icing between layers and on top and sides of cake. Yield: one 8- or 9-inch cake.

Icing:

6 tablespoons butter, softened
1 egg yolk
3 cups powdered sugar
½ teaspoon salt
1 tablespoon plus 1½ teaspoons cocoa
1 teaspoon ground cinnamon
About 1½ tablespoons hot coffee

Cream butter and egg yolk in a medium mixing bowl. Sift sugar, salt, cocoa, and cinnamon; add alternately with 1 tablespoon plus 1½ teaspoons hot coffee to butter mixture. Beat until smooth. (Add a few more drops of coffee, if necessary, to make mixture a spreading consistency.) Yield: enough icing for one 8- or 9-inch cake.

Virginia Nut Cake

⅓ cup shortening
⅓ cup butter, softened
1½ cups sugar
3 eggs
2⅔ cups all-purpose flour
2 teaspoons baking powder
1 teaspoon salt
1 cup milk
1 teaspoon vanilla extract
1⅓ cups chopped pecans or walnuts
Creamy Caramel Icing
Finely chopped pecans (optional)

Cream shortening, butter, and sugar in a large mixing bowl; add eggs and beat thoroughly. Combine dry ingredients; add alternately with milk to sugar mixture, beating well after each addition. Stir in vanilla and pecans.

Pour batter into 3 greased and floured 8-inch cakepans or one 13- × 9- × 2-inch baking pan. Bake at 350° for 25 to 30 minutes for layers and 35 to 40 minutes for pan cake. Cool in pans 10 minutes; remove from pan and complete cooling on wire racks.

Frost with Creamy Caramel Icing and top with chopped pecans, if desired. Yield: one 8-inch cake or 12 to 16 servings.

Creamy Caramel Icing:

¾ cup firmly packed brown sugar
¼ cup plus 2 tablespoons butter
⅛ teaspoon salt
About ¼ cup half-and-half or milk
About 2 cups powdered sugar
¾ teaspoon vanilla extract

Combine brown sugar, butter, and salt in a small saucepan and cook over low heat until butter is melted. Add ¼ cup half-and-half; stir well, and remove from heat.

Add 2 cups sugar and beat until mixture is of spreading consistency; add more sugar or half-and-half, if necessary. Stir in vanilla. Yield: enough for one 8-inch or one 13- × 9- × 2-inch cake.

Black Walnut Loaf Cake

½ cup butter, softened
1 cup sugar
4 eggs, separated
1 teaspoon vanilla extract
2 cups all-purpose flour
2 teaspoons baking powder
¾ teaspoon salt
½ cup milk
1 cup chopped black walnuts

Cream butter and sugar in a medium mixing bowl. Beat in egg yolks, one at a time; stir in vanilla. Combine dry ingredients; reserve ¼ cup. Add flour mixture alternately with milk to butter mixture, beginning and ending with flour mixture. Combine reserved ¼ cup flour mixture with walnuts, stirring to coat walnuts; stir into batter.

Beat egg whites until stiff; fold into batter. Pour batter into a greased and floured 9- × 5- × 3-inch loafpan. Bake at 350° for 50 to 60 minutes, or until wooden pick inserted comes out clean. Cool in pan on wire rack for 5 minutes; remove from pan and cool completely on wire rack. Yield: 1 loaf.

Feud Cake

Legend has it that two neighborhood families claimed the honor of being the originator of this cake. The argument turned into a family feud. The two families are forgotten—but not the cake.

6 eggs, separated (at room temperature)
¾ cup sugar
¼ cup all-purpose flour
2 teaspoons baking powder
½ teaspoon salt
5 cups finely chopped pecans
2 teaspoons vanilla extract
¾ cup powdered sugar
Whipped cream
Chopped pecans

Beat egg yolks with sugar in a medium mixing bowl for about 10 minutes. Stir in flour, baking powder, salt, pecans, and vanilla.

Beat egg whites until foamy in a large mixing bowl; add powdered sugar gradually, and beat until stiff peaks form. Fold meringue into pecan mixture. Pour batter into 3 greased and floured 9-inch cakepans. Bake at 350° for 10 to 12 minutes. Cool in pans 10 minutes; remove from pans and complete cooling on wire racks. Spread whipped cream and generously sprinkle pecans between layers and on top of cake. Yield: one 9-inch cake.

Strawberry Meringue Nut Torte

1½ cups cracker crumbs
1 cup chopped pecans
2 teaspoons baking powder
6 egg whites
2 cups sugar
2 teaspoons almond extract
1 cup whipping cream, whipped
1 quart ripe strawberries, capped, halved, and rinsed

Combine cracker crumbs, pecans, and baking powder in a medium mixing bowl.

Beat egg whites until stiff in a large mixing bowl; gradually add sugar, beating well after each addition. Stir in almond extract; fold in cracker crumb mixture. Spread mixture into 2 greased and floured 9-inch cakepans; bake at 325° for 40 minutes. Remove from pans to wire racks to cool; spread whipped cream and arrange strawberries between layers and on top of cake. Yield: 8 servings.

Oatmeal Cake

1 cup quick-cooking oats, uncooked
1¼ cups hot water
½ cup margarine, softened
1 cup sugar
1 cup firmly packed brown sugar
2 eggs
1⅓ cups all-purpose flour
1 teaspoon soda
1 teaspoon ground cinnamon
1½ teaspoons salt

Stir oats into hot water in a small saucepan; let stand 20 minutes. Cream margarine and sugar in a medium mixing bowl; beat in eggs. Add oatmeal mixture, beating well. Combine dry ingredients; add to oatmeal mixture. Pour batter into a greased and floured 13- × 9- × 2-inch baking pan. Bake at 350° for 35 to 40 minutes. Yield: 12 to 16 servings.

Pineapple-Meringue Cake

½ cup butter, softened
1¼ cups sugar, divided
4 eggs, separated
½ cup cake flour
¼ teaspoon salt
1 teaspoon baking powder
¼ cup milk
1 teaspoon vanilla extract
¾ cup chopped nuts
Pineapple Filling (recipe follows)

Cream butter and ½ cup sugar in a medium mixing bowl. Add egg yolks, and mix well. Sift flour, salt, and baking powder together; add alternately with milk to butter mixture. Pour batter into 2 greased and floured 8-inch cakepans.

Beat egg whites in a small mixing bowl until foamy; add ¾ cup sugar gradually, and beat until stiff peaks form. Stir in vanilla and spread on top of batter in cakepans. Sprinkle nuts on top; bake at 325° for 20 to 25 minutes. Cool in pans.

Place one layer, meringue side down, on a serving platter; spread Pineapple Filling on top. Place second layer over filling, meringue side up. Yield: one 8-inch cake.

Pineapple Filling:

½ cup whipping cream, whipped,
   or 1 cup commercial
   whipped topping
1 tablespoon plus 1½ teaspoons
   powdered sugar
1 cup canned crushed pineapple,
   drained
¼ teaspoon vanilla extract

Combine all ingredients in a small mixing bowl; mix well. Yield: enough filling for one 8-inch cake.

Irish Potato Cake

2 cups sugar
½ cup cocoa
½ cup shortening
1 cup milk
3 eggs
1 cup cold mashed potatoes
2 cups all-purpose flour
⅛ teaspoon salt
1 teaspoon ground cinnamon
1 teaspoon ground cloves
2 teaspoons baking powder
1 cup chopped pecans
1 cup candied cherries, halved

Combine sugar, cocoa, and shortening in a large mixing bowl; cream until light and fluffy. Beat in milk; add eggs, one at a time, beating thoroughly after each addition. Add potatoes; beat well.

Combine dry ingredients; add to batter, and beat until smooth. Fold in pecans and cherries. Pour into a greased and floured 10-inch tube pan. Bake at 350° for 1 hour or until a toothpick inserted comes out clean. Cool in pan 10 minutes; remove to a wire rack and turn right side up to cool completely. Yield: one 10-inch cake.

Sour Cream Pound Cake

1½ cups butter, softened
3 cups sugar
6 eggs
3 cups all-purpose flour
¼ teaspoon soda
¼ teaspoon salt
1 cup commercial sour cream
1 teaspoon vanilla extract

Cream butter and sugar in a medium mixing bowl. Add eggs, one at a time, mixing well after each addition. Combine flour, soda, and salt; add alternately with sour cream to butter mixture and beat well. Stir in vanilla. Pour batter into a greased and floured 10-inch tube pan and bake at 325° for 1 to 1½ hours, or until cake springs back when lightly touched and has separated from sides of pan. Yield: one 10-inch cake.

Crusty Pound Cake

1½ cups butter, softened
3 cups sugar
6 eggs
1 tablespoon vanilla extract
1 teaspoon almond extract
3 cups all-purpose flour
½ teaspoon salt

Cream butter well in a large mixing bowl; add sugar gradually, mixing until texture is fine and mealy. Add eggs, one at a time, beating after each addition. Add flavorings.

Combine flour and salt. Stir flour mixture into batter, beating just until flour is moistened. Do not overbeat. Pour into a greased and floured 10-inch tube pan. Bake at 325° for 1 hour and 25 minutes, or until a toothpick inserted comes out clean and cake shrinks slightly from sides of pan. Cool in pan 15 minutes. Turn out onto a wire rack; turn right side up and complete cooling. Yield: one 10-inch cake.

Million Dollar Pound Cake

3 cups sugar
1 pound butter, softened
6 eggs (at room temperature)
4 cups all-purpose flour
¾ cup milk
1 teaspoon almond extract
1 teaspoon vanilla extract

Combine sugar and butter; cream until light and fluffy. Add eggs, one at a time, beating well after each addition. Add flour to creamed mixture alternately with milk, beating well after each addition. Stir in flavorings. Pour batter into a well-greased and floured 10-inch tube pan. Bake at 300° for 1 hour and 40 minutes or until cake tests done. Yield: one 10-inch cake.

Butterscotch-Mocha Pound Cake

1 (6-ounce) package butterscotch-flavored morsels
2 tablespoons instant coffee powder
¼ cup water
1 cup butter or margarine, softened
1½ cups sugar
3 cups all-purpose flour
½ teaspoon soda
¼ teaspoon salt
¾ cup buttermilk
4 eggs

Combine butterscotch morsels, coffee powder, and water in top of a double boiler; place over boiling water, and stir until smooth. Set aside. Combine butter and sugar; cream well. Stir in butterscotch mixture. Combine flour, soda, and salt; add to creamed mixture alternately with buttermilk, beating well after each addition. Add eggs, one at a time, beating well after each addition. Pour batter into a greased and floured 10-inch Bundt pan. Bake at 350° for 55 to 60 minutes. Cool 10 to 15 minutes; remove from pan. Yield: one 10-inch cake.

Raisin Cake

This was originally known as "Waldorf War Cake" as it was baked during World War I when there was a shortage of granulated sugar and eggs.

2 cups firmly packed brown sugar
2 tablespoons shortening
2 cups plus 1 teaspoon hot water, divided
2 cups raisins
1 teaspoon salt
1 teaspoon ground cinnamon
¼ teaspoon ground cloves
1 teaspoon soda
3 cups all-purpose flour

Combine brown sugar, shortening, 2 cups water, raisins, salt, cinnamon, and cloves in a medium saucepan; bring to a boil over medium heat. Reduce heat; simmer for 5 minutes. Remove from heat; cool completely.

Dissolve soda in 1 teaspoon hot water; add with flour to cold raisin mixture. Pour batter into a greased 13- × 9- × 2-inch baking pan; bake at 300° for 45 minutes or until tests done. Yield: 12 to 16 servings.

Prune Cake

1 cup chopped prunes
1 cup sugar
¾ cup shortening
3 eggs
2 cups all-purpose flour
1 teaspoon ground nutmeg
1 teaspoon ground cinnamon
1 teaspoon soda
½ teaspoon ground allspice
½ teaspoon ground cloves
½ cup commercial sour cream
Frosting (recipe follows)

Cook prunes in boiling water to cover for 5 minutes. Drain and set aside.

Cream sugar and shortening in a medium mixing bowl; add eggs, one at a time, beating well after each addition. Combine flour, nutmeg, cinnamon, soda, allspice, and cloves; add alternately with sour cream to sugar mixture. Fold in prunes, and pour batter into a greased and floured 13- × 9- × 2-inch baking pan. Bake at 350° for 20 to 25 minutes. Do not overbake. Cool and ice with frosting. Yield: 12 to 16 servings.

Frosting:

½ cup raisins
½ cup commercial sour cream
1 cup sugar
2 tablespoons butter or margarine
½ cup chopped nuts
Milk (optional)

Cook raisins in boiling water to cover for 5 minutes. Drain and set aside.

Combine next 3 ingredients and cook over low heat, stirring constantly, about 20 minutes or until mixture thickens. Remove from heat and cool, stirring occasionally, making sure mixture does not harden. Beat again; stir in nuts and raisins. (Add milk to thin frosting, if necessary.) Yield: enough frosting for a 13- × 9- × 2-inch cake.

Sponge Cake

3 eggs, separated
1 cup sugar
¼ cup water
1 cup all-purpose flour
2 teaspoons baking powder
1 teaspoon lemon juice

Beat egg yolks with sugar in a medium mixing bowl; add water and beat well. Combine flour and baking powder; stir into egg mixture. Beat egg whites until stiff; fold into batter. Stir in lemon juice. Pour batter into a greased and floured 13- × 9- × 2-inch baking pan. Bake at 325° for 35 to 40 minutes or until a toothpick inserted in center comes out clean. Yield: one 13- × 9- × 2-inch cake.

Tipsy Cake

1 Sponge Cake (page 215)
1½ to 1¾ cups whole blanched
    almonds
1 cup sherry
3 eggs
¾ cup sugar
2 tablespoons cornstarch
4 cups milk, scalded
1 tablespoon vanilla extract
1 tablespoon rum or sherry
2½ to 3 cups whipping cream,
    whipped
1 cup flaked coconut
Maraschino cherries (optional)

Place Sponge Cake on a deep serving platter; press almonds gently into cake, upright, about ¾ inch apart. Chop remaining almonds and reserve. Pour sherry over cake.

Beat eggs well in a medium saucepan; stir in sugar and cornstarch, and mix well. Add warm milk and cook slowly over medium heat, stirring constantly, until thickened. Cool; stir in vanilla, reserved chopped almonds, and rum. Pour about 1½ cups custard over cake.

Spread whipped cream and sprinkle coconut over entire cake; dot cake with maraschino cherries, if desired. Serve remaining custard with cake. Yield: 12 to 16 servings.

Miss Gertrude's White Layer Cake

A caramel frosting can be made that never needs to be caramelized. The caramel fudge, which turns a soft pale gold as the cream and sugar cook down, is possibly Chattanooga's favorite dessert.

¾ cup shortening or butter
2 cups sugar
2 teaspoons baking powder
3 cups sifted cake flour
1 cup milk
1 teaspoon vanilla extract
5 egg whites, stiffly beaten
Miss Gertrude's Caramel Icing

Cream shortening and sugar in a large mixing bowl until smooth. Combine baking powder and flour; add to sugar mixture alternately with milk, mixing well. Stir in vanilla. Fold in egg whites. Pour batter into 2 greased and floured 9-inch cakepans and bake at 350° for 25 to 30 minutes or until done. Cool in pans 10 minutes; remove cakes and complete cooling on wire racks. Frost with Miss Gertrude's Caramel Icing. Yield: one 9-inch cake.

Miss Gertrude's Caramel Icing:

Butter
¼ cup light corn syrup
3 cups sugar
2 cups whipping cream
¼ cup butter
1 tablespoon vanilla extract

Butter a medium saucepan; combine remaining ingredients except vanilla in saucepan and bring to a boil over medium heat. Cook, stirring occasionally, until mixture reaches soft ball stage (234° to 240°). Stir in vanilla; let cool slightly and beat until creamy. Yield: enough icing for a 2-layer cake.

Yellow Loaf Cake

2 cups sugar
1 cup shortening
5 eggs
3 cups cake flour
2½ teaspoons baking powder
½ teaspoon salt
1 cup milk
1 teaspoon vanilla extract

Cream sugar and shortening in a medium mixing bowl until light and fluffy; add eggs, one at a time, beating well after each addition. Sift dry ingredients together; add to creamed mixture alternately with milk, beating well after each addition. Stir in vanilla. Pour batter into a greased and floured 9- × 5- × 3-inch loafpan; bake at 350° for 1 hour or until wooden pick inserted comes out clean. Yield: one loaf.

Black Walnut Dream Bars

½ cup butter or margarine, softened
1 cup all-purpose flour
1½ cups firmly packed light brown sugar, divided
2 eggs
1 teaspoon vanilla extract
2 teaspoons all-purpose flour
½ teaspoon baking powder
¼ teaspoon salt
1 cup chopped black walnuts
1½ cups flaked coconut

Combine butter, flour, and ½ cup brown sugar in a small mixing bowl, mixing with hands or a pastry blender. Spread mixture in bottom of a greased and waxed paper-lined 13- × 9- × 2-inch baking pan. Bake at 350° until lightly browned, about 10 minutes.

Beat eggs in a medium mixing bowl; add 1 cup sugar gradually, beating constantly. Add vanilla. Combine dry ingredients; blend into egg mixture. Stir in walnuts and coconut. Spread over pastry. Bake at 325° for 20 minutes or until firm and lightly browned. Cool and cut into bars. Yield: 3 dozen bars.

Brownies

1 cup butter or margarine
2 cups sugar
4 eggs, beaten
1½ cups all-purpose flour
¼ teaspoon salt
½ cup plus 2 tablespoons cocoa
2 teaspoons vanilla extract
1 cup chopped pecans

Melt butter in a medium saucepan over low heat; cool. Stir in sugar and eggs. Mix flour with salt and cocoa; stir into butter mixture with remaining ingredients. Pour into a greased 13- × 9- × 2-inch baking pan; bake at 325° for 35 minutes. Cool and cut into squares. Yield: 3 dozen brownies.

Lemon Bars

1 cup plus 2 tablespoons all-purpose flour, divided
½ cup butter or margarine, softened
¼ cup powdered sugar
1 cup sugar
2 eggs, beaten
½ teaspoon baking powder
3 tablespoons lemon juice
Grated rind of 1 lemon
¼ cup powdered sugar

Combine 1 cup flour and butter, mixing well with a pastry blender or fingers; stir in ¼ cup powdered sugar. Press mixture into an ungreased 8-inch square pan. Bake at 350° for 20 minutes.

Combine sugar, eggs, 2 tablespoons flour, baking powder, lemon juice, and rind; blend well. Pour lemon mixture over baked mixture. Bake at 350° for 25 minutes more. Sprinkle with ¼ cup powdered sugar while warm; cut into bars and remove from pan. Yield: 16 bars.

Note: For a party, cut into 1-inch squares to make 64 servings.

Bars and Squares 217

Pecan Bar Cookies

½ cup butter or margarine, melted
2 cups firmly packed brown sugar
2 eggs
1 teaspoon vanilla extract
2 cups self-rising flour
1 cup chopped pecans

Combine butter and sugar in a medium mixing bowl; beat in eggs and vanilla. Gradually add flour, mixing well. Stir in pecans. Pour into a greased 13- × 9- × 2-inch baking pan. Bake at 350° for 20 minutes. Cool and cut into bars. Yield: about 2½ dozen bars.

Pecan Sticks

1 cup butter or margarine, softened
1 cup sugar
1 egg, separated
2 cups all-purpose flour
1 tablespoon ground cinnamon
1 cup chopped pecans

Cream butter and sugar; add egg yolk, flour, and cinnamon, and mix well. Spread in a greased 13- × 9- × 2-inch baking pan; pat mixture down with hands. Spread unbeaten egg white over top; remove excess egg white. Sprinkle pecans on top and press down. Bake at 350° for 35 minutes. Cut into strips while still warm. Yield: about 2 dozen sticks.

Frosted Apricot Jewels

1¼ cups all-purpose flour
¼ cup sugar
1½ teaspoons baking powder
¼ teaspoon salt
½ cup butter or margarine, softened
1 (3-ounce) package cream cheese, softened
½ cup flaked coconut
½ cup apricot preserves
Frosting (recipe follows)
Pecan halves

Combine flour, sugar, baking powder, and salt; cut in butter and cream cheese until mixture resembles coarse meal. Add coconut and preserves, mixing well.

Drop dough by teaspoonfuls onto ungreased cookie sheets. Bake at 350° for 15 to 18 minutes or until lightly browned. Cool completely on a wire rack. Spread each cookie with frosting, and top with a pecan half. Yield: about 3 dozen.

Frosting:

1 cup sifted powdered sugar
1 tablespoon butter or margarine, softened
¼ cup apricot preserves

Combine all ingredients, and beat until smooth. Yield: 1 cup.

Benne Seed Wafers

¾ cup butter or margarine
1½ cups firmly packed brown sugar
2 eggs
1¼ cups all-purpose flour
¼ teaspoon baking powder
½ cup toasted benne (sesame) seeds
1 teaspoon vanilla extract

Cream butter and sugar. Add eggs; beat well. Combine flour, baking powder, and benne seeds. Blend into creamed mixture; add vanilla. Mix thoroughly.

Drop by teaspoonfuls onto greased cookie sheets, allowing space for cookies to spread. Bake at 325° for 12 to 15 minutes. Yield: 7 dozen.

Coconut Island Cookies

3 (1-ounce) squares unsweetened
    chocolate
¼ cup strong coffee
½ cup shortening
1 cup firmly packed brown sugar
1 egg
2 cups all-purpose flour
½ teaspoon salt
½ teaspoon soda
⅔ cup commercial sour cream
1 cup flaked coconut, divided
Chocolate Frosting

Combine chocolate and coffee in a small saucepan; place over low heat, stirring until chocolate is melted. Set aside to cool.

Combine shortening and brown sugar, creaming until light and fluffy; beat in egg and chocolate mixture. Combine flour, salt, and soda; add to creamed mixture alternately with sour cream, mixing well after each addition. Stir in ⅓ cup coconut.

Drop dough by teaspoonfuls onto greased baking sheets. Bake at 375° for 12 to 15 minutes. Frost with Chocolate Frosting while warm, and sprinkle with remaining coconut. Let stand on wire racks until frosting sets. Yield: about 6 dozen.

Chocolate Frosting:

1½ (1-ounce) squares unsweetened
    chocolate
¼ cup commercial sour cream
1 tablespoon butter or margarine
1 to 1½ cups sifted powdered sugar

Combine chocolate, sour cream, and butter in a small heavy saucepan; place over low heat, stirring until chocolate is melted. Remove from heat, and stir in enough powdered sugar to make frosting a spreading consistency. If necessary, reheat occasionally to maintain consistency. This may be used to frost other cookies. Yield: 1¼ cups.

Coconut Macaroons

3 egg whites, at room temperature
1 cup sugar
¼ cup all-purpose flour
3 cups flaked coconut

Beat egg whites at high speed of electric mixer until soft peaks form; add sugar gradually, beating at medium speed, until mixture is stiff and glossy. Sift flour over beaten egg whites; fold in. Fold in coconut. Drop onto lightly greased cookie sheets by teaspoonfuls. Bake at 350° for 10 to 12 minutes or until golden. Yield: about 3 dozen.

Date Macaroons

2 egg whites, at room temperature
1 cup powdered sugar
1 cup chopped dates
1 cup chopped nuts
1 teaspoon vanilla extract

Beat egg whites in a medium mixing bowl until soft peaks form; beat in sugar gradually. Add remaining ingredients; drop by teaspoonfuls onto greased baking sheets. Bake at 350° for 10 to 12 minutes or until a delicate brown. Cool slightly before removing from sheets. Yield: 2 dozen.

Date-Nut Balls

½ cup butter or margarine
¾ cup sugar
1 (8-ounce) package dates, chopped
2½ cups crisp rice cereal
1 cup chopped pecans
Flaked coconut or powdered sugar

Combine butter, sugar, and dates in a medium saucepan. Bring to a boil; cook, stirring constantly, 3 minutes. Stir in cereal and pecans; cool to touch. Shape into 1-inch balls, and roll each in coconut or powdered sugar. Yield: about 4 dozen.

Cherry Delights

1 cup butter or margarine, softened
½ cup sugar
½ cup light corn syrup
2 eggs, separated
2½ cups all-purpose flour
2 cups finely chopped pecans
    or walnuts
Candied cherry halves

Combine butter and sugar, creaming until light and fluffy. Add corn syrup, egg yolks, and flour; mix well. Chill.

Lightly beat egg whites. Shape dough into 1-inch balls; dip each in egg whites, and coat with nuts. Press a cherry half, cut side down, into center of each.

Place cookies about 1½ inches apart on greased baking sheets. Bake at 325° for 20 minutes. Yield: 4 dozen.

Fruitcake Cookies

½ cup butter or margarine, softened
½ cup firmly packed light brown
    sugar
2 eggs, beaten
¼ cup buttermilk
1½ cups self-rising flour
½ teaspoon soda
½ teaspoon ground allspice
½ teaspoon ground cinnamon
1 cup chopped candied cherries
1 cup chopped candied pineapple
1 cup chopped dates
1½ cups raisins (optional)
3 cups pecans, chopped

Combine butter and sugar, creaming until light and fluffy. Add eggs, buttermilk, flour, soda, and spices; mix well. Stir in remaining ingredients. Drop by teaspoonfuls onto greased baking sheets. Bake at 300° for 25 minutes. Yield: about 7 dozen.

Fig Preserve Cookies

1 cup shortening
1 cup firmly packed brown sugar
1 egg
1 cup fig preserves
1 cup chopped pecans or walnuts
1 teaspoon vanilla extract
1¾ cups all-purpose flour
½ teaspoon salt
2 teaspoons baking powder

Cream shortening and sugar well in a large mixing bowl. Add egg; beat well. Add preserves, pecans, and vanilla. Combine dry ingredients; mix into first mixture.

Drop by teaspoonfuls 2 inches apart onto greased baking sheets. Bake at 325° for 20 minutes. Yield: 6 to 7 dozen.

Honey Wafers

3 egg whites
½ cup honey
1 cup graham cracker crumbs
½ cup chopped pecans

Beat egg whites in a large mixing bowl until stiff. Gradually beat in honey; stir in crumbs and pecans. Drop by teaspoonfuls onto well-greased cookie sheets. Bake at 300° about 8 minutes or until set and delicately browned. Yield: about 3 dozen wafers.

Mincemeat Cookies

1 cup butter or margarine, softened
½ cup sugar
3 eggs, well beaten
1 teaspoon soda
1½ tablespoons hot water
½ teaspoon salt
3¼ cups all-purpose flour, divided
1½ cups raisins
1 cup chopped walnuts
1 cup prepared mincemeat

Combine butter and sugar in a large mixing bowl, creaming until light and fluffy. Add eggs and soda dissolved in hot water. Beat in salt and half the flour. Add raisins, walnuts, mincemeat, and remaining flour; mix well. Drop by teaspoonfuls onto greased baking sheets; bake at 350° about 10 minutes or until browned and done. Yield: 9 dozen.

Aggression Cookies

A thin, crisp, and easy cookie to make. The original instructions said to put everything together and "mash, knead, and squeeze (hence 'Aggression') . . . form into balls midway between English walnut and filbert size."

    3 cups firmly packed brown sugar
    3 cups butter or margarine (or 1½
        cups of each)
    2 teaspoons vanilla extract
    1 teaspoon salt
    1 tablespoon soda
    3 cups all-purpose flour
    6 cups quick-cooking oats, uncooked
    Butter
    Sugar

Combine sugar with butter in a large mixing bowl; beat until light and fluffy. Add vanilla and salt. Combine soda and flour, and beat into sugar mixture. Beat in oats, 1 cup at a time. Mix with hands when it becomes too stiff for the electric mixer.

Form dough into small balls about 1 inch in diameter. Place on ungreased cookie sheets. Flatten with the bottom of a small glass buttered and dipped in sugar. (The glass will need to be buttered only a few times, but dip in sugar for each cookie.) Bake at 350° for 10 to 12 minutes. Yield: about 15 dozen.

Oatmeal Cookies

    ¼ cup plus 1 tablespoon hot water
    2 cups firmly packed brown sugar
    ⅔ cup butter or margarine, softened
    2 eggs, well beaten
    4 cups quick-cooking oats, uncooked
    2 cups all-purpose flour
    1 cup raisins
    1 cup flaked coconut
    1 teaspoon soda
    2 teaspoons baking powder

Pour hot water over brown sugar in a large mixing bowl, and stir until dissolved. Add butter; mix well, and add eggs. Combine remaining ingredients and add to sugar mixture gradually, beating well.

Drop by teaspoonfuls onto greased baking sheets and spread slightly with a knife. Bake at 350° about 10 to 12 minutes or until brown. Yield: about 5 dozen.

Best-Ever Sugar Cookies

    2 cups sugar
    2 eggs
    1 teaspoon soda
    2 teaspoons water
    1 cup buttermilk
    1 cup butter or shortening, melted
    2 to 3 teaspoons vanilla extract
    ½ teaspoon salt
    1 teaspoon baking powder
    5 to 6 cups all-purpose flour
    Sugar

Combine sugar and eggs; beat well. Dissolve soda in water; add to sugar mixture with buttermilk, butter, and vanilla. Beat well. Stir in salt and baking powder; gradually stir in flour. Cover; chill at least 1 hour.

Shape dough into balls. Place on greased baking sheets. Flatten with a fork dipped in sugar; bake at 400° for 10 minutes or until lightly browned. Yield: about 5 dozen.

Black-Eyed Susans

½ cup butter or margarine, softened
½ cup sugar
½ cup firmly packed brown sugar
1 egg
1½ tablespoons warm water
1 teaspoon vanilla extract
1 cup peanut butter
1½ cups all-purpose flour
½ teaspoon salt
½ teaspoon soda
About ½ cup semisweet chocolate
    morsels

Combine butter and sugar, creaming until light and fluffy; add egg, warm water, vanilla, and peanut butter; beat mixture well.

Combine dry ingredients; add to creamed mixture, mixing well. Using a cookie press with a flower-shaped disc, press dough onto lightly greased cookie sheets. Place a chocolate morsel in the center of each flower.

Bake at 350° for 8 minutes or until lightly browned. Remove to wire racks, and cool completely. Chill 30 minutes. Yield: about 10 dozen 1-inch cookies.

Candy Cane Cookies

½ cup shortening
½ cup butter or margarine, softened
1 cup powdered sugar
1 egg, slightly beaten
1 teaspoon almond extract
1 teaspoon vanilla extract
2½ cups all-purpose flour
1 teaspoon salt
½ teaspoon red food coloring
½ cup finely crushed peppermint
    candy
½ cup sugar

Combine first 8 ingredients in a large bowl, and mix well. Divide dough in half; add food coloring to one portion, mixing well. Cover and chill at least 2 hours.

On a lightly floured surface, roll a teaspoonful of each dough (plain and colored) into a 4-inch-long rope. (Dough will be dry.) Place ropes side by side, and carefully twist together; curve one end down to resemble a cane. Repeat procedure with remaining dough.

Place cookies on ungreased cookie sheets, and bake at 375° for 9 minutes or just until edges begin to brown. Combine candy and sugar, mixing well. Remove cookies from cookie sheet while warm; immediately coat with candy mixture. Yield: about 4 dozen.

Cream Cheese Crescents

1 cup butter or margarine, softened
1 (8-ounce) package cream cheese,
    softened
2 cups all-purpose flour
¼ teaspoon salt
¾ cup finely chopped walnuts
⅓ cup sugar
1½ teaspoons ground cinnamon
Powdered sugar

Combine butter and cream cheese, creaming until well blended. Combine flour and salt; add to creamed mixture, mixing well. Shape dough into 8 balls; wrap each in plastic wrap, and chill at least 2 hours.

Roll each ball of dough into an 8-inch circle on a lightly floured surface; cut into 8 wedges. Combine walnuts, sugar, and cinnamon; sprinkle ¼ teaspoon mixture over each wedge of dough. Starting at wide edge of dough, roll up each wedge; shape into a crescent. Place point side down on ungreased cookie sheets.

Bake crescents at 350° for 12 minutes or until lightly browned. Cool and dust with powdered sugar. Yield: about 5 dozen.

Filled Cream Cheese Horns

1 (8-ounce) package cream cheese, softened
1 cup margarine
1 egg yolk
1 tablespoon milk
1 tablespoon sugar
2¾ cups all-purpose flour
1 teaspoon baking powder
1 cup canned apricot, prune, or nut pie filling or preserves

Beat cream cheese, margarine, egg yolk, milk, and sugar in a medium mixing bowl until creamy. Combine flour and baking powder; beat into cream cheese mixture. Dough will be sticky. Cover and chill at least 8 hours or overnight.

Roll dough ⅛ inch thick on floured surface. Cut into 3-inch squares with a fluted pastry wheel. Place a teaspoonful of filling on one corner of each square; roll up and bend to crescent shape. Place on greased cookie sheets and bake at 400° for 10 minutes or until set but not brown. Yield: about 4 dozen.

Date-Nut Pinwheel Cookies

1 (8-ounce) package dates, chopped
1 cup sugar
1 cup hot water
1 cup very finely chopped walnuts
2 cups firmly packed brown sugar
1 cup butter or margarine, softened
2 eggs
3½ cups all-purpose flour
½ teaspoon soda
½ teaspoon cream of tartar
½ teaspoon salt
1 teaspoon vanilla extract

Combine dates, sugar, and hot water in a medium saucepan; cook over medium heat until thickened (about 6 to 8 minutes), stirring constantly. Remove from heat, and stir in walnuts; set aside to cool.

Combine brown sugar and butter, creaming until light and fluffy; beat in eggs. Combine flour, soda, cream of tartar, and salt; stir into creamed mixture. Add vanilla; mix well.

Divide dough into thirds. Roll each portion into a 12-inch square on waxed paper; spread with one-third of date mixture. Lifting up edge of waxed paper, gently peel off dough and roll up jellyroll fashion. Wrap rolls in waxed paper, and chill overnight.

Cut dough into ¼-inch slices, and place 2 inches apart on greased cookie sheets. Bake at 350° for 8 to 10 minutes. Cool cookies on wire racks. Yield: about 6 dozen.

Flaky Egg Cookies

12 eggs
2 cups butter, softened
1 cup sugar
4 to 4½ cups all-purpose flour
Topping (optional; recipe follows)

Hard-cook 8 eggs; separate hard-cooked eggs. Mash or sieve yolks only; reserve whites for other uses. Separate remaining eggs; reserve egg whites for topping.

Add butter and sugar to sieved yolks, beating until creamy. Add flour and mix well; beat in 4 egg yolks. Chill dough.

Roll out a fourth of the dough at a time on a floured surface to about ⅛-inch thickness. Cut with a floured 2-inch cutter. Place on lightly floured cookie sheets. Cover with topping, if desired; bake at 375° for 8 to 10 minutes or until very lightly browned. Yield: 12 dozen.

Topping:

4 reserved egg whites
1 cup finely ground nuts
½ to ¾ cup sugar

Beat egg whites until creamy but not stiff. Brush sparingly on tops of unbaked cookies. Mix pecans and sugar; sprinkle over cookies. Yield: enough topping for 12 dozen cookies.

Old-Country Gingersnaps

1 cup shortening
1 cup sugar
1 cup molasses
2 eggs
¼ teaspoon salt
1 teaspoon ground ginger
1 teaspoon ground cinnamon
1 tablespoon soda
2 tablespoons warm water
1 tablespoon vinegar
6 to 6½ cups all-purpose flour

Cream shortening and sugar. Add molasses and eggs, beating well. Blend in salt, ginger, and cinnamon. Dissolve soda in water; Add vinegar and let it foam; beat into cookie mixture. Gradually add enough flour to make a firm dough. Working with one-fourth of the dough at a time, roll out ⅛ inch thick on a floured surface. Cut with a floured cutter; place on greased cookie sheets. Bake at 400° about 3 minutes. Yield: about 12 dozen.

Ginger Crackles

2 cups all-purpose flour
1 teaspoon ground ginger
2 teaspoons soda
1 teaspoon ground cinnamon
½ teaspoon salt
¾ cup shortening
1 cup sugar
1 egg
¼ cup molasses
½ to 1 cup sugar

Combine dry ingredients. Cream shortening in a large mixing bowl; gradually add 1 cup sugar. Beat in egg and molasses. Stir dry ingredients into creamed mixture; blend thoroughly. Roll into balls the size of large marbles; roll in sugar. Place 2 inches apart on ungreased cookie sheets. Bake at 350° for 12 to 15 minutes. Yield: about 4 dozen.

Lemon Cheese Logs

1 cup sugar
1 cup butter or margarine, softened
1 (3-ounce) package cream cheese, softened
1 egg yolk
2½ cups all-purpose flour
1 cup finely chopped walnuts
½ teaspoon salt
½ teaspoon grated lemon rind
1 (6-ounce) package semisweet chocolate morsels
Decorator candies

Combine sugar, butter, and cream cheese; cream until light and fluffy. Add egg yolk, beating well. Stir in flour, walnuts, salt, and lemon rind; mix well. Cover and chill at least 2 hours.

Shape dough by teaspoonfuls into 2-inch logs by rolling between palms of hand. (Dough will be dry.) Place cookies on ungreased baking sheets; bake at 325° for 12 minutes or until lightly browned. Cool completely on wire racks.

Melt chocolate morsels in a small saucepan over low heat. Dip one end of each log in melted chocolate, and sprinkle with decorator candy. Let stand on wire racks until chocolate sets. Store between layers of waxed paper in an airtight container. Cookies may be frozen. Yield: 12 dozen.

Little Ears

Recipe originated in Lithuania, where it was a traditional wedding cookie.

5 egg yolks
½ cup sugar
¼ cup plus 1 tablespoon whipping cream
2 tablespoons rum or brandy
About 3 cups all-purpose flour
Vegetable oil for deep frying
Powdered sugar

Beat yolks and sugar together in a large mixing bowl until light. Add cream and rum. Gradually add enough flour to make a stiff dough. Roll out to a ⅛-inch thickness on a floured surface; cut into 4-inch-long diamond shapes with a knife. Make a ¾-inch slit crosswise in center of each diamond. Pull one end of diamond through slit. Fry in oil heated to 365° until light brown; drain on paper towels. Sprinkle with powdered sugar. Yield: about 5 dozen.

Molasses Board Cookies

    ¾ cup butter or margarine, softened
    1 cup molasses
    1 cup sugar
    2 eggs, beaten
    6 cups all-purpose flour
    ½ teaspoon salt
    1 teaspoon ground ginger
    2 teaspoons soda
    ¾ to 1 cup commercial sour cream

Mix butter, molasses, and sugar in a large mixing bowl until blended. Add eggs and beat well. Combine dry ingredients and stir into molasses mixture alternately with enough sour cream to make a dough which can be easily handled.

Roll out half the dough at a time about ⅓ inch thick on a lightly floured board; slice into 5- × 3-inch bars. Place on lightly greased baking sheets and bake at 350° about 10 to 12 minutes. Yield: 4 dozen.

Never-Fail Cookies

    2 cups sugar
    1 cup butter or margarine, softened
    1 cup milk
    1 teaspoon soda
    1½ teaspoons vanilla extract
    1½ teaspoons lemon extract
    7 to 7½ cups all-purpose flour

Combine sugar and butter in a large mixing bowl; cream until light and fluffy. Add milk in which soda has been dissolved; beat well. Add flavorings. Gradually add flour, beating on low speed, then by hand, until dough is firm enough to be rolled easily. Turn out onto a floured surface. Working with one-sixth of the dough at a time, roll out thinly and cut with a floured 2-inch cookie cutter. Place on lightly greased cookie sheets, and bake at 350° about 10 minutes or until lightly browned. Yield: about 9 dozen.

Pecan Christmas Cookies

    8 cups finely chopped pecans
    ¼ pound citron, finely chopped
    6 cups all-purpose flour, divided
    2 tablespoons baking powder
    2 tablespoons ground cinnamon
    1 teaspoon ground cloves
    2 teaspoons ground nutmeg
    6 eggs
    4½ cups sugar
    1 tablespoon melted butter or
        margarine
    1 egg white
    1 tablespoon water
    ¼ pound candied cherries,
        thinly sliced

Place pecans and citron in a paper bag with 1 cup flour; mix well to separate bits of citron. Stir remaining flour with baking powder and spices. Beat eggs in a large mixing bowl at medium speed of electric mixer until light; gradually beat in sugar. Add butter; gradually beat in flour mixture, blending well. Stir in citron mixture. Form into four or five 1- to 2-inch rolls; wrap in waxed paper and chill for easier handling.

To bake, slice thinly; place on lightly greased cookie sheets. Beat egg white with water; brush on each cookie. Place a thin cherry slice on top. Bake at 350° about 12 minutes. Remove from pan at once. Yield: about 12 dozen.

Peanut Butter Cookies

This recipe dates back to the Oklahoma Land Rush.

¼ cup creamy or crunchy peanut butter
¼ cup margarine, softened
½ cup sugar
¼ cup firmly packed brown sugar
1 egg, beaten
About ¾ cup all-purpose flour
¼ teaspoon salt
¼ teaspoon soda

Blend peanut butter, margarine, and sugar in a medium mixing bowl; add egg, mixing well. Stir in flour, salt, and soda. (Add more flour if dough is not stiff enough to shape.) Shape into a roll about 2½ inches thick. Wrap in waxed paper and chill overnight.

Cut into slices ¼ inch thick. Bake at 350° for 10 minutes. Yield: about 2½ dozen.

Raisin-Filled Cookies

1 cup sugar
½ cup shortening or margarine
½ cup milk
1 egg
3 cups all-purpose flour
1 tablespoon baking powder
¼ teaspoon salt
Raisin Filling

Combine sugar and shortening in a large mixing bowl, beating until creamy. Beat in milk and egg. Combine dry ingredients and add to mixture, beating well.

Working with half the dough at a time, roll out on a floured surface about ⅛ inch thick and cut into 2-inch rounds. Place 1 teaspoon filling on half the rounds and top with remaining rounds. Seal edges by pressing with fork. Place on greased baking sheets. Bake at 400° about 15 minutes or until light brown. Yield: 6 dozen.

Raisin Filling:

¾ cup sugar
1 tablespoon all-purpose flour
1 cup boiling water
1 cup chopped raisins
1 teaspoon vanilla extract
1 tablespoon butter or margarine

Combine sugar and flour in a small saucepan. Add water and raisins. Cook over medium heat, stirring constantly, for 8 to 10 minutes or until thickened. Remove from heat and stir in vanilla and butter. Cool. Yield: enough filling for 6 dozen cookies.

Sand Tarts

½ cup butter or margarine, softened
1 cup sugar
2 eggs
1 egg, separated
1¾ cups all-purpose flour
2 teaspoons baking powder
1 tablespoon sugar
½ teaspoon ground cinnamon
½ cup chopped almonds

Combine butter and sugar in a large mixing bowl; beat until creamy. Beat in 2 eggs and 1 egg yolk. Combine flour and baking powder; add to mixture, mixing well. Working with half the dough at a time, roll out ⅛ inch thick on a floured surface. Cut with a cookie cutter; beat egg white and brush on cookies. Combine sugar and cinnamon, mixing well; sprinkle a few grains of sugar mixture on top of each cookie, and top with almonds. Arrange on greased cookie sheets and bake at 350° for about 8 minutes. Yield: about 5 dozen.

Scotch Cookies

4 cups all-purpose flour
1 tablespoon ground cloves
1 tablespoon ground cinnamon
1 tablespoon ground allspice
2 tablespoons soda
2 cups firmly packed dark brown
    sugar
2 cups firmly packed light brown
    sugar
1 cup butter, softened
⅓ cup shortening
4 eggs, well beaten

Combine flour, spices, soda, and sugar in a large mixing bowl. Add butter and shortening; blend thoroughly. Cover tightly; let stand overnight. Add eggs to flour mixture; mix well and chill.

Roll dough into balls the size of large marbles. Place 2 inches apart on greased cookie sheets; bake at 325° about 8 minutes. Do not brown; remove from oven while golden and slightly raised. (They will be crisp and rather chewy, but hard if overbaked.) Will keep well stored in tins. Yield: 9 dozen.

Thimble Cookies

1 cup sugar
1 cup molasses
1 tablespoon soda
1 teaspoon cream of tartar
1 cup shortening
⅔ cup hot water
1 teaspoon vanilla extract
5 cups all-purpose flour
1 teaspoon ground ginger
1 teaspoon ground cinnamon
1 teaspoon salt
Filling (recipe follows)

Beat sugar, molasses, soda, and cream of tartar in a large mixing bowl until mixture foams. Add shortening, water, and vanilla; beat well. Stir dry ingredients together; blend into first mixture. Chill overnight.

Working with one-fourth of the dough at a time, roll out ⅛ inch thick on a floured surface; cut with 2½-inch cutter. Cut a thimble-size hole in the center of half the cookies. Place a teaspoonful of filling in center of whole cookies; top with cookies with hole in center. Press edges together; place on greased cookie sheets. Bake at 400° for 10 minutes. Yield: about 3 dozen.

Filling:

1 cup raisins, ground
¾ cup sugar
2 tablespoons all-purpose flour
Dash of cream of tartar
1 cup warm water

Combine all ingredients in a medium saucepan; cook over low heat, stirring constantly, until thickened. Cool. Yield: enough filling for about 3 dozen cookies.

Black Walnut Ice Box Cookies

1 cup butter or margarine, softened
1 cup firmly packed brown sugar
2 cups sugar
2 eggs, well beaten
1 cup finely chopped black walnuts
½ teaspoon salt
1 teaspoon vanilla extract
4 cups all-purpose flour
3 packages dry yeast

Combine butter and sugar in a large mixing bowl; cream thoroughly. Beat in eggs, walnuts, salt, and vanilla. Combine flour and yeast; stir into butter mixture, blending well.

Shape dough into three or four 1- to 2-inch rolls; wrap each roll in waxed paper. Chill overnight. Cut into thin slices; place on lightly greased cookie sheets and bake at 350° about 10 minutes or until lightly browned. Yield: about 10 dozen.

Plain Pie Pastry

1 cup all-purpose flour
⅓ teaspoon salt
1 teaspoon sugar (optional)
⅓ cup shortening
About 3 tablespoons ice water

Stir dry ingredients together. Cut in shortening with pastry blender until some of the particles resemble very coarse meal, while others are as large as peas. Sprinkle 3 tablespoons water over, stirring with a fork; mix with a firm stirring motion. A few more drops of water may be needed; when pastry is ready, it forms clumps and clings together when lightly squeezed with the hand. Form into a ball; it will be necessary to use pressure, and work quickly so as not to soften the shortening.

Roll out on floured surface to ⅛-inch thickness. A well-floured pastry canvas is ideal because it puts less extra flour into the crust than a board and makes for easy placement of the crust into the shell. Tip the rolled pastry over the hand and wrist by lifting the canvas with the other hand. Ease pastry loosely down into the pan; trim pastry, leaving 1-inch overhang. Fold loose edges under. Form fluted rim. For a baked pastry shell, prick crust all over with a fork to avoid pastry shrinking during baking. Bake at 425° for 10 to 12 minutes. If not to be prebaked, simply fill and bake according to recipe directions. Yield: one 9-inch pastry shell.

Note: Recipe may be doubled or tripled for additional pastry shells.

Basic Pastry

½ cup water
1 tablespoon vinegar
1 egg
4 cups all-purpose flour
1 tablespoon sugar
2 teaspoons salt
1¾ cups shortening

Combine water and vinegar in a small bowl; beat in egg, and set aside. Combine flour, sugar, and salt in large bowl; cut in shortening until mixture resembles very coarse meal. Gradually add enough liquid mixture, stirring with a fork, until mixture holds together. Roll out on floured surface, one-fourth at a time, to make four 9-inch pastry shells. Yield: four 9-inch pastry shells.

Brown Sugar Pie

2 eggs
2 cups firmly packed brown sugar
¼ cup butter or margarine, softened
1 tablespoon milk
Juice and grated rind of ½ lemon
1 unbaked 9-inch pastry shell

Combine all ingredients in the order given, mixing well. Pour into pastry shell and bake at 425° for 10 minutes; reduce heat to 350° and bake 30 minutes, or until filling is softly set and pastry shell is browned. Yield: one 9-inch pie.

Nashville Chess Pie

½ cup butter or margarine, softened
1½ cups sugar
1 teaspoon cornmeal
1 teaspoon vinegar
1 teaspoon vanilla extract
3 eggs
1 unbaked 9-inch pastry shell or
    individual pastry shells

Cream butter and sugar in a medium mixing bowl until light and fluffy. Add cornmeal, vinegar, and vanilla, mixing well. Beat in eggs, one at a time. Pour into pastry shell or individual shells. Bake at 425° for 10 minutes; reduce heat to 375° and bake an additional 25 minutes, or until pastry is crisp. Yield: one 9-inch pie.

Mama's Custard Pie

3 eggs
¼ cup sugar
1 tablespoon all-purpose flour
¼ teaspoon salt
1 teaspoon vanilla extract
2 cups milk
1 unbaked 9-inch pastry shell
2 tablespoons butter or margarine

Beat eggs lightly in a medium mixing bowl. Combine sugar with flour and stir in. Add salt and vanilla. Gradually stir in milk. Pour into pastry shell and dot with butter. Bake at 425° for 10 minutes; reduce heat to 325° and bake about 30 minutes, or until filling is set and pastry browned. Yield: one 9-inch pie.

Note: If meringue custard pie is desired, use 4 eggs and save 2 of the whites for meringue.

Caramel Meringue Pie

2 cups sugar, divided
½ cup water
3 egg yolks, beaten
⅔ cup all-purpose flour
Dash of salt
3 cups milk
1 teaspoon butter or margarine
1 teaspoon vanilla extract
1 baked 9-inch pastry shell
Meringue (recipe follows)

Place 1 cup sugar in a large skillet over medium heat and cook, stirring constantly, until sugar is melted and caramel-colored. Add water carefully to syrup and boil over medium heat about 1 minute. Stir a small amount of hot mixture into egg yolks; gradually stir egg mixture into remaining hot mixture, stirring constantly.

Combine remaining 1 cup sugar, flour, salt, and milk in the top of a double boiler; stir in hot caramel mixture and add butter. Cook over boiling water until mixture is thickened. Remove from heat and stir in vanilla; pour into pastry shell. Top with meringue and bake at 350° for 10 minutes or until meringue is browned. Cool before slicing. Yield: one 9-inch pie.

Meringue:

3 egg whites
6 tablespoons sugar

Beat egg whites until foamy. Gradually add sugar; continue beating until stiff peaks form. Yield: meringue for one 9-inch pie.

Chocolate Pie

1½ cups sugar
3 tablespoons cocoa
3 tablespoons all-purpose flour
Dash of salt
1 egg, beaten
3 eggs, separated
1½ cups boiling water
1½ teaspoons vanilla extract
1 baked 9-inch pastry shell
¼ cup plus 2 tablespoons sugar

Mix 1½ cups sugar, cocoa, flour, and salt in a large saucepan. Stir in 1 egg; beat 3 egg yolks and add to cocoa mixture, mixing well. Pour boiling water over cocoa mixture, stirring constantly. Cook and stir over medium heat for 5 to 10 minutes or until mixture thickens. Remove from heat and add vanilla. Pour into pastry shell.

Beat 3 egg whites until foamy in a small mixing bowl; add remaining sugar gradually, beating until mixture forms stiff peaks. Spoon on top of pie; bake at 350° about 10 minutes or until meringue is browned. Yield: one 9-inch pie.

Note: Meringue may be omitted and whipped cream used as topping instead.

For an interesting variation, pour chocolate mixture into individual tart shells and put a dollop of peanut butter on top before spooning on meringue.

Sorghum Molasses Pie

1 cup sugar
1 tablespoon butter or margarine, softened
1 cup molasses
1 cup sorghum
3 eggs
Juice of 1 lemon
1 unbaked 9-inch pastry shell
Ground nutmeg

Mix sugar and butter in a medium mixing bowl; add molasses and sorghum. Beat eggs until fluffy in a medium mixing bowl; stir in molasses mixture and add lemon juice. Mix well and pour into pastry shell. Sprinkle nutmeg lightly over top; bake at 350° for 45 minutes or until a knife inserted in center comes out clean. Yield: one 9-inch pie.

Note: Molasses may be omitted and sorghum increased to 2 cups; 2 tablespoons vinegar may also be substituted for lemon juice, if desired.

Lemon Cream Pie

1 cup sugar
¼ cup plus 1 tablespoon cornstarch
¼ teaspoon salt
2 cups milk
3 egg yolks, beaten
3 tablespoons butter or margarine
2 teaspoons grated lemon rind
⅓ cup lemon juice
Meringue (recipe follows)
1 baked 9-inch pastry shell

Combine sugar, cornstarch, and salt in heavy saucepan. Add milk gradually, stirring until smooth. Cook over low heat, stirring constantly, until thickened, about 10 minutes.

Stir a small amount of hot mixture into egg yolks. Combine egg yolks with remaining hot mixture and continue cooking and stirring for about 5 minutes or until thickened. Remove

from heat; add butter, lemon rind, and juice; blend thoroughly.

Pour filling into pastry shell. Spread meringue on top, sealing to edge of crust. Bake at 350° for 12 to 15 minutes, or until golden brown. Cool thoroughly before cutting. Yield: one 9-inch pie.

Meringue:

3 egg whites (at room temperature)
¼ teaspoon salt
1 teaspoon lemon juice
6 tablespoons sugar

Combine egg whites, salt, and lemon juice in a medium mixing bowl. Beat at high speed of electric mixer until soft peaks form. Add sugar, 1 tablespoon at a time, beating constantly until stiff and glossy. Yield: meringue for one 9-inch pie.

Daiquiri Pie

1 envelope unflavored gelatin
1½ cups sugar, divided
½ teaspoon salt
4 egg yolks
½ cup lemon juice
2 tablespoons lime juice
1 teaspoon grated lemon rind
6 drops green food coloring
½ cup light rum
4 egg whites
½ cup whipping cream, whipped
1 baked 9-inch pastry shell
Chocolate shavings or grated lime rind (optional)

Combine gelatin, 1 cup sugar, and salt in top of a double boiler. Beat egg yolks with lemon and lime juice; stir into gelatin mixture. Cook over boiling water, stirring constantly, about 10 to 12 minutes or until gelatin is dissolved and mixture thickened. Remove from water; stir in lemon rind, food coloring, and rum. Set in a bowl filled with ice cubes and water. Cool, stirring occasionally, about 30 minutes or until mixture is thick and mounds when dropped from a spoon.

Beat egg whites in a large mixing bowl at high speed of an electric mixer until soft peaks form. Add ½ cup sugar, 2 tablespoons at a time, beating well after each addition. Continue beating until stiff peaks form. Fold gelatin mixture and whipped cream into egg whites. Pour half of mixture into pastry shell. Chill, along with rest of mixture, for 20 minutes. Spoon remaining mixture in center of pie, mounding high. Chill at least 4 hours or overnight. Garnish with shaved chocolate or grated lime rind, if desired. Yield: one 9-inch pie.

Key Lime Pie

> 2 (15-ounce) cans sweetened
>   condensed milk
> 6 egg yolks
> 1 cup lime juice
> 1 baked 9-inch pastry shell
> Whipped cream

Beat first 3 ingredients together. After the lime juice has thickened the egg yolks, spoon mixture into pastry shell. Chill. Serve topped with whipped cream. Yield: one 9-inch pie.

Montgomery Pie

> ½ cup sugar
> ½ cup molasses
> 1 egg
> 1 cup water
> 2 tablespoons all-purpose flour
> Juice and grated rind of ½ lemon
> 1 unbaked 9-inch pastry shell
> Topping (recipe follows)

Combine first 6 ingredients, mixing well; pour into pastry shell. Spoon topping over all; bake at 350° for 35 to 40 minutes or until lightly browned and crusty on top. Yield: one 9-inch pie.

Topping:

> ¼ cup butter or margarine
> ⅔ cup sugar
> 1 egg
> 1¼ cups all-purpose flour
> ½ teaspoon soda
> ½ cup sour milk or buttermilk

Cream butter and sugar; add egg and beat well. Combine flour and soda; add alternately with milk to egg mixture, mixing well. Yield: topping for one 9-inch pie.

Osgood Pie

> ½ cup butter or margarine
> 2 cups sugar
> 4 egg yolks, beaten
> 1 cup raisins
> 1 cup chopped pecans
> ½ teaspoon ground cinnamon
> ½ teaspoon ground cloves
> 4 egg whites, stiffly beaten
> 1 unbaked 9-inch pastry shell

Cream butter and sugar in a medium mixing bowl. Add egg yolks, raisins, pecans, and spices. Fold in egg whites. Pour into pastry shell. Bake at 325° for 50 minutes. Yield: one 9-inch pie.

Tennessee Jelly Pie

> ½ cup butter or margarine, softened
> 1 cup sugar
> 1 teaspoon cornmeal
> 2 teaspoons half-and-half
> ½ cup tart jelly
> 2 eggs, beaten
> 1 unbaked 9-inch pastry shell

Cream butter and sugar; beat in cornmeal and half-and-half. Blend in jelly, then eggs. Pour into pastry shell and bake at 400° for 10 minutes; reduce heat to 250° and bake about 15 to 20 minutes, or until filling is firm. Yield: one 9-inch pie.

Joshua's Pie

1 cup sugar
1 cup all-purpose flour
1 unbaked 9-inch pastry shell
1 teaspoon vanilla extract
1 cup milk

Mix sugar and flour and pour into pastry shell. Stir vanilla and milk together and pour over dry mixture. *Do not stir.* Bake at 350° for 25 minutes; reduce heat to 300° and bake about 20 minutes, or until crust and filling are browned. Yield: one 9-inch pie.

Jeff Davis Pie

1 cup plus 2 tablespoons sugar,
    divided
3 tablespoons all-purpose flour
1 egg
2 egg yolks
1 cup half-and-half
1 cup milk
1 teaspoon ground cinnamon
¼ teaspoon ground nutmeg
¼ teaspoon ground cloves
1 teaspoon vanilla extract
2 tablespoons butter or margarine
1 baked 9-inch pastry shell
2 egg whites

Combine 1 cup sugar, flour, egg, and egg yolks in the top of a double boiler. Add half-and-half and milk. Cook over boiling water, stirring constantly, until thickened. Remove from heat; add spices, vanilla, and butter, stirring until butter melts. Pour into pastry shell.

Beat egg whites at high speed of an electric mixer until soft peaks form. Add 2 tablespoons sugar gradually, beating until stiff peaks form. Top pie with meringue and bake at 350° for 10 minutes or until top is browned. Yield: one 9-inch pie.

Note: Nutmeg is the only spice used in some Jeff Davis pies.

Old-Fashioned Sugar And Cream Pie

1 cup sugar
¼ cup all-purpose flour
Dash of salt
1¼ cups half-and-half
1 unbaked 9-inch pastry shell
Butter or margarine
Ground nutmeg (optional)
Ground cinnamon (optional)

Combine first 4 ingredients in pastry shell. Dot with butter and sprinkle with nutmeg and cinnamon, if desired. Bake at 450° for 15 minutes; reduce heat to 350° and continue baking for 20 to 25 minutes or until bubbly. Yield: one 9-inch pie.

Fried Apple Pies

2 (6-ounce) packages dried apples
2 cups water
½ cup to ¾ cup sugar
Pastry (recipe follows)
Vegetable oil

Combine apples and water in a large saucepan; bring to a boil. Reduce heat; cover, and simmer about 30 minutes or until tender. Cool. Mash slightly if necessary. Stir in sugar. Set aside.

Divide pastry into thirds; roll each third out on waxed paper to ¼-inch thickness. Cut into 5-inch circles. Place about 2 tablespoons of apple mixture on half of each pastry circle. To seal pies, dip fingers in water, and moisten edges of circles; fold in half, making sure edges are even. Using a fork dipped in flour, press pastry edges firmly together.

Heat ½ inch of oil to 375° in a large skillet. Cook pies until golden brown on both sides, turning only once. Drain well on paper towels. Yield: 1½ dozen.

Pastry:

 3 cups all-purpose flour
 1 teaspoon salt
 ¾ cup shortening
 1 egg, beaten
 ¼ cup water
 1 teaspoon vinegar

Combine flour and salt; cut in shortening until mixture resembles coarse meal. Combine egg and water; sprinkle over flour mixture. Add vinegar, and lightly stir until mixture forms a ball.

Wrap pastry in waxed paper; chill at least 1 hour or until ready to use. Yield: pastry for about 1½ dozen 5-inch pies.

Deep-Dish Apple Pie

 8 cooking apples, peeled and
  thinly sliced
 1¼ cups sugar
 3 tablespoons all-purpose flour
 1½ teaspoons ground cinnamon
 ¼ teaspoon ground nutmeg
 ⅛ teaspoon salt
 3 tablespoons butter or margarine
 Pastry (recipe follows)

Arrange apple slices in a lightly greased 9-inch square baking dish. Combine sugar, flour, cinnamon, nutmeg, and salt; sprinkle over apples, and dot with butter. Top with pastry, and bake at 400° for 40 minutes or until golden brown. Yield: 6 to 8 servings.

Pastry:

 1¼ cups all-purpose flour
 ¼ teaspoon salt
 2 tablespoons shortening
 ¼ cup cold butter or margarine
 3 to 4 tablespoons cold water

Combine flour and salt; cut in shortening. Cut butter into small pieces, and add to flour mixture; cut in until mixture resembles coarse meal. Stir in only enough water to

moisten flour; form dough into a ball. Wrap in plastic wrap, and chill 30 minutes.

Roll dough to ¼-inch thickness on a lightly floured surface, and cut into 1-inch-wide strips. Arrange lattice fashion over filling. Yield: pastry for one 9-inch pie.

Applesauce Pie

 2 egg yolks
 ½ cup sugar
 1 tablespoon melted butter or
  margarine
 1 cup milk
 1 teaspoon cornstarch
 ½ teaspoon vanilla extract
 1½ cups applesauce
 1 unbaked 9-inch pastry shell
 Meringue (optional; recipe follows)

Beat egg yolks with sugar in a medium mixing bowl; add butter. Blend in milk, cornstarch, vanilla, and applesauce. Pour into pastry shell. Bake at 375° for 60 to 70 minutes or until knife inserted at center comes out clean. Top with meringue if desired, and return to oven 5 to 10 minutes or until lightly browned. Yield: one 9-inch pie.

Meringue:

 2 egg whites
 ¼ teaspoon cream of tartar
 5 tablespoons sugar
 ½ teaspoon vanilla extract

Beat egg whites with cream of tartar until almost stiff; gradually beat in sugar. Fold in vanilla. Yield: enough meringue for one 9-inch pie.

Fruit and Vegetable Pies 233

Banana Rolls

Pastry (recipe follows)
¾ cup butter or margarine, softened
1 to 2 teaspoons ground nutmeg
1⅓ cups sugar
4 bananas, peeled
⅓ cup water
Sugar
Butter or margarine

Divide pastry into 4 equal parts; roll each part into an 8-inch circle. Spread each circle with butter; and sprinkle with nutmeg and sugar. Place a whole banana on top and roll up, jellyroll fashion.

Place four rolls in a 13- × 9- × 2-inch baking pan; pour ⅓ cup water over all. Sprinkle a little sugar on top and dot with butter. Bake at 375° about 45 minutes or until brown. Serve warm. Yield: 4 servings.

Pastry:

1½ cups all-purpose flour
½ teaspoon salt
½ cup shortening
3 to 3½ tablespoons ice water

Combine flour and salt; cut in shortening until mixture resembles coarse meal. Add water slowly, stirring with a fork, until mixture clings together. Yield: pastry for 4 rolls.

Cherry Pie Deluxe

1¼ cups sugar
3 tablespoons all-purpose flour
3 tablespoons butter or margarine, softened
2 eggs, beaten
1 teaspoon vanilla extract
¼ teaspoon salt
1 (16-ounce) can pitted sour cherries, drained
1 unbaked 9-inch pastry shell
Vanilla ice cream (optional)

Combine sugar and flour in a medium mixing bowl. Add butter and eggs, beating well. Add vanilla, salt, and cherries. Pour filling into pastry shell. Bake at 400° for 10 minutes; reduce heat to 300° and bake for 30 to 40 minutes, or until filling is set. Delicious served slightly warm, topped with vanilla ice cream, if desired. Yield: one 9-inch pie.

Old English Date Pie

2 eggs
¾ cup sugar
½ teaspoon salt
1 teaspoon ground cinnamon
¼ teaspoon ground nutmeg
¼ teaspoon ground allspice
¼ teaspoon ground cloves
1 (8-ounce) carton commercial sour cream
1 tablespoon fine bread or cookie crumbs
1 cup dates, chopped
1 unbaked 9-inch pastry shell
½ cup flaked coconut

Beat eggs; add sugar, salt, spices, sour cream, and crumbs. Beat well, and stir in dates. Pour into pastry shell and sprinkle coconut over top. Bake at 425° for 10 minutes; reduce heat to 350° and bake 40 minutes, or until filling is set and top is lightly browned. Yield: one 9-inch pie.

Fresh Fig Pie

Pastry for double-crust 9-inch pie
3 tablespoons all-purpose flour
¾ cup plus 1 tablespoon sugar,
   divided
¼ teaspoon ground allspice
3 cups peeled sliced figs, divided
Butter or margarine
3 tablespoons lemon juice
2 tablespoons butter or margarine

Line a 9-inch piepan with half the pastry; set aside. Mix flour, ¾ cup sugar, and allspice in a small mixing bowl. Place 1 cup figs in pastry shell. Sprinkle with one-third of flour mixture. Repeat until all is used. Dot with butter. Sprinkle with lemon juice. Roll out remaining pastry; cut several slits in pastry. Cover pie with pastry; seal edges. Sprinkle top with 1 tablespoon sugar and dot with 2 tablespoons butter. Bake at 325° for 35 minutes. Yield: one 9-inch pie.

Seedless Grape Pie

Pastry for four 9-inch pies
6 cups green grapes
2 cups sugar
½ teaspoon salt
1 tablespoon lemon juice
2 tablespoons all-purpose flour
Butter or margarine
Sugar

Divide pastry into 4 portions. Roll out each portion on a floured surface to fit a 9-inch piepan. Line 2 piepans with pastry.

Slip skins from grapes; set skins aside. Place grapes in a large saucepan and bring to a boil; remove from heat and run mixture through a sieve. Mix grape juice with the skins; add sugar, salt, and lemon juice. Mix thoroughly. Divide grape mixture between bottoms of 2 pastry shells; sprinkle each with 1 tablespoon flour. Dot each filling with butter and lightly brush edges of pastry with cold water.

Cut remaining pastry into strips and place in lattice-fashion over each pie. Sprinkle with sugar. Bake at 425° for 10 minutes; reduce heat to 325° and bake for 40 minutes. Yield: two 9-inch pies.

Fried Peach Pies

1 (8-ounce) package dried peaches
Sugar
2 cups all-purpose flour
1 teaspoon salt
2½ teaspoons baking powder
¼ cup shortening
⅔ cup milk
Vegetable oil for deep frying

Soak fruit in water to cover for several hours or overnight. Cook in water in which fruit was soaked until fruit is tender, stirring occasionally. Remove from heat; mash until smooth, and add sugar to taste. Set mixture aside to cool.

Combine dry ingredients in a bowl. Cut in shortening with two knives or a pastry blender. Add milk and mix well. Knead lightly on a floured surface; roll out pastry. Cut out pastry circles using a 5-inch saucer as a measure. Place about 3 tablespoons of peach mixture on half of each pastry circle. Fold other side over and crimp pastry edges with a fork. Prick finished pies in 2 or 3 places. Fry in deep hot oil until pies are browned. Remove from oil and drain well. Yield: about 12 pies.

Fruit and Vegetable Pies 235

Peach Cobbler Supreme

About 8 cups sliced fresh peaches
2 cups sugar
2 to 4 tablespoons all-purpose flour
½ teaspoon ground nutmeg
1 teaspoon almond extract
⅓ cup melted butter or margarine
Pastry for double-crust 9-inch pie

Combine peaches, sugar, flour, and nutmeg; set aside until syrup forms. Bring peaches to a boil and cook over low heat 10 minutes or until tender. Remove from heat; add almond extract and butter, stirring well.

Roll out half of pastry to ⅛-inch thickness on a lightly floured board; cut into a 10- × 8-inch rectangle. Spoon half of peaches into a lightly buttered 10- × 8-inch baking dish; top with pastry. Bake at 475° for 12 minutes or until golden brown. Spoon remaining peaches over baked pastry.

Roll out remaining pastry and cut into ½-inch strips; arrange in lattice design over peaches. Return to oven for 10 to 15 minutes or until top is lightly browned. Yield: 8 to 10 servings.

Georgia Peach Pie

½ cup firmly packed brown sugar
½ cup sugar
⅛ teaspoon salt
3 tablespoons tapioca
5 cups sliced fresh peaches (5 to 6 medium peaches)
⅛ teaspoon almond extract
Pastry for 1 double-crust 9-inch pie
1 tablespoon butter or margarine
½ teaspoon sugar (optional)

Combine sugar, salt, and tapioca; pour over peaches, and mix gently. Sprinkle mixture with almond extract. Line a 9-inch piepan with pastry. Pour in peach mixture. Dot with butter. Roll out remaining pastry and place over pie. Seal edges by fluting; prick top with

fork. Top crust may be brushed with cold water and sprinkled with a small amount of sugar before putting pie in oven, if desired. Bake at 450° for 10 minutes; reduce heat to 375° and bake for 40 minutes or until golden brown. Yield: one 9-inch pie.

Texas Pecan Pie

1½ cups firmly packed brown sugar
½ cup sugar
¼ cup water
2 tablespoons all-purpose flour
½ teaspoon salt
2 eggs, well beaten
½ cup evaporated milk
1½ cups pecan halves
¼ teaspoon vanilla extract
Pastry Shell (recipe follows)

Combine first 5 ingredients in bowl; mix well. Add eggs and milk, blending thoroughly. Stir in pecans and vanilla. Pour into pastry shell; bake at 400° for 10 minutes. Reduce heat to 350° and bake 35 to 40 minutes longer, or until set and brown. Cool before cutting. Yield: one 9-inch pie.

Pastry Shell:

1½ cups all-purpose flour
½ teaspoon salt
⅔ cup shortening
3 tablespoons water

Stir flour and salt together. Cut in shortening with pastry blender or fork until consistency of coarse meal. Add water; stir gently with fork. Gather pastry into a ball; place in piepan. With fingertips, spread pastry along bottom and sides of piepan, shaping a high, fluted edge. Yield: one 9-inch pastry shell.

Favorite Pecan Pie

    1 unbaked 9-inch pastry shell
    3 eggs
    1 cup sugar
    1 cup light corn syrup
    2 tablespoons melted butter or
        margarine
    ⅛ teaspoon salt
    1 teaspoon vanilla extract
    About 1½ cups pecan halves

Prick bottom and sides of pastry shell; bake at 400° for 5 minutes. Set aside to cool. Beat eggs until light and lemon colored; add sugar and corn syrup, beating until fluffy. Add butter, salt, and vanilla; stir well. Pour filling into pastry shell. Top with pecan halves. Bake at 300° for 1 hour and 45 minutes or until center is firm. Yield: one 9-inch pie.

Georgia Squash Pie

    ¾ cup sugar
    1 tablespoon all-purpose flour
    ¼ teaspoon salt
    1 teaspoon ground cinnamon
    ½ teaspoon ground nutmeg
    ¼ teaspoon ground ginger
    ¼ teaspoon ground mace
    1½ cups cooked mashed squash
        (Hubbard, butternut, or acorn)
    2 eggs, lightly beaten
    1½ cups milk
    2 tablespoons melted butter or
        margarine
    1 unbaked 9-inch pastry shell
    Whipped cream
    Sugar
    Vanilla extract

Combine sugar, flour, salt, spices, and squash, mixing well. Stir in eggs, milk, and butter. Pour into pastry shell and bake at 425° for 10 minutes. Reduce heat to 325°; bake 30 to 40 minutes, or until filling is set. Serve warm with whipped cream flavored with sugar and vanilla. Yield: one 9-inch pie.

Sweet Potato Pie

    2 cups cooked mashed sweet potatoes
    ½ cup butter or margarine, softened
    2 eggs, separated
    1 cup firmly packed brown sugar
    ¼ teaspoon salt
    ½ teaspoon ground ginger
    ½ teaspoon ground cinnamon
    ½ teaspoon ground nutmeg
    ½ cup milk
    ¼ cup sugar
    1 unbaked 9-inch pastry shell
    Additional spices (optional)
    Whipped cream
    Orange rind

Combine sweet potatoes, butter, egg yolks, brown sugar, salt, and spices; mix well. Add milk, blending until smooth.

Beat egg whites until foamy; gradually add ¼ cup sugar, beating until stiff. Fold into sweet potato mixture. Pour filling into pastry shell; sprinkle with additional spices, if desired. Bake at 400° for 10 minutes. Reduce heat to 350°, and bake 30 additional minutes. When cool, garnish with whipped cream and orange rind. Yield: one 9-inch pie.

Sweet Potato Cobbler

    Pastry for double-crust 9-inch pie
    3 cups sliced cooked sweet potatoes
    1 cup sugar
    Butter or margarine
    1 teaspoon ground nutmeg
    ½ teaspoon ground cinnamon
    1¼ cups water

Roll ⅔ of crust and place in bottom of an ungreased 10-inch square baking dish or 9-inch skillet. Combine sweet potatoes and sugar; put on top of bottom pie crust. Roll out remaining pastry and cut into strips; layer strips across pan in a lattice pattern; dot with butter. Sprinkle with nutmeg and cinnamon. Pour water over top of dish and bake at 350° for 45 to 60 minutes. Yield: 8 servings.

Never-Fail Baked Custard

1 quart milk
5 eggs, separated
¼ cup plus 1 tablespoon sugar
1 teaspoon vanilla extract

Warm milk over low heat; cream yolks and sugar thoroughly in a large mixing bowl. Add milk slowly to creamed mixture. Beat egg whites until stiff but not dry; fold into milk mixture. Stir in vanilla. Pour into an ungreased 2-quart casserole; set in pan of hot water. Bake at 325° about 60 minutes or until knife inserted in center comes out clean. Yield: 6 servings.

Brûlée

2 cups sugar, divided
2 quarts milk, scalded
12 egg yolks
3 tablespoons cornstarch
2 tablespoons cold milk
½ teaspoon salt
2 tablespoons vanilla extract
1 cup whipping cream, whipped (optional)
¼ cup chopped pecans (optional)

Cook 1½ cups sugar in an iron skillet over medium heat, stir constantly, until sugar melts and turns pale brown. (Melt sugar slowly; custard will have a more delicate flavor.) Pour caramelized sugar very slowly into scalded milk, stirring constantly. Set aside.

Beat egg yolks in a large mixing bowl for 3 minutes at medium speed of an electric mixer. Dissolve cornstarch in milk; add milk mixture, remaining sugar, and salt to eggs; beat 3 minutes longer at low speed. Stir yolk mixture into the caramelized mixture, blending thoroughly. Set pan of brûlée in a container of cold water until cool. Stir in vanilla; chill. Serve with pecans, if desired. Yield: about 10 servings.

Charlotte Russe

2 cups whipping cream
1 teaspoon vanilla extract
½ cup sugar
Sherry to taste
½ tablespoon unflavored gelatin
¼ cup cold milk
¼ cup warm milk
5 egg whites, stiffly beaten
Ladyfingers, split

Whip cream until stiff in a large mixing bowl; stir in vanilla, sugar, and sherry as desired. Soften gelatin in cold milk; add warm milk. When cool, add to cream mixture, beating constantly. Fold in beaten egg whites. Pour into a 1½-quart glass bowl lined with ladyfingers; chill. Yield: 6 servings.

Tennessee Boiled Custard

¾ to 1 cup sugar, divided
4 cups milk, divided
3 eggs, well beaten
2½ tablespoons all-purpose flour
⅛ teaspoon soda
1 teaspoon vanilla extract

Combine ½ cup sugar and 3 cups milk in top of a double boiler. Heat over boiling water. Combine eggs, remaining sugar, flour, soda, and remaining milk in a medium mixing bowl. Blend well; pour through a strainer into hot milk mixture, stirring constantly. Cook over boiling water, stirring frequently, for 10 to 15 minutes or until mixture will coat a metal spoon. Stir in vanilla; cool. Yield: 4½ cups.

Peach Cobbler Supreme (page 236) is one of the many bonuses of the peach season.

Colonial Tavern Bread Pudding

4 eggs
1 cup sugar
1 quart milk, scalded
1½ cups fine dry breadcrumbs
Salt
½ teaspoon lemon extract
Half-and-half

Beat eggs until mixed, but not light. Stir in sugar, hot milk, breadcrumbs, salt, and lemon extract.

Pour into an ungreased 2-quart baking dish; set dish in a pan with an inch of hot water in it. Bake at 350° for 1 hour or until set and slightly brown. Serve warm with half-and-half. Yield: 6 servings.

Biscuit Pudding

12 large cold biscuits
2 cups sugar
About 4 cups milk
½ cup butter or margarine
3 eggs, beaten
1 teaspoon ground nutmeg
Whipped cream

Crumble biscuits into large mixing bowl. Heat sugar, 4 cups milk, and butter in saucepan until butter melts and skim forms; pour over crumbs. Mixture should be very "soupy"; add a little more milk if necessary. Stir in eggs and nutmeg; beat until smooth. Pour into greased 2-quart baking dish. Bake at 350° for 40 to 45 minutes, or until set and browned. Serve with whipped cream. Yield: 8 servings.

Many of our favorite Southern puddings like this Banana Pudding (page 241) have an egg custard base.

Banana Pudding

½ cup sugar
⅓ cup all-purpose flour
¼ teaspoon salt
2 cups milk, scalded
2 eggs, separated
1 teaspoon vanilla extract
About 25 vanilla wafers
4 bananas, sliced
¼ cup sugar

Combine ½ cup sugar, flour, and salt in top of double boiler. Mix well and stir in milk. Cook about 15 minutes, stirring constantly. Beat egg yolks until thick and lemon colored. Gradually stir one-fourth of hot mixture into yolks; add to remaining hot mixture, stirring constantly. Cook 2 minutes longer. Remove from heat, and add vanilla. Cool. Line a 1-quart baking dish with half of vanilla wafers. Add a layer of sliced bananas. Top with half of pudding. Repeat layers. Beat egg whites until soft peaks form. Gradually add sugar and beat until stiff. Spread meringue over pudding and bake at 350° for 12 to 15 minutes. Yield: 6 servings.

Cherry Pudding

½ cup butter or margarine, softened
1 cup sugar
1 egg
2 teaspoons baking powder
1½ cups all-purpose flour
⅔ cup milk
1 teaspoon vanilla extract
2 cups pitted cherries, drained
Milk or half-and-half (optional)

Beat butter and sugar in a large mixing bowl until creamy. Beat in egg and baking powder. Add flour and milk alternately; stir in vanilla. Fold in fruit. Pour into a greased 9- × 5- × 3-inch loafpan; bake at 375° for 1 hour or until done. Serve warm; pour milk over top, if desired. Yield: 6 to 8 servings.

Kentucky Tombstone Pudding

6 egg yolks
1 cup sugar
1 teaspoon all-purpose flour
1 cup sherry
24 almond macaroon cookies
Dash of cream of tartar
Dash of salt
2 egg whites
2 tablespoons sugar
½ cup whole almonds

Beat egg yolks in a medium saucepan until thick and lemon colored. Mix 1 cup sugar and flour, and beat into yolks. Add sherry and cook over low heat, stirring constantly, until thickened.

Arrange cookies in a 9-inch square baking dish. Pour egg yolk mixture over cookies.

Add cream of tartar and salt to egg whites; beat until stiff, gradually adding 2 tablespoons sugar. Beat until sugar is dissolved.

Pour egg whites over custard, spreading to edges of pan.

Decorate top by placing almonds on end; bake at 300° for 15 minutes or until lightly browned. Serve hot. Yield: 8 servings.

Indian Pudding

¼ cup cornmeal
1 teaspoon salt
⅓ cup molasses
½ teaspoon ground cinnamon
½ teaspoon ground ginger
4 cups milk, divided

Combine cornmeal, salt, molasses, and spices in a small saucepan and bring to a boil over medium heat. Remove from heat; stir in 2 cups milk and pour into a greased 1½-quart casserole. Bake at 300° for 1½ hours, stirring often. Stir in remaining 2 cups milk; continue baking at 300° for 1 hour. Yield: about 8 servings.

Lemon Pudding

3 cups day-old breadcrumbs
1 quart scalded milk
1 teaspoon salt
3 eggs, beaten
1 teaspoon lemon extract
Lemon Sauce (recipe follows)

Place breadcrumbs in a large mixing bowl; pour hot milk over breadcrumbs. Stir in salt; cover and let stand 30 minutes. Beat in eggs and flavoring, beating until perfectly smooth. Pour into a buttered 2½- or 3-quart baking dish; bake at 400° for 45 minutes. Serve warm with Lemon Sauce. Yield: 12 servings.

Lemon Sauce:

¾ cup powdered sugar
¼ cup butter or margarine, softened
2 tablespoons lemon juice

Combine ingredients and beat until smooth. Yield: ½ to ¾ cup.

Orange Pudding

6 oranges, peeled and sectioned
½ cup sugar, divided
1½ tablespoons cornstarch
4 cups milk
4 eggs, well beaten
½ teaspoon vanilla extract

Place orange sections in a large glass serving bowl and sprinkle with half the sugar. Set aside.

Combine remaining sugar and cornstarch in the top of a double boiler. Slowly add milk, stirring to keep mixture smooth; cook over boiling water, stirring constantly, until mixture is well warmed; stir in eggs. Cook over boiling water, stirring constantly, 10 to 15 minutes or until mixture will coat a metal spoon; stir in vanilla. Pour over oranges; cool. Do not stir until completely cooled. Serve in individual compotes. Yield: 10 to 12 servings.

Maple Velvet

2⅔ cups firmly packed light brown
    sugar
2 cups commercial sour cream
2 teaspoons maple extract
2 cups whipping cream
8 cups fresh blueberries, washed

Combine sugar, sour cream, and maple extract in a large mixing bowl; beat at low speed of an electric mixer until sugar is dissolved. Whip cream; fold into sour cream mixture. Chill until serving time. Fold in berries; serve in individual compotes. Yield: 8 to 10 servings.

Maple Cottage Pudding

1 tablespoon butter or margarine
3 tablespoons sugar
1 egg, beaten
½ cup milk
1 cup all-purpose flour
2 teaspoons baking powder
½ teaspoon salt
1 cup maple syrup
¼ cup chopped nuts
½ cup whipping cream, whipped
    (optional)

Cream butter and sugar in a medium mixing bowl; beat in egg, milk, flour, baking powder, and salt.

Bring syrup to a boil in a small saucepan; pour into an 8- or 9-inch square baking pan. Pour batter on top of syrup. Bake at 375° for 25 minutes. Invert onto serving dish; sprinkle nuts over top. Serve with whipped cream, if desired. Yield: 6 servings.

Two-Step Snow Pudding

¼ cup cornstarch
½ cup sugar
Dash of salt
2 cups water
4 egg whites
1 teaspoon vanilla extract
Custard (recipe follows)

Mix cornstarch, sugar, and salt in a medium saucepan; stir in water. Cook, stirring constantly, until mixture boils and becomes clear and thickened. Place egg whites in a medium mixing bowl; beat at high speed of electric mixer until stiff. Beating at low speed, slowly pour hot mixture into egg whites. Add vanilla; mix thoroughly. Pour into a 2-quart glass serving bowl; cool. Make a slight depression in center of the egg white mixture; slowly pour cooled custard into the depression. Custard will go to the bottom and the "snow" will rise to the top. Chill overnight. Yield: 10 servings.

Custard:

2 tablespoons cornstarch
½ cup sugar
Dash of salt
3½ cups milk
4 egg yolks, beaten
1 teaspoon almond extract

Mix cornstarch, sugar, and salt in a medium saucepan; stir in milk gradually. Bring to a boil over medium heat, stirring constantly. Stir a small amount of the hot mixture into yolks; stir yolks into remaining hot mixture. Stir over low heat until slightly thickened; stir in flavoring. Cool. Yield: about 3¾ cups.

Brownie's Persimmon Pudding

1 quart fresh persimmons
1½ cups all-purpose flour
1 teaspoon soda
½ teaspoon ground nutmeg
2 teaspoons ground cinnamon
1 teaspoon ground ginger
1 teaspoon baking powder
3 eggs, beaten
1¼ cups sugar
2½ cups milk
½ cup melted butter or margarine
Whipped cream

Wash persimmons and put through a sieve; there should be 2 cups of pulp. Stir flour, soda, spices, and baking powder together in a large mixing bowl. Beat eggs with sugar. Blend flour mixture with sugar mixture; add persimmon pulp. Stir in milk and butter. Pour into a greased 9-inch square baking dish; set dish in a larger pan with about an inch of water in it. Bake at 350° for 45 minutes or until set. Serve warm with whipped cream. Yield: 8 servings.

Old-Fashioned Sweet Potato Pudding

½ cup butter or margarine
4 cups grated uncooked sweet potatoes
1 cup cane syrup
1 cup milk
1 teaspoon salt
1 teaspoon ground ginger
1 teaspoon ground cinnamon
½ cup chopped pecans
2 eggs, well beaten
1 cup whipping cream, whipped (optional)

Melt butter in a 2-quart baking dish. Combine remaining ingredients except cream; blend thoroughly. Pour into melted butter in baking dish; stir well, and bake at 350° for 20

minutes. Use a spatula to turn the crusted edges underneath; bake 15 minutes longer to allow crust to re-form. Turn again, and bake 10 to 15 minutes longer. Top each serving with whipped cream, if desired. Yield: 8 servings.

The Queen Of All Puddings
La Reine des Poudings

2 cups breadcrumbs
4 eggs, separated
1 cup sugar
1 quart milk
1 cup currants
1 cup raisins
1 tablespoon melted butter or margarine
Juice of 1 lemon
Grated rind of ½ lemon
¼ cup powdered sugar
1 cup tart jelly

Soak breadcrumbs in water for about 1 hour. Drain thoroughly. Lightly beat egg yolks in a large mixing bowl with sugar; add milk and breadcrumbs, beating lightly.

Cook currants and raisins in boiling water for 5 minutes; drain. Add currants, raisins, butter, lemon juice, and lemon rind to breadcrumb mixture. Beat thoroughly; pour into a greased 2½-quart baking dish and bake at 350° for 30 minutes or until center is almost set.

Beat egg whites until frothy; gradually add powdered sugar and beat until stiff. Warm jelly slightly and stir to make it easy to spread. Spread a thin layer of jelly over cooked custard and spread a thin layer of beaten egg whites over jelly; continue layering, ending with egg whites. Brown in oven at 350° for 10 minutes. Serve chilled. Yield: 8 servings.

Woodford Pudding

½ cup butter or margarine, softened
1 cup sugar
3 eggs
1 cup blackberry jam
1 teaspoon soda
1 tablespoon buttermilk
1½ cups all-purpose flour
Ground cinnamon and nutmeg
    to taste
Caramel Sauce

Cream butter and sugar in a large mixing bowl. Add eggs and jam; dissolve soda in buttermilk; stir into jam mixture. Combine flour and spices, and add to jam mixture. Pour into a greased 8-inch square baking pan; bake at 325° for 45 minutes or until pudding is firm but soft. Cut into squares; serve with Caramel Sauce. Yield: 8 servings.

Caramel Sauce:

1 cup firmly packed brown sugar
2 tablespoons butter or margarine
1½ cups boiling water

Combine all ingredients in 1-quart saucepan; stir until sugar is melted. Bring to a boil over high heat. Remove from heat and serve hot over Woodford Pudding or any steamed pudding. Yield: about 2 cups.

Rich Peach Ice Cream

1 quart whipping cream
2½ cups sugar, divided
3 cups finely chopped ripe peaches
Dash of salt

Scald whipping cream and 1¼ cups sugar in top of double boiler, stirring to dissolve sugar. Pour mixture into a 1-gallon hand-turned or electric ice cream freezer; freeze until thickened.

Puree peaches by mashing or by processing in container of electric blender. Combine 1¼ cups sugar, salt, and peach puree; stir until sugar dissolves. Remove dasher; stir pureed mixture into custard. Return dasher, and freeze until firm. Let ripen 1 hour before serving. Yield: ½ gallon.

Crème De Menthe Parfaits

This is better prepared one day early and frozen in the glasses overnight.

¾ cup water
1 cup sugar
1 cup canned crushed pineapple,
    drained
1 tablespoon crème de menthe
Few drops of green food coloring
    (optional)
Vanilla ice cream

Bring water and sugar to a boil in a medium saucepan. Add pineapple, and boil 10 minutes. Remove from heat; stir in crème de menthe and food coloring, if desired. Layer syrup with ice cream in parfait glasses, beginning and ending with syrup. Yield: 5 to 6 servings.

Louisiana Vanilla Ice Cream

6 eggs
1¾ cups sugar
1 (14-ounce) can sweetened
    condensed milk
1 (13-ounce) can evaporated milk
1 tablespoon vanilla extract
Milk

Beat eggs until light and frothy. Add sugar; stir to dissolve. Blend in condensed and evaporated milk and vanilla. Pour into a 1-gallon hand-turned or electric freezer; add milk to fill container three-fourths full. Yield: 1 gallon.

Note: To make peppermint ice cream start freezing ice cream as directed above; when thick and beginning to freeze, take lid off freezer and stir in 1½ cups crushed peppermint candy. Return lid and finish freezing.

Spiced Peaches

2 (29-ounce) cans cling peach halves
1⅓ cups sugar
1 cup cider vinegar
4 (3-inch) sticks cinnamon
2 teaspoons whole cloves

Drain peaches, reserving syrup. Combine peach syrup, sugar, vinegar, cinnamon sticks, and cloves in a saucepan. Bring mixture to a boil; then lower heat, and simmer 10 minutes. Pour hot syrup over peach halves; let cool. Chill thoroughly before serving. Store in refrigerator. Yield: about 4 pints.

Buttermilk Pecan Pralines

2 cups sugar
1 teaspoon soda
1 cup buttermilk
2 tablespoons butter or margarine
2½ cups broken pecans
1 teaspoon vanilla extract
About 24 pecan halves

Combine sugar, soda, buttermilk, and butter in a large, heavy Dutch oven; cook over high heat 5 minutes, stirring constantly. Add broken pecans; cook, stirring constantly, over medium heat until candy thermometer registers 230°. Remove from heat; stir in vanilla. Beat just until mixture begins to thicken.

Working rapidly, drop mixture by tablespoonfuls onto lightly buttered waxed paper. Place a pecan half on each praline; cool. Store in airtight container. Yield: 24 pralines.

Serbian Crêpes Suzette

3 eggs, well beaten
1 cup half-and-half
½ cup all-purpose flour
3 tablespoons sugar
½ teaspoon salt
Butter
Fillings (recipes follow)
Powdered sugar or commercial
  sour cream

Combine first 5 ingredients, beating until smooth. Brush the bottom of a 6-inch crêpe pan with butter; place over medium heat until hot. Pour 1½ to 2 tablespoons batter into pan; tilt pan in all directions so batter thinly covers the pan. Cook about 1 minute.

Lift edge of crêpe to test for doneness. Crêpe is ready for flipping when it can be shaken loose from pan. Flip crêpe, and cook about 30 seconds on other side. Place on a towel to cool.

Spread each crêpe with about 1 tablespoon desired filling. Roll crêpe; sprinkle with powdered sugar or spread top with sour cream. Place on greased cookie sheet and bake at 350° about 10 minutes. Yield: 4 to 6 servings.

Cottage Cheese Filling:

1 cup cottage cheese
1 egg yolk, beaten
Sugar to taste
Lemon juice (optional)

Combine all ingredients, mixing well. Yield: about 1 cup.

Orange Filling:

1 cup orange marmalade
Ground cinnamon
1 teaspoon cognac or orange liqueur

Combine all ingredients, mixing well. Yield: about 1 cup.

Note: Fillings can also be made from sour cream, whipped cream, fruit syrups, or jelly.

Southernisms

"Southernism" is a term commonly used to denote a trait of language or behavior which is characteristic of the South or of a Southerner. I would like to pick up that term and extend it into the field of food because I believe there is another level of meaning to some of the cooking we call "Southern."

Why do I consider biscuits made in a food processor not a Southernism, while feeling positive that biscuits made in an old-fashioned bread bowl are? Why is poke sallet ("all you can find; it cooks down") a Southernism and spinach soufflé not?

Well, there are many old Southern ways with food that simply do not lend themselves to modern recipe form, i.e., the ingredients listed with standard measurements followed by laconic instructions. They are wonderful as they stand and would lose too much in translation. I would rather not tamper with them.

Others do permit themselves to be measured and timed by the clock but represent delicious dishes that seem to me to be on the brink of an undeserved extinction. We might need them someday, who knows? At any rate, I would rescue them if I could. So much for motivation; perhaps when these culinary Southernisms are spread out for us to read and use and enjoy, we may want to keep them.

The notion of Southernisms entered my head after I met Mamie Gammon, a talented Memphis restaurateur who became the first licensed black caterer in her city. Speaking of her childhood and of the many dishes she learned from her mother, she said, "My mother made potato fried pies and sold them at the laundry near our home. My brothers pulled hot food there in their wagon: hot peas, neckbones, ham, baked hash. We could have been the first 'chuck wagon' in Memphis. We missed the boat."

Potato fried pie was a new concept to me; I could not let it pass. Here is Mrs. Gammon's recipe.

Potato Fried Pie

"Mash potatoes and season them with sugar, nutmeg, cinnamon, and butter. Cut rounds of biscuit crust, fill with the potato mixture, seal the edges, and fry them in oil or shortening."

Yes, it is a sweet pastry, and good. I am not sure how widely it is known, but I think of it as pure Memphis since that is where I found it. A word of caution about Southernisms: do not stop an oral recipe in mid-air with a question such as, "How much sugar?" The answer would depend upon how many potatoes had to be sweetened and how sweet the cook wanted to make them. The number of potatoes would depend, in turn, upon how many servings were desired. A recipe that has become a Southernism does not deal in superfluous details.

But the concept of potato fried pie is easy to assimilate, compared with an outlandish dish called "frocking," an amazingly delicious mixture of tomatoes and soda crackers. It was explained to me by Myree Sanders of Gordo, Alabama. She knows the origin of the dish well enough, but the name appears to be untraceable. Until new evidence turns up on that score, it seems safe to assume that frocking is another word for dressing.

"The frocking recipe originated in West Alabama in the early part of this century when the bobwhite quail were plentiful," according to Mrs. Sanders. "The tomato and cracker mixture was used as stuffing for the birds but was mixed to a drier consistency than I use now with chicken. No broth was used, just butter and a little water.

"The stuffed birds were placed in a white cloth sack, tied, placed in a wet brown paper bag, and tied again. Then the whole thing was wrapped in layers of wet paper and baked under the ashes in an open fireplace for many hours, until the birds steamed and tendered.

"Since quail are not easy to acquire any more, we now substitute chicken and add broth, cream of chicken soup, and lots of butter for richness."

Here is how Mrs. Sanders prepares the dish today.

Frocking

1 (3½- to 4-pound) hen or
    fryer
1 tablespoon salt
¾ pound saltine crackers
2 (1-pound 12-ounce) cans
    whole tomatoes with
    juice

1 large onion, chopped
¼ cup vinegar
2 to 2½ cups chicken broth
½ cup butter or margarine,
    melted
Salt and pepper to taste

Place hen in a kettle with cold water to cover; add salt. Simmer about 1 hour, until barely tender; reserve.

Crumble crackers into a large mixing bowl. Add tomatoes, breaking them up with the hands. Add remaining ingredients, mixing well. Pour into roasting pan; cover and bake at 325° for 1½ hours.

Remove from oven; place whole hen in center of frocking. Cover and continue to bake an additional 1½ hours. Yield: 6 servings.

Note: If quail is used instead of chicken, place uncooked quail on uncooked frocking; bake at 325° for 3 hours. One (10¾-ounce) can undiluted cream of chicken soup may be added for richness.

Before the days of commercial light bread and prepared snacks, hot cornbread and biscuits were enjoyed once or twice every day, and the leftovers were the basis of snacks while the supply lasted.

Down in Columbus, Mississippi, Wanda Beasley still serves one of her childhood favorite combinations, hot biscuits with tomato gravy. "I serve it now for a light supper, but we used to have it for breakfast with bacon and preserves. After school, we'd poke a hole in the side of a cold biscuit and fill it with molasses."

Old-Time Biscuits

"A biscuit bowl or pan was always kept on hand filled with flour. The bowl was made by hewing out a block of wood; then it was smoothed to a fine finish by scraping with a piece of broken glass. The more use of the bowl, the more successful the biscuits. As these bowls are now very scarce, one may be improvised by using a wide, flared vegetable bowl or deep platter.

"Into the center of the bowl already containing a ½-inch layer of flour, sift 2 cups of flour. Using the fist, make a hole in the center of the mound of flour, making a depression deep enough to add 1 cup buttermilk in which ½ teaspoon soda has been dissolved. (Adding the soda to the milk makes it fizz.) Into the milk, drop ⅓ cup shortening. Pinch the shortening into small pieces with the fingers, gradually working a small amount of flour into the dough. Finally, a ball of dough will form. (Using the fingers takes practice and feels messy in the beginning. Amateurs may prefer to start the dough with a spoon.)

"Dough should be handled as little as possible. When consistency is right, not sticky, roll the dough out and cut with a biscuit cutter. However, the old-timey way is to pinch off a little dough about the size of a golf ball for a large biscuit and roll in the palm of the hand until smooth; then flatten and place in the hot greased biscuit pan. My family preferred to turn the biscuits over in order to dab a little of the grease on both sides for a crustier biscuit. Bake at 375° for about 10 to 12 minutes. Yield: about 8 large biscuits."

Tomato Gravy

⅓ cup chopped onion
3 tablespoons bacon
    drippings or oil
2 tablespoons all-purpose
    flour

2 cups stewed or canned
    tomatoes
1 teaspoon salt
¼ teaspoon pepper
1½ cups water (optional)

Sauté onion in the drippings in a large black iron skillet. Add the flour and brown slightly. When the flour and onion are slightly browned, add tomatoes at once and stir until thickened. Season with salt and pepper. Water may be added if needed. Serve over large, crusty homemade biscuits. (Recipes begin on page 163.) Yield: about 2 cups.

Most Southernisms, as I see them, are basic, no-frill foods, long on the old-time kitchen staples such as greens, pork, corn, and flour. In one recipe, poke sallet is not only boiled but is fried afterward in bacon drippings. In another, dressing is made into patties and fried instead of being baked in or with chicken.

The necessary arts of canning and preserving are honored traditions in the South. Tomato jam, apple chutney, and watermelon pickle were and are frugal and delightful ways to utilize seasonal abundance. Mincemeat, laced with brandy in order to make it shelf-stable, is another way of saving something good for later. Southerners did not invent mincemeat; that amalgam of sweet and savory goes back through the English to medieval times. But they continue to make it, substituting venison (especially the tongue) for ox or mutton.

It is significant, I believe, that Southernisms include so many sweets. Most of them are comparatively inelegant, consisting of little more than staples plus sweetening. The humble sweet potato or green tomato, sugared, becomes pie filling, and vinegar gives tartness to a nonlemon pie. If sugar runs short, there is always the syrup from sugarcane or sorghum to make a fine custard pie. And biscuit dough becomes dessert when stewed as dumplings in sweet syrup or when used as crust for fruit cobbler.

To make a cobbler, Mrs. Beasley uses her "old-time biscuit" dough and a quart of home-canned fruit. Here is her recipe.

Fruit Cobbler

"Just add a little more shortening to the dough and put a little less soda in the buttermilk. Line a deep bowl or pan with half the dough and pour in the fruit. Sprinkle with equal parts of flour and sugar, about a quarter of a cup of each, mixed. Some fruits take more sugar.

"Sprinkle the fruit with cinnamon, nutmeg, and a few dots of butter. Cover with the rolled-out top crust and sprinkle some more sugar and cinnamon on top. Sometimes, if the fruit is very juicy, I cut up a little of the dough and make a few small dumplings to add to the filling. Put on the top crust and bake the cobbler at 375° for about 30 minutes."

The prevalence of such homely desserts is testimony that in the South, a taste of sweetness, or pleasure food, ranks in importance close behind the staff of life.

Unhampered by the Puritan proscriptions that prevailed in the northern colonies, the South has always maintained a friendly interest in spirits. With dandelions, elderberries, and blackberries growing wild in the fields, homemade wine was within the reach of anyone with the barest knowledge of the fermentation process. Aunts and grandmothers prolonged their lives by taking medicinal draughts of wine, while the masculine members of the family occasionally made use of stronger spirits distilled from that most useful of American grains, corn.

This chapter, then, is an informal sharing of recollections of good things. Some of the recipes give scant instructions, relying heavily on the common sense of the cook. We may be a couple of generations away from the necessity of making hominy at home or grinding our own filé powder, but so long as there are Southerners who remember how to do it, the urbanization of the South appears wonderfully incomplete.

Sun-Preserved Strawberries
Use equal weights of sugar and strawberries. Put the strawberries in the preserving kettle in layers, sprinkling sugar over each layer. The fruit and sugar should not be more than four inches deep. Place the kettle on the stove and heat the fruit and sugar slowly to the boiling point. When it begins to boil skim carefully. Boil 10 minutes, counting from the time the fruit begins to bubble. Pour the cooked fruit into platters, having it about two or three inches deep. Place the platters in a sunny window in an unused room, for three or four days. In doing this be sure to keep protected from flies. In that time the fruit will grow plump and firm and the syrup will thicken almost to a jelly. Put this preserve, cold, into jars or tumblers.
Progressive Farmer magazine

Southernisms

Smoked Apples

We did these apples about 80 years ago, using a wooden barrel and we made a lot at a time. I haven't eaten any of these in a long time. . . .

Select good, firm apples; peel, core, and slice as desired. Put apples in a basket which may be suspended at the top of a large barrel or box. Place a hot brick or live coals in a vessel and place it under the basket. Cover tightly with a well-fitting lid or a heavy blanket.

When this preparation is all made, open the top just enough to drop in the sulphur. Use 1 tablespoon sulphur to half a bushel of apples. Cover and let stand until smoking has ceased, about 30 minutes.

Remove apples and store in covered jars. Apples may shrink in the jars; additional fruit may be added.

Catfish Stew

Take 3 medium-sized catfish, say 8 pounds. Cut off and place the heads in the bottom of a large kettle. Sprinkle over them your seasoning, consisting of 2 tablespoons butter, ¼ teacup of chopped onion, 2 tablespoons salt, 1 pod of red pepper. Then arrange cut-up fish in layers with sliced bread. Sprinkle with black pepper; pour over the whole 1 quart of water and 1 quart of good, rich milk. Cover with a plate and cook for 1 or 2 hours over a slow fire until moderately dry.

Picnic Chicken

Dress as many chickens as the occasion requires; joint and boil until tender in as little water as possible, salting just before they are done. Take up; remove the skin and take all meat from the bones. Break the bones and boil them with the skin a little while longer in the water; then strain it to have ready to moisten the chicken.

Place a layer of dark meat, then a layer of white in a bowl or crock, seasoning each layer with pepper and salt. Moisten with broth. Put on weights until cold. Slice with a sharp knife. This is especially nice for picnics.

Filé (Real Cajun-Style)

Filé (fee-lay): The finely-ground sassafras leaves which add such an exotic flavor to gumbo.

In the month of August, during the full moon, break branches (in fully matured leaf) from a sassafras tree. Hang branches to dry in a shaded, ventilated place for about 2 weeks. Expose to bright sunlight 1 to 1½ hours before grinding finely in a mill. Store in amber jars, tightly sealed, in a cool place, or in the refrigerator for even longer lasting quality.

Ham Bone And Cornmeal Dumplings

The smokehouse had a board roof, boxed-up walls, and a dirt floor, but it had a lock on the door. A big box in one corner held the family's supply of meat. I was always pleased when the hams and shoulders were trimmed down to just a little meat on the bone. I'd take the bone to the chop block, hack it into small pieces, and put it in an iron kettle hung over the fireplace. After it boiled awhile, I'd move it to the wood cook stove.

Take about 2 handfuls of meal, and sprinkle it with salt and black pepper. Scald the meal just enough to make it stick together. Form into balls; then flatten the balls into cakes. Drop into the boiling meat broth.

Turkey Bone Gumbo

1 meaty turkey carcass
½ cup bacon drippings
1 cup all-purpose flour
2 large onions, chopped
3 cloves garlic, chopped
1 green pepper, chopped
4 stalks celery, chopped
2 quarts hot turkey or chicken broth
Dash of hot sauce
2 bay leaves
1 tablespoon parsley flakes
1 teaspoon dried basil leaves
2 to 3 cups chopped turkey
1 pound smoked sausage, cut into
    bite-size pieces
1 tablespoon salt
½ teaspoon pepper
1 bunch green onions, chopped
Hot cooked rice

Place turkey carcass in large soup kettle with water almost to cover. Bring to a boil; cook over low heat for 1½ hours or until meat falls from bones. Drain turkey; reserve broth. Remove turkey from carcass; chop turkey, and set aside.

Heat bacon drippings in kettle; add flour gradually. Cook over low heat, stirring constantly, until a rich brown roux is formed, about 25 minutes. Add onion, garlic, green pepper, and celery; cook until vegetables are tender. Add broth, hot sauce, bay leaves, parsley, and basil. Simmer 1 hour. Add reserved turkey, 2 to 3 cups chopped turkey, and sausage; cook 15 minutes longer. Add salt, pepper, and green onion; cook an additional 10 minutes. Serve over hot cooked rice. Yield: about 12 to 15 servings.

Boiled Peanuts

1 gallon fresh green peanuts
2 cups salt

Wash peanuts and place in a large pot. Cover with water; add salt. Boil until tender. Let stand in same water until cool.

Barbecued Pecans

2 tablespoons melted butter or
    margarine
¼ cup Worcestershire sauce
1 tablespoon catsup
⅛ teaspoon hot sauce
4 cups pecan halves
Salt (optional)

Combine first 4 ingredients; stir in pecans, and mix well. Spread pecans evenly in a shallow baking pan. Bake at 300° for 30 minutes, stirring frequently. Drain on paper towels, and sprinkle with salt, if desired. Yield: 4 cups.

Danish Lettuce

1 tablespoon butter or margarine
¼ cup water
1 medium onion, chopped
8 large stalks celery, chopped
¾ pound (about 4 cups) leaf lettuce
1 teaspoon salt
¼ teaspoon pepper

Melt butter in heavy 3-quart saucepan. Add water, onion, and celery; simmer 5 minutes.

Wash lettuce and cut crosswise into 1-inch lengths. Drain well between paper towels. Add lettuce to saucepan, packing it down with a spatula. Bring mixture to a boil; cover, reduce heat, and simmer 20 minutes. Remove from heat, and stir in salt and pepper. Yield: 6 to 8 servings.

Note: This side dish is also delicious combined with equal amounts of mashed potatoes, stirring only enough to half-blend.

Poke Sallet

Gather all the sallet you can find (it cooks down). Pick 6- or 7-inch shoots. Wash and clean; swim the shoots in plenty of water in a big pot and boil until tender.

Meanwhile, slice a pan of country bacon and fry out the grease. When the poke is tender, drain off the water it was cooked in and cover it with cold water. Squeeze it out of the cold water into the hot bacon grease. Salt to taste, and cook slowly until hot through. Serve with the fried bacon and hot cornbread.

Blackberry Cordial

Boil blackberries, adding a little water to keep them from scorching. When they are soft, put the juice through a jelly bag. Add to each quart of juice:

> 2 cups sugar
> ½ stick of cinnamon
> 2 tablespoons whole cloves
> ½ ounce blade mace or whole allspice

Boil these ingredients for 20 minutes. Strain. Add ¼ cup brandy to each ¾ quart juice (after bottling juice). Put tops (corks) on bottles and drink when depressed.

Dandelion Wine

To one quart of dandelion blossoms add 1 gallon of boiling water and 2 lemons and 2 oranges which have been cut into thin slices. Let stand for 24 hours. Strain and add 1 yeast cake and 1½ pounds of sugar. Keep the mixture in a stoneware crock for 10 days while the liquid ferments. Strain through a cloth and mix in 1½ pounds of sugar; the wine can then be bottled. Use corks for bottling.

Elderberry Blossom Wine

Put 9 pounds of brown sugar into 3 gallons of water and bring it to a boil. Remove from heat. Add a quart of elderberry blossoms. When this is lukewarm, stir in 2 gills (10 fluid ounces) of potato yeast. Then pour this into a crock that has 3 pounds of raisins in it. Keep here for 6 days. Stir vigorously once each day. After the 6 days, strain and bottle without corking. When it stops working, cork tightly.

Hominy

Here is an old recipe for hominy made with baking soda.

Select corn (field corn), shell, and put in iron or enamel kettle. Soak the corn overnight. Place over medium heat; add water to cover, and to each quart of corn, add 3½ rounded tablespoons of baking soda. Let boil slowly (stirring a few times) until hulls slip off readily. If corn is very dry, you may need more soda. The corn should then be thoroughly washed in water, rubbing in palms of hands to remove shells. Cook two or three times for 15 minutes, pouring off water and adding clear water. Add water and cook until tender.

To serve, fry in favorite seasoning, boil in cream, or cook with dry beans.

Grated Corn Muffins

When corn ears get too hard to fry, use a coarse grater to get corn off cob. Use 1 cup cornmeal for each 2 ears of corn. Add 1 teaspoon soda and 1 teaspoon salt for that amount, and enough water to make a batter just thin enough to pour into hot, greased muffin irons. Bake fast (475° for about 20 minutes); add butter while hot.

Corn Pone

Sift 3 cupfuls yellow cornmeal with 1 teaspoon salt, ½ teaspoon soda, and 3 tablespoons of melted bacon drippings. Add just enough buttermilk to make a stiff dough. Wet both hands with water; divide dough into 3 parts. Shape each into a football-shaped pone; place on a well-greased black iron skillet. Pat with more drippings and bake at 400° until golden brown.

Fried Dressing

Moisten 6 slices crumbled day-old bread with weakened broth or melted margarine. Crumble and add salt and pepper to taste, 1 large stalk celery, chopped, and 1 medium onion, minced. Beat 1 egg and add to above to hold together. Let mixture stand to absorb moisture. Add chopped chestnuts, if desired. Drop by tablespoonfuls into hot shortening in a skillet; flatten with spatula and fry until done. (Can be made into cakes before frying.) Will keep stored in the refrigerator until next day for frying.

My grandmother got this recipe from her mother, and she knows of no one else who ever prepared dressing this way.

Butter Roll

Variations of Butter Roll come from several states. In Mississippi and Arkansas, nutmeg is used instead of vanilla for flavoring. And, instead of boiling water poured over the top, a syrup is made of milk and sugar in the pan before adding the rolls.

3 cups all-purpose flour
1 tablespoon baking powder
1 teaspoon salt
⅓ cup lard
1 cup milk

Mix all together with finger tips. Knead until smooth on biscuit board. Roll out ¼ inch thick. Spread with ¾ cup soft fresh-churned butter; sprinkle 1½ cupfuls sugar on top. Roll up jellyroll fashion. Cut into 1½-inch pieces; stand in a large pudding pan. Slowly pour enough boiling water over the rolls to cover. Sprinkle 1 teaspoon vanilla extract on top. Bake at 350° until brown, about 1 hour. Serve with whipped cream. Yield: 8 servings.

Favorite Doughnuts

1 cup sugar, 1 cup of milk,
2 eggs beaten as fine as silk,
Salt and nutmeg (lemon will do),
Of baking powder teaspoons 2,
Lightly stir the flour in
Roll on pie board not too thin,
Cut in diamonds, twist in rings,
Drop with care the doughy things
Into fat that briskly swells
Evenly the spongy cells
Watch with care the time for turning,
Fry them brown just short of burning,
Roll in sugar, serve when cool,
Price a quarter for this rule.

Caramel Dumplings

Caramelize ½ cup sugar in an iron skillet, being careful not to burn. Gradually stir in 2 cups boiling water, 1 cup sugar, and 2 tablespoons butter. Boil for 10 minutes, stirring occasionally. Make dough for Baking Powder Biscuits (page 163). On a floured surface, roll dough with the hands to form small balls. Drop balls into boiling syrup; cover, reduce heat, and simmer exactly 20 minutes. Serve with unsweetened whipped cream. Yield: 6 to 8 servings.

Jam Dumplings

2 cups jam or preserves (any flavor)
3 cups water
1 recipe Baking Powder Biscuits
   (page 163)

Make a syrup of the jam and water in 3-quart saucepan. When the syrup has come to a boil, reduce heat and drop biscuit dough on top by teaspoonfuls. Cover at once; simmer for 12 minutes.

Remove dumplings and arrange in a deep serving dish. Pour the remaining syrup around dumplings and serve hot. Yield: about 8 servings.

Shaver Pie

Mash about 2 cups of cooked, home-dried apples. Add sugar to taste (about ½ cup), ¼ cup butter, ½ teaspoon cinnamon, and a dash each of cloves, nutmeg, and salt.

Make pastry for a double-crust pie (page 228). Roll out ⅓ of the dough at a time on a floured surface; cut a 7- or 8-inch circle from each, reserving trimmings from each piece to combine and roll out into a fourth circle. Fill each circle with ¼ of the filling. Fold to half-moon shape, moistening edges to seal. Place on a large greased cookie sheet. Bake at 400° for 20 minutes or until browned; cool.

When pies are cool, cut them into pieces and place in a large serving bowl. Make the following sauce and pour it, while still hot, over the cooled pies. Yield: 6 to 8 servings.

Sauce:

2½ cups milk or half-and-half
¾ cup sugar
1 tablespoon cornstarch
Dash of ground cinnamon

Combine ingredients in a saucepan; cook over low heat, stirring constantly, until thickened. Do not boil.

Green Tomato Pie

Make pastry for a double-crust 9-inch pie (page 228). Arrange bottom crust in piepan. Sprinkle with a little flour. Slice fresh green tomatoes thinly and fill crust; it will take about 4 cups. Add 1 cup sugar and ½ cup butter. Add ½ teaspoon cinnamon or nutmeg. Pour 3 tablespoons vinegar over filling; put on top crust. Bake at 400° for 10 minutes; reduce heat to 350° and bake 20 to 25 minutes. Serve hot. Yield: one 9-inch pie.

Muscadine Pie

Pop pulp from 1 quart of muscadines or scuppernongs. Save hulls. Cook pulp until seeds turn loose; strain in a colander to remove seeds. Combine seedless pulp with hulls and cook until tender. Mix 2 cups grape filling with 1 cup sugar and 1 tablespoon flour; pour into a pastry-lined 9-inch piepan. Cover with lattice top. Bake at 350° for about 40 minutes or until set and brown. Yield: one 8-inch pie.

Syrup Custard Pie

1 cup sugar
3 tablespoons all-purpose flour
2 cups cane syrup (sorghum or
   molasses)
4 eggs, beaten
1 cup half-and-half
2 tablespoons melted butter
1 unbaked 9-inch pastry shell

Combine sugar and flour in mixing bowl; add syrup, eggs, half-and-half, and butter. Pour into pastry shell. Bake at 325° for about 45 minutes or until set. Yield: one 9-inch pie.

Raisin And Vinegar Pie

½ cup raisins
¼ cup butter or margarine, softened
½ cup plus 2 tablespoons sugar
½ teaspoon ground cloves
¼ teaspoon ground allspice
½ teaspoon ground cinnamon
½ teaspoon vanilla extract
2 eggs, separated
¼ cup vinegar
¼ cup water
1 unbaked 9-inch pastry shell

Cook raisins in boiling water to cover for 5 minutes. Drain raisins and set aside. Cream butter and sugar; beat in spices and vanilla. Stir in egg yolks, vinegar, water, and raisins. Beat egg whites until stiff; fold into mixture. Pour into pastry shell and bake at 350° for 1 hour. Yield: one 9-inch pie.

Tyler Pies

1 cup butter
3 cups sugar
4 eggs
¼ cup all-purpose flour
1 cup milk
1 teaspoon vanilla extract
Dash of nutmeg
2 unbaked 8-inch pastry shells

Cream butter and sugar together; add eggs and beat well. Add flour, milk, and flavorings. Pour into pastry shells. Bake at 400° for 10 minutes; reduce heat to 350° and bake 25 to 30 minutes. Yield: two 8-inch pies or 12 small tarts.

Note: 1½ cups coconut may be added for delicious coconut pies; 9-inch pastry shells may be used.

Old-Fashioned Sweet Potato Pie

2 unbaked 9-inch pastry shells
3 medium sweet potatoes, baked or boiled
1½ cups sugar
½ cup water
½ cup butter or margarine
2 tablespoons vinegar

Lay bottom crust in a deep dish 9-inch pie-pan. Slice potatoes and place in crust. Cover with strips of pastry. Combine sugar, water, butter, and vinegar in a small saucepan; bring to a boil over medium heat and boil for 10 minutes or until slightly thickened. Pour over pie. Bake at 350° for about 45 minutes or until lightly browned. Yield: one 9-inch pie.

Skillet Pudding

1 cup firmly packed brown sugar
2 cups boiling water
6 tablespoons butter, divided
1½ teaspoons vanilla extract, divided
½ cup sugar
½ cup milk
1 cup all-purpose flour
1 teaspoon baking powder
½ teaspoon salt
½ cup raisins

Combine brown sugar, water, 2 tablespoons butter, and 1 teaspoon vanilla in a 10-inch skillet. Set aside.

Combine sugar and remaining butter in a mixing bowl, creaming well. Blend in milk.

Stir or sift flour with baking powder and salt; stir into milk mixture. Add vanilla and raisins. Spoon this batter over the original brown sugar mixture in the skillet. Bake at 350° for 25 minutes. Yield: 8 servings.

Note: This old-fashioned recipe is best served warm and is delicious with whipping cream poured over.

Rosy Chutney

1 (3-inch) stick cinnamon, broken
    into pieces
2 tablespoons mustard seeds
10 whole cloves
1½ cups red wine vinegar
2¾ cups sugar
2 teaspoons salt
2 cups (about 2 large) peeled seeded
    minced tomato
2 cups (about 1 large) unpeeled
    minced tart apple
1 cup minced onion
1 cup minced green pepper
1 cup minced celery

Tie spices in a cheesecloth bag. Place in a 6-quart saucepan. Add vinegar, sugar, and salt; bring to a rolling boil. Reduce heat, and simmer 10 to 15 minutes. Remove spice bag, and add remaining ingredients; return mixture to a boil. Reduce heat; simmer about 30 minutes, stirring constantly, until thick and clear. Cool. Place in a covered container, and refrigerate. Yield: 1 quart.

Southern Chutney

1 quart white vinegar
1 pound mangos, sliced (if mango
    not available, green pears or
    semiripe quince may be used)
3 pounds cooking apples
1 pound brown sugar
1 ounce chile peppers, finely cut
1 cup seedless white raisins
½ pound dried lemon peel,
    finely cut
½ pound preserved ginger
2 cloves garlic, crushed
2 ounces mustard seed
2 teaspoons salt
2 teaspoons powdered sugar

Bring vinegar to a boil. Add peeled and sliced mangos and apples; cook until soft.

Then add brown sugar, chile peppers, raisins, lemon peel, ginger, and garlic. Season with mustard seed, salt, and powdered sugar. Cook for 15 minutes; then seal sterilized jars.

Apple Chutney

4 pounds apples
1 pound raisins
1 pound sultanas
1½ pounds sugar
1 quart vinegar
2 ounces salt
2 ounces bruised ginger
1 ounce red chiles or red pepper

Peel, core, and slice apples; place in a stone crock. Chop raisins and sultanas; add along with remaining ingredients. Let stand days. Boil up until apples look like jam; pack into jars.

Apple Butter

12 to 13 pounds whole apples
5 pounds sugar
½ cup vinegar
¼ cup cinnamon candies

Core and slice apples (do not peel). Place apples in a large kettle with a small amount water; cook until soft. Press apples through sieve.

Combine cooked apples, sugar, and vinegar in a large, deep roasting pan; mixing well. Bake at 325° for 5 hours, stirring occasionally. Add cinnamon candies, stirring well. Cook about 1 additional hour or until thickened. Yield: 15 cups.

Homemade Mincemeat

If kept moistened with brandy, mincemeat will keep through winter.

Boil and chop finely 3 pounds beef or venison tongue. Add 4 pounds finely chopped suet, 4 pounds brown sugar, 1 pound finely sliced citron, 4 pounds raisins, 3 pounds currants, 4 pounds finely chopped apples; add 1 tablespoon each of ground mace, cloves, and cinnamon; then add 2 nutmegs, coarsely ground. Mix with enough brandy to wet well.

Mason-Dixon Mincemeat

3 pounds lean beef, cooked
   and chopped
½ pound beef suet
2 teaspoons salt
3 quarts water
6 pounds apples, peeled
   and chopped
1 cup vinegar
2 quarts apple cider
½ cup lemon juice
1 cup orange juice
1½ cups molasses
3 cups sugar
½ cup citron, chopped
2 pounds seeded raisins
1 pound seedless raisins
2 pounds currants
1 cup tart jelly
1 tablespoon nutmeg
1 tablespoon ground cloves
2 teaspoons allspice
4 teaspoons cinnamon
Grated rind of 1 lemon and 1 orange

Cook meat in salted water until tender. Let stand in liquid overnight. The next day add other ingredients. Cook slowly in open kettle for two hours or until liquid has cooked into fruit. While hot, fill jars and seal; process 15 minutes in boiling water. Yield: 12 pints.

Corn Relish

20 ears fresh corn
1 cup chopped green pepper
1 cup chopped sweet red pepper
1 cup chopped onion
1 cup chopped cucumber
1 cup chopped green tomatoes
1½ cups sugar
2½ tablespoons mustard seeds
1 teaspoon celery seeds
½ teaspoon ground turmeric
3 cups vinegar
2 cups water

Drop corn into boiling water; boil 5 minutes; remove and plunge into cold water. Drain; cut corn from cob. Combine corn with remaining ingredients in a large pot and boil for 15 minutes, stirring occasionally. Keep mixture boiling hot while packing it loosely into sterilized jars. Fill jars to within ½ inch of top. Seal jars. Process in boiling water bath (water to cover top of jars) for 15 minutes. Remove jars and cool. Yield: 5 to 6 pints.

Vegetable Relish

1 (16-ounce) can shoepeg corn
1 quart cooked string beans
1 quart cooked lima beans
8 green peppers, chopped
1 small head cabbage, shredded fine
3 tablespoons mustard seeds
1 cup all-purpose flour
½ cup yellow mustard
½ cup salt
½ cup sugar
3 tablespoons paprika
2 cups vinegar

Place first 7 ingredients in a preserving kettle. Cover with equal parts of vinegar and water. Bring to a boil and cook for 35 minutes. Place remaining ingredients in a bowl. Stir to dissolve; then add to the boiling mixture. Cook 15 minutes; fill glass jars and seal. Store in a cool, dry place. Yield: 9 to 10 pints.

Aunt Willie's Pickles

Choose 5- or 6-inch pickling cucumbers. Wash and put in a gallon jar. Pour boiling water over cucumbers and cover.

On the second day pour off water, rinse cucumbers, and cover cucumbers in fresh boiling water. Repeat on days 3 and 4.

On the fifth day drain, rinse, and slice in ¼-inch slices. Mix the syrup, bring to a boil, and pour over pickles:

    1 quart vinegar
    8 cups sugar
    2 tablespoons salt
    2 tablespoons allspice (place in
        cheesecloth bag)

Days 6, 7, and 8 pour off syrup, bring to a boil, and pour back over cucumbers.

On day 9 let pickles stand in hot syrup for 30 minutes. Drain, bring syrup to boil, place pickles in jars, cover with boiling syrup, and seal. Yield: 6 pints.

Pickled Beets

    3½ quarts small fresh beets
    2 cups sugar
    3½ cups vinegar
    1½ cups water
    1 tablespoon whole allspice
    1½ teaspoons salt
    2 sticks cinnamon

Remove stems and roots from beets; wash and peel. Place beets in a large kettle; cover with water. Bring to a boil. Reduce heat; cover and simmer until tender.

Combine remaining ingredients in a large saucepan. Bring to a boil. Reduce heat; cover and simmer 15 minutes.

Pack beets into hot sterilized jars, leaving ½-inch headspace. Remove cinnamon sticks from syrup. Bring syrup to a boil. Pour boiling syrup over beets, leaving ½-inch headspace. Cover with lids; screw bands tight. Process 30 minutes in boiling-water bath. Yield: about 6 pints.

Pickled Sweet Corn

Select sweet corn ready for immediate use; silk and cut away impurities. Place in the wash boiler, cover with water, and bring to a quick boil. Boil 5 minutes and remove immediately. Refill the boiler with corn and boil each batch 5 minutes. Six dozen ears will fill a 2-gallon jar.

As soon as corn is cooled, cut from cob with a sharp knife. Sprinkle a layer of salt in a large jar, then 3 quarts of corn, and 1 quart of salt; pound down until solid with wooden potato masher. Repeat layers until jar is filled; put a plate and heavy weight on top. In 2 or 3 days a scum will rise. Remove it carefully; put in more corn and a layer of salt on top, tie a clean cloth over it, and set in a cool place. It will keep for months.

Plum Sauce

    7 pounds pitted plums, chopped
    5 pounds sugar
    1 pint apple vinegar
    ½ teaspoon ground cloves
    1 teaspoon ground cinnamon
    1 teaspoon ground allspice

Put plums, sugar, and vinegar in a large cooking vessel. Add spices; cook until the juice gets thick, but not too long, as spices will make it too strong. It should be about the consistency of marmalade. (Some plums have more natural pectin than others and will thicken more quickly.) Fill sterilized jars and process in boiling water bath for about 10 minutes. Yield: about 6 pints.

Citron Preserves

Cover completely 9 pounds of cut-up citron with 7 pounds of sugar; let stand overnight. Start cooking in the morning, adding 6 cut-up lemons after mixture begins to cook. Cook for 2½ hours, stirring often. Test a spoonful by cooling on a saucer to see if preserves are of jelly consistency. Fill 4 pint jars. Watermelon preserves are made the same way.

Corncob Jelly

12 bright red corncobs (or white cobs colored with a little food coloring)
3 pints water
1 (1¾-ounce) powdered fruit pectin
3 cups sugar

Boil corncobs in water 30 minutes. Remove and strain. Add enough water to make 3 cups. Add fruit pectin and bring to a boil. Add sugar and boil 2 to 3 minutes. Pour in jelly glasses and seal. Yield: about 3 cups.

Crabapple Jelly

5 pounds crabapples, stemmed and coarsely chopped
5 cups water
1 (1¾-ounce) package powdered fruit pectin
9 cups sugar

Combine crabapples and water in a large Dutch oven. Bring to a boil. Reduce heat; cover, and simmer about 10 minutes. Mash crabapples; simmer 5 additional minutes. Place in a jelly bag and squeeze out juice.

Return juice to Dutch oven. Add pectin. Bring quickly to a hard boil, stirring occasionally. Add sugar at once. Cook and stir until mixture returns to a full rolling boil (cannot be stirred down). Cook and stir 1

additional minute. Remove from heat, and skim off foam with a metal spoon.

Pour immediately into hot sterilized jars, leaving ½-inch headspace. Seal with a ⅛-inch layer of paraffin. Place lid on jar, screw band tight. Yield: about 5 pints.

Fig Preserves

6 quarts firm figs
½ cup soda
6 quarts boiling water
6 pounds sugar
4 quarts water

Sprinkle clean figs with soda and cover with 6 quarts of boiling water. Let stand 10 minutes. Drain and rinse in cold water.

Boil 6 pounds of sugar and 4 quarts water for 10 minutes. Skim. Add figs. Cook until figs are transparent (about 2 hours). Lift out figs and put in a shallow pan. Pour syrup over figs and cover them. (If syrup is not thick enough, cook it longer.)

Let figs stand overnight. They will absorb the syrup during the night and be nice and plump. Pack in sterile jars; cover figs with syrup, up to ½ inch from top. Seal. Process for 25 minutes at simmer. Yield: 14 to 15 pints.

Tomato Jam

4½ pounds ripe tomatoes
4½ cups sugar
1½ cups vinegar
1 tablespoon broken stick cinnamon
½ teaspoon ground allspice
1 teaspoon ground cloves

Peel and quarter tomatoes; place in a preserving pan. Add remaining ingredients; cook slowly, stirring frequently, until thickened. Pack into jars.

Acknowledgments

Excerpt from *A Bowl Of Red* by Francis X. Tolbert. Reprinted by permission of Doubleday & Company, Inc. Copyright ©1953 by Francis X. Tolbert.

Recipes for Cornmeal Rolls and Sweet Potato Biscuits from *A Kitchen Affair: Loved Recipes* by Unitarian Church, Lexington, Kentucky. Reprinted by permission of the Unitarian Church Women's Alliance, Lexington, Kentucky. Copyright ©1968 by Unitarian Church.

Recipe for Crawfish Bisque À La Bon Ton courtesy of Bon Ton Restaurant, New Orleans.

Quotation on page 46 from *Autobiography* by William Allen White. Copyright ©1946 by Macmillan Publishing Co., Inc., New York, renewed 1974 by Macmillan Publishing Co., Inc., and W. L. White.

Recipe for Joseph Carrico Barbecue Sauce courtesy of Joseph Carrico.

Recipes for Clam Fritters, Carolina Shrimp Casserole, King Or Spanish Mackerel, Low Country Paella, and Sautéed Crabmeat Plantation from *Catch-of-the-Day . . . Southern Seafood Secrets* by Ginny Lentz and Margaret Terrell. Reprinted by permission of Wimmer Brothers, Memphis. Copyright ©1978 by Ginny Lentz and Margaret Terrell.

Recipes for Brown Oyster Stew With Benne (Sesame) Seeds, Philpy, Baked Custard, and Charlotte Russe from *Charleston Receipts* by Junior League of Charleston, Inc. Reprinted by permission of Junior League of Charleston, Inc., Charleston Receipts Committee, Charleston, South Carolina. Copyright ©1950 by The Junior League of Charleston, Inc.

Recipes for East Tennessee Ham, Easy Oven Hamburgers, Roast Leg Of Lamb, Miss Gertrude's White Layer Cake, and Nashville Chess Pie from *Chattanooga Cookbook* by Helen Exum. Reprinted by permission of Chattanooga News Free Press, Chattanooga, Tennessee. Copyright ©1970 by Helen Exum.

Recipe for Seafood Gumbo Filé Chez Pastor courtesy of Chez Pastor Restaurant, Lafayette, Louisiana.

Recipes for Chicken Mousse, Cream De Volaille, and Chicken Mayonnaise from *Crossroads Cookery*. Reprinted by permission of the Women's Club of Hagerstown, Maryland. Copyright ©1961.

Recipes for Southern Lacy Edge Corn Cakes, Colonial Tavern Bread Pudding, Brownie's Persimmon Pudding, and How To Cure A Fine Old Virginia Ham from *Culinary Gems From The Kitchens Of Old Virginia* by Irene Lawrence King. Reprinted by permission of Dodd, Mead and Company, Inc., New York. Copyright ©1952 by Irene Lawrence King.

Recipes for Hamburg-Vegetable Soup, Coconut Macaroons, Date Nut Bread, and Marmalade Bread from *Family Favorites* by the Women of Buechel Presbyterian Church, Louisville, Kentucky.

Recipes for Turkey Hash, Pendennis Club Style, Chicken Divan, Beef Ragout, and Lemon-Topped Round Steak from *Famous Kentucky Recipes* by Cabbage Patch Circle. Reprinted by permission of Cabbage Patch Circle, Louisville, Kentucky. Copyright ©1952 by Cabbage Patch Circle.

Recipes for Lentil Soup, Rich Homemade Bread, Quick Herb Rolls, Hot Water Hoecake, Banana Bread, and Lemon Bars from *Favorite Fare*. Reprinted by permission of The Woman's Club of Louisville, Inc., Louisville, Kentucky. Copyright ©1968 by The Woman's Club of Louisville, Inc.

Recipe for Hot Pants Chili from *Foods From Harvest Festivals And Folk Fairs* by Anita Borghese (Thomas Y. Crowell). Reprinted by permission of Harper & Row, Publishers, Inc., New York. Copyright ©1977 by Anita Borghese.

Recipes for Venison Swiss Steak, Cream Of Turkey Soup, Old-Fashioned Brown Bread, Two-Hour Whole Wheat Rolls, Banana-Peanut Butter Bread, and Cranberry Bread from *Fredericksburg Home Kitchen Cookbook*. Reprinted by permission of Cookbook Committee, Fredericksburg PTA, Fredericksburg, Texas. Copyright ©1978 by Mrs. Wesley A. Gold, Business Manager.

Recipes for Turnip Greens and Potato Fried Pie courtesy of Mamie Gammon, Memphis, Tennessee.

Recipe for Turkey Loaf from *Golden Anniversary Cookbook*. Reprinted by permission of Daviess County Extension Homemakers, Owensboro, Kentucky. Copyright ©1975.

Information on page 123 on Colonial Virginia used by permission of Virginia Polytechnic Institute's publication *"History of Colonial Foods in Virginia."*

Recipe for Chicken-Fried Steak courtesy of Kay's Restaurant, Tulsa, Oklahoma.

Recipes for Veal Divine and Chicken And Oyster Casserole from *Kentucky Cooking New and Old* by Colonelettes, Inc. Reprinted by permission of Colonelettes, Inc., Louisville, Kentucky. Copyright ©1951 by Colonelettes, Inc.

Recipes for A Small Burgoo, Woodford Pudding, Spoon Rolls, and Derby Breakfast Yeast Biscuits from *Kentucky Hospitality—A 200 Year Tradition*. Reprinted by permission of Kentucky Federation of Women's Clubs, Louisville, Kentucky. Copyright ©1976 by Kentucky Federation of Women's Clubs.

Recipe for Boone Tavern Spoon Cakes from *Look No Further* by Richard T. Hougen. Reprinted by permission of Abingdon Press, Nashville, Tennessee. Copyright ©1951 by Richard T. Hougen.

Recipes for Split Pea Soup, Corn Biscuit Strips, Bran Rolls, Bran Muffins, Dill Bread, and Cheese Bread from *Lunch at the Yellow Daisy*. Reprinted by permission of Youth Home Auxiliary, Little Rock, Arkansas. Copyright ©1978 by Youth Home Auxiliary.

Quoted material on page 11 by permission of Mrs. Marie Louise Comeaux Manuel.

Recipes for Pocket Steak, City Chicken, Meat Loaf With Herbs, Veal In Casserole, and Chicken In Aspic from *Maryland Cookery*. Reprinted by permission of Maryland Home Economics Association, Laurel, Maryland. Copyright ©1948 by Maryland Home Economics Association.

Recipes for Eastern Shore Crab Cakes, Southern Maryland Stuffed Ham, Fresh Lima Beans, and Striped Bass Stuffed With Crabmeat from *Maryland's Way*, The Hammond-Harwood House Cook Book by Mrs. Lewis R. Andrews and Mrs. J. Reaney Kelly. Reprinted by permission of Mrs. Lewis R. Andrews and Mrs. J. Reaney Kelly, Annapolis, Maryland. Copyright ©1963 by The Hammond-Harwood House Association.

Recipes for Roasted Quail, Sweet Potato Cobbler, Corn Pudding Supreme, Moravian Sugar Cake, Scalloped Cheese And Cabbage, and Fried Green Apples from *Mountain Cookbook* edited by Ferne Shelton. Reprinted by permission of D.D. Hutchinson d/b/a Hutcraft, Highpoint, North Carolina. Copyright ©1964 by Ferne Shelton Hutchinson.

Recipes for Jeff Davis Pie, Dutch Loaf (Potato Bread), Love Feast Buns, and Lady Baltimore Cake from *North Carolina and Old Salem Cookery*. Reprinted by permission of Elizabeth Hedgecock Sparks. Copyright ©1955 by Elizabeth Hedgecock Sparks.

Recipe for Chicken-Sausage Gumbo (450 gallons) courtesy of W. T. Oliver.

Recipes for Shrimp Stew and Seafood Corn Sticks from the *Original Ocracoke Cookbook*. Reprinted by permission of United Methodist Women, Ocracoke, North Carolina.

Recipes for Winter Okra Soup, Chicken Soufflé, and The Queen Of All Puddings from *Original Picayune Creole Cook Book*. Reprinted by permission of The Times-Picayune Publishing Corporation, New Orleans. Copyright ©1971 by The Times-Picayune Publishing Corporation.

Recipes for Baked Parsnips, Sorghum Molasses Pie, Seedless Grape Pie, Honey-Glazed Onions, and Egg Soup from *Ozarks Cookery* by Eula Mae Stratton. Reprinted by permission of The Ozarks Mountaineer, Branson, Missouri. Copyright ©1975 by The Ozarks Mountaineer.

Recipes for Traditional Maryland Oyster Stew, Deviled Crab Deluxe, Old Line Oyster Pie, Pan-Fried Oysters, Bay Country Oyster And Fish Dish from *Peninsula Pacemaker*. Reprinted by permission of Maryland Seafood Marketing Authority.

Recipes for Okra Seafood Gumbo and Shrimp And Ham Jambalaya courtesy of Earl Peyroux.

Recipe for Chorizo courtesy of Por Que No Restaurant, Louisville, Kentucky.

Recipes for Apricot Nut Loaf, Oatmeal Muffins, German Pancake, Little Party Biscuits, and Raspberry Breakfast Bread from *Prescriptions For Cooks* by Jefferson County Medical Society Auxiliary. Reprinted by permission of Jefferson County Medical Society Auxiliary, Louisville, Kentucky. Copyright ©1962 by the Jefferson County Medical Society Auxiliary.

Recipes for Beaufort Cream Of Crab Soup, Country Captain, Georgia Peach Pie, Okra Pilâu, Tarragon Celery, and Bluffton Boil from *Savannah Sampler Cookbook* by Margaret DeBolt. Reprinted by permission of The Donning Company, Publishers, Norfolk, Virginia. Copyright ©1978 by Margaret DeBolt.

Recipes for Doves, Crème De Menthe Parfaits, Daiquiri Pie, and Jezebel Sauce For Ham from *Something Southern, A Collection of Recipes*. Reprinted by permission of the Junior Service League of Americus, Georgia, Inc. Copyright ©1976 by the Junior Service League of Americus, Georgia, Inc.

Recipes for Cream Of Celery Soup and Fried Chicken from *Southern Cooking* by Mrs. S. R. Dull. Reprinted by permission of Grosset & Dunlap, Inc., Publishers, New York. Copyright ©1941 by Grosset & Dunlap, Inc.

Recipes for Gregg Chili, Broccoli Bisque, Carrot Ring, Spanish Hominy, and Sesame Hash Browned Potatoes from *The Collection: A Cookbook* by the Junior League of Austin, Texas. Reprinted by permission of the Junior League of Austin, Inc., Austin, Texas. Copyright ©1976 by the Junior League of Austin, Texas.

Recipes for Ragout Of Lamb, Breaded Veal Cutlets, and Veal Croquettes from *The Crescent Hill Woman's Club Cookbook* and *The Derbytown Winners Cookbook*. Reprinted by permission of The Crescent Hill Woman's Club, Louisville, Kentucky. Copyright ©1975 by The Crescent Hill Woman's Club.

Recipes for Kentucky Tombstone Pudding, Baked Stuffed Zucchini, Ham With Purple Plums, Pork Tenderloin Braised In Wine, and Casserole Of Veal And Mushrooms Devonshire from *The Farmington Cookbook*. Reprinted by permission of Farmington (Historic Homes, Inc.), Louisville, Kentucky. Copyright ©1968 by Farmington (Historic Homes, Inc.).

Recipes for Gazpacho, Boliche, Alcachofras (Artichokes), Chateaubriand, and Spanish Bean Soup from *The Gasparilla Cookbook* by The Junior League of Tampa. Reprinted by permission of The Junior League of Tampa, Florida. Copyright ©1961 by The Junior League of Tampa.

Recipes for Fresh Fig Pie, Potato Latkes, and Serbian Crêpes Suzettes from *The Melting Pot: Ethnic Cuisine In Texas*. Reprinted by permission of The University of Texas Institute of Texan Cultures at San Antonio, Texas. Copyright ©1977 by Institute of Texan Cultures.

Recipes for Boiled Peanuts, Papa's Favorite Quail And Oyster Stew, Easy Spinach Supreme, and Dill Potatoes from *The Pick Of The Crop* by North Sunflower PTA. Reprinted by permission of Wimmer Brothers Books, Memphis, Tennessee. Copyright ©1979 by Ann Grittman, Editor.

Recipes for Pineapple-Nut Muffins, Never-Fail Popovers, Sally's Beaten Biscuit, and Buttermilk Biscuits from *The Queen's Daughters' Recipes*. Reprinted by permission of The Queen's Daughters, Louisville, Kentucky. Copyright ©1957 by The Queen's Daughters.

Recipes for Dry Barbecue Mixture, Mopping Sauce For Barbecue, and Barbecue Sauce from *The Wide, Wide World Of Texas Cooking* by Morton Gill Clark (Funk & Wagnalls). Reprinted by permission of Harper & Row, Publishers, Inc. New York. Copyright ©1970 by Morton Gill Clark.

Recipes for Fried Green Tomatoes, Cornish Hens With Basting Sauce, Venison Parmesan, and Filé from *Tony Chachere's Cajun Country Cookbook, Inc.* Reprinted by permission of Tony Chachere, Opelousas, Louisiana. Copyright ©1972 by Anthony Chachere.

Recipes for Irish Lamb Stew and Smothered Chicken from *Tried & Tested Recipes of Oldham County Homemakers' Clubs*. Reprinted by permission of Oldham County Homemakers' Association, LaGrange, Kentucky. Copyright by Oldham County Homemakers' Association.

Recipes for Gumbo D'Herbes and Fig Preserves reprinted by permission of the Home Economics Department of the University of Southwestern Louisiana, Lafayette, Louisiana.

Recipes for Delicate Cornmeal Muffins, Ham Loaf, Cinnamon Rolls, and Strawberry Meringue Nut Torte from *What's Cooking In Fleming County, A Book of Favorite Recipes*. Reprinted by permission of Flemingsburg Evening Homemakers, Fleming County, Kentucky. Copyright ©1974 by Circulation Service, Inc.

Recipes for Catfish Chowder, Pan-Fried Fish, Turkey-Almond Casserole, Chicken Roquefort, Veal Paprika, Owendaw, Herb-Roasted Lamb Shanks, Lamb Curry, Veal Birds, Veal Scallopini Valdosta, and Turkey Tetrazzini from *Woman's Exchange Cook Book*, *Volume I* and *Volume II*. Reprinted by permission of The Woman's Exchange of Memphis, Inc., Memphis. Copyright ©1976 by The Woman's Exchange of Memphis, Inc.

Recipe for Brandied Chicken from *Woodford Recipes*. Reprinted by permission of Lathrem's Print Shop. Copyright ©1959 by Woodford Memorial Hospital Auxiliary, Versailles, Kentucky.

Index